The **Intext** Series in *Economics*

Public Finance and
Public Policy Issues

Public Finance and Public Policy Issues

Martin Schnitzer
Virginia Polytechnic Institute and State University

Yung-Ping Chen
University of California, Los Angeles

Intext Educational Publishers
College Division of **Intext**
Scranton / San Francisco / Toronto / London

Contents

Part III   Resource Allocation in the Federal Sector

Part IV   Federal Expenditures and National Priorities

Public Finance and
Public Policy Issues

Introduction

Economic Goals in a Free Society

There is general consensus that the economic objectives of American society are full employment, price stability, economic growth, and a balance of payments equilibrium. Each goal is incapable of precise definition and the attainment of one may not necessarily assist in achieving the others. One acceptable definition of full employment is that it is a situation in the economy which is characterized by an absence of involuntary unemployment. There have to be allowances for frictional and seasonal unemployment. Frictional unemployment refers to the fact that at any given time a certain number of workers will be temporarily out of work because of imperfections in the labor market. Some workers will be in the process of changing jobs, while others will be experiencing temporary layoffs. Seasonal unemployment, as the name implies, means that a certain number of workers are unemployed as a result of seasonal variations in output. Many economists, for purposes of public policy, define "full employment" at an arbitrary rate, such as 96 percent.

Price stability is another economic goal. Again, the problem is one of definition. Many economists believe that a gradual rise in the price level has a beneficial effect on the level of economic activity. But what is a gradual rise in the price level? Eventually a point is reached where a substantial rate of inflation occurs. Inflation could be defined as simply an increase in the overall price level as measured by some statistical device, such as index numbers. This allows for relative price changes which are necessary to allocate resources in a free society. But this then requires price reductions for some goods in order to prevent inflation, because some prices will be bid up in the process of reallocating resources, made necessary by changed tastes and new products.

1

Economic growth is also an objective. It can be defined as an increase in real per capita income. Continued increases in the output of goods and services form the basis for an increase in the standard of living for families and individuals in a society. Moreover, it is not difficult to reconcile the goal of full employment with economic growth, for economic growth is necessary to absorb new entrants into the labor force and to accommodate those workers who are technologically unemployed. However, there is the problem of defining what is an acceptable rate of growth. A high rate of growth can lead to an eventual conflict with the goal of price stability. To a certain extent there is also a conflict between economic growth and the quality of the environment. Economic growth results in part in smoke and fumes from more cars, litter from more cans produced, and pollution of streams from the increased output of factories.

A fourth goal is an equilibrium in the balance of international payments. In particular, in 1971 the balance of payments problem has assumed an importance almost equal to the goals of full employment, price stability, and economic growth. The balance of payments is really a balance of claims and counterclaims between the United States and other countries. Disequilibrium occurs when there is an imbalance in these claims either in favor of the United States or the other countries. When an unfavorable balance of payments occurs, which has happened in the case of the United States, then there is a drain on short-term capital, currency and bank deposits, and gold reserves.

There are other goals which are also important. One such goal is a more equitable distribution of income. There is concern in the United States over the fact that a substantial number of persons receive incomes which are less than adequate in terms of maintaining a basic standard of living. It is necessary to insure all citizens of a minimum living standard, to provide equality of opportunity in employment, and to bring about a more equitable income distribution. Admittedly, the last objective is extremely hard to define. What is the right degree of income inequality? It is apparent, however, that western society has favored arrangements that are designed to achieve some redistribution of income. National governments are generally the most effective of all government instruments to undertake income redistribution because the opportunities to circumvent their actions are most limited.

However, a considerable amount of government intervention is an indispensable condition for the achievement of these goals. This intervention takes two forms. First of all, the government directs the coordination of economic policy, and its various administrative decisions determine some of the boundaries or rules to which business firms and other economic units must pay attention in their own planning and decision making. Second, it participates more directly in the economy through the use of taxation and transfer payments to redistribute income and purchase which affect the allocation of resources. Within this framework provided by the government, consumers and producers have freedom to determine their actions as they see fit.

A shift in attitude toward a greater role for the federal government in economic policy occurred during the Kennedy Administration. What is commonly called the "new economics" came to the fore. As practiced by the Kennedy and Johnson Administrations, the "new economics" reflected the belief that economic stability—full employment without inflation—could be achieved through the use of fine tuning adjustments of the country's fiscal and monetary machinery. It was felt that the maintenance of a high level of aggregate demand would solve such problems as a high rate of unemployment and a low rate of economic growth. The federal budget assumed an active role in economic policy making.

The importance of the federal government budget cannot be minimized. It exerts a strong influence on the national economy in terms of the level of expenditures and taxes, and whether or not it is balanced, and the composition of expenditures and taxes. The budget tends to be the focal point in the presentation and implementation of a government's economic policy. It is often used as a means of publicizing the government's wishes regarding the behavior of particular sectors, individuals, or firms in the economy, either as an attempt to improve the chances of success of given measures proposed, or at times a substitute for any such measures.

The budget can be used as a flywheel to change the level of economic activity in the economy. Taxes represent a withdrawal of income from the income stream, while government expenditures represent an injection of income into it. When the government's income, as represented by taxes and other revenues, exceed expenditures, the net effect is to dampen down the level of economic activity in the economy. On the other hand, when government expenditures exceed revenues, the net effect is to stimulate the economy. Budgetary surpluses or deficits, then, can be used to effect changes in the level of economic activity.

The significance of the federal budget can be measured by its size relative to the gross national product. Budgetary receipts for the 1972 budget are estimated at $202 billion. The vast bulk of these receipts comes from various tax sources. When tax revenues are compared to the projected gross national product of approximately $1 trillion, it can be said that the budget diverts around 20 percent of the gross national product from the private to the public sectors. Budgetary outlays are estimated to be $229 billion for 1972. These outlays, which take the form of direct expenditures on goods and services, and transfer payments, which redistribute income between income groups, represent a direct and indirect contribution to the size of gross national product.

The federal budget is a unified budget; in its accounting structure, it follows closely the recommendations made in the October, 1967, Report of the President's Commission on Budget Concepts. This new unified budget replaces the three separate sets of budget concepts used in recent years: the administrative budget, the consolidated cash budget, and the national income accounts budget. In common with the latter two concepts, the new budget not only includes general fund transactions, but also all trust accounts. It covers lending as well as spending, but each category is shown in separate "loan accounts" and "expenditure accounts" respectively. "Expenditures" represent income-generating purchases of goods and services, transfer payments which enhance the purchasing power of the private sector, grants-in-aid to state and local governments, and subsidies. Net lending in the loan accounts affects the liquidity of the private sector in terms of the composition of its total assets and liabilities.

In practice, the actual allocation of funds among the major end purposes of government has been the accidental result of a myriad of independent budget decisions rather than the outcome of systematic choices. What became necessary was a mechanism to permit the following types of choices to be made: between greater welfare and economic growth, between active and passive defense, between agriculture and education, between air and surface transportation facilities, between direct federal operations and grants to state and local governments, and so forth. Moreover, activities cease to be productive or need to be made more efficient. Some sort of cost-benefit analysis for policymaking decisions became an economic imperative.

The Planning-Programming Budgeting System developed as a result of the need to improve decision making with respect to resource allocation. It is a tool of business-type management which Secretary of Defense McNamara introduced at the Pentagon and which is now being applied gradually to civilian government decision making. It attempts to shift the emphasis in budgeting from inputs to major purposes to be accomplished. It poses the fundamental question and challenge—can the purposes of government be accomplished in a more effective and economical way? It provides a format for presenting data and the methodology for analyzing it. This format takes the form of a comprehensive Program and Financial Plan for each government agency, which is updated periodically and systematically. An early and essential step is determining, for each agency and department, the output-oriented categories which cover its area of responsibility. The Plan itself records an agency's proposed activities, measured in both physical and financial terms.

In the early 1960's, a high rate of unemployment and a low rate of economic growth were the major United States public policy issues. Traditional concepts of public finance underwent a major change; government fiscal policies came to be viewed as instruments for influencing the magnitude and direction of income flows throughout the economy. As the unemployment rate was reduced and as the rate of economic growth started to expand, the issue of poverty came to the fore. There developed the realization that a considerable segment of society subsisted on very low incomes. The idea at stake was whether the federal government, by one means or another, should take upon itself to guarantee that every individual and family receive a certain level of income each year.

However, by the beginning of the 1970's, it was apparent that in addition to the problem of poverty, other problems had developed which required solution. One area in which the federal government has shown flagrant neglect is in the care of natural resources. Land, air, and water have been spoiled freely. Decay of physical facilities and the need for better housing are problems in most cities. State and local governments, overburdened with conflicting demands and requirements for more expenditures, find themselves in need of additional revenue sources.

There is widespread agreement that America's welfare system is in trouble. First of all, it is a categorical program—it makes no provision for general relief to people who do not fit its categories. Second, the decision to operate the program lies with the states, and, within certain limitations, so does the determination of who is eligible for benefits, how much can be granted, and under what conditions. A result is wide disparity in program coverage and administrative practices from state to state. Third, there is the burgeoning cost of welfare expenditures which has forced many cities to the verge of bankruptcy. Recession-based job layoffs have contributed to the increase in welfare expenditures. Inflation has also made welfare services much more expensive than they were only five years ago.

Financial pressures on state and local governments reflect a drastic change in the overall makeup of the U.S. tax dollar. Increasingly, the collection of public money depends upon personal and corporate income taxation, a form of levying largely reserved for the federal government. Meanwhile, the traditional base for municipal taxation—real estate—has stagnated, largely because of the move of businesses and middle-class families to the suburbs and the concomitant growth of inner city slums. Revenue from real estate taxes is further reduced by the tax-exempt status of government and other institutional holdings. Yet the burden of building new schools, hospitals, and other shrines to the nation's prosperity falls most heavily on the states and cities.

I

Macroeconomic Policy Objectives

A

Economic Goals and Problems in the United States Economy

The readings in Section A are designed to reflect the policy goals which have developed in the United States. The first reading is the Employment Act of 1946. It reflects a milestone in governmental public policy in that it gave legislative sanction to the view that the federal government has a direct responsibility for the level of employment and income prevailing in the economy. The second reading, "Objectives of Economic Policy and Measures of Performance," by the Committee for Economic Development attempts to define acceptable policy goals for the economy. It is significant to note that full employment is no longer the primary policy goal—other goals now receive equal priorities.

The third through sixth readings are taken from the Annual Reports of the Council of Economic Advisers. Each reading reflects policy goals and some of the problems involved in achieving them. The reading, "The Objective of Maximum Employment," which is as relevant in 1971 as it was in 1962, discusses the reasons for concern with high employment, and analyzes the appropriate uses of employment policies. The next reading, "Transition to Full Employment Growth," discusses the problems of balancing a high rate of employment with price stability and increasing real output. The reading, "The Unemployment-Inflation Dilemma," pertains to the important and extremely difficult problem which has confronted the economy during 1970 and 1971, namely, reducing the rate of unemployment while at the same time reducing the rate of inflation. The reading, "The United States and the International Economy," discusses the

9

balance of payments problem. The last reading, "State of the Union Message," by President Richard M. Nixon, describes the policy goals set by the Administration for the 1970's.

Employment Act of 1946, as Amended, with Related Laws*

(60 Stat. 23)

[Public Law 304—79th Congress

AN ACT To declare a national policy on employment, production, and purchasing power, and for other purposes.

Be it enacted by the Senate and House of Representatives of the United States of America in Congress assembled,

Short Title

Section 1. This Act may be cited as the "Employment Act of 1946."

Declaration of Policy

Sec. 2. The Congress hereby declares that it is the continuing policy and responsibility of the Federal Government to use all practicable means consistent with its needs and obligations and other essential considerations of national policy, with the assistance and cooperation of industry, agriculture, labor, and State and local governments, to coordinate and utilize all its plans, functions, and resources for the purpose of creating and maintaining, in a manner calculated to foster and promote free competitive enterprise and the general welfare, conditions under which there will be afforded useful employment opportunities, including self-employment, for those able, willing, and seeking to work, and to promote maximum employment, production, and purchasing power.

*Joint Economic Committee, *Employment Act of 1946, as Amended, with Related Laws*, United States Congress, 1966, pp. 1–4.

Economic Report of the President

Sec. 3. (a) The President shall transmit to the Congress not later than January 20[1] of each year an economic report (hereinafter called the "Economic Report") setting forth (1) the levels of employment, production, and purchasing power obtaining in the United States and such levels needed to carry out the policy declared in section 2; (2) current and foreseeable trends in the levels of employment, production, and purchasing power; (3) a review of the economic program of the Federal Government and a review of economic conditions affecting employment in the United States or any considerable portion thereof during the preceding year and of their effect upon employment, production, and purchasing power; and (4) a program for carrying out the policy declared in section 2, together with such recommendations for legislation as he may deem necessary or desirable.

(b) The President may transmit from time to time to the Congress reports supplementary to the Economic Report, each of which shall include such supplementary or revised recommendations as he may deem necessary or desirable to achieve the policy declared in section 2.

(c) The Economic Report, and all supplementary reports transmitted under subsection (b) of this section, shall, when transmitted to Congress, be referred to the joint committee created by section 5.

. . .

Council of Economic Advisers to the President

Sec. 4. (a) There is hereby created in the Executive Office of the President a Council of Economic Advisers (hereinafter called the "Council"). The Council shall be composed of three members who shall be appointed by the President, by and with the advice and consent of the Senate, and each of whom shall be a person who, as a result of his training, experience, and attainments is exceptionally qualified to analyze and interpret economic developments, to appraise programs and activities of the Government in the light of the policy declared in section 2, and to formulate and recommend national economic policy to promote employment, production, and

---

[1] In the original Act, before amendments, this read: "within sixty days after the beginning of each regular session (commencing with the year 1947)". This was changed to "at the beginning of each regular session" in the Legislative Reorganization Act of 1946, Public Law 601, 79th Congress, 1st session.

purchasing power under free competitive enterprise. The President shall designate one of the members of the Council as Chairman.[2]

(b) The Council is authorized to employ, and fix the compensation of, such specialists and other experts as may be necessary for the carrying out of its functions under this Act, without regard to the civil service laws and the Classification Act of 1949,[3] as amended, and is authorized, subject to the civil service laws, to employ such other officers and employees as may be necessary for carrying out its functions under this Act, and fix their compensation in accordance with the Classification Act of 1949, as amended.

(c) It shall be the duty and function of the Council—

(1) to assist and advise the President in the preparation of the Economic Report;

(2) to gather timely and authoritative information concerning economic developments and economic trends, both current and prospective, to analyze and interpret such information in the light of the policy declared in section 2 for the purpose of determining whether such developments and trends are interfering, or are likely to interfere, with the achievement of such policy, and to compile and submit to the President studies relating to such developments and trends;

(3) to appraise the various programs and activities of the Federal Government in the light of the policy declared in section 2 for the purpose of determining the extent to which such programs and activities are contributing, and the extent to which they are not contributing, to the achievement of such policy and to make recommendations to the President with respect thereto;

(4) to develop and recommend to the President national economic policies to foster and promote free competitive enterprise, to avoid economic fluctuations or to diminish the effects thereof, and to maintain employment, production, and purchasing power;

(5) to make and furnish such studies, reports thereon, and recommendations with respect to matters of Federal economic policy and legislation as the President may request.

[2] The original Act, before amendments, read: "The President shall designate one of the members of the Council as chairman and one as vice chairman, who shall act as chairman in the absence of the chairman."

[3] Originally Classification Act of 1923. This act was completely rewritten in 1949.

(d) The Council shall make an annual report to the President in December of each year.

(e) In exercising its powers, functions, and duties under this Act—

> (1) the Council may constitute such advisory committees and may consult with such representatives of industry, agriculture, labor, consumers, State and local governments, and other groups as it deems advisable.

> (2) the Council shall, to the fullest extent possible, utilize the services, facilities, and information (including statistical information) of other Government agencies as well as of private research agencies, in order that duplication of effort and expense may be avoided.

(f) To enable the Council to exercise its powers, functions, and duties under this Act, there are authorized to be appropriated such sums as may be necessary.

. . .

Joint Economic Committee

Sec. 5. (a) There is hereby established a Joint Economic Committee, to be composed of eight Members of the Senate, to be appointed by the President of the Senate, and eight Members of the House of Representatives, to be appointed by the Speaker of the House of Representatives. In each case, the majority party shall be represented by five members and the minority party shall be represented by three members.

(b) It shall be the function of the joint committee—

> (1) to make a continuing study of matters relating to the Economic Report;

> (2) to study means of coordinating programs in order to further the policy of this Act; and

> (3) as a guide to the several committees of Congress dealing with legislation relating to the Economic Report, not later than March 1,[4] of each year (beginning with the year 1947) to file a report with the Senate and the House of Representatives containing its findings and recommendations with respect to each of the main recommendations made by

---

[4] In the original act, before amendments, this read: "May 1". This was changed to "February 1" in the Legislative Reorganization Act of 1946, and subsequently to "March 1" in Public Law 405, 80th Cong., 2d sess.

the President in the Economic Report, and from time to time to make such other reports and recommendations to the Senate and House of Representatives as it deems advisable.

(c) Vacancies in the membership of the joint committee shall not affect the power of the remaining members to execute the functions of the joint committee, and shall be filled in the same manner as in the case of the original selection. The joint committee shall select a chairman and a vice chairman from among its members.

(d) The joint committee, or any duly authorized subcommittee thereof, is authorized to hold such hearings as it deems advisable, and, within the limitations of its appropriations, the joint committee is empowered to appoint and fix the compensation of such experts, consultants, technicians, and clerical and stenographic assistants, to procure such printing and binding, and to make such expenditures, as it deems necessary and advisable. [The cost of stenographic services to report hearings of the joint committee, or any subcommittee thereof, shall not exceed 25 cents per hundred words.][5] The joint committee is authorized to utilize the services, information, and facilities of the departments and establishments of the Government, and also of private research agencies.

(e) To enable the joint committee to exercise its powers, functions, and duties under this Act, there are authorized to be appropriated for each fiscal year such sums as may be necessary, to be disbursed by the Secretary of the Senate on vouchers signed by the chairman or vice chairman.

(f)[6] Service of one individual, until the completion of the investigation authorized by Senate Concurrent Resolution 26, 81st Congress, as an attorney or expert for the joint committee, in any business or professional field, on a part-time basis, with or without compensation, shall not be considered as service or employment bringing such individual within the provisions of sections 281, 283, or 284 of title 18 of the United States Code, or of any other Federal Law imposing restrictions, requirements, or penalties in relation to the employment of persons, the performance of services, or the payment or receipt of compensation in connection with any claim, proceeding, or matter involving the United States.

---

[5] Amended by Public Law 624 (84th Cong., 2d sess.) as follows: "Compensation for stenographic assistance of committees paid out of the foregoing items under 'Contingent expenses of the Senate' hereafter shall be computed at such rates and in accordance with such regulations as may be prescribed by the Committee on Rules and Administration, notwithstanding, and without regard to any other provision of law." (70 Stat. 360.)

[6] This subsection no longer in effect.

Objectives of Economic Policy and Measures of Performance*

Prior to the onset of the Great Depression of the 1930's, the major *explicit* goal of public economic policy in the United States was to maintain stability of the price level. With this goal achieved, it was believed that the natural forces operating in the economy normally would assure expanding employment, economic growth, and equilibrium in international payments. Then the 1930's brought financial collapse, industrial stagnation, severe and protracted unemployment, and disorder in the international system of trade and payments. These conditions shook the faith of those who believed in the capacity of the economy automatically to provide sustained growth and high employment. Toward the end of World War II there was great concern about assuring postwar economic stability. This led to passage of the Employment Act of 1946 which made explicit the responsibility of the government to take deliberate action, in concert with private parties, to maintain high employment and economic growth.

With the same goals in mind this Committee in 1947 first enunciated its stabilizing budget policy. Since that time the United States has become increasingly concerned about maintaining steady economic growth. In addition the country has come to adopt the view that the framing of domestic objectives must take into account the balance-of-payments position of the United States and world economic development generally.

The stabilization policy originally proposed by the CED did not, of course, provide an answer for all problems of economic instability. Moreover, the country is now even more aware that attainment of stable economic growth will not meet the full range of the nation's economic and social needs. In recent years, the country has become concerned about dealing with specific problems of a largely social character. The problems of urban decay and of hard-core poverty are getting increasing attention. The assurance of equal opportunities for the many underprivileged groups in our society calls for the greatest efforts. Not all of these needs can be met by fiscal and monetary policy measures alone. However, the government must consider the impact of fiscal and monetary policies on public and private programs designed to alleviate these problems.

*Committee for Economic Development, from *Fiscal and Monetary Policies for Steady Economic Growth*, January 1969, pp. 23-35.

The purposes of this policy statement are as follows:

To specify and describe the objectives for the over-all economic performance of the United States economy;

To state the manner in which we should measure our major objectives;

To suggest the role that fiscal and monetary policies can play, first, in enlarging the capacity of the economy to perform and, second, in achieving full and stable use of this capacity.

What do we want economic policy to do for the nation? Any discussion of this question will usually identify the four major objectives of policy discussed briefly in Chapter 1—high employment, price stability, economic growth, and equilibrium in our balance of payments.

High Employment

While there had been much previous discussion of the concept of high or full employment, the passage of the Employment Act in 1946 has forced us to think about high employment in measurable terms. Once "maximum" employment was legislated as a goal, it was realized immediately that this did not imply a zero rate of unemployment. There is of necessity some irreducible level or frictional level of unemployment of the labor force at any moment of time in an economy where people are free to work at the job of their choice in the location of their choice, and where production is subject to seasonal influences, shifts in consumer preferences, and changing skill requirements. Unemployment will also persist because some people are not sufficiently well-educated or trained to fill jobs that are available and because of union restrictions on entry into certain occupations in some areas.

For many years an unemployment level of 4 percent of the labor force has been widely used to represent a condition of "high employment." It has become increasingly clear, however, that there is little economic justification for the notion that the target for high employment should be set in terms of a constant fraction of the labor force. We believe that rather than specifying a target for high levels of employment in this way, the economy should take as its employment goal the more general objective of a level of demand for labor which is adequate to absorb those actively seeking employment at wage rates which the market places are willing to pay for their capabilities, i.e., their productivity.

CHART 1. CIVILIAN EMPLOYMENT
(Millions Employed)

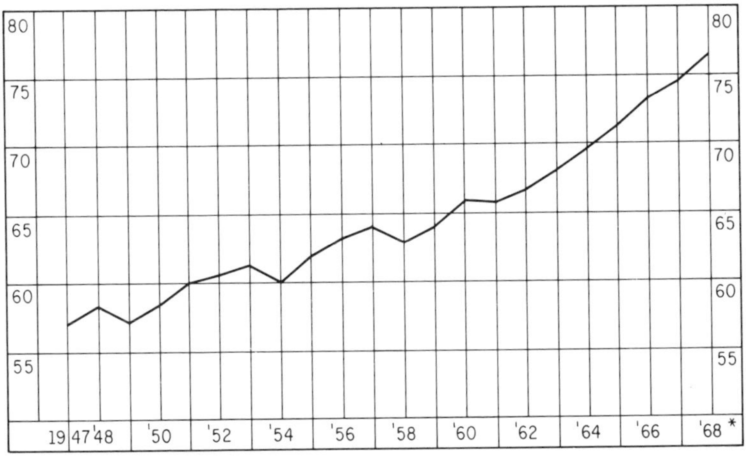

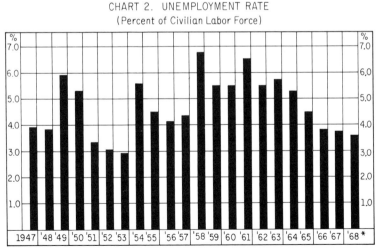

We feel that better insights as to whether this objective is being met can be obtained by a more careful collection and analysis of statistics on job vacancies and on the characteristics of the unemployed. Such an analysis will give additional insight as to how much of the unemployment can be alleviated by measures to expand total demand as contrasted with the contribution that can be made by

CHART 2. UNEMPLOYMENT RATE
(Percent of Civilian Labor Force)

* Average through October. Unemployment rate is based on seasonally adjusted data.
Source: U. S. Department of Labor, Bureau of Labor Statistics.

better labor market information and job training programs.[1] A primary requirement of our high employment policies is the compilation and utilization of data on unfilled job vacancies by location and skill together with unemployment data by similar categories.

However, the absence of such data on a national scale in the United States, and the difficulties that European countries have had in utilizing their job vacancy statistics as guides to stabilization measures, both argue against the immediate substitution of job vacancy and unemployment statistics for the more familiar measure of unemployment as a percent of the labor force.

We believe that our ultimate objective for high employment should be the maintenance of a level of demand for labor which will provide jobs for those seeking employment at wages which the market places are willing to pay for their capabilities, i.e., their productivity. Until job vacancy and unemployment data are improved so that progress toward this objective can be calculated, the present measure of unemployment as a percent of the labor force will have to be used.

Rather than measure achievement of this high employment objective by reference to a simple per cent of the unemployed to the total labor force, information more useful as a guide to fiscal, monetary, and labor market policies would be derived from an analysis of unemployment by skill, age, color, location, duration of unemployment, and by an analysis of job vacancies. If the composition of the unemployed does not match the composition of the available job opportunities, the appropriate measures to expand employment lie in the area of the improvement of labor market information, job training, and increased mobility of labor. If job vacancies are smaller than the number of unemployed capable to fill such positions, the need is for fiscal and monetary policy measures to expand demand and thereby expand job opportunities.

It should be clear that the level of employment which this country can attain will increase as we improve our information about the labor market, as manpower training programs increase and update skills, and as we continue to make progress in the integration of minority groups into the labor force.

Price Stability

This Committee has repeatedly affirmed the desirability of maintaining stability in the price level. Inflation results in arbitrary and

---

[1] Another CED subcommittee is currently studying how training and placement can best meet this problem.

CHART 3. INCREASE OF PRICE LEVELS

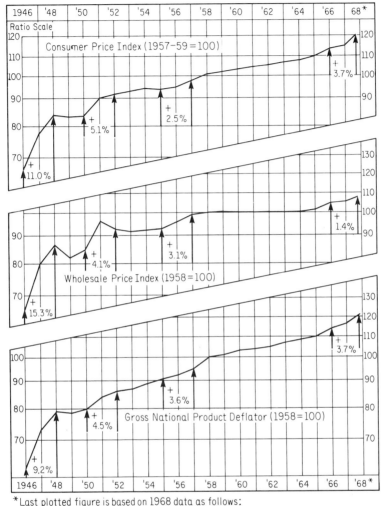

*Last plotted figure is based on 1968 data as follows:
  Consumer Price Index – 9 months average;
  Wholesale Price Index – 10 months average;
  GNP deflator – 3 quarters' seasonally adjusted average.

Note: Percentages shown on graphs are average annual rates of change for period
  indicated between arrows.
Source: U.S. Department of Commerce, Office of Business Economics.

regressive changes in the distribution of wealth and income. It retards
economic growth by diverting resources and energy from the production of goods and services to attempts by both businesses and individuals to lessen the impact of inflation on their own economic
positions. These attempts to protect individual positions from the

effects of inflation frequently give rise to social, political, and economic strife among the different sectors of our society.

This Committee believes—as we think most people believe—that inflation is an evil which cannot be tolerated.[2] Appreciation of the full significance and danger of inflation can be made clear in the following example. A 3 percent rate of inflation in one year if continued as an average, would double the level of prices in roughly 23 years. Clearly, doubling prices in about a generation would work serious hardship upon large groups of our population. In its simplest terms, inflation is a cruel tax on people who live on fixed incomes. This is not a small group. Pensioners, holders of annuities and life insurance policies, investors in bonds and other fixed-money obligations, government employees, private schools, hospitals and other endowed institutions—these and many other groups and organizations suffer when the value of money goes down. In an economy of abundance, it is grossly unfair to place such heavy burdens on those who frequently are least able to protect themselves.

Just as important as the unfairness of the effects of inflation upon the distribution of the national income are its adverse effects upon the total size of the real national income. Inflation is a severe tax upon savings in the form in which most of the population must, in fact, save. And a large flow of savings is the indispensable condition for the rapid growth of productive employment and real national output.

General price stability is not only good for the domestic economy but also protects the nation's competitive position in the world economy from the adverse balance-of-payments effects of price increases greater than those experienced by other major trading nations. Our merchandise trade surplus has dwindled sharply since 1965. The merchandise trade account showed a surplus of only $400 million at an annual rate for the first three quarters of 1968. The substantial weakening of what had come to be considered our great strength in the balance of payments is due in part to the relatively more rapid rise of prices in the United States than was experienced by our major trading partners. Clearly domestic price stability is an important means for the achievement of balance-of-payments equilibrium.

If policy is to be directed at maintaining price stability, it is essential that a reliable measure of price movements be the basis for measuring whether this objective is met. The more widely used mea-

[2] *Defense Against Inflation: Policies for Price Stability in a Growing Economy,* a Statement on National Policy by the Research and Policy Committee of the Committee for Economic Development, New York, 1958, Chapter I.

sures of price movements in the American economy are the Consumer Price Index, the Wholesale Price Index, and the "Implicit GNP Deflator."[3] We believe that the Consumer Price Index is the single most reliable of these major indexes for measuring price stability. It is a measure of changes in the prices of goods and services purchased by urban wage and salary workers. The observed prices are weighted by the quantities purchased in a base period. Although the present index is sometimes called the "Cost-of-Living Index," the popular title is a misnomer. As explained by the Price Statistics Review Committee:

> It is often stated that the Consumer Price Index measures the price changes of a fixed standard of living based on a fixed market basket of goods and services. In a society where there are no new products, no changes in the quality of existing products, no changes in consumer tastes, and no changes in relative prices of goods and services, it is indeed true that the price of a fixed market basket of goods and services will reflect the cost of maintaining (for an individual household or an average family) a constant level of utility. But in the presence of the introduction of new products, and changes in product quality, consumer tastes, and relative prices, it is no longer true that the rigidly fixed market basket approach yields a realistic measure of how consumers are affected by prices. If consumers rearrange their budgets to avoid the purchase of those products whose prices have risen and simultaneously obtain access to equally desirable new, low-prices products, *it is quite possible that the cost of maintaining a fixed standard of living has fallen despite the fact that the price of a fixed market basket has risen*[4] [Italics added]

We recommend that the economy ought to aim for stability in the Consumer Price Index after allowing for the inability of this index fully to reflect quality changes in goods and services produced. As noted earlier, during the period 1959–1964, when wholesale prices remained level, this index rose by 1.4 percent per annum, which many believe is about equal to estimated improvements in quality that are not adequately reflected in the index Our objective, in short, should be a price level stable enough so that neither income nor wealth are unfairly redistributed and so that expectations of inflation do not become substantial elements in business and individual decisions.

[3] $$\frac{\text{GNP in Current Dollars}}{\text{"Real" Current GNP at Base Period Prices}} = \text{"Implicit GNP Deflator"}$$

[4] *The Price Statistics of the Federal Government: Review, Appraisal, and Recommendations,* a Report to the Office of Statistical Standards, Bureau of the Budget, prepared by the Price Statistics Review Committee of the National Bureau of Economic Research, No. 73, General Series, New York, 1961, p. 51.

Economic Growth

A high rate of economic growth has been a major American preoccupation. Rising levels of output substantially improve the economic well-being of the average citizen and also provide an output of increasing variety, scope, and quality to satisfy the wide spectrum of needs and interests of the population. Domestic economic growth also enables this country to help raise standards of living throughout the world. A dynamic, expanding economy eases the social and economic changes and transitions required by a society which demands social improvement and is experiencing rapid technological change. Competing demands for higher incomes, better jobs, and rising standards of living are more easily reconciled if total output is expanding rapidly than if it is rising slowly. Finally, growth provides all the segments of our society with the challenge and the opportunity for achievement that distinguish a vibrant from a stagnant society. **We regard economic growth as an important objective, although not as an end in itself, because it is a means and a prerequisite for the attainment of both economic and other fundamental goals.**

The expansion of the economy's capacity to produce can be viewed as being determined by the enlargement of the labor force and the improvement in productivity. Over the postwar era the trend in productivity gains per man hour in the private economy has been somewhat over 3 percent a year. However, no attempts are made to measure improvements in the efficiency of government workers, and the Department of Labor arbitrarily sets them at zero. Therefore, the measured trend rate of increase in output per man hour for the *total* economy is just over 2.5 percent a year. With the trend in total man hours worked currently growing at about 1.5 percent a year, this implies the rate of potential output is expanding at about 4 percent a year. **We recommend that the objective be to maintain a rate of growth in productivity per man hour at least equal to the 2.5 percent trend. We also recommend that continuing attempts be made to improve this performance.** Our recommendation to maintain and, if possible, to advance the rate of increase in productivity reflects a belief that the improvements in economic well-being arising from more rapid increases in output outweigh the costs of the foregone consumption necessary to provide the larger savings and capital formation required to improve productivity.

Equilibrium in the Balance of Payments

The existence of conditions conducive to a large volume of international trade and capital flows is an important element in any pro-

CHART 4. U.S. MERCHANDISE TRADE
(Billions of Dollars)

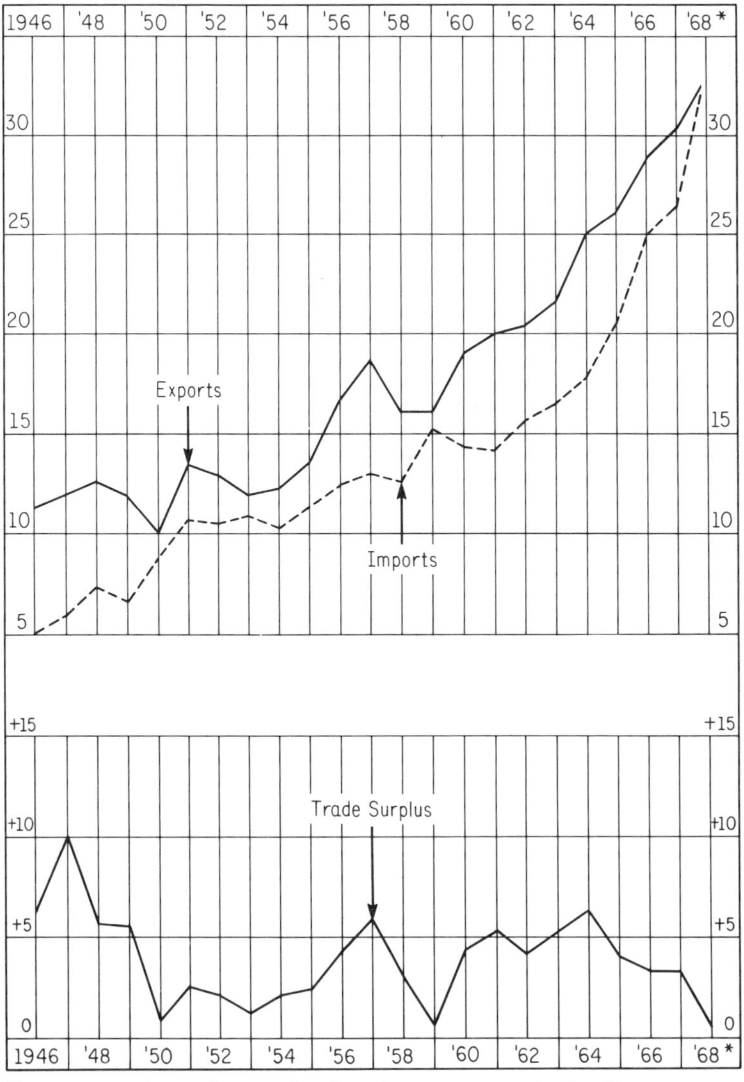

*Average annual rate of seasonally adjusted quarterly totals for first 3 quarters.
Source: U. S. Department of Commerce, Office of Business Economics.

gram for increased productivity and growth in the United States, as well as in other countries. Trade enables countries to emphasize their production in those areas where their productivity is relatively greatest. A country should exploit most intensively the production of goods and services in which its own productivity is highest in comparison with other things it might produce.

Capital flows also raise productivity and standards of living. The flow of capital to those areas where its use results in the greatest increases in output benefits both parties to the transaction. Capital flows of this kind improve productivity and income levels in the country in which they are invested. They also generate more income for the lending country than would be true if the capital were invested less productively at home. Thus, encouragement of trade and capital flows and the creation of conditions conducive to these flows in both the United States and in all other countries is an important element in any program for increased productivity and growth in this country.

The flows of trade, capital, and services among countries require a system of payments and means of settling net deficits and surpluses. Outpayments from the United States need not always be balanced by inflows from abroad; for example, foreigners may choose to hold dollar balances. **Balance-of-payments equilibrium would be attained when on average the deficits in our international accounts are equal to the additional dollars the rest of the world voluntarily wishes to add to its holdings at existing exchange rates when there are no direct or indirect government controls over international trade or capital transactions imposed for balance-of-payments reasons.** It is unlikely that long-run equilibrium in the international payments of the United States can be achieved unless it succeeds in achieving its objectives of high employment, stable prices, and steady growth.

We regard this definition of equilibrium in our international accounts as operationally more meaningful than the deficit measured on the Liquidity basis or on the Official Reserve Transactions basis.[5]

If the United States is to continue to play its part in financing the growth of world trade, increases in foreign private holdings of liquid dollar assets, of cash and credit, may be necessary to support international business. Similarly foreign official institutions may also

---

[5] A deficit as measured on the *Liquidity* basis occurs when short-term claims on the United States held by private and official foreigners increase and there is not an equivalent increase in United States official reserve assets, or when United States reserve assets decline and this decline is not offset by a reduction in foreign official and private short-term claims on the United States. By the *Official Reserve Transactions* method of calculation, a deficit occurs when short- and certain long-term claims on the United States held by official foreign monetary authorities, governments, and international institutions increase and there is not an equivalent increase in United States official reserve assets; or a deficit occurs when United States reserve assets decline and this decline is not offset by a reduction in short- and certain long-term claims on the United States held by official foreign monetary authorities, governments, and international institutions.

desire to increase their holdings of liquid dollar assets. Therefore, on our definition of equilibrium, so long as foreigners, both private and official, wish to increase their dollar holdings, the elimination of a deficit in our international accounts measured on either a Liquidity or Official Reserve Transactions basis would be inimical to the flow of goods and services among nations. Moreover, it would not necessarily be conducive to maintenance of international equilibrium.

The United States, of course, should move through fiscal and monetary policies to reduce its balance-of-payments deficit along lines recommended elsewhere in this statement when it is faced with the prospect of persistent losses of reserves. Action to reduce the deficit would also be required when our government had to exert pressures on other nations to add to their dollar holdings or to refrain from exchanging their dollar claims for American reserve assets. The introduction of direct or indirect controls or other restrictions over trade or capital flows is evidence that our payments are not in equilibrium and is an undesirable means of reducing United States payments deficits.

Of course, at any particular time foreign official and private holders may for a variety of reasons find themselves with more or less dollars than they wish to hold. Changes in United States reserves would then result. Thus, we must maintain a level of reserves sufficient to meet temporary demands, as well as to insure that in the event of persistent deficits the nation will not be forced to take drastic emergency action. Our reserves must be sufficient to give us time to implement in an orderly fashion the measures which will eventually correct the imbalance.

*The Objective of Maximum Employment**

Reasons for Concern over Unemployment

The great depression led this Nation, and most other nations of the free world, to assume national responsibility for the human tragedy and economic waste of involuntary unemployment. Unemployment had previously been regarded as almost solely the personal

*Council of Economic Advisers, from *Economic Report of the President* together with the *Annual Report of the Council of Economic Advisers*, January 1961, pp. 40–48.

responsibility of the individual; now it came to be acknowledged as a charge on the conscience of the Nation. The mass unemployment of the 1930's led to new understanding: that to be unemployed is not to be unemployable; that job opportunities for individual workers depend on national economic circumstances beyond their control.

There are three principal reasons why involuntary unemployment is a national concern: (1) the human obligation to prevent and to relieve economic distress, (2) the basic principle of a free economy that an individual should be able to choose freely how to use his time, whether to work for pay or not, and (3) the economic waste of leaving productive resources idle.

Preventing Economic Distress

First, a wealthy nation cannot in good conscience permit its citizens to be inadequately nourished, clothed, or housed; its sick to be denied medical care; or its young to be deprived of schooling. Unemployment insurance and public assistance are recognitions of this social obligation. But they are not substitutes for the opportunity to earn income from useful employment. For the breadwinner and his family, unemployment means a reduction in living standards. Only about three-fifths of the unemployed in 1961 were receiving unemployment insurance benefits. Even those who were insured generally found weekly benefits a pale shadow of their lost wages. When the unemployment insurance program was inaugurated in the late 1930's, the goal was to provide benefits equal to about half of previous earnings. As Table 1 indicates, benefits now do not meet this standard. The Administration proposed permanent legislation to

TABLE 1

Weekly Earnings in Selected Industries, and Unemployment
Insurance Benefits, 1961

Item	Weekly average, 1961
Unemployment insurance benefits, all industries[1]	$33.80
Weekly earnings, selected industries:[2]	
Retail trade	64.04
Manufacturing	92.34
Telephone communication	92.75
Wholesale trade	93.32
Bituminous coal mining	112.10
Class I railroads	112.41
Contract construction	117.66

[1] For State programs only; see Table B-23.
[2] Gross earnings for production workers or nonsupervisory employees; see Table B-27.
Source: Department of Labor.

strengthen the unemployment insurance system in this and other respects.

For all too many, unemployment has not been simply an uncomfortable interlude between jobs but a catastrophe of long duration; almost one-third of those unemployed in December 1961 had been out of work for 15 or more weeks and one-sixth had been unemployed for at least 27 weeks. Family savings vanish when unemployment is prolonged.

Unemployment is not a perfect measure of the incidence of economic distress. Failure to find work does not entail poverty for some unemployed persons: women whose husbands have good jobs, young people who can fall back on well-to-do parents, older people who have assured livelihoods from property incomes or annuities, people who earn an adequate annual income from work at a seasonal occupation during part of a year. On the other hand, there are many causes of economic distress other than unemployment. Some persons, though employed, suffer from reduced and inadequate incomes resulting from failure to obtain more than part-time or occasional work, or to earn decent returns from long hours of self-employment on the farm or in the shop. Other individuals are not regarded as unemployed simply because, discouraged by a lack of suitable opportunities, they have abandoned the search for jobs. Included in this group are individuals with personal disabilities who can find jobs only when labor markets are tight.

Nevertheless, changes in unemployment are indicative of changes in the over-all magnitude of economic distress. The same conditions of general prosperity which lead to lower unemployment figures also lead to lower rates of involuntary part-time idleness, to better rewards from self-employment, and to more job opportunities for persons on the fringes of the labor force. While effective measures to provide adequate job opportunities will not solve all problems of economic distress, they will solve a substantial share of them. And without successful policy against general unemployment, other attacks on poverty and insecurity stand little chance of success.

Assuring Free Choice

The second reason for national concern over unemployment is the basic principle of a free economy, embodied in the Employment Act, that "useful employment opportunities" be afforded "for those able, willing, and seeking to work." A free society abhors forced idleness as well as forced labor. This principle does not apply a means or needs test for job-seekers. It acknowledges that mature individuals should be able to choose for themselves how they spend their time, as between gainful employment, housework, leisure, and education. Involuntary unemployment can destroy morale and freedom of choice whether or not the individual is in economic need. Americans want to work. Neither welfare programs nor personal means can erase the frustration of the individual who is forced to conclude that society does not need or want his contribution. The general preference for gainful work over unemployment, however well compensated, is demonstrated by the low levels of unemployment in areas with buoyant labor markets, in occupations with ample job opportunities, and in the population at large during years of prosperity.

Avoiding Economic Waste

Finally, excessive unemployment is a waste of productive resources. When these resources are left idle, the useful goods and services they could have produced are forever lost to the Nation. These losses would be enormously wasteful at any time. They are dangerous in a decade when the economy must not only meet compelling domestic needs but underwrite the defense of freedom throughout the world. In coupling maximum production and purchasing power with maximum employment, the Employment Act recognizes the losses of national output and real income associated with unemployment. An estimate of these losses in present circumstances is attempted below. Changes in the unemployment rate are roughly indicative of changes in the "gap" between realized and potential production. The same measures of policy which will lower unemployment will also raise national output closer to capacity to produce. The national economic losses associated with unemployment are, of course, quite independent of the individual circumstances of the unemployed. If housewives, elderly persons, and teenagers on vacation from school are eager and able to produce useful goods and services, it is foolish and wasteful for the Nation to forego their contributions.

Measures of Unemployment

The global measure of unemployment as a percentage of the civilian labor force, provided monthly by the Current Population Survey and published by the Bureau of Labor Statistics, is the best single measure of the economic distress, the frustration of free choice, and the economic waste associated with unemployment. But there are other measures of independent interest. Four of these measures, along with the global rate, are shown in Chart 1:

CHART 1. MEASURES OF UNEMPLOYMENT
Percent Unemployed

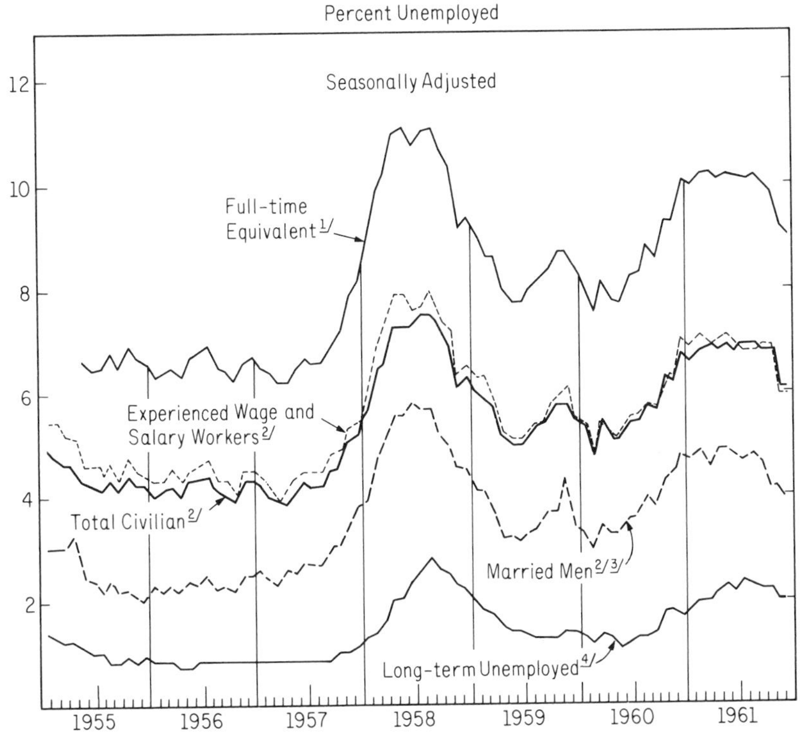

1/ Unemployed plus full-time equivalent of part-time employed as percent of civilian labor force. Excludes self-employed and unpaid family workers.

2/ Percent of civilian labor force in group.

3/ Married men living with their wives.

4/ Persons unemployed 15 weeks or more as percent of civilian labor force.

Sources: Department of labor and council of economic advisers.

(1) The unemployment rate among *experienced wage and salary workers*—those who have already held at least one job. This measure excludes the self-employed and new entrants to the labor force. (2) The unemployment rate among *married men living with their wives*. This measure relates to individuals whose commitment to the labor force is permanent and necessary to the support of their families. It does not cover all individuals with such a commitment, and conceptually it is inappropriate both as a measure of economic waste and as an indicator or involuntary unemployment among persons "able, willing, and seeking to work." (3) A *full-time equivalent* measure which (a) adds to the wholly unemployed the full-time equivalent of work lost by involuntary part-time employment and (b) sub-

tracts the self-employed from both the labor force and civilian employment on the grounds that they are not subject to the risk of unemployment. This concept has merit as a measure of economic waste and of imbalance in markets for hired labor. (4) The number of *long-term unemployed*, those who have been jobless for more than 15 weeks, as a percentage of the labor force. This rate is an important measure of the financial and social distress caused by the concentration of prolonged unemployment on a small fraction of the labor force.

The differences among these measures reveal more clearly than any single measure the anatomy of unemployment. But they show no systematic tendency to widen or narrow. If due allowance is made for volatility in month-to-month movements all five measures tell the same story about changes in economic conditions.

Full Employment as the Objective of Stabilization Policy

The goal of the Employment Act is "maximum employment," or—to put it the other way round—minimum unemployment. Ideally, all persons able, willing, and seeking to work should be continuously employed. Involuntary unemployment is an individual and social evil. No one would prefer for its own sake a higher rate of unemployment to a lower one. But zero unemployment is unattainable. A more meaningful figure is needed to give content to the realistic and forceful declaration of policy in the Employment Act. A feasible interim goal must reflect a balancing of employment and production objectives with other considerations of national policy, within the limits set by the existing characteristics of the economy. Such a goal is set forth in the discussion which follows. We must not forget, however, that any practical unemployment goal is only a temporary compromise, and its attainment must never be an occasion for relaxation, but rather an incentive to search out ways to achieve a still lower rate.

The partial conflict which exists between minimum unemployment and certain other national objectives—and which imposes the necessity of striking a balance between them—results mainly from the fact that these other objectives are served by stability of the general price level. Given the existing structure of the economy and the nature of the processes by which prices and wages are determined, a serious attempt to push unemployment close to zero would produce a high rate of price inflation. The result would be a weakening of the competitive position of U.S. products in world markets, an arbitrary redistribution of real income and wealth, and a threat of even more serious consequences if expectations of further inflation should become dominant.

Happily, however, the conflict between the goals served by price stability and the goal of minimum unemployment is only partial. Stabilization policy—policy to influence the level of aggregate demand—can strike a balance between them which largely avoids the consequences of a failure in either direction. Furthermore, the degree of conflict can be diminished by private and public policies which improve the functioning of labor and product markets.

There are various possible causes of unemployment, on the one hand, and of inflationary pressure, on the other. These causes may be grouped into (1) those related to aggregate demand and (2) those related to the structure and functioning of markets. It is necessary to distinguish carefully between these two groups of causes in setting an appropriate target for stabilization policy.

The relation of aggregate demand and of structural causes to unemployment may be briefly described as follows:

(1) The total effective demand for goods and services—by consumers, businesses, and governments—may be insufficient to employ all the persons seeking work at existing wage rates.

(2) Workers may be idle while vacancies are unfilled. This may arise because the workers live too far away from the available jobs, are not qualified for them, or simply are unaware of their existence. In a dynamic economy, there will always be workers between jobs, some seeking new positions out of preference, some displaced by economic and technological change. New entrants to the labor force will similarly be unemployed while locating jobs suitable to their qualifications and preferences. The length of "frictional" unemployment for any one worker, and the size of the pool of frictionally unemployed, depend on how smoothly the labor market functions, how well the skills, experience, and qualifications of workers match the specifications of available jobs, how ready workers are to change residence and occupation, how adequate are facilities for training and retraining, and how rapidly displacements resulting from economic change are occurring. Structural unemployment may be regarded as an extreme form of frictional unemployment. It occurs when inability or failure to make the necessary adjustments concentrates unemployment of long duration on displaced workers in particular areas and occupations, while elsewhere jobs are seeking workers of quite different qualifications.

Similarly, aggregate demand and the structure of markets are related to the price level, as follows:

(1) Inflation may result from excessive aggregate demand. De-

mands for goods and services by consumers, businesses, and governments may add to a total which exceeds the amount that the economy can supply. Prices will be bid up in all markets, and, as business firms try to expand output in order to seize the profit opportunities presented, increases in wages and in costs of materials will follow. The resulting rise in incomes will reinforce and renew the process. In less extreme circumstances, aggregate demand may press hard upon, but not exceed, the economy's productive capacity. Increases in prices and wages may occur nevertheless, reflecting the need to obtain additional output by using labor and capital more intensively—by making greater use of overtime labor, by attracting workers from great distances, by making employment attractive to persons formerly not in the labor force, and by making use of obsolescent capacity and inefficient production techniques.

(2) Upward pressure on prices may originate in those sectors of the economy where competitive forces are weak and large corporations and unions have a considerable degree of discretion in setting prices and wages. (This discretion, and the public interest in its responsible exercise, are discussed in Chapter 4.) There are two ways in which wage and price decisions in these sectors may put upward pressure on the general price level. First, prices may be increased when demand is not strong in the aggregate or even in the specific industries involved. Because the prices of these industries affect costs elsewhere, increases in their prices tend to spread throughout the economy. Second, prices in these sectors may remain constant in the face of declining demand, although they rise in times of increasing demand. The result in the long run is an upward drift in prices in these industries, which again tends to be transmitted to the whole economy.

Expansion of aggregate demand is clearly the specific remedy for unemployment caused by a deficiency of aggregate demand. Excessive aggregate demand, however, is a source of inflationary pressure. Consequently, the target for stabilization policy is to eliminate the unemployment which results from inadequate demand without creating a demand-induced inflation. A situation in which this is achieved can appropriately be described as one of "full employment," in the sense that further expansion of expenditure for goods and services, and for labor to produce them, would be met by only minor increases in employment and output, and by major increases in prices and wages. Correspondingly, expansion of demand beyond full employment levels would involve a major sacrifice of the objectives by price stability, and only a minor gain with respect to the goal of maximum employment.

The selection of a particular target for stabilization policy does not commit policy to an unchangeable difinition of the rate of unemployment corresponding to full employment. Circumstances may alter the responsiveness of the unemployment rate and the price level to the volume of aggregate demand. Current experience must therefore be the guide.

In the existing economic circumstances, an unemployment rate of about 4 percent is a reasonable and prudent full employment target for stabilization policy. If we move firmly to reduce the impact of structural unemployment, we will be able to move the unemployment target steadily from 4 percent to successively lower rates.

The recent history of the U.S. economy contains no evidence that labor and commodity markets are in general excessively "tight" at 4 percent unemployment. Neither does it suggest that stabilization policy alone could press unemployment significantly below 4 percent without creating substantial upward pressure on prices.

When unemployment was about 5 percent, as in 1959 before the steel strike and in the first half of 1960, the economy showed many independent symptoms of slack, notably the substantial underutilization of plant and equipment capacity. The wholesale price index fell at a rate of 0.2 percent a year in the 15 months April 1959–July 1960; and at the consumer level, prices of commodities other than food rose at a rate of only 0.6 percent.

The economy last experienced 4 percent unemployment in the period May 1955–August 1957, when the unemployment rate fluctuated between 3.9 percent and 4.4 percent (seasonally adjusted). During this period, prices and wages rose at a rate which impaired the competitiveness of some U.S. products in world markets. However, there is good reason to believe that upward pressures of this magnitude are not a permanent and systematic feature of our economy when it is operating in the neighborhood of 4 percent unemployment. The 1955–57 boom was concentrated in durable manufactured goods—notably automobiles (in 1955), machinery and equipment, and primary metals. The uneven nature of the expansion undoubtedly accentuated the wage and price pressures of those years. Moreover, the review of the present price outlook in Chapter 4 points to a recent strengthening in the forces making for price stability. The experience of 1955–57 is nevertheless sobering, and experience at higher levels of activity will be needed to indicate whether stabilization policy can now undertake a more ambitious assignment than 4 percent unemployment.

There is no precise unemployment rate at which expansion of aggregate demand suddenly ceases to affect employment and begins to affect solely the general price level. The distinction between aggregate demand effects and structural effects is a matter of degree, both for employment and for the general price level. Sufficiently high levels of aggregate demand can, and have in the past, cut deeply into frictional and structural unemployment. When vacancies are numerous, the time required to find an attractive job is reduced. When there are vacancies everywhere, no one needs to travel far to find a job. And when no applicant for a job meets its exact specifications, the specifications may well be adjusted. Similarly, the degree of inflationary pressure arising from discretionary price and wage setting is not independent of the general strength of demand. Presumably, this pressure could be entirely eliminated by sufficient weakness in aggregate demand if that were the sole objective of stabilization policy.

But while stabilization policy would not be an ineffective cure for either one or the other of these economic ailments, it would be an extremely expensive cure. On the one hand, attempting to reduce frictional and structural unemployment by a highly inflationary expansion of demand would court disaster in our balance of payments position. On the other hand, an attempt to restrict aggregate demand so severely as to eliminate all risk of an increase in the general price level might well involve keeping the economy far below full employment. This would mean sacrifice rather than achievement of both of the major goals that price stability serves: Equity would be sacrificed because the economy as a whole, and the unemployed in particular, would suffer as a result of the manner in which a few individuals and groups exercise their economic power. Eventually, the balance of payments would also be weakened: under conditions of prolonged unemployment and excess capacity, the investment needed to keep our exports competitive in quality and cost would be unlikely to occur.

The 4 percent interim goal refers to the global measure of unemployment as a percentage of the civilian labor force. An objective stated in terms of any of the other measures of unemployment discussed above would have the same implications for stabilization policy, for the various measures tell the same story with respect to the degree of over-all tightness in the economy. The particular numerical statement of the goal must, of course, change with the unemployment concept used. For example, 4 percent in terms of the global measure is roughly equivalent to a rate of 2 1/4 percent among married men living with their wives; the latter figure, though lower, is at least as serious as the former in its implications for the human consequences of unemployment. Corresponding figures for the other measures of unemployment are 4 1/4 percent among experienced wage and salary workers, 6 1/4 percent for the full-time equivalent concept, and, if the 4 percent global rate is long sustained, a two-thirds of one percent rate of long-term unemployment.

Unemployment of 4 percent is a modest goal, but it must be emphasized that it is a goal which should be achievable by stabilization policy alone. Other policy measures, referred to in the next section and discussed in detail in Part II of this chapter, will help to reduce the goal attainable in the future below the 4 percent figure. Meanwhile, the policies of business and labor, no less than those of Government, will in large measure determine whether the 4 percent figure can be achieved and perhaps bettered in the current recovery, without unacceptable inflationary pressures.

*The Transition to Full Employment Growth**

At the end of 1970 total output should be rising, and the price level should be rising significantly less rapidly than at the beginning of the year. Nevertheless, total output will be below its potential and the rate of inflation, while declining, will probably still be too high. The transition to an economy growing along the path of potential output at full employment with reasonable price stability will not have been completed.

The problem then will be to raise the rate of increase of real output while continuing to reduce the rate of inflation. This will be essentially a continuation of the 1970 problem. There will, however, be two differences.

Whereas in 1970 it is necessary that real output should rise by less than its potential, at some point it will be necessary that output should rise somewhat more rapidly than potential for an interval. This would be the only way for actual output, starting below potential, to regain the potential.

This temporary period of regaining potential output will have to be negotiated cautiously to avoid reviving inflation. The possibility of doing this should be strengthened by another development. As persistence of policy brings the actual inflation rate down, the expected rate of inflation will also fall, and this will influence both

*Council of Economic Advisers, from *Economic Report of the President* together with the *Annual Report of the Council of Economic Advisers*, February 1970, pp. 65-71.

buyers and sellers of goods and services (including labor). Workers will accept smaller increases in money wages if expected price increases are smaller. Interest rates will be lower because lenders will no longer want as much compensation for the expected fall in the value of money and borrowers will be less ready to give such compensation. In other words, the inflationary momentum that resisted antiinflationary policy strongly in its early phases will subside.

With the economy starting from a position below potential, and inflationary expectations reduced, an increase of demand sufficient to restore output to its potential rate need not revive inflation if it does not occur too rapidly. Just how fast it will be safe to proceed can be much better judged after the behavior of the economy in 1970 is tested.

It is impossible to state a target for reduction of unemployment and the rate of inflation in the years just ahead. As both are reduced, the costs and benefits of further reduction must be weighed. It would be foolish to predict now where the margin of improvement in unemployment and inflation lies.

But after 1970 we will have a clear guide for the *direction* of policy: lower inflation, and lower unemployment.

The Stabilization Problem in the Longer Run

The main lesson of stabilization policy in 1969 was the importance of avoiding in the future the kind of inflationary situation and pervasive inflation-mindedness that had built up by the end of 1968. Starting from that situation a major change in the behavior of the economy and in expectations was required, a change that would run against the current of strong ongoing forces. No one could tell how fast that change could be successfully accomplished or the degree of monetary and fiscal restraint required to accomplish it.

The objective of stabilization policy in 1970 will be to move us toward a position where the main goal can be continuity. That position will have been reached when inflation has been brought down to a significantly slower rate, and real output is growing at about its potential rate. At that point growth of the GNP in current dollars at a steady and moderate rate, such as 6 percent per year, would serve to support steady growth of output at its potential rate with a far better performance of the price level than has been experienced in recent years.

The problem then will be threefold:

1. To stabilize the rate of growth of money GNP as far as feasible at a pace that will permit the economy to produce its potential.

2. To adapt the economy so that it lives better with whatever remaining instability may develop; and

3. To press on with measures to reduce both inflation and unemployment further.

Stabilizing the Growth of GNP

The stabilize the growth of GNP will require avoiding destabilizing moves in fiscal and monetary policies and instead using these policies to offset, or at least constrain, destabilizing forces arising in the private economy. One difficulty is that the attempt to use fiscal and monetary policies to counter fluctuations arising in the private economy may itself be destabilizing, if moves are not made in the right amounts and at the right times.

Stabilization by Fiscal Policy. Fiscal policy should avoid large destabilizing swings occurring at random or contrary to the clear requirements of the economy. The big upsurge of Federal spending (nondefense as well as defense spending) after mid-1965, which was unmatched by any general tax increase for 3 years, is a major example of such a destabilizing movement.

The likelihood of achieving economic stability would not be greatly affected by the size of the surplus or deficit, within a reasonable range, if that size were itself stable or changing only slowly, and if the effects on liquidity resulting from secular increases or decreases in the Federal debt were offset by monetary policy. Therefore, it should be possible to decide on the desired full-employment surplus or deficit on grounds other than stability, and without sacrificing stability if the target itself is kept reasonably stable. If the budget position changes sharply in the short run in the absence of marked shifts in private demand, the adaptation of the private economy and the compensatory force of monetary policy may not come into play quickly enough to prevent large swings in overall economic activity. This is a major lesson the the 1970's.

The considerations which should govern the decision about the average size of the surplus deficit are discussed in Chapter 3. Except as a result of a national emergency, there is probably no reason for this decision to change in a way that would radically alter, from year to year, the size of the surplus or deficit that would be the objective under conditions of high employment.

If the surplus or deficit position of the budget that would be yielded by a steadily growing, full-employment GNP were kept stable, the actual figure would, of course, automatically respond to changes in the pace of the economy. If the economy were to grow unusually slowly in any year, receipts would rise slowly also, and the surplus would be below normal (or the deficit would be enlarged further). These variations in the size of the surplus or deficit would tend to stabilize the growth rate of the GNP. The question is in what circumstances and how to go beyond this and vary expenditure programs and tax rates to offset fluctuations in the private economy. There is now abundant experience with the obstacles to effective and flexible use of tax changes for this purpose. Moreover, recent experience and analysis suggest that the stabilizing power of temporary income tax changes may not be as great as had been hoped, and it might become less if they were used frequently, because people would tend to adjust their behavior to what they regard as the normal rate of taxation. Nevertheless, there will be situations in which tax rates must be changed in order to maintain the desired longrun deficit or surplus position and there may also be circumstances in which the effort should be made to use a temporary tax change to offset destabilizing shifts in private demand.

The possibility of varying the rate of increase of Federal spending in the interest of stability is somewhat greater though still limited. Although tax and expenditure decisions are both politically sensitive, the fact that the President has some discretion to adjust the timing of expenditures within the limits of legislation avoids some of the complications that beset tax changes. Moreover, the effect of expenditure changes on economic activity can probably be more reliably foreseen than the effect of temporary tax changes. It is true that the part of the total expenditures that is open to deliberate variation is small, because of legal and implied commitments. Nevertheless, some variations can, in fact, be made, as they were in 1969, and it would be unwise to rule out the attempt to do more of this when the economic necessity is clear. Furthermore, it is possible to broaden the "automatic stabilizers" in Federal expenditure, as the Administration has proposed in the Manpower Training Act and Employment Security Amendments mentioned earlier.

The possibility of using debt management as an instrument of stabilization policy has been severely inhibited by the 4 1/4-percent interest rate ceiling on Government bonds. This ceiling has forced the Federal Government to sell only short or intermediate securities since 1965. Raising or eliminating the ceiling to realistic levels, or eliminating it, would provide the Federal Government with a desirable degree of latitude in conducting its financing operations.

Stabilization by Monetary Policy. Monetary policy can be devoted somewhat more singlemindedly to maintaining stability than can fiscal policy. Nevertheless, there are a number of difficulties in its use. Apparently the effects of changes in monetary policy are felt in the economy with widely varying and often long lags. Therefore, if policy that is intended to have a restrictive effect is continued until the effect is visible, the lagged consequences of what has been done may show up in excessive contraction. The attempt to counter this by a sharp reversal in policy to an expansive posture may, after a while, generate inflationary rates of expansion. In the present state of knowledge there is no ideal solution for this problem. Prudence, therefore, suggests the desirability of not allowing monetary policy to stray widely from the steady posture that is likely on the average to be consistent with long-term economic growth, even though forecasts at particular times may seem to call for a sharp variation in one direction or another.

The suggestion that monetary policy might well be steady, or at least steadier than it has been, raises the question of the terms in which this stability is to be measured. There is abundant evidence that the steadiness of monetary policy cannot be measured by the steadiness of interest rates. Interest rates will tend to rise when business is booming and inflation is present or expected; they will tend to decline in the opposite circumstances. Better results might be obtained by concentrating more on the steadiness of the main monetary aggregates, such as the supply of money, of money plus time deposits, and of total bank credit. This still leaves questions of policy to be resolved when these aggregates are tending to move in different directions, or at different rates of change, as they often do. There is no substitute for trying to understand in particular cases what the significance of the divergences is and what they indicate about the underlying behavior of the supply of liquidity.

Improving our Economic Data

Since the Federal Government has the responsibility for keeping the economy on a noninflationary growth path with high employment, it must have at its disposal the tools for accurately measuring on a timely basis the performance of the economy at the national level. The Government now publishes a broad array of economic statistics that serve this purpose. These statistics, particularly those relating to economic activity in the short run, have grown over the years in volume and quality and have served the Nation well. But our demands for economic data of high quality keep outrunning the supply. The Federal Government is not alone in requiring better statistics, since to an increasing extent businesses have been making use of economic data for planning their own operations. Indeed, never before have so many businesses watched so closely the economic indicators that appear each month or quarter.

More accurate measurement of economic performance would improve the management of policy in a number of ways. It would tell us more certainly where we have been. Elementary as this may sound, it is of crucial importance. Too often this is a fundamental problem for the policymaker. The economy, or some important part of it, may be on a somewhat different course from that indicated by the data. Or economic series that purport to measure the same thing, or almost the same thing, may move in contradictory directions. Sometimes a series that moves in one direction one month moves in the opposite direction when revised the following month. The first requirement for making judgments about where the economy is going or what policies are needed is an accurate picture of where we have been.

Accurate data are also needed in order to help analyze the past and find relationships that have some degree of stability. Accomplishing this aim is obviously only partly a question of statistics; the economy is, of course, more than a mechanism. For example, swings in sentiment and attitudes in our affluent economy have a powerful effect on the inclinations of consumers and businesses to spend. Consumer behavior has been especially difficult to predict in recent years, and may be more complex than had been thought previously. Business decisionmaking is equally complex. Yet economic analysis is a continuing search for patterns of regularity that can be helpful in forming judgments about the economy. And the first requirement for this search is reliable basic data. The Administration has proposed substantial improvements in many of the key economic statistics, including, for example, those relating to retail sales, construction, the service industries, international prices, and job vacancies.

Having data on a timely basis is also important for the policymaker. This is particularly important if there is reason to think that the economy may be shifting its course. This Nation probably has more timely statistics than any other economy, but clearly much improvement is in order here. Early in 1969 the President directed the Director of the Bureau of the Budget to take action that would secure prompter issuance of monthly and quarterly statistical series by Federal agencies. The Bureau of the Budget issued a set of guidelines governing release of major economic indicators, and the statistical agencies have already achieved a considerable speedup. Further progress depends heavily on obtaining prompter reporting from the business community.

Living with Instability

If the American people assign sufficient priority to doing so, they should be able to enjoy a higher degree of economic stability than in the past. Still, some instability will remain, and this emphasizes the importance of improving the operation of the economy so that the remaining instability will cause less pain and inefficiency. The most obvious and probably most important step in this direction is improvement of the unemployment compensation system. Proposals of the Administration to accomplish this have been discussed earlier in this chapter. Improvement of labor markets—through better provision for retraining and movement of workers—would also help to prevent the concentration of unemployment on a small group of workers who are substantially injured by it.

On the inflation side, also, some useful steps can be taken. The distortions introduced into the economy by the presence of interest rate ceilings of various kinds—on savings deposits and shares, on guaranteed and insured mortgages, on loans generally under State usury laws—have become evident in this inflationary period. When market interest rates rise certain uses of credit are shrunk disproportionately because of these ceilings. The need to free the economy of these rigidities is discussed in Chapter 4.

The construction industry has experienced much greater fluctuations in conjunction with general economic instability than most other industries. This has been painful to the workers and contractors in the industry and harmful to the growth of its productivity. Steps to reduce this extreme instability are also discussed in Chapter 4.

The Continuing Problems of Inflation and Unemployment

The present anti-inflation effort should reduce the rate of inflation substantially and demote inflation from its position as the Nation's most important economic problem. Still the problem of getting the inflation rate down further, while at the same time maintaining high employment, will probably remain. This will require persistent efforts to reduce the inflation that occurs when demand is growing sufficiently to keep employment high. One of the most hopeful lines of attack will be to improve the adaptation of the labor force—in skills and location—to the pattern of demand for labor. This will shorten the interval of job-search for persons losing or leaving old jobs or entering the labor force, in given conditions of the labor market. It will permit an increasingly high rate of employment to be attained without so strong a pressure of demand as to cause inflation. Manpower programs to move in this direction by better training programs, application of computer technology to job placement and general overhaul of the Nation's job exchange system, have already been discussed. Evaluation of experience with them should permit further development of improved methods. Measures to improve the competitiveness of product markets to assure that business policies will freely and flexibly adapt to changes in market demand will also contribute to reducing the average rate of inflation that accompanies high employment. Some of these measures are considered in Chapter 4.

There is no inherent reason why a high employment economy must be an inflationary economy—even a mildly inflationary economy. After the series of inflationary episodes since World War II, the transition to a stable condition of high employment without inflation will come slowly. But with persistent attention and effort it is attainable.

The Unemployment-Inflation Dilemma *

The dilemma of having to balance our efforts between reducing unemployment faster and reducing inflation faster is not new. This itself is worth recognizing, because if the problem were truly new, the thinking and experience of the past would be of little value. In fact the dilemma has been one of the central concerns of economics and of economic policy throughout this generation. The problem came to the fore as early as 1936 and 1937 when the economy, although still at a very low level, was recovering from the Depression and prices began to rise. President Roosevelt called public attention to what he believed to be the dangers of the price increases. There were many who thought that the ending of the recovery in the sharp recession of 1937–38 was due to the earlier price rise, which they attributed to concentrations of economic power. This belief was one of the motives for the establishment of the Temporary National Economic Committee (TNEC) to investigate the concentration of economic power.

*Council of Economic Advisers, taken from *Economic Report of the President* together with the *Annual Report of the Council of Economic Advisers*, February 1971, pp. 75–85.

The work of the TNEC led to no conclusions on this point, because its report did not come until the war had superseded earlier concerns. Nevertheless, the problem of reconciling full employment and price stability was prominent in wartime thinking about the postwar economy. This was one of the reasons why some were reluctant to accept what they interpreted as the overly ambitious commitment to full employment implicit in the original "Full Employment Bill," an attitude that led to a less ambitious commitment in the Employment Act as enacted in 1946.

Discussion of the possibility of full employment without inflation continued in the first 10 years after the war. This was a period in which contemporary experience was dominated by the effects of wars, controls, and their aftermath, and it was not generally considered that it could provide much light on the characteristics of a normal peacetime economy. The events of 1955–57 intensified the concern with the problem. We then had the first full employment achieved in normal conditions since 1929, and it was accompanied by a disturbing increase in the inflation rate. From the third quarter of 1954 to the third quarter of 1957, prices (as measured by the GNP deflator) rose at an annual rate of 3.1 percent, reaching a peak annual rate of 5.4 percent in one quarter. Six quarters after the recession began the inflation rate was still 2 percent, and this contributed to the idea of inflation as a permanent problem. This experience lay behind the statements contained in the *Economic Report of the President* during that period about the need for responsible restraint in raising prices and wages.

In the upswing that followed, however, most measures of the general price level stabilized, and this stability continued through 1965. From mid-1958 to the end of 1965 the rate of inflation averaged 1.5 percent per year, as measured by the GNP price deflator, and 1.3 percent by the consumer price index. At the time this moderate rate of inflation was considered as being, for all practical purposes, "reasonable price stability." The experience, however, did not resolve questions about the compatibility of full employment and price stability. Unemployment was high during all of this period, although declining from 7.1 percent in early 1961 to 5.0 percent by the end of 1964 and to 4.5 percent in mid-1965. Some thought that the prolonged period of little inflation would create an environment stable enough so that a gradual reduction of the unemployment rate to 4 percent could be achieved without speeding up the inflation. Evidence that the inflation rate was holding steady at a low level as unemployment fell towards 4.5 percent encouraged this hope. But in fact the GNP price deflator began to rise soon after unemployment fell below 4 percent at the end of 1965, and there had been evidence of the beginnings of a rise in wholesale prices before that. This rise in the inflation rate and its sequel left several important questions unanswered. Would the inflation rate have increased if the drop in the unemployment rate from 5 percent to 4 percent had occurred more gradually? Would the inflation rate have stabilized at the still moderate figures registered late in 1965 if demand had remained just sufficient to keep unemployment at 4 percent? Or was some higher rate of inflation the inevitable accompaniment of the 4-percent unemployment rate?

Demand kept rising rapidly, although not without some interruptions, after the end of 1965, reducing the unemployment rate below 4 percent and pushing the inflation rate still higher. While this was happening, that is, until about the middle of 1969, the dilemma of policy disappeared. Unemployment had been driven down to a level where symptoms of labor shortages and tight labor markets were widespread. In those circumstances the proper course of policy was clear. Restrictive policy which would restrain inflation would carry with it little, if any, cost in the form of undesirable effects on employment. For the time the appropriate direction of policy was unambiguous.

The dilemma reasserted itself in early 1970 when we again experienced high and, for a time, rising inflation rates along with rising unemployment rates. This was a natural transitional combination, in view of the rapid inflation we had been experiencing. Once the rise of total demand was restrained, the effects were first felt on the real side of the economy—on output, employment, and unemployment—with prices continuing to rise as a result of forces set in motion earlier.

The Goals of Policy

There are several reasons for believing that from this point forward a further reduction of the inflation rate will be consistent with reduction of the unemployment rate:

1. A reduction of the inflation rate has already begun. This is reflected in most broad measures of the price level.

2. There is a lag between the emergence of slack in the economy and its effect on the inflation rate so that the full effects on prices of the sluggish economy in 1970 have yet to be felt.

3. If, as expected, employment rises at a moderate rate during 1971, sufficient slack will still remain in the economy to exert downward pressure on the rate of inflation.

4. With output rising fast enough to cut into the unemployment

rate, a high rate of productivity growth should continue through 1971. Stern cost-cutting measures in 1970 have put businesses in a postion to achieve more favorable trends in costs per unit of output as operating rates improve. This will help to limit the pressures of these costs on prices.

To go beyond these general statements of direction and try to estimate how much unemployment and inflation could be reduced, we must move cautiously. However, some approximate judgments seem consistent with recent as well as earlier experience. Confining the economic expansion to a pace which would keep unemployment about where it now is, in the neighborhood of 5.5 to 6.0 percent, would permit a significant decline in the rate of inflation during 1971 and 1972. To allow so high an unemployment rate to persist for so long a time, however, would be inconsistent with the Employment Act—and undesirable even if there were no Act. On the other hand, trying to restore what has been commonly regarded as "full employment"—a 4-percent unemployment rate—within the present planning period that extends to the end of fiscal year 1972 would entail risks on the inflation side. Although this latter path might be consistent with some further reduction of the inflation rate, there is a serious risk that the inflation rate would start rising again if the 4-percent unemployment rate were approached as rapidly as such timing would imply.

There is a feasible path between these extremes that would better meet the Nation's present requirements by allowing significant progress to be made against both inflation and unemployment. This is a path that would see the unemployment rate reduced to the 4-1/2-percent zone by the second quarter of 1972 and the inflation rate, as measured by the GNP deflator, declining to approach the 3-percent range at the same time. Total output would have to rise significantly faster than the growth of potential output, or employment would rise only in proportion to the growth of the labor force and would not cut into unemployment. The necessary rate of increase of total output, however, would not have to exceed the rates that have been achieved during past periods of economic recovery.

The general goal, which is more important than the precise numbers, is that the rate of unemployment should decline as fast as is consistent with a reasonably steady and durable decline in the rate of inflation. We believe that the numbers we have proposed—an unemployment rate in the 4-1/2-percent zone and an inflation rate declining to approach the 3-percent range by mid-1972—are feasible representations of that goal. But the numbers are themselves not the fundamental goal.

It has to be recognized that achievement of this goal would still leave the economy short of the ideal with respect to both unemployment and inflation. As things turn out, the economy may yield better results on both sides than are projected here. But it would be unrealistic to count on such an outcome, and irresponsible to hold out to the American people the idea that there are readily available policies which would achieve it. The long and accelerating inflationary boom that was set off beginning in late 1965 left the country with this unemployment-inflation dilemma, whose severity was only subsequently appreciated. But to move firmly along the path laid out would relieve the anxiety about the economy from which the country has been suffering for many years and generate confidence in further progress.

Improving the Unemployment-Inflation Choice

How rapidly we can move in expansion of the demand for output, with associated increases in production and employment, will depend heavily on the capability of the economy to resist the inflation of prices and costs. In many directions we see accumulating evidence of public weariness with a continuing deterioration in the purchasing power of its money. Surveys of public sentiment reveal it sharply. Widespread public support for direct price and wage controls clearly reveals public frustration with inflation even if the full consequences that these controls would have in distortions and black markets are not perceived. Developments which persistently force costs and prices upward will simply prolong unemployment and the sluggish spending inclination of consumers. And growing confidence in prospects for a reasonably stable price level would make a major contribution to invigorated consumer spending and improved economic conditions generally.

Broad fiscal and monetary policies must continue to play the basic role. How expansive these policies can be, however, will depend on what more can be done to enable the economy to translate rising demand into rising output, employment, and real incomes rather than into a more rapidly rising cost-price level. This list of other possible actions, beyond the prudent management of fiscal and monetary policies, is long and varied. The problem is to select those which would be, on balance, helpful. It is not solved by saying that reliance on fiscal and monetary restraint alone will make the process of disinflation slower and more painful than we would like. That is a restatement of the problem, not a solution to it.

As a basis for thinking about the problem, several points must be borne in mind:

1. The free market system of determining prices and wages, even with its imperfections, serves exceedingly well in shaping what gets produced and by whom, and how the resulting income gets distributed. These are key questions in any economy, and no effective substitute for this market economy has been found that answers them better. We take the free market system for granted, like the air we breathe, and become conscious of the benefits of either only after they have been lost.

2. There is now a great deal of experience to indicate that the superficially attractive route of voluntary controls is unlikely to lead to a solution. By "voluntary controls" is meant a system in which the Government, or a quasi-independent board selected by the Government, specifies comprehensive standards of wage-price policy to be observed voluntarily by labor and business, without any similarly comprehensive means of enforcement by Government. The basic deficiency in this approach is that it counts on a large number of people to acquiesce in conduct that they find contrary not only to their own interests but also to their view of fairness, propriety, and efficiency. The great initial attraction of the idea, that it makes the public think something effective is being done, is also one of its adverse consequences because it distracts attention from the real nature of the problem.

3. At the same time, it is evident that some price and wage increases that are going on are not adaptations to current basic market conditions and are not consistent with efficient operation of the economy. To some extent this simply reflects a lag in adjustment to the change in market conditions that has taken place in the past year. But in some cases the behavior of prices or wages can be explained only by a combination of this factor with an unusual degree of insulation from competitive market forces.

4. In some cases the insulation from market forces is due to acts of commission or omission by the Federal Government. This may be true, for instance, in industries that are protected from foreign competition by import quotas or voluntary arrangements with similar effect. In these cases the Government has the instruments at hand for correcting the problem. This does not, in itself, make the correction easy. Those who have been the beneficiaries of a shelter from competitive forces would certainly feel aggrieved by changes in conditions on which they have come to rely.

Government policy must find its way among all these considerations. Short of an emergency of a kind which does not exist, mandatory comprehensive price and wage controls are undesirable, unnecessary, and probably unworkable. The Government should not rely upon pseudo-solutions for real problems and should not delude the public about doing so. But there are cases where price or wage increases not justified by competitive market forces are contributing to the prolongation of the inflation and to unemployment as well. In some of these cases the Government has means of correction available that do not interfere with market performance but tend rather to improve it.

What is called for is a policy of doing what can effectively be done, wherever it can be done, and not pretending to do more. The Administration set out on this course with the President's speech of June 17, 1970, and has since then been following it with increasing force.

In June the President directed the Council of Economic Advisers to issue a periodic *Inflation Alert* to call attention to specific cases or general features of exceptionally inflationary wage or price behavior. The purpose of these reports was to bring to bear on important wage and price decisions a more informed and sharply focused public attention. The Council will continue to issue the *Inflation Alert* approximately every 3 months. Certain points made in the December 1970 issue, prompted by developments in the immediately preceding period, are worth reiterating.

1. Apart from temporary aberrations the general price level tends to rise by the excess of wage increases over productivity increases. Productivity cannot be counted on for long to rise more than about 3 percent per year, although this rate will probably be exceeded during the next year. This means that a continuing 7-percent annual rate of increase of employee compensation per hour would commit the economy to a continuing inflation rate of about 4 percent.

2. We shall not make progress in reducing the inflation rates if the gains we hope to make on the labor cost front are offset by too rapid increases of profit margins.

3. If the inflation is to be slowed down, all wages that have not kept up with the inflation of prices cannot catch up in any short period. On the average, labor compensation has kept pace with the inflation and productivity increases, but some wages have led and some have lagged. If those that have lagged were to catch up quickly, while the leaders did not fall back—as they surely would not in a short period—then the cost-price spiral is given another turn, prices rise further, and new laggards are created who feel they have to catch up.

4. To embody in wage agreements covering two or three future years provisions for wage increases based on the assumption that

prices will continue to rise at recent peak rates is not a reasonable response to our present situation. If this were done generally it would be a recipe not only for permanent rapid inflation but also for persistent unemployment, because the Government would be bound to try to check the inflation by generally restrictive policies. On the other hand, in some cases escalator clauses, which relate future wage changes to actual variations in the cost of living rather than to the expectation of continued inflation as its peak rate, may have a role to play during the adjustment to a more stable price level.

The President's June 1970 speech also announced the establishment of the Regulations and Purchasing Review Board to correct Government policies which unnecessarily contribute to inflation. It has under consideration a number of problem areas on which recommendations will be forthcoming. Examples of these are the management of import restrictions, regulations which unduly increase the cost of bidding on small Government projects, design and procurement methods for Government buildings, and the administration of the Davis-Bacon Act, which requires that contractors on Federal construction projects pay "prevailing" wages (a provision which in practice may have exerted an inflationary effect on construction wage rates and costs).

It is the general policy of this Administration that where it has a legitimate role the Government should act to correct market conditions that prolong inflation, or whose correction can have a favorable effect on the price level. In line with this policy the Administration last fall took two steps to restrain increases of crude oil prices. It relaxed limitations on the importation of oil from Canada and permitted production of oil on Federal offshore leases without restriction by State regulatory commissions.

Following the announcement of a large increase in prices of some steel products in January 1971 the President directed the Cabinet Committee on Economic Policy to investigate economic conditions in the steel industry which were giving rise to such increases. To be taken into account in this review is the voluntary agreement by producers of steel in Japan and the European Economic Community to limit their sales of steel in the United States, an agreement negotiated by the U.S. Government. One subject to be investigated is how the interests of U.S. users of steel, including many industries which themselves face foreign competition, can best be correlated with the interests of U.S. producers in these international steel arrangements.

Rapidly rising construction costs have been a serious concern for the past 2 years. In 1969 the Administration took steps to reverse price increases in lumber; the impact on construction is one reason for concern about steel price increases. The Administration has also moved to check the extraordinary wage and price increases in the construction industry. The wage increases have been occurring despite high unemployment in the industry. On January 18, 1971, the President met with leaders representing construction workers and employers and asked them to submit a plan for stopping the exceptionally large wage and price increases that are raising the cost of new homes and other buildings and causing unemployment in the industry itself. An effective resolution of these problems by parties in the industry would avert the need for changes in the legal provisions affecting the construction labor market. The public interest cannot condone continuing massive increases in these costs at a time when American families need more homes and many in the industry are unemployed and need jobs. The rising demand for houses, highways, and buildings must produce more construction and not be dissipated in higher costs and prices.

To regularize the increasingly active Federal role in particular labor or product markets, the Council's function of alerting against inflation has been broadened. By a decision taken in January the Council of Economic Advisers will report immediately to the Cabinet Committee on Economic Policy on any exceptionally inflationary wage or price developments so that the Cabinet Committee can consider appropriate Federal action.

The measures the Administration is taking will contribute to the capability of the economy to resist inflation as it moves along a rising path in 1971–72. They will not relieve the country of the consequences of past errors which have caused us to live for a longer time with both more unemployment and more inflation than anyone would like. They will still leave us dependent upon a course of steady but not excessive economic expansion as the way out of this dilemma. But they give the Nation additional assurances that 1971 can be a year not only of diminishing rates of inflation but also of rising employment and output.

The Path of the Economy in 1971

Some of the factors that will determine the course of the economy in 1971 are present and visible, others may be present but not now clearly seen, and still others are, from the standpoint of the Federal Government, matters of policy still to be decided or at least subject to revision.

The most obvious of the present conditions is that the year 1970 ended with unemployment in the neighborhood of 6 percent and output in the fourth quarter about 6-1/2 percent below its potential. As explained in Chapter 1, the fourth quarter was significantly depressed by the automobile strike. This carries with it the probability of a large rise in output in early 1971 to rebuild inventories and meet customers' demands for motor vehicles. Also, apprehension that there may be a steel strike after midyear is likely to cause some larger than usual additions to steel inventories in advance. These two factors will provide a special boost to total output in the first half of the year but they also involve the danger of a subsequent letdown. The assurance of a reasonably smooth and even expansion throughout the year must be a special concern of economic policy in 1971.

Aside from these transitory influences, there are several conditions that promise a strong rise of output during the year. The sharp rise in housing starts which occurred in the second half of 1970, the large inflows of savings into thrift institutions in the same period, and the beginning of a decline in mortgage interest rates all point to a much increased rate of residential construction in 1971 as compared with 1970. How fully these promising developments translate into more housing and more jobs will depend heavily on progress in stabilizing labor and other costs in the industry.

The increased availability of funds and lower interest rates, especially during the second half of 1970, permitted State and local governments to increase their borrowing substantially, and this will support an acceleration of State and local expenditure.

On the other hand, the most recent survey of anticipated plant and equipment expenditure of business, made by the Department of Commerce and the Securities and Exchange Commission in late November and December, suggests a year-to-year rise of 1-1/2 percent. This does not allow for 1971 business purchases of automobiles and trucks not bought in 1970 because of the strike. It also does not allow for the effects of the liberalization of depreciation allowances for tax purposes that was announced in early January 1971 and went into effect retroactively to January 1. This liberalization will initially add about $2.6 billion in calendar 1971 to the after-tax cash flow of business. It will stimulate investment by increasing the after-tax rate of return on machinery and equipment.

The catch-up after the auto strike and the stocking up in anticipation of a steel strike are likely to lead to a high temporary rate of inventory accumulation in the first half of 1971. Apart from this, however, there is nothing in the relationship between inventories and sales as the year opens to suggest that a change in the rate of inventory accumulation will be an active element in the economy for the year as a whole.

The Federal Budget proposed by the President implies an increase of $17.0 billion in expenditures on the national income accounts basis between calendar 1970 and calendar 1971. Federal purchases of goods and services would decline $1.9 billion, the reduction in defense spending more than offsetting a rise in nondefense purchases.

The first instalment of revenue sharing together with other programs would result in $6.6 billion of increased grants to the States, and these will support increased State and local expenditures. Also, there would be an increase of $12.0 billion in transfer payments to individuals, resulting in part from a proposed 6-percent increase in Social Security benefits effective January 1, 1971. On the other side of the Budget there will be the reduction of revenues resulting from the depreciation revision.

There is, of course, no counterpart of the Federal Budget to represent the probable course of monetary policy during 1971. In practice one of the important features of monetary policy as an instrument of economic stabilization is its capability for being adapted quickly and flexibly to emerging developments. As a basis for considering what the outcome for the year would be with a specified combination of policies, it is convenient to assume that the money stock will continue to grow at about the rate that has prevailed since the turn early last year.

There is little doubt that this combination of conditions and policies will bring forth a substantial rise of total output during the year. But the *rate* of expansion is critical for attainment of the Nation's economic goals, and this rate is uncertain. The outcome will depend upon the level of personal savings, the response of business investment to an actual upturn of sales and profits, the effects of rising construction costs on the housing market, the influence of the depreciation reform on business planning, the degree to which individuals and businesses want to rebuild their liquidity, and many other factors. The combination of such variables will determine whether, under present policies, there is a vigorous cumulative cyclical recovery such as has occurred after some economic declines or only a gradual rise.

There is a considerable body of opinion that expects the gross national product for 1971 to be in the range between $1,045 billion and $1,050 billion, which would be an increase of 7 to 7-1/2 percent above that for 1970. This is a possible outcome. However, it seems more likely that with present policies the outcome would be higher than that and could be as high as $1,065 billion.

A $1,065 billion GNP for 1971 would be consistent with satisfactory progress towards the feasible targets suggested above—that is, towards an unemployment rate in the 4-1/2-percent zone and an inflation rate approaching the 3-percent range by mid-1972. This calculation involves estimates of the rates of increase of productivity and the labor force, which may in fact turn out differently, so that the connection between the unemployment-inflation targets and the 1971 GNP is not a rigid one. Nevertheless, although emerging information may later suggest a different view, the figure of $1,065 billion for the GNP in 1971 is an appropriate intermediate target of a policy whose ultimate goal is not a dollar total but a desired behavior of prices, unemployment, and real output. It is reasonable to expect that with an increase of the GNP to $1,065 billion in 1971, the rate of price increase would be declining through the year, the unemployment rate would also end the year significantly lower than at the end of 1970, and real output would show a strong gain.

For the GNP to reach $1,065 billion in 1971 would require an increase comparable to the increases after the low points of the economy in 1954, 1958, and 1961. If the rise in the money stock were to continue at the 1970 rate, the ratio of money to the GNP would then decline at about the average rate of the period 1952-70. Although this is a possible development, it is not a certainty. In the earlier recoveries cited, a major stimulus to the sharp rise of demand and output was a change from running down inventories to building them up. This is less likely in 1971 than after the earlier adjustments, which were much more severe.

A GNP in the neighborhood of $1,065 billion in 1971 is a good present estimate of the figure consistent with the targets for unemployment and inflation. It is feasible, and its realization with the proposed budget and complementary monetary policy is a reasonable expectation.

It will be necessary to maintain an appropriate balance between our international responsibilities and domestic objectives of economic policy in decisions about how to combine or "mix" the different instruments of policy. And the economy remains a highly complex system which, even with its patterns of regularity, does not respond to policy changes in simplistic and invariant ways. For these reasons we must be prepared, as new evidence appears, to make promptly the necessary policy adjustments.

The President's Budget for 1972 is based on the principle that expenditures should not exceed the revenues that the tax system would yield under conditions of full employment. This is an important principle. It permits the Federal budget to support the economy when the economy is weak, by allowing the Federal budget to move into a deficit under those conditions. But it retains the fiscal discipline of budget balancing by drawing a line beyond which expenditures may not go without tax increases. Moreover, keeping the full employment budget balanced, even when the economy is below full employment, prevents the Government from incurring commitments to higher expenditures and lower taxes that would unduly encumber the future. The Budget for fiscal 1972 provides for the most urgent needs that should be met through Federal expenditures. Moreover, the yield of the present tax system will be required later to meet foreseeable expenditures to which the Government is already largely committed. Therefore, still further increases of expenditures beyond this Budget or cuts in taxes would not have been consistent with fiscal discipline.

In the past year monetary policy has moved towards a greater degree of stability in the rate of increase of the monetary aggregates, notably the stock of currency plus demand deposits. This is, as was stated in last year's *Economic Report of the President*, a desirable direction. The financial and economic system is thus given a more stable monetary framework within which to operate.

The reasons for a new stability in fiscal and monetary policy are weighty. But the need to press forward to reduce unemployment and inflation is also great. After the economic instability we have experienced in the past 5 years the parameters of the system cannot be located with precision and may well be in flux. It would be unwise to try to freeze a course of policy which is expected to carry us through the difficult months ahead without change. A course of flexibility and determination, with cooperation and division of labor among the several instruments of economic policy, will be needed, and if followed will lead to the goals we all seek.

The United States and the International Economy*

The international economy has undergone a remarkable transformation in the past decade. For many years after World War II, import quotas, discriminatory trade practices, and exchange restrictions on all forms of international payments characterized the bulk of

*Council of Economic Advisers, from *Economic Report of the President* together with the *Annual Report of the Council of Economic Advisers*, January 1963, pp. 91-96.

international transactions. Though further progress needs to be made, much of this restrictive legacy has now been swept away. This transformation culminated in the formal acceptance by the major European countries in early 1961 of the currency convertibility requirements of the International Monetary Fund. It is a notable achievement and has far-reaching implications for the U.S. economy and U.S. economic policy.

Among the factors facilitating this development has been a massive redistribution of the world's gold and foreign exchange reserves. At the end of 1948, the United States held 71 percent of the free world's monetary gold stock; by June 1962, the U.S. share had fallen to 40 percent. During the same period, Western Europe's share grew from 15 percent to 44 percent. In addition, foreign official holdings of liquid dollar assets rose by nearly $9 billion. This redistribution ended the excessive concentration of reserves which had been brought about by the political upheavals in Europe in the 1930's, World War II, and the requirements of postwar reconstruction. In achieving balance of payments surpluses which rebuilt reserves, continental European countries gained greater freedom of action to promote economic expansion and to reduce restrictions on international transactions.

The redistribution of reserves was brought about partly through deficits in the international payments of the United States, which led to large transfers of gold and liquid dollar assets to Europe. These U.S. payments deficits have persisted beyond the point where they improve the distribution of the world's monetary reserves. Indeed, continuing large payments deficits by the United States could create doubts about the stability of the dollar and threaten the efficient operation of the international payments systems. As a result, the U.S. Government has had to pay close and constant attention to the net financial outcome of its transactions, and those of its citizens, with the rest of the world. Important measures have been taken to improve the payments position of the United States, and domestic economic policy has been framed with attention to the balance of payments and the position of the dollar. International transactions of the United States are discussed in the first section of this chapter.

The relaxation of many restrictions on trade and payments and the redistribution of world reserves have not been the only factors transforming the world economy. The progress of the European Economic Community (EEC) toward a rapidly growing, unified, tariff-free market encompassing six European countries—and possibly more in the future—has already profoundly altered world economic relationships. The EEC offers a domestic market broadly comparable to the United States and an import market even larger. Liberal access to this market will be vital to future foreign trade; exclusion by restrictive import tariffs or other barriers could seriously affect the trade and economic development of many countries of the free world. The emerging EEC and the relationship of the United States to it are discussed in the second section of this chapter.

It is now generally acknowledged that the responsibility of the industrial nations for providing capital and technical knowledge to other countries for economic development requires more than the occasional and sporadic efforts made before the mid-1950's. Systematic economic development of the low-income parts of the free world—within a span of time that is very short by historical standards—has become a major objective of western foreign policy. Carrying out this gigantic task will require considerable transfers of capital and technical skill. It will result in large shifts in the structure of world production and trade, and will require substantial adjustments in both advanced and developing countries. Some of these problems are discussed in the third section of this chapter.

These developments have one common characteristic: they bring countries economically closer together. They tend to integrate the free world economy. Markets will become more unified, competition will be keener, and differences among nations in techniques of production will diminish. Substantial progress toward our foreign economic objectives will be made, but new challenges for economic policy, national and international, will arise. Some of these problems and recent efforts to find solutions are discussed in the final section of this chapter.

U.S. International Transactions

The United States as World Trader, Investor, and Banker

The United States is by far the largest producing nation in the world, accounting for more than 40 percent of total industrial production of the free world. Its 188 million inhabitants place it fourth among nations in population, and its unequalled level of per capita income makes it the world's largest domestic market and largest source of savings.

As trader. The basic purpose of our foreign trade is to exchange goods produced efficiently in the United States for goods which we can produce relatively less efficiently or not at all. International trade lowers costs and raises standards of living both at home and abroad. Foreign trade accounts for a much larger part of transactions of the U.S. economy than is generally appreciated. Even though our merchandise exports are only about 4 percent of total gross national product (GNP), they amount to nearly 9 percent of our total production of movable goods. For some products, overseas demand is exceptionally important; it provides over half the market for such diverse U.S. products as rice, DDT, and tracklaying tractors. Imports by the United States provide materials essential for production and also permit Americans variety and diversity in their consumption. Crucial products like nickel and cobalt come almost entirely from foreign sources.

U.S. exports and imports are a major part of world trade. In the first three quarters of 1962, U.S. merchandise imports were nearly 14 percent of total world imports. For some countries and some commodities, of course, the U.S. market is far more important than this average share implies. For example, U.S. coffee imports are usually over half of total world imports of coffee.

U.S. citizens pay large sums for services provided by foreigners—transportation of goods and persons, food and lodging for American tourists and businessmen traveling abroad, interest, dividends, and profits on the funds of foreigners invested in American enterprise or securities. In addition, the United States spends overseas nearly $3 billion (gross) a year for its own military defense and, indeed, for the defense of the entire free world. This expenditure is made in part directly by the U.S. Government and in part by more than one million U.S. servicemen and their dependents stationed abroad.

The United States is also a major supplier of goods and services, accounting in 1961 for nearly 18 percent of total world exports of merchandise, for nearly one-fourth of world exports of manufactures, and for nearly one-third of world exports of capital goods. It is a principal exporter of many agricultural goods, especially cotton, wheat, tobacco, soybeans, and poultry, and it exports large amounts of military equipment to its allies—some on a grant basis, some for cash payment.

The very size of the United States in the world economy lends to its economic activity and its economic policies special importance and interest abroad. Its rate of unemployment, economic growth, and commercial and financial policies are closely charted and carefully watched throughout the world.

As saver and investor. A nation as large and wealthy as the United States is naturally an important source of savings for the entire world, and national savings move abroad both as private investment and as official foreign aid. Its advanced technology invites emulation abroad, and the profitability of duplicating American technology draws American savers and investors beyond domestic borders. Its need for foreign resources to supply American production attracts private U.S. development capital. In addition, the United States has accepted heavy responsibility for the economic development of emerging nations, which require public as well as private capital.

Private long-term investment abroad by U.S. residents has risen markedly in the past decade, from an annual average of $0.9 billion in 1952–55 to $2.5 billion in 1958–61. Much of this increase has gone to Europe.

The U.S. Government provided $3.2 billion to foreign countries and international lending institutions in the first three quarters of 1962—in the form of development loans, Export-Import Bank export credits, sales for local currencies, commodity and cash grants, technical assistance, and contributions to international institutions. This was 12 percent more than in the corresponding period in 1961. U.S. foreign aid to the developing nations has risen markedly since 1954, and under new programs, notably the Alliance for Progress in Latin America, U.S. economic assistance is expected to continue to be high. Total aid expenditures are, however, still below those reached in the late 1940's under the Marshall Plan to assist European recovery.

Both private investment outflows and government aid are appropriate for a high-output, high-saving country such as the United States, and both are expected to yield considerable economic and political returns in the long run. Government and private lending and equity investment add substantial amounts each year to the net foreign assets of the United States, which have risen steadily in the past decade. Their contribution to the growth of U.S. national wealth is shown in Table 12, Chapter 3. But in the short run, both also aggravate the U.S. balance of payments deficit. To reduce the impact of the foreign aid program on the balance of payments, a large part of foreign aid expenditure has been tied to the purchase of goods and services in the United States. In the first three quarters of 1962, 76 percent of government grants and capital outflows resulted in no direct dollar outflow, compared with 65 percent two years earlier. Recent changes in the tax treatment of earnings on foreign investments (described in Appendix A) were designed to achieve more equitable tax treatment between U.S. investment at home and abroad. They should reduce the outflow of investment funds to the extent that these funds were attracted by various tax privileges available in several other countries, and should also increase the repatriation of foreign earnings. Thus these changes should improve the U.S. payments position, at least in the short run when improvement is crucially needed.

Though foreign aid and investment absorb only a small part of U.S. savings, the United States is providing a substantial part of the total flow of savings across national boundaries, especially of the flow to the developing nations. The Development Assistance Committee (DAC) of the 20-nation Organization for Economic Cooperation and Development (OECD) estimates that the United States in 1961 supplied 57 percent of official foreign aid and 44 percent of private long-term investment flow from DAC members to the less developed countries.

As banker. Since the end of World War I, and especially in the past 15 years, the U.S. dollar has emerged as the principal supplement to gold as an international store of value and medium of exchange. The important position of the United States as a market for goods and as a source of goods and savings, its well-developed, extensive, and efficient financial markets, and its long-standing policy of buying gold from, and selling it to, foreign monetary authorities at a fixed price have all made the U.S. dollar an attractive form in which to hold international reserves. Foreign monetary authorities hold more than $12 billion—over one-quarter of their total gold and foreign exchange reserves—in liquid dollar assets, mostly in the form of U.S. Treasury bills and deposits in American banks. In addition, foreign private parties hold $8 billion in dollar assets, and international institutions nearly $6 billion.

These large outstanding claims on the United States indicate the importance attached by the rest of the world to the dollar as an international currency, and the significance of the United States as an international banking center. For a number of years, the deficit in the U.S. balance of payments was financed to a large extent by increases in foreign dollar holdings which enabled foreign governments and nationals to acquire earnings assets and at the same time add to their liquid resources. In recent years, about one-fourth of our over-all deficit has been settled in gold, but the growth in dollar holdings abroad was continued on a significant scale. The rise in dollar holdings has been an important element in the growth of international liquidity.

But these large balances also make the dollar peculiarly vulnerable. A decline of confidence in the dollar, resulting in widespread conversion of dollars into gold, would create a serious problem for the international payments system and for the economic progress of the free world. Therefore, satisfactory progress in reducing the U.S. payments deficit is essential at this time.

The United States still holds large gold and foreign exchange reserves. Last summer the President reaffirmed U.S. determination to defend the existing parity of the dollar and indicated the country's willingness to use its entire gold stock, if necessary, to do so. In addition to the $16 billion in gold and convertible currencies held by the United States, stand-by arrangements have been entered into with a number of individual countries, and the United States has extensive drawing rights on the International Monetary Fund. The Fund itself was strengthened in October when a special borrowing arrangement, supplementing the Fund's resources by as much as $6 billion, came into force. The final section of this chapter will describe how international cooperation in the past few years has developed new and more effective techniques to protect the dollar and the international payments system against speculative attack.

The balance of payments in 1962. A record of the international transactions of the United States is presented in the balance of payments accounts, compiled by the Department of Commerce (Table 14). For the year 1962 as a whole, the over-all payments deficit of the United States was around $2 billion—a decline from $2.5 billion in 1961 and $3.9 billion in 1960 (Chart 12). Although U.S. imports have risen substantially above their 1961 recession low, rising commercial exports have offset a part of the increase. Earnings from American investments abroad continued their upward trend of the past few years. Net military expenditures abroad were offset substantially by accelerated payments by Germany against current and future delivery of materials for national defense. The German Government has agreed to offset fully U.S. defense expenditures in Germany by military purchases in the United States, thus both bolstering the German defense contribution and reducing the net impact of our military spending abroad. More recently the Italian Government has also agreed to substantial military purchases in the United States.

U.S. foreign aid expenditures rose further in the first three quarters of 1962, but since they were increasingly tied to purchases of U.S. goods and services, the direct outflow of dollars actually fell slightly below that in the corresponding period of 1961. Private long-term investment abroad continued at a rate of about $2.5 billion a year. In the first three quarters of 1962 the deficit on goods and services, Government assistance, and long-term capital—the so-called basic accounts—was slightly larger (at an annual rate) than in 1961.

TABLE 14

United States Balance of International Payments, 1951-62

(Billions of dollars)

Type of transaction	1951-55 average	1956-60 average	1958	1959	1960	1961	1962[1]
Current account and unilateral transfers	- 0.6	0.8	-0.1	-2.3	1.3	2.4	2.1
Merchandise trade balance	2.4	3.9	3.3	1.0	4.7	5.4	4.7
Exports	13.4	17.8	16.3	16.3	19.5	19.9	20.8
Imports	-11.0	-13.8	-13.0	-15.3	-14.7	-14.5	-16.1
Military expenditures	-2.3	-3.2	-3.4	-3.1	-3.0	-2.9	-3.0
Income on foreign investments, net[2]	1.6	2.2	2.2	2.2	2.3	2.8	3.1
Other services, net[3]	.3	.2	.2	.1	-.1	-.1	.1
Government nonmilitary grants	-2.1	-1.7	-1.6	-1.6	-1.7	-1.9	-1.9
Pensions and remittances	-.6	-.7	-.7	-.8	-.8	-.9	-.9
Long-term capital account	-.9	-3.0	-3.5	-1.9	-3.2	-2.9	-2.7
U.S. direct investment[4]	-.7	-1.7	-1.2	-1.4	-1.7	-1.5	-1.2
Other private U.S. investment	-.2	-.9	-1.4	-.9	-.8	-1.0	-1.1
Government loans (less repayments)[5]	-.2	-.8	-1.0	-.4	-1.1	-.9	-1.1[7]
Foreign long-term capital[6]	.3	.4	.1	.7	.4	.5	.7[7]
Balance on entries above ("basic" accounts)	-1.5	-2.3	-3.7	-4.2	-1.9	-.5	-.6
U.S. private short-term assets and nonliquid liabilities	-.2	-.5	-.4	.1	-1.4	-1.3	-.6
Errors and omissions	.4	.4	.5	.4	-.6	-.6	-.7
Over-all balance [deficit (-)]	-1.2	-2.3	-3.5	-3.7	-3.9	-2.5	-1.9
Sales (-) of gold and convertible currencies	-.2	-.7	-2.3	-.7	-1.7	-.7	-.7[8]
Increase (-) in liquid liabilities to foreigners	-1.0	-1.6	-1.3	-3.0	-2.2	-1.7	-1.3[8]

[1] First 3 quarters, seasonally adjusted annual rate (except as noted).
[2] Excludes subsidiary earnings not repatriated.
[3] Includes foreign military purchases in the United States.
[4] Excludes reinvested subsidiary earnings, amounting to $1.0 billion in 1961.
[5] Includes changes in holdings of nonconvertible foreign currencies.
[6] Excludes reinvested subsidiary earnings, amounting to $0.2 billion in 1961.
[7] Includes certain increases in nonliquid U.S. Government liabilities to foreigners.
[8] Unadjusted annual rate.

NOTE.—Minus signs indicate payments to foreigners.
Detail will not necessarily add to totals because of rounding.
Sources: Department of Commerce and Council of Economic Advisers.

The net recorded outflow of short-term capital declined sharply, reflecting in part a reduction in the flow of bank credit to Japan as its payments position improved.

U.S. balance of payments developments during the course of 1962 reflected the Canadian exchange crisis of May and June. Payments to Canada dropped sharply during the first half of the year, but rose again in early summer when an extensive stabilization program brought to a halt speculation against the Canadian dollar, for which a new par value equal to 92 U.S. cents had been established in May.

A substantial contribution to U.S. receipts was made by advance repayments totaling over $660 million by France, Italy, and Sweden of postwar debt to the U.S. Government. In addition, late in 1962 the U.S. Treasury sold 15- and 16-month, nonmarketable securities denominated in foreign currency to Italy and Switzerland, totaling the equivalent of $250 million Debt prepayments of over $660 million had also been received in 1961.

Without these special receipts, the U.S. payments deficit in 1962 would have been $900 million higher. This underlines the importance of policy to correct the balance of payments. The U.S. Government is continuing to carry out and develop programs affecting a wide

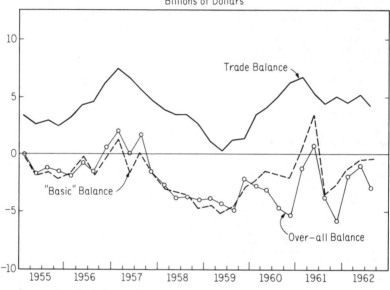

CHART 12. BALANCE OF TRADE AND PAYMENTS
Billions of Dollars

Seasonally adjusted annual rates.
Note: For definitions of different balances see table 14.
Source: Department of Commerce.

variety of transactions ranging from exports to the outflow of funds attracted by higher interest yields abroad. New measures adopted in 1962 are described in the appendix. Particular attention is being given to the share and terms of development assistance extended by other industrial nations and to their share of the common costs of defending the free world. Greater effort on their part would not only increase free world security; at the present time it would also contribute to better balance in international payments. Countries in which U.S. military forces make large expenditures are being urged to offset these expenditures, for example by purchasing military equipment in the United States.

*The State of the Union**

**Mr. Speaker, Mr. President, My Colleagues in the Congress,
Our Distinguished Guests, My Fellow Americans:**

As this 92nd Congress begins its session, America has lost a great Senator, and all of us who had the privilege to know him have lost a loyal friend. I had the privilege of visiting Senator Russell in the hospital just a few days before he died. He never spoke about himself. He only spoke eloquently about the need for a strong national defense.

In tribute to one of the most magnificent Americans of all time, I respectfully ask that all those here rise in silent prayer for Senator Russell.

[All present rose in silent prayer.]

Thank you.

Mr. Speaker, before I begin my formal address, I want to use this opportunity to congratulate all of those who were winners in the rather spirited contest for leadership positions in the House and the Senate, and also to express my condolences to the losers. I know how both of you feel. I particularly want to join with all the Members of the House and the Senate as well in congratulating the new Speaker of the United States Congress. And to those new Members of this House who may have some doubts about the possibilities for advancement in the years ahead, I would remind you that the Speaker and I met just twenty-four years ago in this chamber as freshmen Members of the 80th Congress. As you see, we have both come up in the world a bit since that time.

This 92nd Congress has a chance to be recorded as the greatest Congress in America's history.

In these troubled years just past, America has been going through a long nightmare of war and division, of crime and inflation. Even more deeply, we have gone through a long, dark night of the American spirit. But now that night is ending. Now we must let our spirits soar again. Now we are ready for the lift of a driving dream.

The people of this nation are eager to get on with the quest for new greatness. They see challenges, and they are prepared to meet those challenges. It is for us here to open the doors that will set free again the real greatness of this nation—the genius of the American people.

*President Richard M. Nixon, *Congressional Record*, 92nd Congress, 1st Session, January 22, 1971, pp. 1–5.

How shall we meet this challenge? How can we truly open the doors, and set free the full genius of our people?

The way in which the 92nd Congress answers these questions will determine its place in history. But more importantly, it can determine this nation's place in history as we enter the third century of our independence.

Tonight, I shall present to the Congress six great goals. I shall ask not simply for more new programs in the old framework, but to change the framework itself—to reform the entire structure of American government so we can make it again fully responsive to the needs and the wishes of the American people.

If we act boldly—if we seize this moment and achieve these goals —we can close the gap between promise and performance in American government, and bring together the resources of the nation and the spirit of the people.

In discussing these great goals, I am dealing tonight only with matters on the domestic side of the nation's agenda. I shall make a separate report to the Congress and the nation next month on developments in our foreign policy.

The first of these six great goals is already before the Congress.

I urge that the unfinished business of the 91st Congress be made the first priority business of the 92nd.

Over the next two weeks, I will call upon Congress to take action on more than 35 pieces of proposed legislation on which action was not completed last year.

The most important is welfare reform.

The present welfare system has become a monstrous, consuming outrage—an outrage against the community, against the taxpayer, and particularly against the children it is supposed to help.

We may honestly disagree, as we do, on what to do about it. But we can all agree that we must meet the challenge not by pouring more money into a bad program, but by abolishing the present welfare system and adopting a new one.

So let us place a floor under the income of every family with children in America—and without those demeaning, soul-stifling affronts to human dignity that so blight the lives of welfare children today. But let us also establish an effective work incentive and an effective work requirement.

Let us provide the means by which more can help themselves. This shall be our goal. Let us generously help those who are not able to help themselves. But let us stop helping those who are able to help themselves but refuse to do so.

The second great goal is to achieve what Americans have not enjoyed since 1957—full prosperity in peacetime.

The tide of inflation has turned. The rise in the cost of living, which had been gathering dangerous momentum in the late Sixties, was reduced last year. Inflation will be further reduced this year.

But as we have moved from runaway inflation toward reasonable price stability, and at the same time as we have been moving from a wartime economy to a peacetime economy, we have paid a price in increased unemployment.

We should take no comfort from the fact that the level of unemployment in this transition from a wartime to a peacetime economy is lower than in any peacetime year of the 1960s.

This is not good enough for the man who is unemployed in the Seventies. We must do better for workers in peacetime and we will do better.

To achieve this, I will submit an expansionary budget this year—one that will help stimulate the economy and thereby open up new job opportunities for millions of Americans.

It will be a full employment budget, a budget designed to be in balance if the economy were operating at its peak potential. By spending as if we were at full employment, we will help to bring about full employment.

I ask the Congress to accept these expansionary policies—to accept the concept of the full employment budget.

At the same time, I ask the Congress to cooperate in resisting expenditures that go beyond the limits of the full employment budget. For as we wage a campaign to bring about a widely shared prosperity, we must not re-ignite the fires of inflation and so undermine that prosperity.

With the stimulus and the discipline of a full employment budget; with the commitment of the independent Federal Reserve System to provide fully for the monetary needs of a growing economy; and with a much greater effort on the part of labor and management to make their wage and price decisions in the light of the national interest and their own long-run best interests—then for the worker, the farmer, the consumer, and for Americans everywhere we shall gain the goal of a new prosperity; more jobs, more income and more profits, without inflation and without war.

This is a great goal, and one that we can achieve together.

The third great goal is to continue the effort so dramatically begun last year: to restore and enhance our natural environment.

Building on the foundation laid in the 37-point program I submitted to Congress last year, I will propose a strong new set of initiatives to clean up our air and water, to combat noise, and to preserve and restore our surroundings.

I will propose programs to make better use of our land, and to encourage a balanced national growth—growth that will revitalize our rural heartland and enhance the quality of life throughout America.

And not only to meet today's needs but to anticipate those of tomorrow, I will put forward the most extensive program ever proposed by a President of the United States to expand the nation's parks, recreation areas and open spaces in a way that truly brings parks to the people, where the people are. For only if we leave a legacy of parks will the next generation have parks to enjoy.

As a fourth great goal, I will offer a far-reaching set of proposals for improving America's health care and making it available more fairly to more people.

I will propose:

—A program to insure that no American family will be prevented from obtaining basic medical care by inability to pay.

—A major increase in and redirection of aid to medical schools, to greatly increase the number of doctors and other health personnel.

—Incentives to improve the delivery of health services, to get more medical care resources into those areas that have not been adequately served, to make greater use of medical assistants and to slow the alarming rise in the costs of medical care.

—New programs to encourage better preventive medicine, by attacking the causes of disease and injury, and by providing incentives to doctors to keep people well rather than just to treat them when they are sick.

I will also ask for an appropriation of an extra $100 million to launch an intensive campaign to find a cure for cancer, and I will ask later for whatever additional funds can effectively be used. The time has come in America when the same kind of concentrated effort that split the atom and took man to the moon should be turned toward conquering this dread disease. Let us make a total national commitment to achieve this goal.

America has long been the wealthiest nation in the world. Now it is time we became the healthiest nation in the world.

The fifth great goal is to strengthen and to renew our State and local governments.

As we approach our 200th anniversary in 1976, we remember that this Nation launched itself as a loose confederation of separate States, without a workable central government. At that time, the mark of its leaders' vision was that they quickly saw the need to balance the separate powers of the States with a government of central powers.

And so they gave us a Constitution of balanced powers, of unity with diversity—and so clear was their vision that it survives today as the oldest written Constitution still in force in the world today.

For almost two centuries since—and dramatically in the 1930s—at those great turning points when the question has been between the States and the Federal Government, that question has been resolved in favor of a stronger central and Federal Government.

During this time the Nation grew and the Nation prospered. But one thing history tells us is that no great movement goes in the same direction forever. Nations change, they adapt, or they slowly die.

The time has now come in America to reverse the flow of power and resources from the States and communities to Washington, and start power and resources flowing back from Washington to the States and communities and, more important, to the people, all across America.

The time has come for a new partnership between the Federal Government and the States and localities—a partnership in which we entrust the States and localities with a larger share of the Nation's responsibilities, and in which we share our Federal revenues with them so they can meet those responsibilities.

To achieve this goal, I propose to the Congress tonight that we enact a plan of revenue sharing, historic in scope, and bold in concept.

All across America today, States and cities are confronted with a financial crisis. Some already have been cutting back on essential services—for example, just recently San Diego and Cleveland cut back on trash collections. Most are caught between the prospects of bankruptcy on the one hand and adding to an already crushing tax burden on the other.

As one indication of the rising costs of local government, I discovered the other day that my hometown of Whittier, California, which has a population of only 67,000, has a larger budget for 1971 than the entire Federal budget was in 1791.

Now the time has come to take a new direction, and once again to introduce a new and more creative balance in our approach to government.

So let us put the money where the needs are. And let us put the power to spend it where the people are.

I propose that the Congress make a $16 billion investment in renewing State and local government. $5 billion of this will be in new and unrestricted funds, to be used as the States and localities see fit. The other $11 billion will be provided by allocating $1 billion of new funds and converting one-third of the money going to the present narrow-purpose aid programs into Federal revenue sharing funds for six broad purposes—for urban development, rural development, education, transportation, job training and law enforcement—but with the States and localities making their own local decisions on how it should be spent within each category.

For the next fiscal year, this would increase total Federal aid to the States and localities by more than 25 percent over the present level.

The revenue sharing proposals I send to the Congress will include the safeguards against discrimination that accompany all other Federal funds allocated to the States. Neither the President nor the Congress nor the conscience of the Nation can permit money which comes from all the people to be used in a way which discriminates against some of the people.

The Federal Government will still have a large and vital role to play in achieving our national purposes. Established functions that are clearly and essentially Federal in nature will still be performed by the Federal Government. New functions that need to be sponsored or performed by the Federal Government—such as those I have urged tonight in welfare and health—will be added to the Federal agenda. Whenever it makes the best sense for us to act as a whole nation, the Federal Government should and will lead the way. But where State or local governments can better do what needs to be done, let us see that they have the resources to do it there.

Under this plan, the Federal Government will provide the States and localities with more money and less interference—and by cutting down the interference the same amount of money will go a lot further.

II

Fiscal Measures and
Stability and Growth

A

Keynesian Economics: An Old or New Dimension?

It is a commonly held belief that Keynesian economics, or the "new economics" as it is called by many, was formally introduced into the United States during the Kennedy Administration. This belief is formally stated in the first paragraph of the Tobin reading which states: "Since 1960 a revolution has occurred in the intellectual basis of macro-economic policy making in the United States." Fiscal policy measures, as practiced by the Kennedy and Johnson Administrations, were largely directed toward influencing the level of aggregate demand so as to bring it into line with the economy's changing productive capacity. A fundamental approach was a massive reduction in both personal and corporate income taxes. It was expected that the tax cuts would operate to stimulate both consumption and investment spending, thus increasing output and the level of employment.

The two readings in Section A present contrasting views over the Keynesian revolution in U.S. economic policy. The first reading, "The Intellectual Revolution in U.S. Economic Policy-Making," is by James Tobin, who was a member of the Council of Economic Advisers during the Kennedy Administration, presents the view that a complete turnabout in economic thinking with respect to the balanced budget, the role of government spending, and other issues was accomplished during the early 1960's. The "new economics" became a reality in terms of its application. The second reading, "Pre-revolutionary Fiscal Policy: The Regime of Herbert Hoover," is by Herbert Stein, a member of President Nixon's Council of Economic Advisers, who presents the view that much of which is claimed as a part of the "new economics" is really not all that new. Some of the ideas expressed in the "new economics" were actually a part of Herbert Hoover's economic policies.

The Intellectual Revolution in U.S. Economic Policy-Making*

I.

Since 1960 a revolution has occurred in the intellectual basis of macro-economic policy-making in the United States. I say *macro-economic* because the policies mainly affected are the national fiscal and monetary measures that relate to the stability and growth of the economy as a whole rather than the host of governmental regulations, subsidies, and taxes bearing on specific individuals, industries, and regions. I say revolution even though professional economics in the United States cannot claim any spectacular breakthrough in economic theory or econometric knowledge. In our universities economists analyze the problems of stabilization and growth with much the same tools that they, along with economists on this side of the Atlantic, have used for the past ten or even thirty years.

What has profoundly changed is the view of the economic mechanism commonly accepted by men of affairs, the models which influential laymen unconsciously employ. Five years ago an immense gulf separated the macro-economics of the university classroom and scholarly journal from the macro-economics of businessmen, bankers, Congressmen, financial journalists, and editorial writers. It may be difficult for you to understand the extent of this gulf, for nothing like it has existed in the United Kingdom for several decades. Today, at long last, the gulf has been greatly narrowed.

This is a development of the greatest importance. For it is the practical man's economics, not the academician's, that dominates national policy. Scientific economics has not achieved the combination of technical mystery, professional consensus, and public prestige that would induce practical men to accept without question the recommendations of chosen experts. Economics probably does not deserve such status, and in any event it is virtually impossible to disentangle the scientific content of expert advice from its distributive, normative, and political content. Consequently, everyone is his own economic expert. Politicians and business executives quite naturally insist on looking inside the economic physician's black bag. They will not accept the expert's conclusions unless they can follow

*James Tobin, Noel Buxton Lecture at the University of Essex, January 18, 1966.

The text, including footnotes 1 and 4, is unchanged from the original lecture. All other footnotes were added in 1971 for this re-publication.

his reasoning and accommodate it to their own understanding of the economic process.

In the famous peroration of the *General Theory*, Keynes rightly stressed that the theorist wields influence only as his ideas are absorbed, vastly altered and simplified, into the standard intellectual equipment of men of affairs. He was a good prophet for his own theory. The revolution I am discussing is in large part the triumph of Keynesian ideas in the United States.

This intellectual revolution has produced a much greater consensus than existed previously that a steadily growing fully employed economy is both desirable and attainable; that governmental fiscal and monetary powers can contribute greatly to achieving full employment, steady growth, and price stability; and that these powers should be dedicated to economic objectives rather than to other ends. The phobias about public expenditures, budget deficits, and internal public debt which hobbled U. S. economic policy for many years have been largely overcome or forgotten.

I like to think that this revolution did not just happen but was helped along by the economists associated with the Kennedy and Johnson Administrations, and in particular by the President's Council of Economic Advisers, on which I served in 1961-62.[1] I believe that the Council successfully changed the terms of discussion about the economy in Washington and in the nation, and it is this educational effort rather than the series of specific measures advocated and adopted that I propose to recount.

I do not mean to over-emphasize ideas and words. No doubt the main bulwark of the present happy consensus is the long, steady, and balanced expansion of the economy since 1961. Nothing succeeds like success and the perception of success. Keynesian policies suffered for decades in the United States from the popular impression that they were applied in the thirties and failed, that only war restored full employment. Economists can show, and have shown, that this is an error: Keynesian medicine was scarcely tried before 1940, but to the extent it was tried it had the expected results. If the war

---

[1] The Council of Economic Advisers, established by the Employment Act of 1946, consists of a Chairman and two other Members appointed by the President. The membership changes with the political color of the Presidency. The Council is an agency of the Executive Office of the President, responsible directly to the White House rather than to any Cabinet Secretary. The Council advises the President on economic policy, in particular on policies related to the objectives of the Employment Act, "maximum employment, production, and purchasing power." Membership on the Council is a full-time job; in recent years the three members have been university professors on leave from their academic appointments. The Council has a professional staff of 15 to 20 economists and statisticians.

in Europe did the trick, it was because it released the inhibitions on taking Keynesian medicine; the successful stimulus of the economy by defense spending was a point for Keynes, not against him. But sophisticated analysis availed nothing against the popular legend. Keynesian policies needed a success story, not just rationalizations of alleged past failures. Now they have the benefit of a popularly perceived success. Prosperity is attributed to the tax cuts of the past few years. Even if this conclusion had no more to recommend it than the logic of *post hoc propter hoc*, the new legend would influence public opinion for years to come.

But the success of recent fiscal policies was by no means evident to influential American opinion in advance. The first necessity was to create a climate of opinion in which policies like tax reduction would be acceptable. Indeed this was the major job the Council of Economic Advisers faced in 1961. With 7 percent of the labor force unemployed and industrial operating rates below 80 percent of capacity, it did not take deep economic erudition to conclude that the economy needed government measures to expand aggregate demand. To make a politically convincing case for expansionary policy was much more difficult.

Coming to Washington from my ivory tower in 1961, I was amazed by the discussion of economic policy in the national and financial press, in the Congress, in the Executive Branch, in business and trade union circles. I was impressed by its serious tone and substantial volume, but dismayed by the conceptual framework in which the dialogue took place. The participants were for the most part concerned, intelligent, and well informed. But the model of the economy which implicitly underlay their interpretation of events and statistics I, as an academic economist, found surprising and wrong. Yet this semi-professional discussion was far more influential than the analyses of economists.

II.

Let me enumerate some of the intellectual obstacles that in 1961 stood in the way of expansionary policy.

First was the idea of the business cycle. Here is an example of an economist's idea, oversold in its heyday, coming back to haunt the economists of a later era. By 1961 the American economy had experienced four postwar recessions, and ups and downs in business activity were generally accepted as the natural and inevitable rhythm of American capitalism.

For the true believer in cycles, equilibrium is roughly the median of the fluctuations; departures upward in booms and downward in recessions are symmetrical evils. The internal mechanism of the economy tends, unfortunately perhaps, to overshoot equilibrium in both directions. The task of policy is, so far as possible, to dampen these fluctuations both ways. And since the forces of cumulative movement in whatever direction the cyclical wind is blowing are very strong, the proper stance for government is always to "lean against the wind."

A corollary of this manner of thinking is what might be called the first derivative or direction-of-change obsession. That is, if business indicators are moving up, the situation is satisfactory—and stimulus is either unnecessary or dangerous—regardless how low the *levels* of the indicators might be. A psychologically related corollary is neglect of the natural growth of the economy, making it possible to point regularly with satisfaction and pride to the setting of new statistical records in production, employment, profits, and incomes even when their rates of increase fell short of the growth of population and productivity.

The cyclical model, of course, held sway over some economists as well as over most laymen. Professor Arthur F. Burns, a previous Chairman of the Council of Economic Advisers, said in April 1961 that the natural forces of revival would carry the economy to 4 percent unemployment within 18 months, and that any governmental stimulus would therefore be dangerous.

The cyclical model dominated not only public policy but also the calculations and expectations underlying private business decisions. The financial community was attuned to cyclical patterns of interest rates; they regarded it as unnatural and improbable that interest rates would not rise in an upswing and, at least in the beginning, acted accordingly. Non-financial business investment decisions were geared to a fluctuating economy with high average amounts of unemployment and unused capacity. I had occasion to appreciate this when the Council and a group of business economists exchanged five year projections of demand for the economy as a whole and for the industries they represented. The business spokesmen were incredulous of the Council's full employment calculations. Their own pessimistic expectations added up, though they did not individually realize it, to an incredibly stagnant economy with large and growing unemployment. Such expectations were themselves an obstacle to the restoration of full employment. They also affected pricing decisions perversely, as some industries, notably steel, tried to establish prices which would yield normal profits at low rates of capacity utilization.

A second obstacle to expansionary policy was the popular structural diagnosis of unemployment. The rate of unemployment had been higher at each of the three successive postwar cyclical peaks. The expansion of 1959-60 had reduced unemployment only to 5 percent of the labor force before it ended in the spring of 1960. To most adherents of the cyclical model, the increasing average rate of unemployment was indicative of a structural change in the economy. Since cyclical upswings were by definition prosperity and since the economy set new records in every upswing, the rise in umemployment "in the midst of prosperity" obviously required special explanation.

Structural explanations were easy to find and even to buttress with superficial statistical support. The demographic composition of the labor force was changing, so that relatively more people were in the categories most susceptible to unemployment, the old, the young, the Negroes. Automation was alleged to be rapidly eliminating old jobs while creating new ones for which neither the displaced workers nor the new entrants to the labor market were qualified by skill, experience, or location.

The structural diagnosis had a wide appeal—to businessmen and bankers wishing to minimize the unemployment problem; to labor leaders advocating shorter hours to share the work and agreements by employers to slow down technical change; to advocates of special government programs to assist the displaced; to technocratic Utopians sure that the U.S. was on the verge of a new labor-less technology requiring a whole new system of distribution.

Above all, the diagnosis had an almost irresistible appeal to common sense and casual, anecdotal observation. Anyone can see that automatic elevators displace elevator boys, that unemployed coal miners are stranded in West Virginia, that high school dropouts have trouble finding jobs. The leading Republican spokesman in Congress on economic matters, Representative Thomas Curtis, said that unemployment, far from being a problem, was a symptom of the rapid progress of the economy. A distinguished labor economist privately warned me that the Administration should not commit itself to the goal of 4 percent unemployment because the prospective influx of teenagers would make it impossible to achieve.

National unemployment was not widely regarded as a politically urgent problem. The unemployed themselves were not sufficiently numerous or vocal to carry much political weight, except in depressed areas like West Virginia and the Lake Superior region. Many conservatives found false comfort in stories that the U.S. unemployment rate, in particular its striking excess over European rates, was just a statistical illusion fostered by liberals seeking excuses for government action. Eventually President Kennedy found it necessary to appoint a blue ribbon commission to certify the accuracy and purity of the statistics. Even liberals were not greatly exercised. J. K. Galbraith had downgraded full employment in his *Affluent Society*, suggesting that the associated output was not worth the inflationary cost, that the unemployed could be handsomely treated in welfare programs, and that poverty in the U.S. was largely case poverty which would yield to specific programs but not to general economic growth. Early in 1961 Theodore Sorensen, President Kennedy's chief aide for domestic policy, privately expressed skeptical amazement at my obsession with reducing unemployment from 7 to 4 percent. "You want to raise our grade from 93 to 96," he said, "that is, from A- to A. Why should the President spend political good will to do that?" I should say that neither Galbraith nor Sorensen stuck to these views in their subsequent counsel to the President.

A third and major obstacle, of course, was the strong instinctive American opposition to government spending, especially to deficit spending. President Eisenhower had strongly reenforced this feeling. One of the few causes for which he used the Presidential pulpit was to preach against the immorality of burdening our grandchildren with Federal debt. Although his budgets were in fact more in deficit than in surplus, he succeeded in solidifying the image of Republican fiscal rectitude in contrast to liberal Democratic irresponsibility. At the same time, the emerging U.S. balance of payments and gold crisis was attributed, by such high priests of international finance as Per Jacobsson, the Managing Director of the International Monetary Fund, to the lapse of fiscal control which permitted a $12 billion deficit in the recession fiscal year 1958-59.

Many who took a more sophisticated view of fiscal policy nevertheless circumscribed it by their adherence to the cyclical model described above. Recognizing that cyclical fluctuations in tax revenue made annual balance in the budget unfeasible, they prescribed balance over a cycle instead. The liberal *Washington Post*, whose economic editorials were then written by an eminent university colleague of mine, argued in 1963 against a deficit budget on the ground that the government should not throw away what was very likely the last chance to avoid going through a whole cycle without a single surplus. Others, drawn from such diverse positions in the political spectrum as Senator Paul Douglas and Professor Arthur F. Burns, warned against using up fiscal ammunition while the economy was in upswing; none would be left, they said, to combat the next recession.

Taking office in 1961 after a narrow electoral victory and a gold crisis, the Kennedy Administration was determined to avoid the tag of fiscal and financial irresponsibility. I believe the President felt more politically vulnerable on this score than on any other. In Congress the leaders of his own party were fiscal conservatives. Even the liberal Democrats had been intimidated by Eisenhower's fiscal strictures and found in Federal Reserve monetary policies a scapegoat for the sluggishness of the economy. A notable example was Senator Proxmire of Wisconsin, a liberal whom President Eisenhower had some years previously singled out for a fiscal scolding. By 1961 he had convinced himself that deficit spending could not work and confined his economic crusades to attacks on Federal Reserve Chairman Martin.

The Kennedy Administration further hemmed itself in by the stirring call for dedicated sacrifice the President issued in his inaugural address. However appropriate this stance was to the international situation, its belt-tightening implication was a handicap to domestic policy in an economy where resources lay idle for lack of spending.

Consequently the new Administration did not at its outset adopt or even espouse expansionary fiscal policy. An interregnum task force headed by Professor Paul Samuelson, its sights already lowered by considerations of political acceptability, tentatively suggested in January 1961 a $2 billion temporary tax reduction. Even this was never seriously considered. In his first State of the Union Message January 30, 1961, the President pointed out that he was constrained by the spending and revenue estimates for the next fiscal year already submitted by his predecessor. "Within that framework," he pledged, "barring the development of urgent national defense needs or a worsening of the economy, it is my current intention to advocate a program of expenditures which, including revenues from a stimulation of the economy, will not of and by themselves unbalance the earlier Budget." Three days later, in his special economic message, he repeated this pledge and endorsed the general philosophy of cyclical budget balance: "This Administration is pledged to a Federal revenue system that balances the budget over the years of the economic cycle. . . ."

In spite of these constraints, the Administration contrived a modest recovery program, concentrating on the acceleration of already scheduled Federal expenditures, especially those that could be crowded into the Eisenhower fiscal year ending June 30, 1961, and the expansion of extra-budgetary outlays, notably social insurance benefits. Both then and since talented people have devoted great effort and ingenuity to the task of shrinking the size of the politically significant administrative Budget without altering the substance and economic impact of Federal programs—not the most noble or straightforward way to do the Lord's work—Lord Keynes, that is.

The Berlin crisis in the summer of 1961 activated one of the escape clauses in the initial-budget pledge, leading to a defense build-up of some $3 billion in annual rate of expenditure. The Administration was nevertheless inclined, both to maintain untarnished its image of fiscal responsibility and to show seriousness of national purpose by tangible sacrifices, to ask the Congress for tax increases at the same time. Only urgent last-minute objections from the President's economic advisers averted such a perversely deflationary policy. But since the Berlin build-up was clearly unbalancing the fiscal year 1961-62 budget, the President felt it necessary to assure the Congress and the world that "I intend to submit . . . in January [1962] a budget for the next fiscal year [1962-63] which will be strictly in balance." This pledge hampered fiscal policy for still another year, until the President became convinced that the course of "fiscal responsibility" would yield neither balanced budgets nor full recovery. But the new approach, which led eventually to the great tax reduction of 1964, would not have been possible without a change in the general intellectual climate. It is to the efforts of the Kennedy Council of Economic Advisers to make this change that I now turn.

III.

First, the Council established at the outset a definite numerical full employment target, an overall unemployment rate of 4 percent. To his credit President Kennedy espoused this as an Administration goal, even though he could foresee the political embarrassment of failing to achieve it and even though he rated more highly than his advisers the political and economic obstacles in the way. Actually, the Council and the President were only carrying out the mandate of the Employment Act of 1946. The Act declared the achievement of "maximum employment, production, and purchasing power" to be the goal of Federal economic policy and charged the President, with the help of the Council, to set forth at least annually "the levels of employment, production, and purchasing power obtaining in the United States and such levels needed to carry out the policy" of the

Act. But previously the quantitative side of the mandate had usually been cautiously ignored.[2]

Why 4 percent? There were critics on both sides. Many critics inside the government, in the labor movement, in the economics profession, and elsewhere considered 4 percent an intolerably high amount of unemployment. Of course the target was not intended to concede that any unemployment is *per se* desirable. It was simply an estimate of what expansion of aggregate demand in a peacetime market economy could accomplish without encountering unacceptable price inflation because of sectoral and regional shortages and bottlenecks. Indeed the Council always described it as an *interim* target, hoping that the adaptability and mobility of the labor force, as improved by scientific government measures, would eventually permit the economy to absorb higher aggregate demand.

Four percent unemployment, when last experienced in 1955–57, had been accompanied by a rate of inflation generally regarded as too high. The Council suspected that this experience reflected special circumstances rather than permanent structural features of the economy, but it could scarcely suggest a target lower than 4 percent. Indeed conservative critics both within and outside the government considered the unemployment target too low. Their fears were reenforced by the structural diagnosis of unemployment, and their concern to avoid inflation was accentuated by United States balance of payments difficulties.

Further carrying out the mandate of the Employment Act, the

[2] This statement was intended to refer to the practice of the Eisenhower Administration 1953–61. During the Truman administration the Council under the chairmanship of Edwin G. Nourse and Leon Keyserling set quantitative targets for every year from 1948 to 1952. Thus the Kennedy Council was returning to earlier practice, although its full employment targets were stated with more detail and precision. As it stands, the sentence in the text is unfair to the Truman Council and especially to Mr. Keyserling, and I am glad of this opportunity to correct this inadvertent injustice. I am grateful to Walter Salant for calling this to my attention. On the record of the Truman Council see Salant's article, "The Intellectual Revolution in U.S. Economic Policy-Making and the Truman Council of Economic Advisers," *Quarterly Journal of Economics*, forthcoming.

I am also glad to acknowledge two other points that Salant documents. Mr. Keyserling and his colleagues were growth-minded, not cycle-minded. The Truman Council also recognized "the distinction between changes in revenues that result from a decline in economic activity and those that are autonomous causes of change." In emphasizing these items of the "intellectual revolution," I was not claiming professional novelty for the Kennedy Council's use of them in the 1960's. In spite of much previous work by academic and government economists and by the Committee for Economic Development, the ideas of steady growth and the full employment budget had not been absorbed in influential opinion by 1961.

Council calculated the potential Gross National Product corresponding to 4 percent unemployment. Statement of a GNP target was also a considerable innovation. Potential GNP in real terms was estimated to be growing at a trend annual rate of 3 1/2 percent because of increases in population and productivity. The percentage gap between actual and potential GNP was closely correlated with the unemployment rate. According to a rule of thumb known as Okun's Law, after the Yale and Council economist, Arthur M. Okun, now a Council Member, who propounded it, each percentage point by which the unemployment rate exceeds 4 percent is associated with a 3 percent GNP gap. At the beginning of 1961 this gap—the estimated loss of output due to unemployment—was nearly 9 percent, or $45 billion.

In addition to its considerable analytical usefulness, this apparatus served several purposes in the intellectual battle. Contrast it with the cyclical model. Steady growth at full employment, rather than the path of cyclical midpoints, is the normal and desired equilibrium. The damping of fluctuations is not an end in itself; instead departures from full employment are to be minimized. If the state of the economy is to be appraised by reference to its full employment potential, it is a contradiction to speak of high unemployment "in the midst of prosperity." If the gap is large, it is neither a consolation nor an excuse for inaction that activity is increasing and that new statistical records are being set. Indeed the model makes clear that total demand must run ahead, at a rate of 3 1/2 percent per year in real terms, just to keep unemployment the same. Finally, the analysis indicated more dramatically than the unemployment statistic alone the many dimensions and large size of the national loss due to underutilization—in jobs, labor force, production, profits and other incomes, and even government revenues.

In celebrating the decline in unquestioning acceptance of the cyclical model of the economy, I do not mean to imply that fluctuations are a thing of the past. A regular cycle is, I think, no longer regarded as normal and inevitable. Government policy may legitimately be geared to more ambitious aims than the damping of fluctuations. It is recognized that active adjustment of policy may be needed to stay on the proper track, not just to moderate and reverse recessions already underway. Economic stabilization is still a task of great technical and political difficulty, but at least it has been freed of some extraneous ideological and theoretical baggage. Fluctuations and departures from full employment we will doubtless continue to have. But they will reflect forecasting mistakes and inherent limitations in policy tools rather than blind acceptance of "the cycle." This in itself should improve the performance of the economy over the cyclical 1950's. In addition, both Presidents Kennedy and Johnson have, on the urging of the Council, recommended to the Congress procedures for making quick simple temporary changes in income tax rates.[3]

It was of no small importance that the Council's definition and estimation of the targets of government policy under the Employment Act became Administration doctrine, adopted throughout the Executive Branch. The terms in which a problem is stated and in which the relevant information is organized can have a great influence on the solution. Whether in inter-agency debate or in public discussion, it became difficult for government spokesmen to advocate policies that held no prospect of reaching the target in a reasonable time.

The structural diagnosis of increased unemployment was a major obstacle to the acceptance of the Council's target as a measure of the need to stimulate aggregate demand. The structural thesis had many adherents in the Executive Branch, and for almost all journalists and laymen it was a self-evident truth. Economists saying it was an optical illusion were voices in the wilderness. Nevertheless one of the very first undertakings of the new Council in 1961 was a statistical analysis of the possible magnitude of the increase in unemployment that could be attributed to changes in the demographic and industrial composition of the labor force. This turned out to be very small, of the order of one-tenth or one-fifth of one percent.

The Council presented these results, along with the theoretical arguments supporting its own diagnosis that unemployment in excess of 4 percent was attributable to deficiency of demand, in its first testimony to the Joint Economic Committee in March 1961.[4] As indicative of the need for such a presentation, I recall that the very

[3] Although I still believe that tax flexibility is an important device for stabilization, I do not now regard the income tax, personal or corporate, as the best vehicle for temporary changes in taxes. It would be more effective to use durable goods excises and investment taxes or tax credits. Temporary changes in these provide, as temporary changes in income tax rates do not, direct incentives for taxpayers to shift the timing of their expenditures. See my article, "In Defense of the New Economics," *Fortune*, October 1969, pp. 211–212.

[4] The Employment Act of 1946, in addition to establishing the Council of Economic Advisers in the Executive Branch of the Federal government, set up a joint committee of the two Houses of the Congress. The Joint Economic Committee is also concerned with the general state of the economy, relative to the objectives of the Employment Act, and with the adequacy of Federal policies. Besides initiating its own studies and hearings, the Committee receives and evaluates critically the annual Economic Report of the President.

next day the Chairman of the Board of Governors of the Federal Reserve System expressed to the same Committee his belief that much of the increase in unemployment was of a structural character for which expansion of aggregate demand was an inappropriate remedy. An important study by the staff of the Joint Economic Committee supported the Council's view. Subsequently numerous private economists have attacked the problem using a variety of methods and data. Rarely in social science has there been so clear and unanimous a verdict. The structural diagnosis had no empirical foundation. The increase in unemployment since 1957 was due to deficiency of demand. Nevertheless the structural thesis continued to have a great popular following, at least until very recently, when aggregate demand actually has pushed unemployment down virtually to 4 percent.

To avoid recurrence of a frequent misunderstanding, I should say that the Council never denied the existence of structural unemployment. Indeed the Council from the very beginning strongly and repeatedly supported specific labor market policies to reduce such unemployment. But the Council did deny that anything had happened to the economy to make structural unemployment significantly worse. And we fought vigorously the claim that the need for direct policies to combat structural unemployment was a reason for failing to take measures to expand aggregate demand.

Specific labor market policies were one device for minimizing the inflationary risks of aiming aggregate demand at high employment and production targets. Another approach to the same objective was to use the persuasive force of the Presidency to induce trade unions and business corporations to hold down money wages and prices. In 1961 the President, on the Council's suggestion, asked the major steel companies not to increase their prices when the final installment of wage increases granted in their 1959 contract took effect October 1, 1961. The President suggested both to the companies and to the union that such restraint could be matched by moderation in the union's wage demands when a new contract was negotiated in 1962. As everyone knows, this intervention succeeded until the industry announced price increases in April 1962 right after the new contract was signed. The President's angry response induced the industry to rescind this move. Meanwhile the Council had generalized and formalized the approach by setting forth in its January 1962 Report "guideposts for non-inflationary wage and price behavior." I do not propose to discuss the vicissitudes of this policy, but only to indicate how it fitted in to the Council's general intellectual framework and strategy.

Fear of inflation was an important reason for the caution and skepticism regarding expansionary policy voiced by many people both in and out of government. In my opinion the influential public greatly exaggerates the evils of small increases in prices. Anti-inflationary sentiment, like anti-deficit sentiment, hardened during the 1950's. The country needs a dialogue about inflation, but 1961 was not a good time for government officials to start one. Politically a resolute anti-inflationary posture was, and is, required to merit a reputation for fiscal responsibility. Economically, price stability was unusually important because of U.S. balance-of-payments difficulties.

The Council was confident that considerable expansion of demand could occur without pulling up prices. (I think, incidentally, that the success of this prediction—as against the pessimistic inflationary warnings of those who chronically oppose expansionary policy—greatly enhanced the standing of the Council with President Kennedy.) But the behavior of wages and prices at acceptable rates of unemployment was in doubt, and corporations and unions with market power might push up prices even in the face of unemployment and excess capacity. The Council did not wish the course of wages and prices to give any excuse for deflationary measures by the monetary authorities or others.

This was the essential reason for the wage and price guideposts. They were designed to persuade trade unions and business firms with administrative power over wages and prices to make decisions and bargains consistent with the public interest in a stable overall price level. The doctrine that money wage rates should in general rise no faster than the productivity of labor brought the Council in conflict with organized labor, whose economists conveniently claimed that increased money wage rates were the way to generate the demand needed for economic expansion. The price guideposts encountered similar disapproval from business, whose economists argued that only higher profit margins would generate the investment required for economic expansion. The Council argued—correctly as events have shown—that restoration of high utilization of capacity would do wonders for profits.

The guideposts were scarcely novel doctrine. The Eisenhower Council had voiced similar views, without attracting so much attention or criticism. By contrast, the guideposts have had a greater impact and a longer life than their authors originally expected. There are, I think, two main reasons. First, the productivity standard for money wage increase was given precise numerical content. It is less difficult to ignore or distort vague precepts than to get round a

3.2 percent rule. Second, on several strategic occasions the President, first Kennedy and then Johnson, has thrown the weight of his office behind the guideposts.

I come now to the even more difficult battle to unleash fiscal policy. Here the Council introduced two important and related concepts, neither altogether novel in professional economic discussion, into the wider and more influential intellectual form. One was the notion of "fiscal drag," i.e., the simple observation that, in the absence of increases in expenditures or reductions in taxes, the sheer growth of the economy makes the Federal budget ever more deflationary. The second was that a budget program should be evaluated by its hypothetical outcome at full employment rather than by its expected or realized outcome in actuality.

The relationship of the budget to the economy is a two-way street. The government's budget program—its program of expenditures and its tax legislation—affects economic activity. The actual budget outcome depends in turn on economic activity, because of the built-in sensitivity of tax revenues and some expenditures to corporate and individual incomes. The council argued that an increased deficit was not *per se* an indication of expansionary fiscal policy. More frequently it was just the passive reflection of a weakening of the economy. A truer measure of the direction of budget policy can be obtained by standardizing the hypothetical level of economic activity at which successive or alternative budget programs are compared.

The estimates of potential GNP at 4 percent unemployment provided the obvious and natural point of reference. The full employment surplus or deficit implicit in a budget program is a measure of the extent to which the Federal government would augment or absorb the full employment saving of the economy. An increase in the surplus as a percentage of potential GNP is therefore a deflationary change in fiscal policy, and a decrease in the surplus, or increase in the full employment deficit, an expansionary move. Technically this analysis needs to be modified—for reasons connected with the theory of the balanced budget multiplier—for changes in the total size of government purchases of goods and services relative to potential GNP, and perhaps also for the composition of government expenditures and revenues.

But the major thrust of the idea is clear, and I know that it came as a revelation to many informed and intelligent semi-economists or non-economists, including especially the corps of Washington economic reporters. Once again, it was a step forward just to get this type of analysis and calculation adopted routinely in budget deliberations within the Executive Branch. For one thing, of course, full employment budgets generally look better than actual budgets.

This approach, of course, suggested a new way of defining optimal budget policy, i.e., to define it in terms of its hypothetical full employment outcome rather than its actual outcome. As the principle of an annually balanced budget gave way to the principle of a cyclically balanced budget, the next step might seem to be a budget balanced at full employment. But of course this is not the last stop on the road to functional finance, for there is no intrinsic economic virtue in balance at any time or over any period. Instead a logical principle is the following: The budget program should yield a full employment surplus or deficit such that the full employment saving available for private investment would just suffice for the private investment demands that could be expected if the economy were growing at its natural rate, along the track of potential Gross National Product. Depending on economic circumstances, including the size of the budget and the stance of monetary policy, this principle may suggest either a surplus or a deficit; only by accident would it suggest exact balance.

I cannot say that influential lay opinion in the United States has really been brought to this point.[5] I am not sure what the reaction would be if it were true and became evident that an endless sequence of deficits was necessary to maintain full employment. The Council did not, at least in the period I am reporting, believe it was true. For reasons I will shortly explain, the Council believed, in 1961–62 at any rate, that a budget surplus at full employment was feasible and desirable. Even later, when the case for the massive tax cut was being made, the Council and the Administration advanced the paradoxical argument that this was the route to eventual budgetary balance. The political value of the argument is apparent, but I believe it also reflected the Council's continuing belief that a larger fiscal stimulus was required to restore full employment than to maintain it once it was restored.

At the moment the question of budgetary rules, so obsessive in the past, seems to have receded from public attention. Adjustments in the budget from year to year are discussed almost wholly in terms of the requirements of economic stabilization; i.e., the debate concerns what is needed to keep the economy expanding without unacceptable inflation. This year, for example, tax increases may be

[5] In his 1972 budget message, President Nixon adopted the full employment budget, not just as a relevant measure but as the budget that ought to be balanced. As the previous paragraph explains, there is no logical basis for this precept.

indicated. But the issue is being debated in terms of the balance of the economy rather than the mechanical balance of the budget. Indeed many exponents of the "new economics" emphasize that it works both ways. I believe that the economic education of the influential public in recent years may make it easier to enact deflationary as well as expansionary tax changes.

The question of the appropriate budget outcome at full employment is connected with another issue on which I should report. This is the mixture of fiscal policy with other Federal economic measures, in particular monetary and debt management policies. I should not give the impression that the economic advisers of Presidents Kennedy and Johnson were simply agitators and cheerleaders for Keynesian fiscal policies. Some of us, at least, brought to Washington the spirit of what Paul Samuelson has called the "neo-classical synthesis." We knew, or thought we knew, that there were any number of mixtures of policies capable of sustaining full employment. They would differ in the uses of national output, as between government purchases, private consumption, and private investment. Given government expenditures, tightening fiscal policy and simultaneously easing monetary policy could engineer a transfer of resources from private consumption to investment. Higher taxes would repress consumption spending and easier monetary policy would induce private business to invest the additional government saving.

At the same time, acceleration of the economy's rate of growth was a prominent national objective. In 1961 the U.S. seemed to be losing the international growth rate Olympics; we were outclassed by the Soviet Union, Japan and most countries of Western Europe. It was small consolation to have our poor showing matched by other English-speaking countries, the U.K. and Canada. The growth rate was an issue in the 1960 campaign, and the Democratic party national platform boldly promised to raise it to 5 percent a year.

Some of us, myself included, took seriously what Richard Nixon had to his political disadvantage scornfully called growthmanship. We were not optimistic about the 5 percent figure, from which candidate and President Kennedy also backed away. But we did consider an increase in the growth rate above the prevailing 3 1/2 percent trend to be an important objective for the nation and specifically for the Kennedy Administration. While we sympathized with the stress which J. K. Galbraith and other liberals placed on the importance of expanding the public sector, we did not agree that total output and the growth of total output had ceased to be socially important.

We made, moreover, a distinction which is natural for economists but subtle, probably over-subtle, for politicians, journalists, and voters, the distinction between restoring full employment and increasing the long-run rate of growth of *potential* output. In our thinking, growth policy proper referred to the latter rate, and not to the temporary and inherently unsustainable rate of growth in actual GNP during recovery from recession. The distinction is a natural corollary of the "gap" apparatus already described, and indeed we hoped that a by-product of that analysis would be to make the distinction clear. As economists, we thought the restoration of full employment was the easier problem, since it involved only the manipulation of demand to employ idle resources. Sustaining faster growth at full employment is difficult, since it involves increasing the quantity and productivity of resources. We wished to disassociate ourselves and the Administration from those liberal Democratic and trade union economists like Leon Keyserling, Chairman of the Council during the Truman Administration, who always identified growth with expansion of demand, regardless of the availability of unemployed resources.

This growth orientation naturally disposed us to favor a policy mixture which would provide for a high proportion of public and private investment in full employment GNP. This objective, in turn, disposed us to view high potential Federal revenues at full employment as desirable, *provided* the tax system necessary to yield them did not itself prevent full employment. To the extent that these revenues could not for political reasons be invested in the public sector, they could augment the saving available for private investment.

We recognized, of course, that the equivalent private investment demand would not materialize automatically. The restoration of full utilization of capacity and of the corresponding profits, and the upward revision of business expectations colored for so long by low-level business cycles, would stimulate investment demand enormously. But policy measures would be needed too. Some were in fact adopted: a tax credit for investment and a liberalization of depreciation rules. (Incidentally, these proposals were understandably unpopular with labor and doctrinaire liberals and, in the beginning at least, encountered a frigid reception among the businessmen they were designed to assist and motivate.) Unfortunately the aggressively easy monetary policy that was a logical part of the program was not feasible. Although in comparison with other upswings interest rates were quite stable and bank reserves quite plentiful until the end of 1964, I would not say that monetary policy played an active role in stimulating investment. Balance-of-payments difficulties were of course a major reason. As our European official creditors have repeatedly reminded us, the policy mixture that will limit capital outflow while stimulating the home economy is a tight money-easy budget combination, rather than the easy money-tight budget mixture appropriate for domestic growthmanship. However distasteful their pressure for tight money, their advice had at least the merit of removing inhibitions which many influential people felt the gold problem placed on deficit spending.

I know that some critics have felt, at the time and since, that the Council's fascination with the "neo-classical synthesis" and its orientation to long-run growth policy diminished its ardor for the expansionary fiscal policies that were so obviously the first order of the day in 1961. If there is guilt on this score, it belongs to me rather than to my two colleagues on the Council, Chairman Walter Heller and Kermit Gordon, because I was the member most optimistic about the economic feasibility of accelerating growth by an appropriate mixture of fiscal and monetary policies and most persuaded that the gold and balance-of-payments problems could and should be met by means other than tight money and high interest rates. But the fact is that there was no heel-dragging. No opportunity was lost to press for more expansionary budgets and bigger deficits.[6] The Council was unanimous and persistent. Until the summer of 1962 we constantly sought large renewable temporary tax cuts in one form or another, to move the economy back to full employment and to be rescinded if and when private investment revived sufficiently. Thus the full employment surplus implicit in the permanent tax legislation could be prevented from blocking recovery but preserved for its potential contribution to the public sector and to capital formation and long-run growth.

Fortunately or unfortunately, temporary tax reduction to stimulate an already expanding economy was not politically feasible. I have already described the budget-balancing pledges which the pressures of "fiscal responsibility" forced upon the new Administration. Deficit-creating tax cuts for unabashed Keynesian reasons were not

[6] The Council recognized, of course, that the desired fiscal expansion could come from increased federal spending as well as from tax reduction. Within the Administration the Council persistently advocated increased civilian expenditures. The political judgment of the White House was that the budget was increasing as rapidly as the Congress and public would tolerate. In these circumstances it was the duty of the Council to point out, and to advocate, tax reduction as a means of restoring full employment. Those who, like J. K. Galbraith, are critical of the tax reductions of the early 1960's are saying that the economy should have been allowed to stagnate, with high and even rising unemployment, until a consensus for bigger federal spending emerged.

While a third course was theoretically available—aggressively expansionary monetary policy—I have explained in the text the obstacles to its adoption.

respectable. Leaders in Congress,—notably Representative Wilbur Mills, the powerful Chairman of the House Ways and Means Committee—and in the financial community made this very clear in the summer of 1962, when the President had finally concluded that additional fiscal stimulus was needed. The Administration must propose, they said, a serious permanent structural reform, justified not by the momentary need for greater demand but by the secular need to release the energy, incentive, and initiative of American taxpayers from the burdens of outmoded Korean war tax rates. An immediate tax cut to stimulate demand could have been obtained only if the economy actually went into recession. Although the hesitation in the expansion in summer 1962 was frightening—indeed this was a major reason for the President's conversion—no downturn occurred. At this point, the Council shifted its energies wholly to obtaining a large permanent tax reduction at the earliest possible moment. Thanks to the tax reform proposals which were mixed in, the legislation was not proposed until 1963 or enacted until 1964.

Although the "neo-classical synthesis" was not responsible for the excessive tightness of the Administration's fiscal policy in 1961-62, its use in public rationalization of the policy made it a natural culprit. Moreover, the Council over-estimated the speed— though not, I think events are proving, the eventual strength,—of the response of private investment to recovery itself. This was the principal miscalculation in the Council's famous or notorious over-optimistic forecast for 1962. It would be a mistake, however, to conclude that the Administration's belief in this forecast made policy less expansionary than it would otherwise have been. By the inverted logic that often applies to political economy, just the opposite is true. The President has given a pledge to submit a balanced 1962-63 budget as hostage for not raising taxes in the Berlin crisis. Total expenditures in this budget were therefore tied to estimated revenues, and these were higher the more optimistic the economic forecast. When it became clear that neither the economic not the budget forecast could be met, the Administration shifted gears.

Now that the United States economy is approaching the "interim" four percent unemployment target, hard choices about the composition of output actually confront us. The Council's attempt to bring to a wider audience economists' analyses of alternative mixtures of stabilization policies and their implications for growth may yet bear fruit.

Even though it brings new problems and hard choices, the attainment of 4 percent unemployment—after five years of uninterrupted expansion virtually free of inflation—will be an important day in the history of economic policy in the United States. The revolution in public economic thinking in these five years is as remarkable as the reversal in the economic situation itself. Appropriately enough, both triumphs can be celebrated next month along with the twentieth anniversary of the Employment Act of 1946.[7]

*Pre-revolutionary Fiscal Policy: The Regime of Herbert Hoover**

Tourists in Leningrad are shown the cruiser "Aurora," moored in the Neva at the spot from which it fired the shell into the Winter Palace in October, 1917, opening the Revolution. But the guide neglects to say that the Winter Palace was occupied at the time not by the Czar but by Alexander Kerensky, a Social Revolutionary. This does not make the shot any less revolutionary, but it does change the character of the October revolution and the factors which must be called up to explain it.

Just so the story of the "Keynesian" or "Keynes-Kennedy" revolution in fiscal policy of the past thirty-five years is likely to be vague about the nature of the regime against which that revolution was made. A generation of political oratory has left us with the impression that the revolution was really against the "Czar"—against a fiscal policy that disregarded the welfare of the people, served the moneyed classes, and kowtowed to "laissez-faire" and the "balanced budget." Government is imagined to have been either passive and

[7] From the vantage point of 1971, I must, alas, add a much less optimistic postscript. At the time the Buxton lecture was being written in late 1965, the escalation of the war in Vietnam was beginning to produce an inflationary boom. In 1966 the Administration did not take the elementary fiscal measures to neutralize the sharp increase in defense spending. We are still paying for this mistake, economically and intellectually. Because of the inflation of 1966 to date and the recession of 1970–71, the "new economics" has lost much of the public prestige gained before 1966. One result of the disillusionment has been a receptive audience for "monetarism" and for the contention that the government should stop trying to stabilize the economy and stabilize its own policies and actions instead. Although these ideas are far removed from the prevailing notions of 1960, they do represent something of a counter-revolution. The outcome is still very much in doubt.

*Herbert Stein, from *The Fiscal Revolution in America* (Chicago: University of Chicago Press, 1969), pp. 6–26. Reprinted with permission from the University of Chicago Press; © 1969 by the University of Chicago; all rights reserved.

ignorant or, if aware of any economics, aware only of "classical" economics as Keynes later described it, believing in wage reduction as the sovereign remedy for unemployment.

If the picture were correct, explaining the fiscal revolution would be easier than it is. The revolution could be ascribed to the inevitable triumph of truth over error and of humanitarianism over callousness. But the situation was not exactly like that. There was a great depression, and the government did fail to discharge its responsibilities, in fiscal policy and other ways. However, the sins and errors of the old regime were more complicated and so was the process of their correction.

The "New" Economics—of the 1920's

Americans who thought about such things in the 1920's did not regard themselves as the accidental beneficiaries of the workings of the invisible hand in a system of laissez-faire. They believed that theirs was an era of deliberate social engineering. It was a period of research and rationalization, in government as well as in industry.

Reviewing the decade in 1929, Wesley C. Mitchell said:

> From the use of abstruse researches in pure science to the use of broad economic conceptions and the use of common sense, the method of American progress in 1922–28 has been the old method of taking thought.
>
> If the prime factor making for prosperity has been the application of intelligence to the day's work, then Government agencies must be credited with an indispensable, though indirect, part in what has been accomplished.

These were not just the remarks of an American economist who happened to be somewhat out of the mainstream of academic economic orthodoxy. They were the remarks of the economist chosen by Herbert Hoover, when Secretary of Commerce, to write the key section of a report on recent economic changes and chosen again by Hoover, when President, to chair his Research Committee on Social Trends.

Hoover was the most important representative of belief in the deliberate application of thought to social problems. He entered the cabinet in 1921 with a reputation as a liberal and a planner. When President Harding proposed to name him Secretary of Commerce, the conservative Republican leadership of the Senate threatened not to confirm him, but was subdued by Harding's threat not to name Andrew Mellon Secretary of the Treasury if Hoover were not accepted.

Even before he became Secretary of Commerce, Hoover believed the era of laissez-faire to be long gone.

Years later, on July 26, 1933, he was to complain to his friend and economic adviser, Arch W. Shaw:

> I notice that the Brain Trust and their superiors are now announcing to the world that the social thesis of laissez-faire died on March 4. I wish they would add a professor of history to the Brain Trust. The 18th century thesis of laissez-faire passed in the United States half a century ago. The visible proof of it was the enactment of the Sherman Act for the regulation of all business, the transportation and public utility regulation, the Federal Reserve System, the Eighteenth Amendment, the establishment of the Farm Loan Banks, the Home Loan Banks, the Reconstruction Finance Corporation. All are but part of the items marking the total abandonment of that social thesis. However, there are many other subjects upon which I could comment which are not news to you.

Unemployment was high on the list of problems which Hoover regarded, years before it became his personal cross, as requiring thought and social action. In 1921 at his suggestion President Harding convened a conference of leading citizens both to consider how to take care of the unemployed over the winter of 1921–22 and to initiate a long-range study of the problems of unemployment and business cycles. The work of the conference continued in several committees for the next eight years, and Hoover was the guiding spirit in its activities throughout. Hoover's relation to the conference is shown by this excerpt from a report of the 1921 session in the *International Labor Review:*

> For the first time intelligence of a very high order has been brought to bear upon the problems of unemployment in the United States. . . . In the midst of a season called reactionary [Secretary Hoover's] alone among the outstanding national leaders has been the spirit which perceived the dreadful human consequences of involuntary unemployment.

In many speeches Hoover decried the idea that depressions were "acts of God" against which mortals can do nothing. He certainly considered himself to be in the "Do Something" camp. Speaking of the advice he got after the 1929 stock market crash he said:

> Mr. Mellon had only one formula: "Liquidate labor, liquidate stocks, liquidate the farmers, liquidate real estate." . . . Secretary Mellon was not hard-hearted. In fact he was generous and sympathetic with all suffering. He felt there would be less suffering if his course were pursued. . . . But other members of the Administration, also having economic responsibilities—Under Secretary of the Treasury Mills, Governor Young of the Reserve Board, Secretary of Commerce Lamont, and Secretary of Agriculture Hyde—believed

with me that we should use the powers of government to cushion the situation.

Perhaps Hoover was drawing a sympathetic picture of himself. But in May, 1932, by which time Hoover's qualities had been tested, Walter Lippmann concluded:

> For whatever else may be said about Mr. Hoover, however much one may disagree with his policies, it cannot be said that he has overlooked the need of restoring employment. Mr. Hoover's concern with the problem has been quite as sincere and his efforts to deal with it quite as persistent as those of any man living.

Hoover did not believe that the economy would manage itself, but thought the deliberate social application of knowledge was necessary. He particularly recognized the need for purposeful action to deal with unemployment. Moreover, he had a set of ideas about how the economy worked which provided him with the basis for a policy to deal with unemployment. These ideas were not "classical" in the sense later described by Keynes.

Hoover viewed the problem as one of keeping the flow of expenditures and income going. This has already been suggested by his disagreement with the "liquidation" view of Secretary Mellon, and it underlies every approach he made to the Depression, or at least every explanation he gave of what he was doing, even when he was using means that would now be regarded as deflationary. One of his simplest statements was made in a message to the Elks on April 18, 1930, asking them to cooperate in measures to accelerate building construction:

> These measures will provide employment, enlarge buying power, increase the circulation of money, create markets for farms and factories, and assure prosperity and contented homes.

Such statements do not suggest any very sophisticated theory of income determination, but for many practical purposes even a naive theory may be sufficient. Explaining J. M. Keynes' insights before 1936, Lawrence Klein said: "Economists can sometimes go very far in the advocacy of proper, sound policy measures based on an inadequate formal theory." This may be true of Presidents as well as of economists.

Hoover believed that the maintenance of wage rates would contribute to sustaining economic activity and employment. This belief was simply the application to the Depression of the general American high-wage philosophy that became popular in the 1920's. One of Hoover's first acts after the 1929 stock market crash was to summon industrial leaders to the White House and ask them to pledge not to cut wage rates. They agreed, and there was at the time little argument over the wisdom of this policy. Later, of course, wage rates were cut, and by 1932 there emerged some public argument in favor of wage reduction as a cure for unemployment. However, Hoover did not change his position.

More important for the subject of this book are two fiscal policy ideas of the 1920's, shared by Hoover and his contemporaries. One idea was that reduction of tax rates would raise the revenue. The other was that an increase of spending for public works could reduce unemployment in a depression.

In order to yield its beneficial effect upon the revenue, a tax reduction had to be of the right kind. It had to be a cut of the higher income tax rates, which would induce the saving classes to invest in productive United States enterprises rather than put their money in tax-exempt securities or foreign bonds or hoard it or consume it. The additional investment would raise the national income, and therefore the tax base, enough to yield enlarged revenues even at the lower tax rates. No explicit, comprehensive theory of national income determination went with this idea about revenue-raising tax reductions, which is not to deny that one could be constructed. But reductions of federal income taxes in 1924, 1926, and 1928 were each followed by an increase of federal revenues. To some, this seemed proof enough that a tax cut would or could raise the national income and thereby raise the revenue.

The idea of the revenue-raising tax cut was later to be associated with the name of Andrew Mellon, but Mellon himself was cautious in advancing the proposition. His usual statement was that because of the rise of taxable income resulting from tax rate reductions, the revenue loss would be less than otherwise expected. However the important point is the recognition that a tax reduction, at least of a certain kind, could raise the national income.

That increased expenditure on public works could be a powerful instrument against depression unemployment was part of the conventional wisdom of the 1920's, shared by public officials, businessmen, labor leaders, economists and other leaders of public opinion. The 1921 Unemployment Conference, which Hoover inspired, placed great weight on public works as a remedy and did much to establish the acceptability of the policy. The continuing work of the Conference during the 1920's, including the 1923 report on business cycles and the 1929 report on public works, drew further attention to the value of this instrument, but with cautious recognition of the limits set by the availability of useful projects and the difficulty of adapting the timing of the work. These reports were signed by such leaders of the business community as Owen D. Young and John J. Raskob, as well as by William Green of the American Federation of Labor and other people well qualified to reflect and transmit the established doctrine of the 1920's.

As Secretary of Commerce, Hoover was instrumental after the recovery of 1922 in getting several hundred millions of dollars in funds that had been appropriated for federal construction set aside for use later when the economy might need more stimulation. In 1928 he endorsed Senator Jones' Prosperity Reserve Bill, which provided for automatic doubling of federal public works appropriations whenever total construction contract awards fell by a specified percentage below the 1926–27 level. Later in 1928, after the election, came—on paper—Hoover's most daring venture in the use of public works as an anti-depression device. Governor Brewster of Maine announced Hoover's "$3 billion reserve fund" program to the national Conference of State Governors "at the request of Herbert Hoover as an authorized exposition of a portion of his program for stabilizing prosperity." The plan "proposed that federal, state and local governments, in addition to appropriating money the expenditure of which cannot be hastened or postponed, shall make certain credits available, in connection with public works planned well in advance, which credits shall be used only when specified, official indexes of economic conditions show that business appears to be headed for a depression." The total credits to be provided in advance were $3 billion, or about 3 per cent of the gross national product of 1929, which in relation to the gross national product of 1968 would be about $25 billion.

Popular discussion of the expansion of public works during depressions was often vague or silent about how this expansion was to be financed. However, no one demanded, or as a practical matter expected, that it would be financed out of current taxation. Summing up his study of thinking about public works during the 1920's, E. Jay Howenstine, Jr. said:

> Fifth, significant proposals were made on budgetary and financial policy. Cash reserves as a means of financing emergency public works were definitely frowned upon, but the building up of credit reserves or borrowing power, and the authorization in advance of contingency bond issues, so that funds could be readily available in time of need, received widespread approval."

Whether the effectiveness of the emergency public works program was thought to depend upon its being financed by borrowing, or whether borrowing was simply an expedient way of paying in the short run, is not clear. The difference between bond finance and tax finance seems not to have been regarded as *per se* critical for the short run effects of the expenditures. In the long run, expansion of public works in depression would be balanced by restraint in prosperity, and over some appropriate period the total expenditures would be balanced by taxes.

There had been some controversy among economists about whether public works expenditures would bring about a net increase of employment. The answer was seen to hinge upon the effects of the means used to finance the expenditures. The distinction between tax finance and bond finance was not regarded as conclusive, but something more had to be specified about the nature of the taxes and the borrowing and the surrounding monetary conditions before the question could be answered. The upshot of this controversy as it stood at the beginning of the Depression is fairly summarized by Douglas and Director, who said:

> We can conclude therefore that it is possible for government to increase the demand for labor without a corresponding contraction of private demand, and that this is particularly the case when fresh monetary purchasing power is created to finance the construction work.

Hoover and the country confronted the Depression with a package of attitudes and ideas which even today sound modern. They did not believe that they had or wanted laissez-faire. They accepted the need for social action to prevent or correct unemployment. This action was to sustain the flow of expenditures, not to try to put the economy through a salutary liquidation. Wage rates were to be maintained. Public works expenditures were to be expanded, and financed by borrowing if necessary. Even the income-stimulating effect of tax reduction was recognized, although this idea had not been specifically applied to the depression problem.

But obviously this package was not enough. There were other conditions and ideas present which explain the inadequacies and errors of the policies that were actually to be followed.

The President as Leader

Acceptance of the passing of laissez-faire and recognition of the need for social control did not mean elevation of the central government to the role of manager of the economy. The alternative to the automatic, atomistic system was the cooperative system, in which the elements of the society—state and local governments as well as the federal, businesses and associations of businesses, and individuals —worked together consciously and voluntarily to achieve the objectives of the society. This cooperative system required leadership—someone to point the way that the parties should take—and this function might be performed by the President, directly or by assembling the best and most influential minds. But this "indicative" role did not give the central government responsibilities that were otherwise different from those of other elements in the society.

This view of how the system could and should work was at the core of Hoover's outlook. As Food Administrator during the war one of his main activities had been calling upon the American people to eat less meat and make jelly without sugar. As head of Belgian and other European relief programs he had called upon the American people for voluntary support. These were the performances that had made him an American hero. The Unemployment Conference called at his suggestion in 1921 was not called to discuss what the federal government should do, but to discuss what everybody should do. In his remarks opening the conference, Hoover made that clear and warned against excessive reliance upon the federal government. Under his direction, branches were set up in every state where there was serious unemployment, and the state branches set up subcommittees in cities or counties. As he described the program later, *they* (state branches and subcommittees) had responsibility to look after the destitute, while *we* (federal government) undertook national and local drives for money for their use. "We developed cooperation between the federal, state, and municipal governments to increase public works." The subsequent reports which grew out of the Unemployment Conference, down through 1930, distributed their advice impartially to businesses, banks, states and localities.

As Secretary of Commerce, Hoover was the leader of the movement to organize businesses in trade associations for better cooperation with each other and with the government to reduce waste, including the waste resulting from unemployment. Secretary Hoover's emphasis on the collection and dissemination of economic statistics was also based on the belief that with better information more constructive social action might be voluntarily forthcoming.

It is worth noting, as symptomatic of contemporary thinking about how to organize an economy, that the monetary authority was highly decentralized, the twelve Federal Reserve Banks having great independence of the Federal Reserve Board in Washington, which in turn had real independence of the government.

Hoover's inaugural address in March, 1929, had voluntary cooperation for the solution of national problems as one of its main themes. He called a special session of Congress to meet in the next month to do something about the farm problem (and tariffs) and said in his opening message:

> I have long held that the multiplicity of causes of agricultural depression could only be met by the creation of a great instrumentality clothed with sufficient authority and resources to assist our farmers to meet these problems, each upon its merits.

He thereupon proposed creation of a Federal Farm Board to assist *organizations of farmers* to hold their product off the market. The *government* was to provide no subsidy or support. This was not reliance upon the workings of free markets, but neither was it reliance upon the power of the central government.

In someone else the call for cooperation might have been an excuse for inactivity, but not in the case of Hoover. He did more than call for cooperation. He was indefatigable in creating organizations to promote cooperation, and in nagging, wheedling and threatening in an effort to get it.

A similar, but not identical, point was made about Hoover by Lippmann in October, 1931:

> Thus in meeting the depression he has in respect to those elements which are governmental and require his leadership—like tariffs, debts, reparations, political stabilization—been extremely disinclined to act and greatly bewildered by political opposition and public criticism. He does not seem to know how the political functions of the President are exercised effectively, and to be rather dismayed at not knowing. On the other hand, he has had the utmost confidence and boldness in attempting to guide and oversee the industrial life of the country, initiating major policies as to wages, purchases of raw materials, capital investment and what not. Scarcely a week passes but some new story comes out of Washington as to how Mr. Hoover has had somebody on the telephone and is attempting to fix this situation or that.
>
> Thus he spends his energies lavishly in fields where under our political system the President has no powers and no responsibility; he is unable to use his energy successfully on the major political tasks where he alone has the power of leadership and the consequent responsibility. This is the reason why he has fallen under the double criticism that he is both inactive and meddlesome, and that is the reason why his advisers are alarmed at the lack of confidence now so commonly felt about him in high Republican circles.

A generation later Lippmann's list of subjects on which Hoover failed to act seems archaic; indeed, Hoover's preoccupation with international debts and reparations is hard for us to understand. But Lippmann's picture of Hoover trying to manage the economy by talking to its vital forces on the telephone is important.

The attempt to summon up the cooperation of state and local governments and of businesses and banks is better understood if the relatively small size of the federal government at the beginning of the

Depression is appreciated. In 1929 total federal expenditures were about 2.5 per cent of the gross national product, federal purchases of goods and services about 1.3 per cent, and federal construction less than .2 per cent. In 1965, for comparison, these figures were 18 per cent, 10 per cent, and 1 per cent. There was a little more room for action on the revenue side. Receipts were about 3.7 per cent of the GNP in 1929, but by 1931 they had fallen 50 per cent in dollar amount to 2.7 per cent of the diminished GNP. A very large percentage change in the revenue or expenditure side of such small budgets would have been required to make a significant dent in the national economy. Moreover, during the 1920's the size of the federal budget had been fairly constant. The federal government was not then, as it later became, a machine constantly generating new programs and expansions of old ones so that in order to get an emergency increase of expenditures it was only necessary to advance the implementation of plans already in the pipelines. It was perhaps natural in those circumstances that a President should think the most valuable application of his leadership would be in affecting the expenditures of state and local governments and of private businesses rather than in manipulating the expenditures of the federal government.

Several other features of the economic and political scene at the onset of the Depression may be noted here as factors to be encountered later in the story of the fiscal policies and actions of the Hoover administration:

1. Hoover and the other decision-makers of his time were deficient in tools for appraising the economic situation in which they found themselves. At no time did they have even reasonably reliable and current information on the amount of unemployment. Perhaps more important, estimates of the national income, of investment expenditures, and of state and local expenditures were available only long after the event, so that the administration was always in the dark about the quantitative effect of its efforts to sustain the economy by stimulating those categories of expenditures. Moreover, such information as was currently available was interpreted in the light of three recent recessions in 1919, 1924, and 1927, only the first of which had been deep, and none of which had been long. In only one year of the twentieth century had unemployment exceeded 10 per cent of the labor force. That was 1921 when the figure was 11.9 per cent. America was not prepared to visualize a decade in which employment never fell below 14 percent. The only long depression with which anyone in 1930 had any experience had been in the 1890's. Hoover remembered graduating from Stanford in the middle of that depression with $40 in his pocket and beginning to make his

fortune, so it probably did not leave a searing impression on him. Also, the 1929 depression began in the heyday of "business cycle theory," when economists accepted the idea of recurring, regular fluctuations in economic activity, with built-in forces making for declines and recoveries. Thus both recent experience and economic "science" (in an age devoted to science) led to the expectation that strong natural forces would intervene to bring about recovery, and the currently available data were not adequate to show promptly that the expectation was not being fulfilled.

2. The government, if it pursued an anti-depression fiscal policy, or wished to do so, could not assuredly count on the cooperation of the monetary authority—the Federal Reserve System. The Federal Reserve Board's legal independence of the government did not necessarily mean that the Federal Reserve would not cooperate, for example, by helping to finance a government deficit. But the government could not compel cooperation, and cooperation might not be forthcoming, either because the Federal Reserve had a different idea of proper policy or because of legal limits on the Federal Reserve's own capacities.

3. The United States was on a form of gold standard and the leaders of American thinking and policy were committed to maintaining the convertibility of dollars, whether held by foreigners or by Americans, into gold at a fixed price. This required that care be taken to avoid policies which might give rise to a demand for such conversions on a large scale.

4. The idea that government budgets should be balanced had a great deal of force in popular thinking and in the thinking of leaders of government, business, and finance. As has been suggested in the discussion of public works above, and as we shall see in the story of Hoover's fiscal policy, the budget balancing principle left considerable room for maneuvering, but that it was an inhibition to some degree is undeniable.

1930—Anti-Depression Plan A

Hoover's initial response to the stock market crash in October, 1929, was prompt, active, and strictly according to the book. He held a number of conferences with business leaders and public officials and announced his preliminary conclusions in a public statement on November 15. He pointed out that during the period of speculation through which the nation had passed, capital had been diverted to the security markets, leaving a large backlog of investment, including federal, state, and local public works, to be done.

"The magnificent working of the Federal Reserve System and the inherently sound conditions of the banks have already brought about a decrease in interest rates and an assurance of abundant capital—the first time such a result has been so speedily achieved under similar circumstances." As a consequence, private and public investment expenditures might be expected to go forward rapidly.

The President said that any lack of confidence was "foolish," but he took a dim view of trying to sustain the economy by talk.

> My own experience has been, however, that words are not of any great importance in times of economic disturbance. It is action that counts. The establishment of credit stability and ample capital through the Federal Reserve System and the demonstration of the confidence of the Administration by undertaking tax reduction with the cooperation of both political parties, speak louder than words.

The reference to tax reduction is a decision to cut taxes on 1929 incomes, payable in calendar year 1930, by about $160 million—or about 4 percent of annual federal revenues. This decision was to be spelled out on December 4, 1929, in the budget message. Meanwhile, between November 19 and November 23 the President conferred with railroad executives, other businessmen, and labor leaders and communicated with the governors of the 48 states. His objective was to obtain agreements for the maintenance of wage rates and industrial peace and for the enlargement of private investment and public works expenditures.

In his state of the Union message to Congress on December 3, the President reported on these conferences with satisfaction:

> I have, therefore, instituted systematic, voluntary measures of cooperation with the business institutions and with state and municipal authorities to make certain that fundamental businesses of the country shall continue as usual, that wages and therefore consuming power shall not be reduced, and that a special effect shall be made to expand construction work in order to assist in equalizing other deficits in employment. Due to the enlarged sense of cooperation and responsibility which has grown in the business world during the past few years the response has been remarkable and satisfactory. We have canvassed the Federal Government and instituted measures of prudent expansion in such work that would be helpful, and upon which the different departments will make some early recommendations to Congress.
>
> I am convinced that through these measures we have reestablished confidence. Wages should remain stable. A very large degree of industrial unemployment and suffering which would otherwise have occurred has been prevented. Agricultural prices have reflected the returning of confidence. The measures taken must be vigorously pursued until normal conditions are restored.

Of the twenty-eight pages in President Hoover's state of the Union message only one and a half were devoted to the general economic situation, and these came near the middle of the message, between "Alien Enemy Property" and "Agriculture," without any special emphasis. Hoover said later that he did not want to alarm the public. Reports of his meetings with businessmen indicate that he viewed the situation with considerable gravity. Nevertheless he could believe that he had moved with unprecedented speed, energy and sophistication to deal with the situation. Like a good general, the President had estimated his problem and given orders for Plan A to deal with it. That the estimate was inaccurate, and that the orders would not be carried out, because they could not be, he did not know.

The December, 1929, budget message did not mention the business decline except for one use of the phrase "under the present circumstances" which probably refers to it. This phrase occurs in the discussion of the tax reduction, which had been announced on November 15 as part of the program to sustain the economy. The message said, on this score:

> With an estimated surplus of over $225,000,000 this year [fiscal year 1930, from July 1, 1929 to June 30, 1930] and $122,000,000 next year it is felt that some measure of reduction in taxes is justified. Since the fiscal year 1921 four reductions in taxes have been made. Experience has shown that each reduction in taxes has resulted in revenue in excess of the mathematically computed return under the reduced rates. Undoubtedly an increase in the prosperity of business brought forth by tax reduction is partly responsible for this experience. Such reduction gives the taxpayer correspondingly more for his own use and thus increases the capital available for general business. Under the present circumstances I am in favor of a reduction in income taxes to be effective on returns for the calendar year 1929, which will be due March 15, 1930. . . . Our effort will be to conduct our financial requirements so as to continue the benefits of reduced taxation for succeeding calendar years. It would not, however, at this time be safe to extend the period of the reduction. A year hence we will know more definitely whether the condition of our finances justifies a continuation or extension of the reduction.

This is a paradoxical statement. On the one hand the tax reduction seems to be recommended as a step to bring about "an increase in the prosperity of business." On the other hand the tax reduction is justified by the prospect of budget surpluses in the fiscal years 1930 and 1931. But the prospective budget surpluses, especially that for fiscal 1931, depended on the continuation of prosperity.

The most striking feature of the budget, in retrospect, is that it estimated that income tax receipts would be exactly the same in fiscal year 1931 as in fiscal year 1930, before allowing for the recommended tax cut. This implied little or no economic decline between 1929 and 1930. Whether the administration believed these receipts estimates to be probable, whether it put them forward to demonstrate and inspire confidence, or whether it had some other reason for calculating the revenues as they would be under conditions of high employment, the record does not show. In any case, the administration recommended a tax cut, claiming that it would have beneficial effects upon the general economy, while it was consistent with a balanced budget only on the assumption that there would be little or no recession in 1930.

On the expenditure side of the budget, there is no visible sign of the President's intention to increase federal public works in order to increase employment. There is some reference to proceeding "expeditiously" in the federal building program, but this is related to having overcome some previously encountered delays rather than to any current need for urgency. The budget estimates are not classified in a way that permits identification of any total for public works or construction.

Total expenditures for all purposes, excluding debt reduction, were to increase as follows:

Fiscal year 1929, actual	$3,298 million
1930, estimate	3,394 million
1931, estimate	3,468 million

These increases were almost entirely due to rising expenditures of the Federal Farm Board, and were not the result of policies adopted to deal with the business decline.

The budget message does not explain what surely looks like a major discrepancy between the President's talk about pushing forward public works and his financial plan. In fact, the budget messages of the time explain very little.

The budget presented for fiscal year 1931 called for slight change in the budget position. If economic conditions were fairly prosperous throughout 1930, so that the estimated revenues were actually achieved, the budget surplus would be a little smaller in fiscal 1931 than in 1929 or 1930. The excess of receipts over expenditures, excluding expenditures for debt reduction, was estimated as follows:

Fiscal year, 1929, actual	$735 million
1930, estimated	775 million
1931, estimated	678 million

Of course if, as turned out to be the case, 1930 was not a year of prosperity, receipts would be below the estimate and there would be a deficit for fiscal 1931.

Having set its course during November and early December, the administration then entered a period of consolidation. The President went about explaining the new policy of cooperative, responsible application of intelligence to the problem of the day and counting its results. He explained to the press at the Gridiron Club on December 15, that the President not only was the "Chief Executive of the greatest business in the world," but also "must, within his capacities, give leadership to the development of moral, social, and economic forces outside of government which make for betterment of our country." The subjects with which the President was concerned "cover the whole range of human thought, and I do not arrogate to myself the combined knowledge or judgment of the technologists, the philosophers, the scientists, the social thinkers, the economists, and the thousand callings of our people." Therefore he would have to call upon the knowledge of expert citizens. Carrying out this principle, he announced four days later the establishment of a Committee on Social Trends to make a three-year study. Wesley Mitchell, Chairman of the Committee, and the other members, Charles E. Merriam, W. F. Ogburn, H. W. Odum and S. M. Harrison, were all distinguished and modern social scientists of their time.

On January 3, 1930, Hoover announced that "Our drive for increase in construction and improvement work to take up unemployment is showing most encouraging results, and it looks as if the work undertaken will be larger for 1930 than for 1929. He reported responses from states, localities, railroads and public utilities to his appeal for expansion of capital expenditures, but significantly did not refer to expenditures by the federal government itself. In the middle of the year the President addressed the annual Conference of State Governors on the radio, and thanked them for their cooperation in speeding up public works. He estimated that in the first six months of 1930 the amount spent or contracted for in federal, state, and local public works had been at least $1.7 billion, exceeding the figure for the same period of 1929 by over $200 million. By this time the federal government was beginning to participate in the President's program for the nation. On April 22, 1930, the administration had sent to Congress a supplemental request for appropriations for public buildings for the fiscal year 1931 amounting to about $140 million, not all of which was for expenditure in that year. The request noted that "Submission at this time of these additional projects for specific authorization and appropriation will afford employment for many thousands of men engaged in the building trades and allied industries." When the fiscal year 1931 opened, expenditure estimates for that year had been revised upward, by about $100 million over the estimates for fiscal 1931 submitted in the December, 1929, budget message and about $200 million over actual expenditures in fiscal year 1930. The increase was largely due to the speeding up of public works "in order to assist in unemployment together with the increased relief of veterans." Because of these increased expenditures and "possible reduction of revenue arising from slack times" the Cabinet would make an effort to prune the budget. However, this would have to be done "without interfering in the program of aid to unemployment."

In the fall the President announced that investment expenditures of railroads and public utilities in the first eight months of 1930 had been $4.5 billion, compared with $4.0 billion in the same period of 1929. He cited this as evidence of the effectiveness of the new instrument of social policy—voluntary responsible behavior.

The President believed throughout 1930 that his policy was working and would work. He later denied that he ever said that prosperity was just around the corner. However, on May 1, 1930, he told the Chamber of Commerce of the United States, "I am convinced we have passed the worst." When he came to write his memoirs in 1952 he explained this optimism on the ground that Presidents must be encouraging. However, even in 1952 he described the latter part of 1930 as a period in which "the country was steadily and successfully readjusting itself despite some adversities and much licking of wounds."

In June, 1930, a delegation from the National Unemployment League, consisting of several clergymen and other concerned citizens, called on the President in the White House to recommend a $3 billion public works program. The President rejected this idea.

Hoover also turned down a more moderate suggestion for federal spending from a group in whom he might have been expected to have more confidence. On October 17, 1930, the President had established a Cabinet Committee to consider a program for dealing with unemployment during the winter of 1930–31 within the framework of the general philosophy he had already laid down. The appointment of this committee did not result from any belief that the situation was deteriorating, but rather from the thought that improvement of economic conditions would still leave a problem of unemployment relief during the winter. The President named Colonel Arthur Woods, an old associate from the 1921 Conference on Unemployment, to develop suggestions for consideration by the Cabinet Committee. Woods in turn named a committee to work with him.

Shortly after it was appointed, in the fall of 1930, "the Committee in a confidential memorandum recommended that he ask Congress, when it assembled in December, for authorizations and appropriations in the sum of $840,000,000." The committee thought that even if, as was hoped, business turned up in the summer, the amount of unemployment remaining would be large enough to justify the expanded public works program in the second half of 1931. However, the President rejected this advice. While he went along with the idea that the economy needed some immediate stimulation in the form of increased federal expenditures, he would not commit the government to enlarged public expenditures beyond the middle of 1931, by which time recovery was expected to be under way.

For Hoover, at least, this optimism was based in part on the belief that his policy was working. In December he was estimating that the construction work of governments, railroads, public utilities and large business organizations would be $7 billion in 1930 as against $6.3 billion in 1929. For others, things just seemed so bad that they had to get better. Thus, the *Commercial and Financial Chronicle* said in October, 1930:

> No change of any great moment is to be noted in the general situation. The industries of the country still remain in a state of great depression, and he would be a bold man who would undertake to predict, with any great degree of assurance, when the country is to emerge from this unfortunate situation. The most that can be said is that the slump has continued so long and has proceeded so far that it seems hardly tenable to believe that the end is still far off. It is on this idea . . . that a spirit of optimism is growing up in business circles. . . .

Confidence in an imminent upturn was not confined to the naive and the wishful. Reviewing a long career as an economist at the Department of Agriculture, much of it devoted to forecasting, Louis Bean said, "Like most economists we misjudged the information at the end of 1930 and expected that the low point would come in the summer of 1931, and it didn't come until the summer of 1932."

But the Hoover policy was not working. True, public works expenditures had increased, the federal, state, and local total rising from $2,468 million in 1929 to $2,858 million in 1930. Federal spending increased by a third—from $155 million to $209 million—but accounted for a small part of the total rise. However the public works increase was swamped by the decline in private construction, despite the President's appeals and meetings. Private nonresidential construction fell from $5.0 billion to $4.0 billion and residential construction from $4.0 billion to $2.3 billion.

The administration's optimism was clear in the revenue estimates in the December budget message. Receipts for the fiscal year that would end on June 30, 1931, were estimated to be only about 8 per cent below receipts for the year that had ended on June 30, 1930. Receipts for the fiscal year 1932 were estimated to be higher than for fiscal year 1931 and even a little higher than for the fiscal year 1930. These estimates implied in the first place that calendar year 1930 individual and corporate incomes were much better than they actually had been, and in the second place that calendar year 1931 would be much better than calendar year 1930. The level of the national income at the beginning of 1931 was substantially below the average for 1930 so that the estimates implied a very sharp rise during the calendar year 1931.

With these assumptions about the economic prospect the administration's position was that need remained for increasing federal public works expenditures during the remainder of fiscal 1931 (January to June, 1931) but that extraordinary expenditures to support employment should be tapered off after that. The President asked for a supplementary appropriation of $150 million for emergency public works in the fiscal year 1931, saying, "The test of the value of such relief is the ability to pay wages between now and the end of the fiscal year." He estimated that the normal rate of federal expenditures for public works, including loans for shipbuilding, naval vessel construction, and military aviation, had increased from $250 million in fiscal 1928 to $500 million in fiscal 1931, and would continue at the higher rate or more, in the future. His emergency program would raise that to $650 million during the calendar year 1931.

Because of the higher expenditures, both normal and emergency, and the deficiency of the revenues as compared with previous estimates, the President decided that the tax relief given a year earlier could not be continued. Even with the restoration of the one percentage point that had been cut off income tax rates on 1929 incomes and the optimistic assumptions underlying the revenue estimates, the net budget position would shift from a surplus of $180 million in fiscal 1930 to a deficit of the same size in fiscal 1931. The budget for fiscal 1932 would be almost exactly in balance, showing a surplus of $30 million on a total of about $4 billion.

Until the end of 1930, President Hoover had maintained his position as the leader of the activists in dealing with the Depression. After that time his position was increasingly challenged. This challenge came especially from advocates of what were always called "vast" public works programs, the same adjective being used in the press whether the amount involved was $1 billion, $3 billion, or $5 billion—these being the favorite figures. The following list of proposals, certainly incomplete, gives some idea of their frequency, size and sponsorship:

December, 1930	Emergency Committee for Federal Public Works	$1.0 billion
January 5, 1931	90 economists endorse above proposal	
May 1, 1931	National Unemployment League proposal to U. S. Chamber of Commerce	$3.0 billion
June 1, 1931	28 mayors of large cities	$5.0 billion
September 4, 1931	Congressman W. M. White	$8.5 billion
September 5, 1931	Engineering News-Record	$7.0 billion
September, 1931	Petition of 1200 publicists, economists and clergymen	$7.0 billion $3.5 billion
September 7, 1931	League for Independent Political Action	$3.0 billion
September 8, 1931	Senator Wagner	$2.0 billion
September 21, 1931	William Randolph Hearst (later endorsed by 31 economists)	$5.0 billion
September 26, 1931	Dr. John O'Grady	$6.0 billion

As proposals of amounts of money to be spent for federal construction in a short period, perhaps a year or two, these suggestions could not be taken seriously. The federal government could simply not raise its construction expenditures quickly by one or two billion dollars a year, for instance, and have any structures to show for it. Federal construction expenditures were only $210 million in 1930—a small base on which to erect a program of several billion dollars. The larger proposals were intended to finance expansion of state and local public works expenditures, in addition to federal, as were the later $3.3 billion and $4.8 billion programs of the New Deal. But even combined federal, state, and local construction expenditures in 1930 were less than $3 billion. It is significant that the New Deal did not succeed until 1939 in raising the annual amount of public construction by $1.5 billion over the 1930 rate, in 1930 prices.

The impracticability of the "vast" programs appearing almost daily in 1931 did not mean that everything was done, then or later, that could have been done. Probably a reasonable appraisal of the possibilities was contained in a latter from James S. Taylor, Chief of the Division of Public Construction of the Department of Commerce, to Wesley Mitchell on June 3, 1931: "When one gets to very high figures, physical impracticability alone can be used as an argument, but in the field of state highways alone I dare say the State Highway Departments could have spent several hundred millions additional of Federal Funds."

The "vast" public works programs of 1931 probably served to push Hoover a little in 1931 and in 1932 and helped to lay the groundwork for the New Deal efforts. The programs were a training ground for the discussion of Depression fiscal policies. On the other hand, this discussion of $3 billion, $5 billion, and even $7 billion spending programs helped to create in Hoover's mind the idea that he was fighting a war on two fronts. He had to defend the country against the Depression. At the same time he had to defend the country against the wild men, especially dangerous since the Democratic gains in the 1930 Congressional elections, who were prepared to spend any amount of money.

1931—Fiscal Stimulation by Inadvertence

However, neither the big fiscal action of 1931 nor the big fiscal issue, as a practical matter, lay in the field of public works. The big fiscal action was the payment on the veterans' adjusted service certificates, and the big fiscal issue was whether to raise taxes for 1932.

While the administration was slowly raising federal public works expenditures by $60 million, enactment of a law providing for advance payment on the veterans' adjusted service certificates put one billion dollars into the hands of the public at one swoop. True, the money was already theirs—the veterans'. Congress has passed a bonus bill in 1924, promising to pay the veterans of World War I certain amounts in about 1945. A veteran's dependents would immediately receive the full amount to which he was ultimately entitled if he died before 1945. Also, the veteran could borrow a percentage—in 1930 the percentage was 22 1/2—of the "face value" ultimately due. The government was preparing for payment of the total benefit in 1945 by depositing each year in a trust fund an amount which, with interest, would accumulate to the required amount. These annual deposits, out of the general revenue, ran around $110 million.

In the early part of 1931, when many veterans were unemployed and needy, nothing seemed more natural than that the government should pay them what it had promised to pay later anyway. Proposals to this end were introduced in Congress and, after a debate in which the President's opposition was made known, the House passed a compromise suggested by Owen D. Young, conservative industrialist and possible Democratic Presidential candidate. The Young Plan allowed each veteran to borrow at a low rate of interest up to 50 percent of the amount to which he would finally be entitled. This proposal passed the House of Representatives, whereupon the President sent a letter to Senator Smoot, chairman of the Senate Finance Committee, objecting chiefly on the grounds that most of the payments under the bill would go to persons who were not in need, whereas the Treasury's borrowing to finance the payments would absorb credit that might have been used by private business to employ the needy. This argument did not prevent the Senate from passing the bill, nor did it prevent the Congress from repassing the bill over the President's veto.

Payment of the veterans' certificates, although the biggest single fiscal action of the Hoover period, was not a "pure" act of anti-depression fiscal policy. For one thing, the immediate beneficiaries, the veterans, had an exceptional amount of political power in the Congress and sympathy in the country. Moreover, the nature of the transaction was such as to put relatively little demand upon the budget. All but about $100 million of the billion paid to veterans under the act came out of a trust fund, and trust funds were not then considered part of the budget when people talked of balancing the budget. This did not at all relieve the Treasury of the necessity to find the money to make the payments, and probably did not affect the economic consequences of the payments, but it surely made the bill easier to swallow.

As for President Hoover's veto of the bill, perhaps one can say of that what Arthur Schlesinger, Jr., said in explaining and forgiving President Roosevelt's veto of a similar bill four years later: "Opposition to the bonus was one of the virtuous issues of the day; it was considered to show both an enlightened concern for the public welfare as against selfish special interests and a true dedication to economy in government."

The Hoover administration's anti-depression fiscal actions in 1931 were inhibited by the recurrent belief that the corner had been turned and recovery was in sight, and by the small size of the budget with which it worked and the difficulty of increasing expenditures rapidly. Nevertheless, as a result of the automatic decline of revenues with falling incomes, and the payment on the vetrans' certificates, the changes in the budget between 1929 and 1931 were very large relative to the size of the budget, and even of quite substantial size relative to the size of the economy in 1929. Receipts declined by almost 50 per cent and expenditures rose by almost 60 percent. The swing from surplus to deficit was over 3 percent of the 1929 gross national product, or about equivalent to a swing of $25 billion from surplus to deficit relative to the 1968 GNP. E. Cary Brown has made a sophisticated attempt to measure the stimulating effect of fiscal policy on the total demand for goods and services during the 1930's. The method need not be described here, except to say that it applies the common sense of "modern" theories of the impact of fiscal policy and usual judgments about the magnitudes of certain key factors. The conclusion of the Brown study is that the net stimulating effect of federal fiscal policy was larger in 1931 than in any other year of the 1930's except 1934, 1935, and 1936—of which only 1936 (when another bonus payment was enacted over a President's veto) was much larger than 1931. The increase in the stimulating effect of the federal budget from 1929 to 1931 was larger than in any other two-year period. The stimulating effect of the fiscal policy of all governments—federal, state, and local—was larger in 1931 than in any other year of the 1930's.

B

The Budget

The budget of the federal government is essentially an accounting of the government's current financial position—chiefly income, expenditures, and debt—together with the President's recommended fiscal programing of the government, including appropriations sought, for the ensuing fiscal year. In common parlance, the federal budget also has the meaning of the breadth of activities carried on by the government and the amounts of budgeted public funds utilized by the government in the financing of its operations. This is the meaning implied when reference is made to the growth of the federal budget.

The readings in Section B are designed to provide a comprehensive view of the functions of the federal budget. The first reading, "The New Federal Budget," presents the new unified budget which is now used by the federal government. The second reading, "The Federal Budget: A Chart Presentation," by Robert P. Mayo, provides information about the drafting of the budget. The final reading, "The Budget Program by Function," provides a detailed breakdown of the functions of the budget, and presents expenditures by various categories.

The New Federal Budget*

In late January, the President presented Congress a budget for fiscal year 1969 that is radically different in format and in some

*Federal Reserve Bank of Cleveland, *Economic Review*, March 1968, pp. 3-14.

concepts from all other Federal budgets. The new budget statement (The Budget) is designed to replace the administrative budget, the consolidated cash budget, and the national income accounts (NIA) budget.

The new budget format was recommended by the President's Commission on Budget Concepts, which was the first Presidential group to review basic budget concepts since the Budget and Accounting Act was passed in 1921. The Commission was established in March 1967 and submitted its proposals in late 1967. The Administration accepted nearly all of the Commission's recommendations.

This article examines the format of the new budget, including the coverage and accounting basis. The conversion to the new budget format will be a two-stage process. The first stage, representing the reclassification of items, is introduced in the fiscal 1969 budget. The second stage, involving a change in accounting methods, will occur in about two years. This article also provides some historical comparisons of the figures in the new and old Federal budgets and briefly discusses the Federal budget for fiscal year 1969.

The Budget and Financial Plan

The new Federal budget is part of an overall financial plan comprising a set of comprehensive and integrated accounts, which are summarized in Table 1. The accounts consist of four major subdivisions: (1) budget authority; (2) budget receipts, expenditures, and net lending; (3) the means of financing a budget deficit (or disposing of a surplus); and finally, (4) outstanding Federal debt and loans.

The new format gives special attention to legislation and budget authority.[1] The first section ("Budget authority") begins with a statement of the new appropriations requested by the President, and then presents figures on appropriations that will become available automatically in the coming fiscal year because of past Congressional action. The sum of new and past appropriations becomes the "total authority" for the relevant fiscal year (see Table 1, Section I).

The "Budget receipts, expenditures, and lending" section is the heart of the new budget and financial plan. The section is divided into two subaccounts—the expenditure subaccount and the loan subaccount—that separate loan activities from other receipts and expenditure programs (see Table 1, Section II).

---

[1] The term "authority" is redefined in The Budget as "an authorization by an Act of Congress to incur obligations and make payments out of the Treasury for specified purposes."

TABLE 1

Summary of the President's Budget and Financial Plan

  I. Budget authority
    Proposed for action by Congress
    Not requiring action by Congress
      Total authority
 II. Budget receipts, expenditures, and lending
    Expenditure account
      Receipts
      Expenditures (including net lending)
        Expenditure account surplus or deficit
    Loan account
      Loan disbursements
      Loan repayments
        Net lending
    Total budget
      Receipts
      Expenditures and net lending
      Budget surplus or deficit
III. Means of financing
    Borrowing from the public
    Reduction of cash balances, etc.
      Total budget financing
 IV. Outstanding Federal securities and Federal loans, end of year
    Federal securities
      Gross amount outstanding
      Held by the public
    Federal credit programs
      Direct loans outstanding
      Guaranteed and insured loans outstanding

Source: Bureau of the Budget

Within the expenditure subaccount, receipts consist of all tax receipts, fees, trust fund receipts, and receipts derived from sovereign authority; expenditures include all nonloan expenditures and trust fund payments. The difference between total receipts and expenditures is the "expenditure account surplus or deficit." The loan subaccount of The Budget provides a separate treatment of the Government's lending activities. The section shows gross loan disbursements during the fiscal year and deducts loan repayments (and actual sales of loans) to arrive at "net lending."

The separation of expenditure and loan activities provides the Executive Branch, Congress, and the public with a useful measure of the economic or fiscal policy impact of The Budget. That is, the size and direction of the "expenditure account surplus or deficit" indicates whether The Budget is acting to restrain or stimulate the economy. Government lending programs are excluded from the impact measure because such programs involve the exchange of financial assets rather than direct income payments. Although a Government loan increases the purchasing power of the private sector of the economy, borrowers simultaneously assume liability for ultimate repayment. Consequently, the economic impact of a loan is held to be different from a direct expenditure.

The total budget includes both the expenditure subaccount and the loan subaccount, and reflects the whole range of Government activities that require Congressional approval; the total surplus or deficit is the amount to be financed. The term "budget surplus or deficit" refers *solely* to the total budget. Consequently, the new budget eliminates the confusion previously generated by numerous budget concepts and their often conflicting surplus or deficit figures.

The third section of the new Federal budget and financial plan covers the *means of financing* a budget deficit (or disposition of a surplus). This section (see Table 1, Section III) shows the amount of deficit to be financed by borrowing from the public and the amount by other means, such as the drawing down of cash balances. Both Treasury and Federal agency borrowing from the public are included as a means of financing the deficit.

The fourth section of the new budget and financial plan presents data on the level of Federal borrowing and lending at the end of the fiscal year. It shows the gross volume of Federal securities expected to be outstanding and the amount held by the public,[2] as well as the anticipated status of the various Federal credit programs.

Budget Coverage and Accounting Basis

Coverage

The new Federal budget is designed to be a comprehensive accounting of the full range of Government activities—regular agencies, the trust funds, and Government corporations. Table 2 presents the highlights of differences between the new budget and other budget concepts.

The major difference between The Budget and the administrative budget is the inclusion of trust funds in the new budget. Since the consolidated cash budget and the NIA budget include trust funds, the differences between the new budget and the cash and NIA budgets involve the treatment of loans, participation certificates, and seigniorage.

The first difference is that Government loans will be divided into two categories in the new budget. The amount of any subsidy ele-

---

[2] "Public" is defined as outside Government agencies and trust funds. Holdings of Government debt by the Federal Reserve System are included in public holdings because Federal Reserve receipts and expenditures are not included in The Budget.

TABLE 2
Budget Concepts: The New and The Old

	The Budget	NIA Budget	Consolidated Cash Budget	Administrative Budget
I. Coverage				
Receipts				
Regular taxes	Included	Included	Included	Included
Trust fund taxes	Included	Included	Included	Included
Receipts from market-oriented activities	Excluded from receipts, netted against expenditures or outlays	Excluded from receipts, netted against expenditures	Includes some in receipts	Includes some in receipts
Expenditures				
Regular agencies	Included	Included	Included	Included
Trust funds	Included	Included	Included	Excluded
Loans	Excluded from expenditure account; included in total budget outlays	Excluded	Included (net on expenditure side)	Included (net on expenditure side)
Other				
Participation certificates	Treated as borrowing	Excluded	Treated as reduction of payments	Treated as reduction of expenditures
Seigniorage	Excluded from receipts, treated as a means of financing the deficit	Excluded	Excluded from receipts, treated as a means of financing the deficit	Treated as receipt item
Federal home loan banks and land banks	Excluded	Excluded	Included	Excluded
District of Columbia	Excluded	Excluded	Included	Excluded
II. Accounting Basis				
Receipts	Accrual*	Combination, cash and accrual	Cash collections	Cash collections
Expenditures	Accrual†	Deliveries	Cash payments—checks cashed	Cash payments—checks issued

*Presently on a cash collection basis, but are expected to be on an accrual basis in the future.
†Presently on a checks issued basis, but are expected to be on an accrual basis in the future.
Source: Federal Reserve Bank of Cleveland.

ment in the loans[3] will be treated as an expenditure item in the expenditure subaccount. In this way, the "pure" lending activity of the Government will be isolated in the loan subaccount. By including loans, the new budget differs from the NIA budget, which excludes lending activities and other financial transactions.

The second, and in terms of dollar magnitude the most important, difference between the budgets is the handling of sales of participation certificates.[4] In the new budget, participation certificates appear as a debt operation in the "means of financing" section. In other words, sales of participation certificates are given the same treatment as direct borrowing by the Treasury. In the cash and administrative budgets, participation certificates are considered negative expenditures, while the NIA budget excludes them.

The third difference between budgets is that in the new budget the Government's "profits" on coinage operations (seigniorage) are a means of financing the budget deficit. In contrast, seigniorage is a form of revenue in the administrative budget and is excluded in the cash and NIA budgets.

The new budget does not differ from other budget concepts with respect to the treatment of the Federal Reserve System. The payment of "interest on Federal Reserve Notes" to the Treasury by the Federal Reserve continues as a revenue item in the new budget, while other receipts and expenditures of the Federal Reserve Banks are excluded.

Government-sponsored enterprises are omitted from the new budget whenever they are completely privately owned. Conse-

---

[3] A considerable number of Federal loans include a subsidy element that reflects lending at more favorable interest rates than the cost of money to the Government (or the even higher cost of money obtained through private sources). For example, if the Federal Government lends $100 for 40 years on an amortized basis at an interest rate of 2 percent when it has to pay 5 percent to borrow the money from the public for the same term of years, the "loan" is worth only about $63—not $100. (The same annual repayments would be required by a loan of $63 for 40 years at 5 percent as a loan of $100 at 2 percent for the same period of time.) That is to say, the borrower is receiving an asset worth $100, but the Government is getting an asset in return worth only about $63. The difference of about $37 represents a Federal payment to the borrower, which is comparable to an ordinary Government expenditure rather than a loan.

[4] Participation certificates are sold to the public and are interest-bearing instruments representing shares in a pool of Government-held loans. For example, the Federal National Mortgage Association (FNMA) sells beneficial interests, or participations, in mortgages owned by the Association. FNMA also has the responsibility for managing and coordinating the pooling of assets and sale of participation certificates in the capacity of trustee for the Farmers Home Administration, the Office of Education's academic facilities loan program, the college housing and other programs of the Department of Housing and Urban Development, and the Small Business Administration.

quently, the Federal Home Loan banks and the Federal Land banks are excluded from the new budget. The Federal Intermediate Credit banks, Banks for Cooperatives, and the FNMA secondary market operation fund are included since they are not 100 percent privately owned. Activities of the Federal Deposit Insurance Corporation are also included in the new budget. Receipts and expenditures of the District of Columbia are excluded from the new budget, which is the case in both the NIA and administrative budgets.

Accounting Basis

The use of accrual accounting for all Government receipts and expenditures is perhaps the most important innovation to be introduced in the new budget. Broadly speaking, accrual accounting records a receipt of expenditure at the time a credit or liability arises. On the expenditure side, accrual accounting "times" spending when the actual liability is incurred. Use of accrual accounting for spending is particularly significant for goods with long production times, such as planes, missiles, and warships; spending will thus be recorded as work progresses.

In the case of receipts, the new budget will use the accrual method to record corporate profits taxes, and will be similar to the NIA budget in this procedure. The feasibility of introducing the accrual method for personal income and employment taxes is still under study. If a satisfactory accrual accounting basis cannot be developed for these taxes, they will be reported on a cash basis. The use of a cash basis for personal income and employment taxes would probably not impair the usefulness of the new budget, because it is doubtful that individuals keep accrual accounting records or that tax accruals have much, if any, influence on individual behavior. In practice, receipts of the new budget may approximate the NIA budget insofar as the treatment of taxes is concerned.

Because of the lack of historical data on accrual expenditures and the problems involved in establishing an accrual accounting system, it will be at least two years before the new budget can be recorded on an accrual basis. Government agencies will have time in the interim period to develop the necessary accrual accounting records. In addition, loan subsidies will not be included in expenditures for at least two years so that record-keeping methods can be developed.

Federal Budget Receipts and Expenditures, 1965–1969

A comparison of Federal receipts and expenditures under different budget concepts for fiscal years 1965–1969 is shown in Chart 1.

CHART 1. FEDERAL BUDGET RECEIPTS AND EXPENDITURES
Fiscal Years 1965-1969

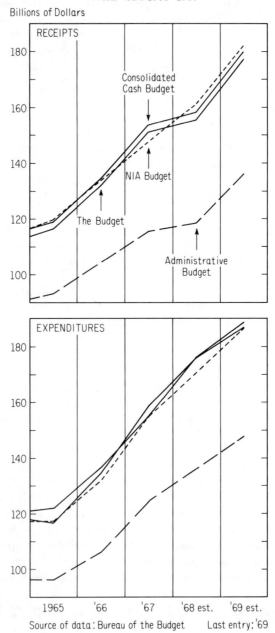

Billions of Dollars

Source of data: Bureau of the Budget   Last entry: '69

Total receipts in The Budget are somewhat smaller than in either the cash or NIA budgets because there is more netting of items in the former.[5] That is, receipts of a particular program or agency, such as the post office, are subtracted from the expenditures of the program or agency, and the net figure is recorded as an expenditure. Administrative budget receipts are much smaller than those in The Budget because trust fund receipts are excluded from the administrative budget.

Total expenditures in The Budget are roughly similar to those in the cash budget, but are slightly greater than in the NIA budget and much greater than in the administrative budget. Spending figures in the new budget are higher than in the NIA budget because lending programs and other financial transactions are included in the former. In the new budget, spending figures are much larger than in the administrative budget, chiefly because participation certificate sales are removed as an offset against expenditures and the trust funds are included.

Federal Budget Surpluses and Deficits, 1965-1969

In The Budget, total receipts are generally smaller than those in the cash and NIA budgets and total outlays are generally larger. As a result, deficits in The Budget are usually larger (or surpluses smaller) than in the cash or NIA budgets. In fact, in each fiscal year from 1961 through 1969, the total deficit in The Budget exceeds the deficit in the NIA budget; the same is true in comparison with the cash budget, with the exception of fiscal year 1965. (See Table 3.)

Chart 2 shows the respective surpluses or deficits under the various budget concepts for fiscal years 1965-1969. In fiscal years 1965 and 1966, the expenditure account of The Budget was virtually in

---

[5] The greater use of netting in the new budget reflects the view that ". . .receipts from activities which are essentially governmental in character, involving regulation or compulsion, should be reported as receipts. But receipts associated with activities which are operated as business-type enterprises, or which are market-oriented in character, should be included as offsets to the expenditures to which they relate." *Report of the President's Commission on Budget Concepts*, Washington: U. S. Government Printing Office, 1967, p. 65. The following categories of receipts are offsets to expenditures in the new budget: receipts of Government enterprises and enterprise funds; permits and fees; hunting and grazing licenses and fees; interest, dividends, rents, and royalties; sales of products; fees and charges for services and benefits of a voluntary character; sales of Government property; repayments of loans and advances; and recoveries and refunds of earlier expenditures. However, the new budget also presents gross figures on receipts and expenditures for those agencies whose receipts are offset against expenditures.

TABLE 3
Four Budget Concepts Fiscal Years 1961–1969 (billions of dollars)

Description	Actual						Estimated		
	1961	1962	1963	1964	1965	1966	1967	1968	1969
The Budget:									
Expenditure account:									
Receipts	$94.4	$99.7	$106.6	$112.7	$116.9	$130.9	$149.4	$155.8	$178.1
Expenditures	96.7	104.7	111.5	118.1	116.7	130.7	153.2	169.9	182.8
Expenditure account surplus or deficit	− 2.3	− 5.0	− 4.9	− 5.4	0.1	0.2	− 3.6	− 14.0	− 4.7
Net lending	1.2	2.4	0.1	0.5	1.2	3.8	5.2	5.8	3.3
Total budget:									
Receipts	94.4	99.7	106.6	112.7	116.9	130.9	149.6	155.8	178.1
Expenditures and net lending	97.9	107.0	111.3	118.7	118.0	134.6	158.4	175.6	186.1
Surplus or deficit	−$ 3.5	−$ 7.4	−$ 4.7	−$ 6.0	−$ 1.1	−$ 3.7	−$ 8.8	−$ 19.8	−$ 8.0
Consolidated Cash Budget:									
Receipts	$97.2	$101.9	$109.7	$115.5	$119.7	$134.5	$153.6	$158.8	$181.2
Payments	99.5	107.7	113.8	120.3	122.4	137.8	155.1	176.0	188.7
Surplus or deficit	−$ 2.3	−$ 5.8	−$ 4.0	−$ 4.8	−$ 2.7	−$ 3.3	−$ 1.5	−$ 17.2	−$ 7.6
National Income Accounts:									
Receipts	$95.3	$104.2	$110.2	$115.5	$120.6	$132.9	$147.6	$161.1	$182.5
Expenditures	98.0	106.4	111.4	116.9	118.3	131.9	155.1	171.1	185.0
Surplus or deficit	−$ 2.7	−$ 1.2	−$ 1.2	−$ 1.4	$ 2.3	$ 0.9	−$ 7.5	−$ 10.0	−$ 2.5
Administrative Budget:									
Receipts	$77.7	$81.4	$86.4	$89.5	$93.1	$104.7	$115.8	$118.6	$135.6
Expenditures	81.5	87.8	92.6	97.7	96.5	107.0	125.7	137.2	147.4
Surplus or deficit	−$ 3.9	−$ 6.4	−$ 6.3	−$ 8.2	−$ 3.4	−$ 2.3	−$ 9.9	−$ 18.6	−$ 11.8

NOTE: Details may not add to totals due to rounding.
Source: Bureau of the Budget.

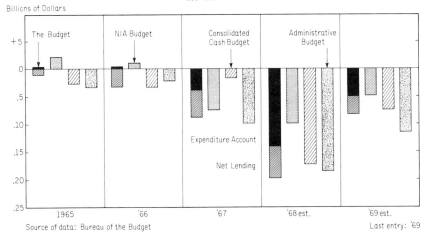

CHART 2. FEDERAL BUDGET SURPLUSES and DEFICITS
Fiscal Years 1965–1969

Billions of Dollars

The Budget   NIA Budget   Consolidated Cash Budget   Administrative Budget

+5

0

.5

.10

Expenditure Account

.15

Net Lending

.20

.25

1965   '66   '67   '68 est.   '69 est.

Source of data: Bureau of the Budget   Last entry: '69

balance (surpluses of $0.1 and $0 2 billion, respectively), but the Government's net lending activities resulted in a total budget deficit in both years. In fiscal years 1967, 1968, and 1969, deficits in the expenditure account combined with net lending activity to yield total budget deficits in The Budget greater than those in either the NIA or consolidated cash budget (see Chart 2).

Irrespective of the budget concept used, the economic or fiscal policy impact of the Federal Government on the economy is best measured by changes in net budget position rather than by the amount of budget surplus or deficit in any fiscal year. Thus, an increase in the amount of budget deficit (or a decrease in the surplus) has a stimulative effect on the economy, while a reduction in the deficit (or an increase in the surplus) has a restraining effect. The fact that The Budget provides a better indication than the other budgets of the impact of the Federal Government on the economy, makes The Budget an important tool of economic analysis. Since Federal lending programs are excluded, the focal point of The Budget in measuring economic or fiscal policy impact is the "expenditure account surplus or deficit." As shown in Chart 3, the "expenditure account" moved in the direction of surplus (restraint) in fiscal year 1966, while the NIA budget moved in the direction of deficit (stimulus). In fiscal years 1965, 1967, 1968, and 1969, the two budget deficits moved in the same direction, but the magnitude of change was greater in the expenditure account of The Budget than in the NIA budget in three of the four years, indicating a greater impact on the

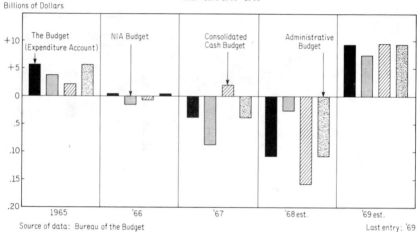

CHART 3. NET CHANGES in FEDERAL BUDGET SURPLUSES and DEFICITS
Fiscal Years 1965–1969

Billions of Dollars

The Budget (Expenditure Account)   NIA Budget   Consolidated Cash Budget   Administrative Budget

1965   '66   '67   '68 est.   '69 est.

Source of data: Bureau of the Budget

Last entry: '69

economy due to Federal activities than suggested by the NIA budget.[6]

When the changes to an accrual basis have been made, the new budget totals, as well as the year-to-year changes in the totals, should eventually provide a better gauge of the fiscal impact of the Government on the economy than that of any other budget concept. Nevertheless, the complexity of the Federal Government's activities should still preclude the use of only one budget number, such as the amount or change in the amount of surplus or deficit, to measure the effect of the Government on the economy. Instead, The Budget should be thought of as a broad financial plan that covers (1) the various ways of channeling the economy's resources to the Federal Government through use of an assortment of taxes and forms of borrowing, and (2) programs designed to serve national objectives.

The Budget for Fiscal Year 1969

Expenditures

As proposed in The Budget, total Federal outlays are estimated at $186.1 billion in fiscal year 1969, an increase of $10.4 billion over fiscal year 1968. Because total Federal outlays consist of the sum of expenditures and net lending, Federal expenditures are budgeted at

---

[6] These differences are due largely to the treatment of corporate taxes on an accrual basis in the NIA budget; hence, the NIA budget presently gives a better indication of impact. Eventually, both measures will be closer in treatment, and the new budget will be better when expenditures are placed on an accrual basis.

$182.8 billion, an increase of $12.8 billion over fiscal year 1968. The difference between the $10.4 billion increase in total outlays and the $12.9 billion increase in total expenditures occurs because net lending activities in fiscal year 1969 are budgeted to decline $2.5 billion from fiscal year 1968, mainly reflecting a $1.9 billion decline in mortgage acquisitions.

As shown in Table 4, the 1969 budget proposes increased spending in every major function, except space research and technology. The largest dollar increase in spending is proposed for the health, labor, and welfare function, up $5.5 billion over 1968. The bulk of the increase ($4.2 billion) in that function is for expanded social security and medicare benefits passed by Congress last year. As proposed in The Budget, the national defense function shows the second largest increase, $3.3 billion.

TABLE 4

Federal Expenditures, by Function Fiscal Years 1967-1969
(billions of dollars)

Function	1967 Actual	1968 Estimate	1969 Estimate	Change 1968–1969
Expenditures:				
National defense	$ 70.1	$ 76.5	$ 79.6	+$ 3.3
International affairs and finance	4.1	4.3	4.5	+ 0.2
Space research and technology	5.4	4.8	4.6	− 0.2
Agriculture and agricultural resources	3.2	4.4	4.5	+ 0.1
Natural resources	2.1	2.4	2.5	+ 0.1
Commerce and transportation	7.3	7.7	8.0	+ 0.3
Housing and community development	0.6	0.7	1.4	+ 0.7
Health, labor, and welfare	39.5	46.4	51.9	+ 5.5
Education	3.6	4.2	4.4	+ 0.2
Veterans benefits and services	6.4	6.8	7.1	+ 0.3
Interest	12.5	13.5	14.4	+ 0.9
General government	2.5	2.6	2.8	+ 0.2
Allowances:				
Civilian and military pay increases	—	—	1.6	+ 1.6
Contingencies	—	0.1	0.4	+ 0.3
Undistributed intragovernmental payments				
Government contribution for employee retirement	- 1.7	- 1.9	- 2.0	− 0.1
Interest received by trust funds	- 2.3	- 2.7	- 3.0	− 0.3
Total expenditures	$153.2	$169.9	$182.8	+$12.9
Net Lending:				
International affairs and finance	$ 0.5	$ 0.7	$ 0.7	—
Agriculture and agricultural resources	1.2	0.9	1.1	+$ 0.2
Housing and community development	1.7	3.3	1.4	− 1.9
All other	1.7	0.9	0.1	− 0.8
Total net lending	$ 5.2	$ 5.8	$ 3.3	− 2.5
Total outlays	$158.4	$175.6	$186.1	+$10.4

NOTE: Details may not add to totals due to rounding.
Source: Bureau of the Budget

All but $400 million of the $10.4 billion increase in total outlays is accounted for by higher social security benefits, additional defense costs, higher military and civilian pay scales, scheduled to become effective July 1, 1968, under existing law, and higher interest payments on the Federal debt. Increases in other types of expenditures are offset by the reduction in planned mortgage lending, as mentioned earlier.

Receipts

As shown in Table 5, total Federal receipts in fiscal year 1969 are estimated at $178.1 billion, an increase of $22.3 billion over 1968.

TABLE 5

Federal Receipts, by Source, Fiscal Years 1967–1969
(billions of dollars)

Source	1967 Actual	1968 Estimate	1969 Estimate	Change 1968–1969
Individual income taxes	$ 61.5	$ 67.7	$ 80.9	+$13.2
Corporate income taxes	34.0	31.3	34.3	+ 3.0
Employment taxes	27.8	29.7	34.2	+ 4.5
Unemployment insurance	3.7	3.7	3.6	− 0.1
Premiums for other insurance and retirement	1.9	2.0	2.3	+ 0.3
Excise taxes	13.7	13.8	14.7	+ 0.9
Estate and gift taxes	3.0	3.1	3.4	+ 0.3
Customs	1.9	2.0	2.1	+ 0.1
Other receipts	2.2	2.4	2.7	+ 0.3
Total receipts.	$149.6	$155.8	$178.1	+$22.3

NOTE: Details may not add to totals due to rounding.
Source: Bureau of the Budget

In addition to revenue throw-off associated with expanding economic activity, the revenue estimates assume the adoption of a temporary 10 percent income tax surcharge, the extension of excise tax rates on telephone calls and automobiles, an acceleration of corporate tax payments, and certain transportation user charges. These measures are estimated to yield about $13.1 billion in fiscal year 1969. The surtax and acceleration of corporate tax payments are expected to increase revenues $2.7 billion in fiscal year 1968 and $10.2 billion in fiscal year 1969. Extension of the excise taxes would prevent a drop in revenues of $0.3 billion in fiscal year 1968 and $2.7 billion in fiscal year 1969. The user charges are expected to provide $0.3 billion in fiscal year 1969.

Economic Impact of the Budget

As indicated earlier, under the new budget format, the best measure of the economic impact of the Federal Government is the expenditure account surplus or deficit, i.e., the difference between direct expenditures and total receipts, excluding lending activity. As shown in Table 6, the expenditure account deficit would amount to

TABLE 6
The Federal Budget Fiscal Years 1967–1969
(billions of dollars)

	1967 Actual	1968 Estimate	1969 Estimate
Receipts, Expenditures, and Net Lending:			
Expenditure account:			
Receipts	$149.6	$155.8	$178.1
Expenditures	153.2	169.9	182.8
Expenditure deficit............	-$ 3.6	-$ 14.0	-$ 4.7
Loan account:			
Loan disbursements	$ 17.8	$ 20.9	$ 20.4
Loan repayments	- 12.6	- 15.1	- 17.1
Net lending.................	$ 5.2	$ 5.8	$ 3.3
Total budget:			
Receipts....................	$149.6	$155.8	$178.1
Outlays (expenditures and net lending).	158.4	175.6	186.1
Budget deficit	-$ 8.8	-$ 19.8	-$ 8.0

NOTE: Details may not add to totals due to rounding.
Source: Bureau of the Budget

$4.7 billion in fiscal year 1969 if all of the proposed tax measures were adopted. As compared with fiscal year 1968, the expenditure account deficit would be reduced by about $9.3 billion, and the reduction would exert a restraining influence on the economy. On the other hand, failure to adopt the income tax surcharge, combined with the approval of all expenditure programs, would yield a sizable expenditure account deficit, forcing the Government to borrow in the nation's credit market an amount of funds comparable to that in fiscal year 1968. In short, even if all the proposed spending programs were approved, adoption of the surtax would increase revenues appreciably, reduce the budget deficit, and work toward restraining the economy in fiscal year 1969 (compared with 1968), as well as reduce the financing needs of the Treasury. On the other hand, if the proposed spending programs were approved without the surtax, the result would be an excessively large budget deficit, further stimulus to economic activity, and continued heavy Treasury demands in credit markets.

Concluding Comments

The new Federal budget presents, for the first time, a comprehensive and interrelated set of accounts that summarize the Federal Government's activities more completely than any other budget concept. As a result, the new budget to some extent eliminates the confusion generated by the three or more different formats presenting various concepts of the budget, in terms of both composition and totals. The new budget format goes a long way in improving understanding of the activities of the Federal Government and should enable the Administration, Congress, and the public to exercise more informed judgments concerning not only Government activities, but also the impact of those activities.

The Federal Budget: A Chart Presentation*

Mr. Mayo: Thank you, Mr. Chairman.

The Budget of the United States Government is addressed to the Congress. Its primary purpose is to present the President's requests for the year ahead for congressional action with regard to new programs and appropriations and to overall fiscal policy. The budget thus serves two major functions simultaneously. It is an aid to decision making as to the efficient allocation of resources among competing claims—both within the Government and between the Government and private sectors of the economy. It also bears an intimate relationship to economic stabilization and growth.

The budget also serves many other purposes. Budget data are used to measure the size of the Government, to assist the Treasury in management of its cash flow and borrowing, to aid national income analysis for economists in our social accounting system, to help the Federal Reserve in the formulation of monetary policy, and to provide data for observers around the world concerned with the impact of Federal Government activity on financial markets and the U. S. balance of payments.

But the budget's role in the context of the President's financial plan to the Congress is primary—a role set up by the Budget and Accounting Act of 1921.

The charts which follow are concerned with (1) a brief description of the Federal budget process and (2) a discussion of the key figures in the current budget.

Chart 1 shows the four essential steps in the Federal budget

*Robert P. Mayo, from "Proceedings of a Symposium on the Federal Budget in a Dynamic Economy," The American Bankers Association, April 1968, pp. 4-22.

CHART 1   THE FEDERAL BUDGET PROCESS

1	Executive Formulation
2	Congressional Action
3	Execution and Control
4	Reporting and Audit

process. First is the responsibility of the Administration for the preparation of the budget for the year ahead. Congressional action on the President's requests then follows. Once that action is completed, proper execution and control logically follows, accompanied by a comprehensive system of reporting budget results—plus the post-audit.

Executive formulation of the budget must be thoughtful and detailed, extending over a relatively long period of time. Chart 2 describes this process. By this time a year ago, work on the 1969 budget—which appeared this January—was already well under way.

Examination of program issues by each of the Government agencies begins in February. By early summer planning figures have been worked out between department heads and the Budget Bureau. Ceilings are suggested for each agency. Each department is given very specific instructions for preparing budget estimates—estimates which are supported by narrative descriptions of services to be performed and a detailed statement of program costs. The fruits of the Planning-Programming-Budgeting system are introduced into the picture.

At the same time the Council of Economic Advisers, the Treasury, and the Budget Bureau—the *troika*—make their initial evaluation of the economic environment in which the new budget is likely to operate, together with rough estimates of Federal revenue.

During the fall, lengthy Budget Bureau hearings are held with

CHART 2   EXECUTIVE FORMULATION*

1967 Feb.-July	1. Program Issues Examined in Agencies
August	2. Planning Figures Established 3. Initial Fiscal Policy Assessment
Sept.-Oct.	4. Detailed Estimates Prepared 5. Revenue Outlook Updated
Nov. Jan. '68	6. Budget Bureau Review 7. Presidential Review 8. Submission to Congress

*1969 Budget

each agency, leading to the preparation of the budget document itself. At the same time more precise assumptions are made as to economic activity, and detailed revenue estimates are prepared by the Treasury. Critical Budget Bureau review of the most sensitive programs with the President follows. By the end of January the initial job of budget formulation is completed for the year beginning the following July 1.

CHART 3   THE BUDGET PRESENTATION

1	The Budget
2	The Appendix
3	Special Analyses
4	Budget in Brief
5	Supplementary Material

The budget presentation has many facets—Chart 3. The President's message, including the key tables and a chart or two, accounts for less than 10 percent of the budget document itself. More than half of the 556-page budget document is taken up with the program analysis of budget authority and outlays by function and by agency.

A detailed description of the budget requests is contained in the *Appendix*, known fondly throughout Washington as the telephone book. This provides much but not all of the material the Congress has requested to help make up its mind on individual programs. It also provides a wealth of information on specific programs that are intimately involved in the forward planning of many American businesses and are highly significant to individual communities and areas.

Of particular significance in interpreting the budget is the 194-page volume, *Special Analyses*. Thirteen in number, these analyses compare budget concepts, segregate investment from operating outlays, analyze credit programs, summarize civilian employment, and present various other aspects of the Government operations which cut across both agency and functional lines. The popular version of the budget is, of course, the 72-page *Budget in Brief*, which is widely used in stimulating public interest and understanding of the budget story.

The press, of course, plays an important role in getting the budget story across. It is not surprising, therefore, that the budget press conference and subsequent press inquiries often produce useful supplementary information not set forth explicitly in the budget itself.

Congress does not act on expenditures. It acts only to provide the authority to spend. This is a common point of misunderstanding on the part of the American people and a common source of confusion in discussing what the Congress does to the President's program.

The legislative budget process is at least as complicated as executive budget formulation. It is set forth in Chart 4. Any new program first must be approved by the Congress in substantive form before the Appropriations Committee even touches it.

CHART 4   THE LEGISLATIVE PROCESS

- On Expenditure and Loan Programs:
  - . . . Substantive Authorizations
  - . . . Appropriations
- On Financing of Programs:
  - . . . Revenue
  - . . . Borrowing

The Congress also must react to the ways in which programs are financed. It must do so in terms not only of the total size of the tax bill and the balance among types of taxes but also with regard to its concern about the ultimate budget surplus or deficit and the restraints which it feels are necessary to put on the Treasury in borrowing the funds the Government needs to pay its bills—notably the public debt limit and the 4 1/4 percent interest rate ceiling.

The appropriations process is far from simple, as shown in Chart 5. Appropriations action in the House of Representatives starts off with the assignment of particular agency appropriation responsibility to one of more than a dozen subcommittees. There are many different types of appropriations, too—annual appropriations, permanent indefinite appropriations, authorizations to spend from debt receipts, contract authorizations, et cetera. Even more detailed information, in the form of agency justifications, is requested of each department

CHART 5   APPROPRIATIONS ACTION

- By The House—
  1. The Subcommittee System
  2. Agency Justification
  3. Marking Up The Bill
  4. Committee Approval
  5. Passage
- By The Senate
- Presidential Approval

head to explain in minute detail just how funds are to be spent within each subsection of the agency.

After completion of a subcommittee's hearings and the preparation of supplementary staff material, the bill will be debated in closed session on a line-by-line basis. This is called marking up the bill. Once the bill is approved by the subcommittee, its chances for full committee sanction are quite good, unless an economy drive or some other overriding circumstance dictates major change. Upon passage of the bill the Senate goes through the same process, although not necessarily in quite as much detail. And if there is disagreement between the two Houses, a joint conference will be needed to work out a compromise.

Each appropriation bill stands on its own feet and must be approved or disapproved by the President on its individual merits. There is no such thing, therefore, as an Appropriations Committee action or congressional action on the budget as a whole—as in nations with a parliamentary form of government. This is true despite many attempts that have been made in this direction and despite conscientious efforts to start off appropriations action with overall testimony by the Secretary of the Treasury and the Budget Director with regard to the state of the Government's finances. Nor does the President have power to delete, through item veto, specific parts of any appropriations bill which he may dislike.

Unfortunately, the timeliness of appropriations action leaves much to be desired. The increasing complexity of the appropriations process has lengthened seriously the time required for congressional action. Many appropriations bills do not complete the legislative cycle until well after the new fiscal year has begun, with resulting confusion and stopgap expedients.

Once money is appropriated, the Budget Bureau immediately reviews spending agency requests which outline needs for funds on a quarter-by-quarter basis. In addition to deciding on the appropriateness of these pending requests, the Budget Director also may establish reserves against appropriations so that they cannot be used immediately. This may be done to provide a cushion against a likelihood of large requests later in the year, to bring authority in line with fiscal policy objectives, or to control appropriations which extend over a period of years. All this is summarized in Chart 6.

Each agency has its own budget office, with authority to make allotments of funds to subdivisions within each agency. Presidential approval of each appropriation bill is also followed by the drawing of appropriation warrants, based on Treasury interpretation of spending authority granted, and this is checked by the General Accounting

CHART 6 EXECUTION AND CONTROL

1	Budget Apportionments
2	Establishment of Reserves
3	Agency Controls
4	Treasury Disbursement

Office. Disbursing officers acting for the Treasury, then proceed with the issuance of checks as approved bills are paid.

The budget reporting function has two basic facets—Chart 7. One essential aspect of budget reporting relates to years not yet completed or yet to begin—the first two lines of the chart. This refers to Budget Bureau publication of appropriate and timely revisions of budget estimates, reflecting the effect of recent expenditure trends, changes in expenditure goals, congressional action, and developments in the economy and in tax collection experience which dictate revised revenue estimates.

CHART 7 REPORTING AND AUDIT

•	Reporting— By Bureau of The Budget By Congress By Treasury
•	Audit General Accounting Office

The absence of such timely budget revisions has done a great deal unfortunately to damage the Administration's reputation for budget credibility, particularly in 1966. The lengthening of the legislative cycle on appropriations means that the Administration can no longer wait until Congress adjourns before submitting a midyear review.

There is also reporting on the budget by the Congress, as appropriations committees seek to build a record of achievement in their action on the President's requests. Some of this reporting has been rather confusing not only to the general public but within the Congress itself; it is hoped that more consistency with the President's format will be forthcoming under the new budget reporting system.

Reporting of actual expenditures and receipts is done by the Treasury, through the Bureau of Accounts, in the daily and monthly Treasury statements, the Treasury monthly bulletin and the Treasury annual report, and the annual combined statement of receipts and expenditures.

The final step in this part of the process is the job the Comptroller General of the United States performs for the Congress through the General Accounting Office. This is the postaudit function which has given GAO the title of "Watchdog of the Treasury."

The President's 1969 budget, as it appeared on January 29, embraced for the first time the new unified concept recommended by last year's President's Commission on Budget Concepts. As shown in Chart 8, the report of the Commission stressed not only the need for concentrating on a single budget instead of three competing forms of budget presentation, but also emphasized the importance of comprehensiveness in the budget—notably through the inclusion of all trust funds and direct loan programs within the overall budget definition.

CHART 8 THE NEW BUDGET CONCEPT

1	A Unified Budget
2	Comprehensive Coverage
3	Emphasis on Congressional Action
4	Expenditures vs. Loans
5	Participation Certificates
6	Emphasis on Financing
7	Netting Proprietary Receipts
8	Accrual Accounting
9	Loan Subsidies
10	Better Public Information

The Budget Commission report stressed also the need for greater emphasis in the budget document on congressional action. It recommended a separation of regular expenditures from direct loan programs for economic analysis purposes. It recommended that sales of participation certificates in outstanding loans of Federal lending programs should be considered as a means of financing, like the sale of Treasury securities, rather than as offsets to expenditures.

It urged more attention to the financing aspects of the budget and suggested new rules for deducting proprietary receipts from budget expenditures. It urged substantial new strides toward placing the entire Government on an accrual rather than a cash basis of accounting. It urged proper definition of the subsidy element in all direct loan programs and appealed also for better public information about the budget.

The first seven of these recommendations are fully reflected in the 1969 budget. The eighth and ninth have been accepted in principle, although it probably will be two years before they can become fully effective. As far as the tenth is concerned the new budget is silent. The very acceptance of the other nine in itself constitutes a major step toward better public information, but only time will tell whether or not the Commission's recommendations on updating of budget forecasts and the need for long-term budget planning are fully embraced.

Let's turn now to the current budget picture and highlight its basic characteristics as presented in January.

The Government is expected to spend $186 billion during the fiscal year 1969, as shown on the left-hand part of Chart 9. This is an

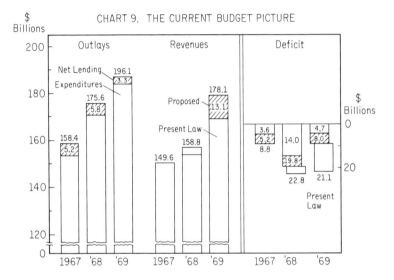

CHART 9. THE CURRENT BUDGET PICTURE

increase of more than $10 billion above the current year. Revenues are projected to reach $178 billion, but $13 billion of that is attributable to the President's tax program. Meanwhile revenues under present law are expected to increase by $12 billion simply because of projected economic growth.

The budget deficit then—even assuming acceptance of the President's tax program—rises from $8.8 billion last year to $19.8 billion this year and then falls to $8 billion next year. Without the tax program the deficit will exceed $20 billion both this year and next year.

The budget presentation also notes the economic significance of the excess of expenditures over receipts in the expenditure account itself, excluding net lending transactions. This excess of expenditures over receipts—again assuming full tax program action—is estimated at $14 billion for the current year and $4.7 billion for fiscal 1969. This segment of the budget deficit is quite parallel to the national income account structure.

The new 1969 budget figures can be compared with figures under old concepts of the budget for reference purposes to satisfy the wishes of those who are familiar with the now outmoded forms of presentation. The figures on the old concepts serve a purpose on an interim basis, but eventually should fade into the background as far as their budget connotations are concerned.

In terms of measuring the overall size of government on Chart 10.

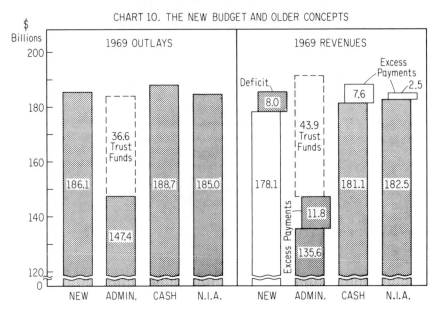

CHART 10. THE NEW BUDGET AND OLDER CONCEPTS

the new total of budget outlays of $186 billion is not materially different from the totals for either cash payments to the public or Federal sector expenditures in the national income accounts (shown as N.I.A. on the chart); nor is it substantially different from the sum of the old administrative budget expenditure figures and trust fund outlays. The same is true on the revenue side.

Small differences in outlays and revenues, however, can still produce sizable differences in the measurement of the net impact of Government operations. The 1969 budget deficit is estimated at $8 billion. On the old administrative basis the excess of expenditures comes to almost $12 billion. On a cash basis the figure is $7.5 billion and on a national income accounts basis $2.5 billion. If you look closely at the budget document you will find that a real effort has been made to deemphasize so-called competing forms of the deficit, retaining, however, such statistical tabulations as are significant for particular purposes.

Budget spending divides logically into three broad functional groups—Chart 11. About $80 billion of the $186 billion of spending

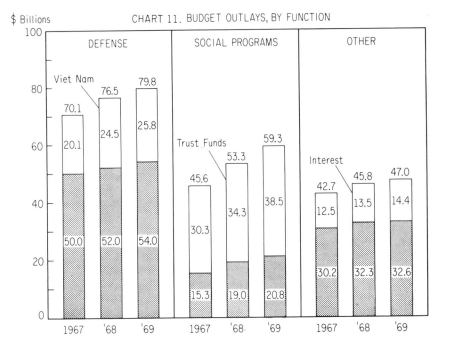

$ Billions   CHART 11. BUDGET OUTLAYS, BY FUNCTION

in fiscal 1969 is attributable directly to national defense, with $26 billion representing estimated direct dollar costs of our involvement in Viet Nam—the left side of the chart. The 1969 increase in the defense budget is significantly less than in other recent years. The turn of military events since the appearance of the budget, however, is responsible for the President's announcement of an increase of $2.5 billion in defense spending above the figures shown here.

Social programs, mostly through the trust funds, continue to show significant increases as shown in the central part of the chart. The 1969 figures reflect, for example, the effect of the new social security benefit increases. Social programs outside of the trust funds are rising much less rapidly in 1969 than in earlier years.

Among "other" expenditures—the right side of the chart—interest on the public debt can be singled out as an important rising cost with recent billion-dollar-a-year increases reflecting both large Government deficits and higher interest rates.

It was mentioned earlier that total budget outlays are rising less rapidly in 1969 than earlier. The left half of Chart 12 shows this slowing down in the rate of increase in the budget—$10.5 billion next year versus $17 billion this year. The President's budget presentation makes a particular point that most of the budget—involving defense, interest, scheduled contract payments, social security, et

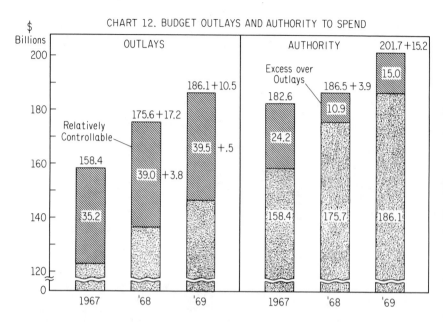

CHART 12. BUDGET OUTLAYS AND AUTHORITY TO SPEND

cetera—is relatively uncontrollable from the Administration's point of view. Figures are presented on "relatively controllable" outlays, therefore, to indicate that in areas where the President feels he has real spending discretion Federal outlays are rising only by $.5 billion from 1968 to 1969.

Outlays may be undertaken only under congressional grant of authority to spend money. The figures are shown on the right half of Chart 12. In each of the three years shown in the budget, authority to spend is well above actual outlays: $24 billion above in 1967, $11 billion above in 1968, and $15 billion above in 1969. Total authority sought of the Congress by the Administration for the 1969 fiscal year exceeds $200 billion. This is $15 billion more than the authority involved in fiscal 1968, providing a base for further increases in Federal spending in 1970 and later years. It is this expanding base which provides an obvious target in any fiscal austerity program.

Let us take the President's authority request of $201.7 billion for 1969 in the upper left-hand part of Chart 13 and tie it into next year's spending stream. Only about $131.3 billion of the new authority sought is actually to be spent in 1969. The rest of the 1969 spending, $54.8 billion, grows out of the unspent authority outstanding when the fiscal year begins on July 1, which is estimated to be $220.7 billion.

Most of the $220.7 billion unspent authority outstanding at the beginning of next year will carry over still another year, however; in

CHART 13. FLOW OF BUDGET OUTLAYS·$ BILLIONS

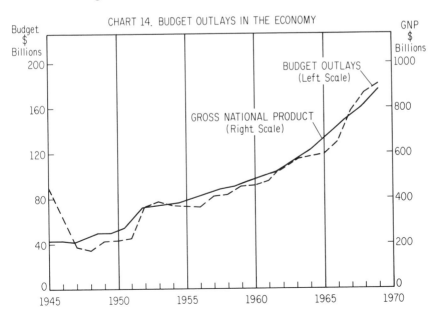

1969 NEW
AUTHORITY

201.7

131.3

1969
OUTLAYS

186.1

UNSPENT
AUTHORITY
JULY 1, '68

220.7 *

54.8

70.4

165.9

UNSPENT
AUTHORITY
JUNE 30,'69

236.4

*Excluding $1.6 billions expiring authority

fact, $165.9 billion of it is in that category. It, in turn, will be joined
by $70.4 billion of new authority which will be available for spend-
ing no earlier than fiscal 1970, so total authority outstanding at the
end of June a year from now is expected to exceed $236.4 billion.

The aggregate size of the budget has significance as a dollar
amount, since the Federal Government is the biggest single organization in the country. It has perhaps even greater significance in relation to the growth of the U. S. economy—Chart 14. Budget spend-

CHART 14. BUDGET OUTLAYS IN THE ECONOMY

Budget
$
Billions

GNP
$
Billions

BUDGET OUTLAYS
(Left Scale)

GROSS NATIONAL PRODUCT
(Right Scale)

ing over the past 20-odd years is charted on the scale on the left, ending up with the $186 billion figure projected for 1969. The second line on the chart ties to the right hand scale and shows our total output of goods and services in the nation.

Since the scales on Chart 14 are on a 5 to 1 ratio, in every year when the budget outlays line is above the GNP line budget outlays are in excess of 20 percent of our nation's production and income. The budget has expanded quite generally at the same rate as the economy during most of the postwar years, except that today Viet Nam has inflated spending to a point where Federal outlays are now larger in relation to the economy than at any time since World War II.

Our symposium subject today relates to spending—not taxes or borrowing—but no presentation of the whole budget picture would be complete without either of them being mentioned.

Budget revenues have, of course, also expanded over the years—from $6 billion in 1939 to $40 billion ten years later, to nearly $80 billion in 1958, and to $178 billion in 1969, as presented in Chart 15. The 1969 corporate income tax estimate is $34 billion. Individual income taxes are expected to total $81 billion; employment taxes, $38 billion; and excises, $20 billion. These 1969 figures include the effect of the President's new tax program.

The share of corporate income taxes in total revenues is slightly larger today than before World War II but smaller than in 1949, even

CHART 15. BUDGET REVENUE TRENDS

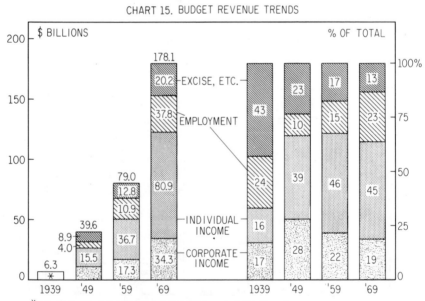

*1.1 corporate, 1.0 individual, 1.5 employment, 2.7 excise, etc.

with the assured surtax. Meanwhile individual income taxes have in recent years come close to providing half of the Government's revenues. After a percentage dip in the early postwar period, employment taxes again account for a quarter of the Government's revenues. At the same time there has been a substantial decline in the importance of excise taxes in the overall revenue picture.

The Federal budget deficit to be financed in the current fiscal year amounts to $20 billion—Chart 16. That figure will fall to $8 billion next year if the tax program is enacted.

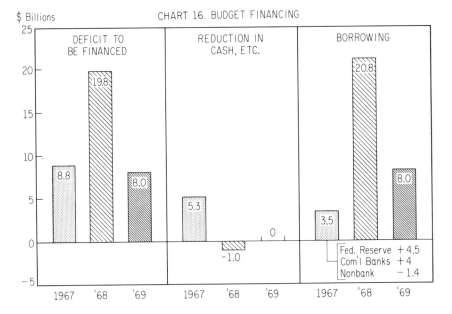

CHART 16. BUDGET FINANCING

The amount of the deficit, of course, does not necessarily equal the Government's need to borrow from the public. The Treasury may draw down excess cash, as it did in 1967, or add to cash, as it may do in 1968. Therefore, a $8.8 billion deficit last year resulted in only $3.5 billion of new borrowing, while the $19.8 billion deficit for this year produces public borrowing requirements of over $20 billion. Changes in taxes receivable and accounts payable will also enter the financing picture when the Government puts its accounts completely on an accrual basis.

The type of public borrowing which the Treasury undertakes to finance the deficit has, of course, significant economic effect. In 1967 more than all the borrowing from the public was accounted for by an increase in Federal Reserve holdings of Government securities so that nonbank investors actually showed a decline. The banking system has also been a heavy participant in the borrowing operations, now largely completed, for the fiscal year 1968.

We will have a national debt of about $298 billion by June, 1969 according to the budget estimates. The figures on Chart 17 reflect U.S. Treasury and Federal agency borrowing from the public.

CHART 17. SIZE OF THE NATIONAL DEBT

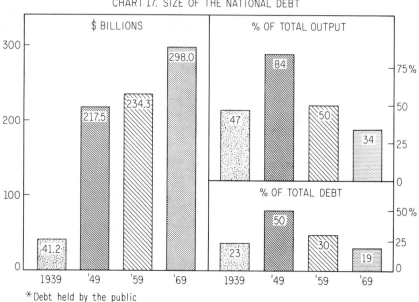

*Debt held by the public

They exclude borrowing from Government agencies and trust funds since those are considered intragovernmental transactions for the purposes of adding up the aggregate figures.

This 1969 estimate of the size of the debt is more than seven times as large as the prewar national debt figure and also shows a significant increase from the fairly level period of debt during the fifties.

In the last analysis, of course, the debt held by the public at the present time is nothing more nor less than the cumulated budget deficit over the history of our nation, representing upwards of $2.5 trillion of Government spending—20 percent of it last year, this year, and next year alone—and a shortfall in revenue of approximately $300 billion.

The national debt today is equal to about one-third of the gross national product—the right side of Chart 17. This is significantly less than the ratio of about one-half, which characterized both pre-World War II and 1959 and well under the figure of twenty years ago, 84 percent.

Since World War II, the public debt has grown less rapidly than the debts of individuals, corporations, and state and local governments, so that the national debt today accounts for one-fifth of total debt outstanding in our economy as against nearly one-third ten years ago, one-half in 1949, and about one-fourth in the prewar period.

Budget expenditures for interest, of course, have been rising, as is shown in Chart 18. Interest payments to the public (excluding inter-

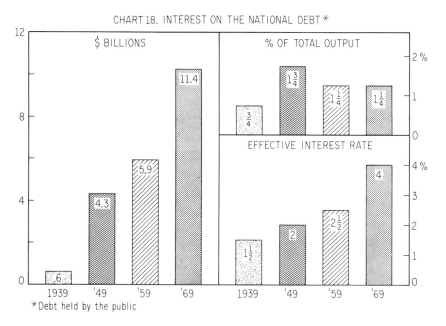

CHART 18. INTEREST ON THE NATIONAL DEBT *

*Debt held by the public

est paid to the trust funds and interest paid less interest received by Federal agencies) now approximate $11.5 billion, almost double the figure only ten years ago. The current figure is equal to 1 1/4 percent of our total current output of goods and services—not much different from ten years ago and midway between the 3/4 of 1 percent in 1939 and the 1 3/4 percent ratio in 1949.

These figures present a less favorable picture of the burden of the debt than is revealed by a glance at the debt figures themselves, since interest rates have risen materially during the last thirty years. An exceedingly rough measurement of average interest rates on Government borrowing from the public shows a steady progression from 1 1/2 percent thirty years ago to 2 percent following World War II, to 2 1/2 percent in 1959, and to an estimate of close to 4 percent for 1969.

Not only are the figures on the national debt of significance in interpreting the budget position of the United States—so also are the outstanding figures on Federal credit programs. As we all know, there are basically two types of Federal credit programs, (1) those involving direct loans by the Government or its agencies—the left-hand side of Chart 19—and (2) those relying on private credit but involving Government guarantees and insurance—the right-hand column of Chart 19.

CHART 19. FEDERAL CREDIT PROGRAMS

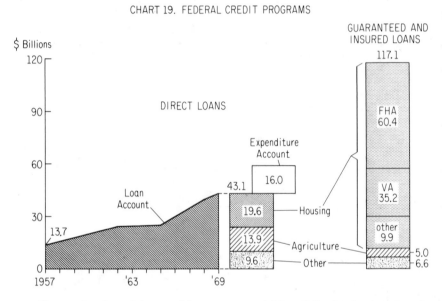

Guaranteed and insured loans are outside of the budget and only appear as budget outlays with regard to administrative costs and defaults. Direct loans, however, are within the budget. They are typically shown as part of the loan account where loans are made with the expectation of full repayment, although they often involve Government subsidy. Some loans, however, may be reflected in the expenditure account of the Government, like any other expenditure, if they are loans in name only, involving such programs as Commodity Credit Corporation nonrecourse loans, and AID (Agency for International Development) loans abroad.

Within the direct loan category there has been a substantial increase in loans outstanding over the years. Most of these are loans for housing. Many are for agriculture or for other purposes such as loans to assist foreign trade and loans to small business.

Housing loans dominate the guaranteed and insured loan picture. There are now $60 billion Federal Housing Administration insured loans outstanding plus $35 billion of Veterans' Administration loans.

There is pressure, of course, to substitute guaranteed and insured loans for direct loans whenever possible, not only because of the desire to stimulate private financing but also from the Government's standpoint in keeping the budget totals lower than they would be otherwise.

The Federal credit picture may be expanded tremendously in the years to come, particularly in the guaranteed and insured field, since many consider such loans essential to the attainment of national goals in fields such as air and water pollution and rebuilding our cities.

Mr. Kennedy: Thank you very much, Bob, for a most informative and very complete picture on the preparation and composition of the budget.

*The Budget Program by Function**

The outlays of the Federal Government are grouped into 13 functional categories according to the general purpose served, regardless of the administering agency. This section describes the trends and anticipated developments in the major programs under each of these functions.

In addition to the outlays estimated in the functional categories, the budget includes several lump-sum allowances.

- $4.0 billion for the proposed general and special revenue sharing programs (this is over and above the $9.5 billion included in the functional totals for grant programs to be converted to special revenue sharing);
- $1.0 billion for pay raises for civilian agencies (the national defense total includes a comparable allowance of $2.4 billion for military and civilian pay raises in the Defense Department); and
- $1.0 billion for unforeseen contingencies and for programs on which detailed proposals have not yet been completely formulated.

Budget *totals* do not include the contributions the Government makes, as an employer, to retirement trust funds for Federal employ-

*Office of Management and Budget, from the "U.S. Budget in Brief," Office of Management and Budget, January 1971, pp. 29–54.

Changing Composition of the Budget
(Dollars in billions)

Function	Percent of total budget							Outlays 1972
	1945	1950	1955	1960	1965	1970	1972	
National defense	85.7	30.4	58.7	49.8	41.9	40.8	33.8	$77.5
International affairs and finance	3.5	11.1	3.0	3.3	3.7	1.8	1.8	4.0
Space research and technology	*	.1	.1	.4	4.3	1.9	1.4	3.2
Agriculture and rural development . .	1.7	6.5	5.9	3.6	4.1	3.2	2.5	5.8
Natural resources	.3	2.9	.7	1.1	1.7	1.3	1.9	4.2
Commerce and transportation	4.4	3.9	1.6	5.2	6.2	4.7	4.8	10.9
Community develop- ment and housing . .	−.2	.6	*	1.1	.2	1.6	2.0	4.5
Education and manpower	.2	.5	.8	1.1	1.9	3.7	3.8	8.8
Health	.2	.6	.4	.8	1.5	6.6	7.0	16.0
Income security	1.2	10.9	13.3	19.7	21.7	22.3	26.5	60.7
Veterans benefits and services	1.2	20.5	6.6	5.9	4.8	4.4	4.6	10.6
General government . .	.8	2.7	1.7	1.4	1.9	1.7	2.2	5.0
Interest	3.7	13.3	8.8	9.0	8.7	9.3	8.6	19.7
Allowances	. . .	. . .	. . .	. . .	. . .	. . .	2.6	6.0
Undistributed deductions	−2.8	−3.9	−1.8	−2.5	−2.6	−3.2	−3.4	−7.8
Total	100.0	100.0	100.0	100.0	100.0	100.0	100.0	229.2

*Less than 0.05%.

ees and interest received by trust funds on their investments in Federal debt securities. These amounts are included in each function and then deducted as lump sums to avoid double counting. The transactions occur solely within the Government accounts, and do not result in any flow of funds to or from the public. Since the same adjustments are made on the receipts side of the budget, the budget surplus or deficit is not affected.

The defense programs recommended in this budget are necessary to provide the strength needed for our security. From our position of strength we seek meaningful negotiations for peace and a reduction or limitation of military forces. It is essential to our policies and to the effectiveness and readiness of our military forces that budget authority and outlays for national defense programs increase.

Our strategic forces are the cornerstone of the free world's deterrent against nuclear attack and must always be sufficient for this crucial role. We seek a negotiated limit or reduction of strategic nuclear forces in the SALT talks. In the absence of such an agreement, and in the face of a formidable Soviet threat, we must proceed with planned improvements.

National Defense

Program	Outlays in millions		
	1970 Actual	1971 Estimate	1972 Estimate
Department of Defense—Military:			
Military personnel	$23,031	$21,698	$20,105
Retired military personnel	2,849	3,394	3,744
Operation and maintenance	21,609	20,380	20,234
Procurement	21,584	18,448	17,936
Research, development, test, and evaluation	7,166	7,281	7,504
Military construction and other	1,059	1,407	2,019
Allowances	—	945	3,580
Deductions for offsetting receipts	-148	-183	-147
Subtotal, military[1]	77,150	73,370	74,975
Military assistance[2]	731	1,130	1,025
Atomic energy[1]	2,453	2,275	2,318
Defense-related activities	79	-54	92
Deductions for offsetting receipts[3]	-118	-278	-898
Total	80,295	76,443	77,512

[1] Entries net of offsetting receipts.
[2] Excludes support to other nations funded directly by the Department of Defense.
[3] Excludes offsetting receipts deducted by subfunction above: 1970, $979 million; 1971, $1,193 million; 1972, $1,113 million.

Our general purpose forces, together with those of our allies, must be adequate to counter a major Warsaw pact attack in Europe or a Chinese attack in Asia, to assist our allies against lesser threats in Asia and simultaneously to contend with a minor contingency anywhere.

Funds in this budget will assist our allies and friends assume a greater share of their own defense. The general purpose forces will be kept modern, fully ready and trained to meet a range of contingencies.

This strategy is already meeting its first tests. By May 1971, authorized troop ceilings in Vietnam will be approximately half the strength approved when this administration took office. Reductions in approved force levels have also been possible in Thailand, Korea, Japan, Okinawa, and the Philippines.

National defense outlays will increase by $1.1 billion over 1971, to $77.5 billion. This increase primarily reflects a rise in outlays for military functions and the military assistance program to provide for:

- a high level of readiness and increased modernization for the general purpose forces;
- a high level of military assistance;
- a more effective research and development effort; and
- progress toward an all-volunteer armed force.

Atomic Energy Commission outlays are estimated to increase

$43 million, to $2.3 billion in 1972. These increases will be partially offset by sales of $920 million from the stockpile of strategic materials.

Department of Defense—Military

This Nation's ability to pay the full cost of an adequate military program has never been questioned. Outlays for the military and military assistance programs will rise. Despite this increase the resources required for our military programs will continue to decline as a percent of Gross National Product (GNP).

Strategic Forces

The function of the strategic forces is to deter nuclear attack or to retaliate decisively should this fail. This capability is assured by three major strategic systems—intercontinental ballistic missiles (ICBM's), submarine-launched ballistic missiles (SLBM's) and bombers—each able to survive a first strike and inflict unacceptable damage upon any aggressor. This budget provides funds to: (1) Continue converting our intercontinental and submarine-launched missile forces to more effective systems; (2) a phased minimum deployment of the Safeguard ABM system; (3) proceed with orderly development of a new manned strategic aircraft; and (4) continue development of an advanced ballistic missile submarine system.

General Purpose Forces

Our general purpose forces, and those of our allies, must be adequate to meet a variety of nuclear and conventional war situations below the level of strategic nuclear exchange. We expect our allies to do more in their own behalf, as many are planning to do; but we must also do our share. We have a vital interest in peace and stability abroad and plan to maintain the capabilities to protect these interests. Withdrawals from Vietnam and the change in our force planning and strategy permit a smaller force structure than in the past. At the same time, Vietnam has limited our ability to meet some military needs elsewhere, particularly in NATO. Military forces must be combat ready and properly equipped to fulfill their role in our strategy for peace.

Land forces will be increasingly tailored to meet a range of contingencies. Armored and mechanized infantry forces will be kept ready with our NATO commitments in mind. Marine Corps divisions and Army airmobile and airborne units will emphasize rapid response.

Ship construction will be budgeted at the highest levels since 1963 to continue the improvement of the fleet. Five high-speed nuclear attack submarines, one nuclear guided-missile frigate, and seven antisubmarine destroyers will be added. It is also necessary to explore new ways to develop better *naval forces* for the late 1970's and 1980's. In this connection, the budget will support: (1) Experimentation with dual use of our aircraft carriers in both attack and antisubmarine warfare roles; (2) initial procurement for a force of high-speed patrol boats with surface-to-surface missile capability; and (3) exploration of concepts for a new class of smaller, faster escort ships.

Tactical air forces contribute to general purpose operations by providing air support for ground actions. To provide for future modernization, development of F-15 and AX air systems for the Air Force will proceed and procurement of the swing-wing F-14 fighters for fleet air defense and Harrier vertical-takeoff-and-landing aircraft for the Marine Corps will be increased.

Research and Development

In order to improve the effectiveness and readiness of our general purpose and strategic forces, increased emphasis will be placed on the development of new weapons, vehicles, and communications systems, and on strengthening the technological base that is essential to our national security.

Military Assistance

Military assistance and sales programs supplement the efforts of other countries to provide for their own defense, and ease the transition of our allies and friends to a position of greater self-reliance—a fundamental requirement for success of the Nixon doctrine.

Atomic Energy

The Atomic Energy Commission is responsible for developing and manufacturing nuclear weapons, improving nuclear power reactors for propulsion of naval vessels and generation of electric power, and providing services to enrich nuclear fuels for atomic powerplants. It also pursues the various peaceful applications of atomic energy, and conducts basic research in the physical and biomedical sciences.

Funds are included for continued development and production

National Defense

Fiscal year	Total outlays (in millions)	Percent of total budget outlays
1972 estimate	$77,512	33.8%
1971 estimate	76,443	35.9
1970	80,295	40.8
1969	81,232	44.0
1968	80,517	45.0
1967	70,081	44.3
1966	56,785	42.2
1965	49,578	41.9
1964	53,591	45.2
1963	52,257	46.9
1962	51,097	47.8
1961	47,381	48.4

of nuclear weapons and development of higher performance naval reactors.

Research on the NERVA nuclear rocket will be reduced in scale. Two plutonium production reactors will be shut down due to a reduction in military requirements. The program to develop a "fast breeder" nuclear power reactor designed to meet future energy needs will be accelerated.

Our foreign assistance programs will be reformed and reorganized in 1972. Legislation will be proposed to give new policy directions to these programs and adapt them to changed world conditions. Recognizing that other nations now have a greater ability and responsibility to deal with their own needs, U.S. assistance will supplement the defense and development efforts of lower income countries. The proposed new foreign assistance structure will clearly distinguish security assistance, which is intended to help less-developed countries defend themselves, and development assistance, which promotes long-term economic growth. Increasing reliance will be placed on multilateral institutions in order to minimize our direct involvement in the affairs of other countries.

Economic and Financial Assistance

International Security Assistance

The proposed security assistance program encompasses both military and economic supporting assistance. By actively encouraging others to mobilize men and resources for their own defense, this program reduces the need to maintain U.S. military forces abroad.

Military assistance, included in the national defense function, is an integral part of international security assistance. Military assistance grants supplement the defense efforts of countries least able to meet the financial costs of equipping their military forces. As their economies improve, these countries will be able to shift from grant assistance to foreign military credit sales.

Supporting assistance provides financial and technical aid to friendly countries whose defense expenditures are an especially heavy drain on their resources. Outlays for supporting assistance will increase, primarily to help Vietnam and Cambodia.

Multilateral Development Assistance

An increasing share of economic assistance will be channeled through multilateral institutions. This reflects the growing capacity of the World Bank group, regional development banks, and the United Nations to manage large capital and technical assistance programs. Additional subscriptions to these institutions are proposed so that the United States may fulfill its international obligations. Outlays for U.S. contributions to these institutions will rise by $80 million in 1972.

Bilateral Development Assistance

Two new U.S. agencies to provide bilateral development assistance are proposed. The International Development Corporation will make loans to selected countries for long-term development. The Corporation will operate in a business-like manner, encouraging borrower initiative and project quality. The International Development

International Affairs and Finance

Program	Outlays in millions		
	1970 Actual	1971 Estimate	1972 Estimate
Economic and financial assistance:			
International security assistance:			
Military assistance[1,2]	($ 593)	($1,175)	($1,025)
Supporting assistance..............	485	504	658
Multilateral development assistance......	337	415	495
Bilateral development assistance........	1,050	1,011	1,056
Other economic and financial assistance...	359	260	427
Food for Peace	937	1,014	952
Foreign information and exchange activities .	235	240	243
Conduct of foreign affairs	398	421	453
Deductions for offsetting receipts.......	−232	−279	−261
Total	3,570	3,586	4,032

[1] Outlays for military assistance are included in the national defense function. They are not included in the totals shown for international affairs and finance.
[2] Excludes trust funds.

Institute will mobilize U.S. scientific expertise and technology to help solve developmental problems of lower income countries.

Other Economic and Financial Assistance

The Overseas Private Investment Corporation supplies a broad range of services to U.S. investors in less-developed countries in order to strengthen the role of private institutions in the development process. The Export-Import Bank will continue to contribute toward the expansion of exports and achievement of a more favorable balance of payments.

The President's Foreign Assistance Contingency Fund will be used to meet unforeseen circumstances requiring economic, military, or humanitarian assistance.

Food for Peace

The United States donates and sells agricultural commodities on favorable terms to friendly nations. This program combats hunger and malnutrition, promotes economic growth in developing nations, and expands export markets for U.S. commodities. More than half of the shipments go to Korea, India, Indonesia, and Vietnam.

Foreign Information and Exchange Activities

Important mutual benefits flow from widened social, educational, and cultural contacts among the people of the world. Cultural and educational exchange activities of the State Department will be expanded. Radio, television broadcasts, motion pictures, libraries, publications, and other activities of the U.S. Information Agency will continue at current levels.

Conduct of Foreign Affairs

The Department of State has overall responsibility for assisting the President in foreign affairs and represents the United States throughout the world. Increases in assessed contributions to international organizations and a special contribution for the expansion of United Nations headquarters will account for most of the $32 million increase in the Department's outlays for foreign affairs. The Arms Control and Disarmament Agency will concentrate on strategic arms limitation and other negotiations and supporting research.

The 1972 budget will allow steady progress in exploiting the

International Affairs and Finance

Fiscal year	Total outlays (in millions)	Percent of total budget outlays
1972 estimate	$4,032	1.8%
1971 estimate	3,586	1.7
1970	3,570	1.8
1969	3,785	2.1
1968	4,619	2.6
1967	4,547	2.9
1966	4,490	3.3
1965	4,340	3.7
1964	4,117	3.5
1963	4,115	3.7
1962	4,492	4.2
1961	3,357	3.4

scientific return from continued exploration of the moon, extending man's capability to live and work in space, continuing unmanned exploration of the planets and the universe, and developing the practical applications of space technology.

Manned Space Flight

Man's epic journeys under the Apollo program have provided important scientific data on the origins of the moon and the solar system. The next step in the manned exploration of space is Skylab, an experimental space station which will test man's ability to live and work in space for up to 56 days and perform experiments related to astronomy and to earth resources. To reduce substantially the cost of future space operations in earth orbit, development will begin on the engine of a space shuttle.

Space Science and Applications

Work will start on the Grand Tour unmanned missions to explore the outer planets. Funds are also provided for the 1975 Viking unmanned exploration of Mars, for development of a High Energy

Space Research and Technology

Program	Outlays in millions		
	1970 Actual	1971 Estimate	1972 Estimate
Manned space flight	$2,209	$1,887	$1,662
Space science and applications	656	631	727
Space and aircraft technology.	516	470	429
Supporting space activities.	374	393	347
Deductions for offsetting receipts.	−6	−13	−13
Total	3,749	3,368	3,151

Space Research and Technology

Fiscal year	Total outlays (in millions)	Percent of total budget outlays
1972 estimate	$3,151	1.4%
1971 estimate	3,368	1.6
1970	3,749	1.9
1969	4,247	2.3
1968	4,721	2.6
1967	5,423	3.4
1966	5,933	4.4
1965	5,091	4.3
1964	4,170	3.5
1963	2,552	2.3
1962	1,257	1.2
1961	744	0.8

Astronomy Observatory to obtain space physics data, and for the launch of an Earth Resources Technology Satellite to demonstrate applications of space technology including crop surveys and geological measurements.

Space and Aircraft Technology

Work will continue on a variety of advanced research and technology programs to support future space and aeronautics projects. One such program is an experimental short takeoff aircraft for improved short-haul transportation.

Federal agriculture and rural development programs enhance farm income by improving agricultural marketing and production and expanding exports; aid in the elimination of hunger and malnutrition; protect consumers by assuring the wholesomeness of meat, poultry and eggs; and contribute to the development of rural areas.

The 1972 budget proposes a special revenue-sharing program to make funds available to enhance rural community development. The budget provides for strengthened efforts to achieve an equitable distribution of Government services between urban and rural communities in areas such as housing, sewer and water facilities, and economic

Agriculture and Rural Development

Program	Outlays in millions		
	1970 Actual	1971 Estimate	1972 Estimate
Farm income stabilization	$4,589	$4,075	$4,227
Rural housing and public facilities	579	60	432
Agricultural land and water resources	344	353	334
Research and other agricultural services	730	816	855
Deductions for offsetting receipts	−41	−42	−43
Total	6,201	5,262	5,804

development. These new efforts, involving direct services and loans, as well as the special revenue sharing funds will further the goal of balanced national growth through revitalization of rural communities. In addition, the provisions of recently enacted farm legislation and the recommendations in the 1972 budget will help maintain the ability of American agriculture to feed and clothe over 200 million people and provide reasonable incomes for our farmers.

Outlays for agriculture and rural development will be $542 million above the 1971 level. Lower net asset sales under various agricultural credit programs account for most of the increase. Other outlay increases are for farm income support, food inspection programs, and distribution of surplus agricultural commodities for school lunch and family feeding programs. These increases will be partially offset by a $275 million reduction from proposed substitution of insured farm operating loans for direct loans. This shift will not decrease the amount of credit available to farmers.

Farm Income Stabilization

The Agricultural Act of 1970 provides the framework for satisfying three basic agricultural goals of the administration: (1) to protect and improve farm income; (2) to provide more flexibility for farmers to make their own farm operating decisions; and (3) to develop greater reliance on the market place, making producers less dependent on Government programs.

In 1972, outlays for farm income stabilization programs will be $4.2 billion. The major portions of these outlays are for farm commodity price support and supply adjustment programs. Due to the corn blight and increased demand for wheat and soybeans, 1971 outlays are below initial estimates. Lower receipts resulting from more normal marketing conditions account for most of the increase in net outlays in 1972. Outlays for both 1971 and 1972, however, will be below the 1970 level.

Provision of surplus agricultural commodities to families and school children is an important part of the administration's overall program to assure adequate nutrition for all our citizens. Although the number of families benefiting from direct distribution of commodities will decline in 1972 as the food stamp program expands, the value of commodities received by each family, and by each school child, will increase.

Rural Housing and Public Facilities

The budget will continue to emphasize loan programs to help low-income rural residents acquire adequate housing. These loans will assist about 132,000 rural families to acquire homes, compared with about 87,000 in 1971.

The Government assists rural communities in developing sewer and water systems through grants and loans. Both loan levels and outlays for grants will increase in 1972.

Rural electric cooperatives have successfully established a private electric bank, and loans from the new bank will supplement the Government's direct loans. Legislation is again proposed to establish a rural telephone bank of mixed and eventually private ownership. The budget provides initial capitalization of the proposed telephone bank, which will extend credit to rural telephone systems at rates more competitive with commercial lending rates.

Agricultural Land and Water Resources

The Government provides technical and financial assistance to farmers to encourage sound conservation practices. Technical conservation services will continue at the 1971 level. The administration has redirected the agricultural conservation cost-sharing program to emphasize practices which provide more environmental benefits at reduced Federal cost. Outlays for this program, which has been renamed the rural environmental assistance program, will be $150 million in 1972.

Research and Other Agricultural Services

Outlays for research and extension programs will increase in 1972. Research on ways to avoid the use of pesticides will receive emphasis. In cooperation with the States, a trial program to manage the use of pesticides will be expanded.

Increases in meat and poultry consumption, implementation of

Agriculture and Rural Development

Fiscal year	Total outlays (in millions)	Percent of total budget outlays
1972 estimate	$5,804	2.5%
1971 estimate	5,262	2.5
1970	6,201	3.2
1969	6,221	3.4
1968	5,943	3.3
1967	4,376	2.8
1966	3,679	2.7
1965	4,807	4.1
1964	5,185	4.4
1963	5,139	4.6
1962	4,123	3.9
1961	3,340	3.4

the Wholesome Meat and Poultry Acts, and the new egg products inspection program will require increased Federal inspection and assistance to States. These regulatory programs will increase by about $13 million.

The Federal Government's natural resources programs are designed to maintain a careful balance among several objectives. Many unique resources, such as park lands and wilderness areas, must be preserved for the enjoyment and use of present and future generations. The Nation's resources must be developed and utilized prudently in order to provide the fuels and raw materials required by our modern industrial economy. At the same time, the environment must be protected from the undesirable side-effects which often accompany resource development and use.

Although the ultimate responsibility for protecting and enhancing the environment rests mainly with State and local government, industry, and the public, the Federal Government is providing vigorous leadership. The high priority that the administration assigns to improving the quality of the environment is reflected by:

- The creation of the Environmental Protection Agency to consolidate and intensify pollution control and abatement activities;
- Increases totaling $1.1 billion in appropriations and $676 million in outlays for water pollution abatement and recreation programs; and
- Additional increases for abating pollution at Federal facilities.

High priority is also assigned to reforming existing programs, as indicated by:

- Proposed legislation which, in addition to doubling the program level, will allow more flexibility in allocating grants for waste treatment facilities in order to increase the program's effectiveness in reducing pollution, and strengthen enforcement authority; and
- Termination of Federal purchases of helium for stockpiling purposes.

Water Resources and Power

Water resources programs develop projects to control water pollution, produce hydroelectric power, control floods, prevent erosion, improve navigation, and provide recreation facilities.

Outlays for these programs will be above 1971 levels due to significant increases in water quality programs and some increases for

Natural Resources

Program	Outlays in millions		
	1970 Actual	1971 Estimate	1972 Estimate
Water resources and power..............	$2,245	$3,025	$3,864
Land management	754	864	830
Mineral resources...................	94	173	68
Recreational resources................	370	536	615
Other natural resources programs	122	133	143
Deductions for offsetting receipts........	-1,105	-2,094	-1,276
Total	2,480	2,636	4,243

water resources development. Proposed legislation will authorize appropriations of $2 billion for waste treatment plant construction grants in 1972. Outlays of $2 million in 1971 and $4 million in 1972 are provided to implement a program authorized under the Refuse Act of 1899 to require permits for discharge of effluents into navigable streams.

Funds are provided for operation and maintenance of power projects being completed in 1971 and 1972, for additional underground electric power transmission research, and for construction of transmission facilities that will integrate Corps of Engineers and Bureau of Reclamation power projects into existing transmission systems and increase system reliability.

Land Management

Public land and national forest programs preserve wildlife, scenic resources, and wilderness areas. At the same time, these programs yield forest products, livestock forage, water and minerals, and afford broad opportunities for recreation. Under land management programs, access roads and trails are constructed and the resources of the lands are protected from damage by fire, insects, disease, erosion, and improper use. Outlays for land management programs will be somewhat below 1971 levels due to unusually high fire-fighting outlays in 1971.

Mineral Resources

Mineral resources programs include research on the conservation and development of minerals and fuels, research in metallurgy and mining, economic and statistical analysis, and coordination of oil and gas activities.

To further antipollution efforts, increased outlays are provided for pilot plant programs to develop low-pollution fuels by coal gasification; for laboratory research in high-efficiency, low-pollution generation of electricity by magnetohydrodynamic processes; and for research in underground waste disposal and urban waste recycling.

Recreational Resources

Recreation programs include management and protection of the national park system, construction and maintenance of park facilities, operation of national wildlife refuges, sport fishery and wildlife research and technical assistance, construction of Federal fish hatcheries, and preservation of historical properties.

The Land and Water Conservation Fund is used to acquire Federal park lands and to assist in the acquisition and development of State and local parks and recreation facilities. The budget recommends that the Land and Water Conservation Fund be fully funded, and that all remaining prior year authorizations for the fund be utilized, except for $20 million to be retained in order to make further payments, if necessary, for Redwood National Park lands. As a result, outlays for recreation programs will rise by $79 million in 1972.

Other Natural Resources Programs

Other natural resources programs include such activities as water resources investigations, geological and mineral resource surveys, and topographic surveys and mapping. Outlays for these programs will increase by $10 million in 1972.

During the past year, legislation was enacted affecting airway and airport development, merchant marine, urban mass transit, railroads, and highway programs.

The recent creation of the Postal Service will permit more extensive use of modern technology and business methods to improve the quality and efficiency of the postal services.

Natural Resources

Fiscal year	Total outlays (in millions)	Percent of total budget outlays
1972 estimate	$4,243	1.9%
1971 estimate	2,636	1.2
1970	2,480	1.3
1969	2,081	1.1
1968	1,655	0.9
1967	1,821	1.2
1966	1,999	1.5
1965	2,028	1.7
1964	1,944	1.7
1963	1,483	1.3
1962	1,665	1.6
1961	1,554	1.6

The newly established National Oceanic and Atmospheric Administration will intensify research and promote improved utilization and protection of the atmosphere and oceans.

Ground Transportation

Major adjustments will be made in 1972 to effect the transition to revenue sharing. Starting January 1, 1972, four major grant programs—urban mass transportation, all Federal-aid highways other than interstate highways, State and community highway safety, and highway beautification—will become part of the special revenue sharing program for transportation. Interstate highway construction and highway and urban transportation research, development and demonstrations will continue as Federal programs.

The Interstate Highway System, now 72 percent complete, is scheduled to be completed within 7 to 8 years. In the highway safety program, efforts to alleviate the problem of drunk drivers will be greatly expanded.

Under a new program to revitalize the Nation's railroad passenger service, the National Railroad Passenger Corporation is being established with responsibility for operating most of the Nation's intercity rail passenger service. The Government will also step up efforts to correct deficiencies in railway safety.

Commerce and Transportation

Program	Outlays in millions		
	1970 Actual	1971 Estimate	1972 Estimate
Ground transportation	$4,632	$ 5,145	$ 5,310
Air transportation	1,223	1,620	1,835
Water transportation.................	902	1,066	1,123
Area and regional development..........	590	747	801
Postal service	1,510	2,353	1,333
Advancement and regulation of business.....	607	711	677
Deductions for offsetting receipts........	-154	-200	-142
Total	9,310	11,442	10,937

Air Transportation

The scope of Federal aviation programs has been significantly broadened by the Airport and Airway Development and Revenue Act of 1970. This act authorizes increased aviation taxes and charges which will partially defray the costs of operating, expanding and modernizing the national airways system. Beginning January 1, 1972, the airport grant program will become part of the special revenue sharing program for transportation.

Commerce and Transportation

Fiscal year	Total outlays (in millions)	Percent of total budget outlays
1972 estimate	$10,937	4.8%
1971 estimate	11,442	5.4
1970	9,310	4.7
1969	7,921	4.3
1968	8,094	4.5
1967	7,594	4.8
1966	7,171	5.3
1965	7,399	6.2
1964	6,511	5.5
1963	5,765	5.2
1962	5,430	5.1
1961	5,062	5.2

In 1972, the Federal Aviation Administration will spend $1.5 billion on the airways system and on airport grants. In order to serve increased aircraft traffic, about 1,500 air controllers and maintenance technicians will be hired by FAA. Modernization and expansion of our airways system will be accelerated. Continued assistance for SST prototype development will help the American aviation industry to maintain world leadership in aircraft production. Outlays for this program will be $281 million in 1972.

Water Transportation

Outlays for the administration's new maritime program will increase by $26 million in 1972. This 10-year program is designed to develop a modern, efficient merchant fleet capable of carrying a larger share of our foreign trade and to eventually reduce the dependence of the shipping industry upon Federal support.

The Coast Guard will devote greater resources to prevention and control of oil spills. It will administer the Oil Pollution Fund, which will be used to defray the costs of oil spill cleanup until damages can be collected from the responsible party.

Area and Regional Development

During the past decade these programs have provided many useful services and developed plans for many areas which will be useful in furthering their economic development. Experience has also proved, however, that State and local governments are in a better position than the Federal Government to determine how their areas can best be developed. Therefore, urban and rural community development revenue sharing programs will be proposed to Congress to replace the present programs.

Postal Service

Legislation enacted in 1970 will convert the Post Office Department into an independent executive agency to be known as the Postal Service.

Increased mail volume and capital investment for modernization of postal facilities will raise postal costs from $9.2 billion in 1971 to $9.9 billion in 1972. Postal revenue is expected to rise from $6.9 billion to $8.6 billion, primarily as a result of an expected rate increase.

Advancement and Regulation of Business

The Department of Commerce will increase assistance to firms suffering economic hardship as a result of competition from imports. The Small Business Administration will provide lending assistance to 7,800 new businesses.

A number of consumer protection committees will be set up by the Federal Trade Commission to coordinate Federal, State, and local programs that help protect the public from fraudulent, deceptive, or unfair advertising and sales practices. The General Services Administration is creating a Consumer Information Center to disseminate information about products.

The emphasis in community development and housing programs in 1972 will be on major program reform. In the past, narrowly defined grant, loan, and loan insurance programs have tended to fragment government at the local level. This has weakened just those institutions of government that must respond to local needs. Similarly, housing programs have become overly specialized, sometimes preventing the construction of badly needed housing simply because certain projects do not fit into one of the precise categories eligible for assistance. Therefore, in 1972, legislation will be proposed to:

- Create a special revenue sharing program for Community Development;

Community Development and Housing

Program	Outlays in millions		
	1970 Actual	1971 Estimate	1972 Estimate
Low- and moderate-income housing aids.....	$1,280	$1,633	$1,948
Community planning, management, and development.....................	2,172	2,701	3,198
Maintenance of the housing mortgage market .	-487	-423	-651
Deductions for offsetting receipts........	...	-53	...
Total	2,965	3,858	4,495

- Provide a new planning and management support program to strengthen State and local decisionmaking capabilities; and
- Simplify and consolidate the multitude of housing programs.

These new and revised programs will gradually eliminate the problems created by the existence of many narrowly defined categorical programs.

Low- and Moderate-Income Housing Aids

These programs help provide decent, safe, and sanitary housing to families who could not otherwise afford it. About 518,000 units of assisted housing will be made available under 1972 commitments. Long-term subsidy contracts will be the principal means of reducing the cost of renting or buying a home.

Community Planning, Management, and Development

Major legislation will be proposed to reform the community planning, management, and development assistance programs of the Department of Housing and Urban Development (HUD) and the Office of Economic Opportunity (OEO). This two-part reform will be implemented during 1972 and become fully effective in 1973.

The present comprehensive planning program will take on a different emphasis, strengthening the executive and managerial capabilities of State and local governments. In recognition of this, commitments under the present program will double in 1972. To complete this portion of the reform, a new program of community development planning and management grants will become operative in 1973. Special revenue sharing for community development will be proposed. Initial funding of $1 billion is requested for 1972, which would be equivalent to a rate of $2 billion in the first full year of operation. These funds will be used in accordance with local needs so that a community need not distort its priorities in order to qualify for aid through narrowly defined categorical programs.

To provide for an orderly transition to the new program, four existing programs, Model Cities, urban renewal, rehabilitation loans, and water and sewer facility grants will be funded for the first 6 months of the year. This will allow ample time for the new program to be enacted and funded after which the older programs will be terminated.

Effective January 1, 1973, community action agencies, now funded through OEO, will be funded through special revenue sharing. The extended transition period is necessary due to the widely varying status of community action within local government structures.

In 1972, HUD's research and technology program will focus on improving housing management and preventing the deterioration and abandonment of housing. Operation Breakthrough will enter the final phases of testing new methods of producing large volumes of housing. A relaxation of the legal and market constraints on the use of such new methods will be sought. OEO will continue to emphasize development of innovative approaches for solving the problems of the poor.

Maintenance of the Housing Mortgage Market

The production and sale of housing depends upon the existence of a smoothly functioning mortgage market. The Government helps maintain such a market by:

- Assisting private housing to compete for needed funds in the capital market by insuring housing mortgages, private securities backed by mortgages, and accounts in savings and loan associations—which invest most of their assets in home mortgages;
- Assuring that all citizens have equal access to sale and rental housing through enforcement of the fair housing laws; and
- Helping to provide property insurance in areas where insurance is not otherwise available through the private market.

Education and general science programs develop the intellectual skills of our people and further the expansion of basic scientific knowledge. Manpower programs develop occupational skills and provide employment opportunities for our workers.

The administration's education, science, and manpower programs reflect reforms which will:

- Improve the allocation of Federal funds by concentrating on areas of greatest need;

Community Development and Housing

Fiscal year	Total outlays (in millions)	Percent of total budget outlays
1972 estimate	$4,495	2.0%
1971 estimate	3,858	1.8
1970	2,965	1.5
1969	1,961	1.1
1968	4,076	2.3
1967	2,616	1.7
1966	2,644	2.0
1965	288	0.2
1964	-185	—
1963	-880	--
1962	589	0.6
1961	191	0.2

- Emphasize carefully planned and evaluated experiments to increase the effectiveness of education and manpower programs;
- Increase support for basic research and research on major social and environmental problems; and
- Decentralize the responsibility for planning and operating comprehensive manpower programs in order to achieve a better match of training resources and local needs.

Elementary, Secondary, and Vocational Education

An important element of the administration's reform of Federal grant programs will be a proposal to adopt a $3 billion special revenue sharing program for elementary and secondary education. This proposal will draw together a large number of present grants into four general areas and give States greater latitude to meet local problems.

Reduction of racial isolation is essential if the Nation's schools are to provide equal educational opportunity. Under the proposed Emergency School Assistance Act, project grants totaling $1.5 billion will be made in 1971 and 1972 to local school districts desegregating under court order or attempting to overcome the disadvantages of racial isolation on their own initiative.

Higher Education

A basic revision of existing student aid programs will be proposed to insure that no qualified student who wants to go to college is barred by lack of funds. Grants, work-study payments, and subsidized loans will be extended to lower income students, and a proposed National Student Loan Association will provide capital to banks and colleges for loans to students of all income levels.

The National Foundation for Higher Education will be created to support reform and innovation at colleges and universities.

Education and Manpower

Program	Outlays in millions		
	1970 Actual	1971 Estimate	1972 Estimate
Elementary, secondary, and vocational education..........................	$3,257	$3,668	$4,063
Higher education	1,381	1,458	1,302
Other education aids..................	429	419	463
General science	464	502	546
Manpower training and employment services. .	1,602	2,017	2,156
Other manpower aids	169	248	308
Deductions for offsetting receipts........	−14	−12	−29
Total	7,289	8,300	8,808

Loans from the private sector will continue to be the major source of funds for the construction of college facilities in 1972. Federal interest subsidies will reduce the cost of such loans.

Other Education Aids

Funds are provided for the creation of a National Institute of Education in HEW to serve as the focal point for educational experimentation.

Funds for the National Foundation on the Arts and the Humanities will almost double in 1972 for the second consecutive year, reflecting a growing commitment to foster the cultural life of the Nation.

General Science

To meet the need for research on urgent national problems and to advance our technology and economic productivity, the budget of the National Science Foundation will be increased by more than 22 percent in 1972, from $506 to $622 million. This will permit the Nation's scientific and engineering talent to undertake research relating to pollution, health, transportation, and other social and environmental problems.

Manpower Training and Employment Services

Reform legislation will again be proposed to give State and local officials the primary responsibility for providing comprehensive services closely related to local conditions and individual needs. Total budget authority of $2 billion would be provided during the first full year under this special revenue sharing measure.

Education and Manpower

Fiscal year	Total outlays (in millions)	Percent of total budget outlays
1972 estimate	$8,808	3.8%
1971 estimate	8,300	3.9
1970	7,289	3.7
1969	6,525	3.5
1968	6,739	3.8
1967	5,853	3.7
1966	4,258	3.2
1965	2,284	1.9
1964	1,751	1.5
1963	1,502	1.3
1962	1,406	1.3
1961	1,227	1.3

The proposed welfare reform also will have an important impact on manpower programs by providing increased job training and child care services to help low-income families become self-supporting. Pending the enactment of welfare reform, the Work Incentive program (WIN) will provide job training for 187,000 public assistance recipients, a 50 percent increase over 1971. An estimated 200,000 children will receive child care services in 1972 under the WIN program.

Computerized job banks will operate in all States by 1972, and efforts will be directed toward further development of the programs necessary to support a nationwide computerized job placement system.

Other Manpower Aids

The Occupational Safety and Health Act of 1970, achieved after decades of effort, will be funded at over $25 million to reduce the incidence of diseases, injuries, and deaths in the workplace. Disabled coal miners will receive additional benefits with the promulgation of State standards for workmen's compensation for "black lung" disease. Federal workers will benefit from a strengthened labor-management relations program.

In 1972, the Federal Government will implement a new comprehensive health strategy for the 1970's. Its design will be based on three principles:

- *Prevention.*—Wherever possible, the need for medical care must be eliminated by the avoidance of illness and injury through effective preventive measures.
- *Equity.*—No American family should be prevented from obtaining a reasonable and basic standard of medical care by inability to pay.
- *Efficiency.*—The productivity of the health system should be raised; shortages and maldistributions of health care resources must be overcome, so that improved health purchasing power leads to the delivery of needed services and brings medical cost inflation under reasonable control.

Part of the strategy will be a new health protection program for all poor families with children. Legislative proposals will be presented to Congress in calendar 1971.

Development of Health Resources

In 1972, the administration will give high priority to development of the Nation's health resources to prevent health problems

Health

Program	Outlays in millions		
	1970 Actual	1971 Estimate	1972 Estimate
Development of health resources:			
Biomedical research (including new initiative in cancer)	$1,200	$1,287	$1,355
Training health manpower (including new support)	449	488	577
Constructing health facilities	315	290	280
Improving the organization and delivery of health services	133	163	168
Providing or financing medical services:[1]			
Medicare	7,149	8,278	9,038
Medicaid	2,727	3,250	3,383
Other	468	509	529
Prevention and control of health problems	561	664	703
Deductions for offsetting receipts[2]	−6	−2	−18
Total	12,995	14,928	16,010

[1] Entry net of offsetting receipts.
[2] Excludes offsetting receipts which have been distributed by subfunction above: 1970, $1,556 million; 1971, $2,119 million; 1972, $1,928 million.

and increase capacity to assure each citizen access to needed health care.

Research to eliminate or control cancer will be greatly intensified through a special $100 million initiative in the 1972 budget. Another special emphasis will be on sickle cell anemia. Research on heart and lung disease, investigating the health hazards of narcotic addiction, alcoholism, and environmental pollutants; preventing the disabilities and disease of infancy and early childhood; and improving our knowledge of human reproduction will also be part of the expanded 1972 research effort.

Outlays to expand the Nation's supply of health personnel and for a new initiative in the support of our health professions schools will rise by $89 million to a level of $577 million. More direct support will be provided for the training of physicians, and a major effort will be undertaken to develop new types of paramedical personnel.

Federal programs to increase the supply of health facilities will emphasize grants to support the construction of outpatient and rehabilitation facilities, and will use interest subsidies and loan guarantees to support hospital construction.

The administration will encourage experiments with organizations that deliver prepaid comprehensive medical services. This effort will include research and technical assistance for private enterprise interested in pursuing this approach to improving the efficiency of the Nation's health care system. Demonstrations of new roles for auxiliary health personnel will also be supported.

Providing or Financing Medical Services

In 1972, Medicare, the largest Federal health program, will ease the burden of medical care costs for virtually all the 20 million aged in the Nation, while Medicaid will help an estimated 19 million poor persons receive necessary medical care. Legislation will be introduced to provide improved cost controls and other modifications in Medicare and Medicaid that will encourage greater efficiency through use of alternatives to costly hospitalization.

In 1972, Federal efforts to provide family planning services will be expanded to support projects capable of serving 3 million women, an increase of 800,000 over 1971. Health services for American Indians and Alaska natives will be expanded. In addition, comprehensive medical services will be provided to approximately 500,000 crippled and mentally retarded children.

Prevention and Control of Health Problems

Disease prevention and control, environmental health problems, and consumer protection are integral parts of this administration's health strategy. Outlays for these activities will rise by $39 million in 1972 to $703 million. Research, treatment, and rehabilitation efforts to combat drug abuse and alcoholism will be intensified.

Federal action to reduce the health dangers of air and water pollution, solid wastes, radiation, and occupational hazards are essential to the administration's efforts to improve and protect the quality of the environment. These activities will receive high priority in 1972, as will efforts to assure drug and food safety.

Health

Fiscal year	Total outlays (in millions)	Percent of total budget outlays
1972 estimate	$16,010	7.0%
1971 estimate	14,928	7.0
1970	12,995	6.6
1969	11,696	6.3
1968	9,672	5.4
1967	6,721	4.2
1966	2,543	1.9
1965	1,730	1.5
1964	1,737	1.5
1963	1,393	1.3
1962	1,139	1.1
1961	873	0.9

Income Security

Program	Outlays in millions		
	1970 Actual	1971 Estimate	1972 Estimate
Retirement and social insurance:			
Social security[1]	$29,695	$35,160	$38,615
Unemployment insurance	3,369	5,888	5,058
Other retirement programs[1]	4,210	4,956	5,357
Public assistance:			
Cash payments	4,142	5,593	6,604
Food stamps	577	1,535	1,971
Other	466	731	713
Social and individual services	1,331	1,684	1,937
Deductions for offsetting receipts[2]	-1	-1	-18
Total	43,790	55,546	60,739

[1] Entries net of offsetting receipts.
[2] Excludes offsetting receipts which have been distributed by subfunction above: 1970, $1,074 million; 1971, $1,110 million; 1972, $1,330 million.

Progress and reform are the distinguishing traits of the Nation's income security programs. Significant advances were made in calendar year 1970:

- Unemployment insurance was extended to 4.8 million additional workers, and special extended benefits will be automatically triggered when warranted by economic conditions.
- The food stamp program was reformed, providing sufficient benefits to purchase a nutritionally adequate diet, free stamps for the poorest families, and adjustments for increases in the cost of living.

The year ahead promises even more dramatic advances. Legislation has been proposed to reform the Nation's basic income security programs:

- *Welfare reform* will fundamentally recast welfare policy in the United States, and cover 11 million people in families of the "working poor" for the first time in our history.
- *Social security* benefits will be adjusted automatically with the cost of living, with the first step being a 6 percent increase on January 1, 1971.

Income security programs account for one-quarter of the total Federal budget and influence the lives of millions. Social security benefits will reach 27 million people in 1972, food stamps will aid 11 million poor, and welfare assistance will be provided to more than 14 million.

Recently, the annual increase in income security programs has approached half or more of the normal growth in Federal revenues.

Retirement and Social Insurance

These programs are designed to cushion the income loss suffered when earnings are interrupted or terminated by old age, disability, death, or temporary unemployment. The benefits are related to prior earnings and are financed principally by payroll taxes on employees and employers.

Proposed improvements in social security include increases in widow's benefits and liberalization of the retirement test (earnings allowed without benefit reduction).

Under proposed amendments, earnings subject to tax will increase from $7,800 to $9,000 beginning January 1, 1971. In the future, the level of taxable earnings would be increased automatically.

Public Assistance

The Federal Government provides cash assistance to those who have little or no other means of support—one-parent families with dependent children, the aged, blind or the disabled. In 1972, the Federal Government will pay 57 percent of total program costs—an estimated $6.6 billion—with the States bearing the remainder.

The proposed *welfare reform* is the most important domestic legislation to be advanced in a generation. It would emphasize greater incentives for work, training, and self-sufficiency. The program will provide national eligibility standards and a Federal income floor; States will supplement these basic payments. A minimum monthly payment will be required for aged, blind, and disabled recipients.

Beginning in 1973, payments will also be made to the working poor for the first time in our history, providing income supplementation to those who are employed full time but simply do not earn enough to support their families.

Extension and reform of the *food stamp program* were early efforts of this administration to eliminate hunger and malnutrition. An estimated 11 million people will be served in the year ahead. The food stamp program will be integrated with the proposed welfare reform.

Social and Individual Services

During the 1960's Congress authorized a series of services to public assistance recipients with 75 percent Federal matching of any State spending designed to combat rising dependency.

Sharply rising costs—uncontrollable under current laws—and the

Income Security

Fiscal year	Total outlays (in millions)	Percent of total budget outlays
1972 estimate	$60,739	26.5%
1971 estimate	55,546	26.1
1970	43,790	22.3
1969	37,399	20.4
1968	34,108	19.1
1967	31,164	19.7
1966	29,016	21.5
1965	25,702	21.7
1964	25,110	21.2
1963	24,084	21.6
1962	22,530	21.1
1961	21,227	21.7

undetermined value of the services provided make this program a prime candidate for reform. A 10 percent growth limit will be sought on outlays and legislation will be proposed to fundamentally restructure the program to encourage better results and greater accountability in the use of funds. An additional $151 million will be spent to upgrade foster care for dependent children and provide special incentives for the adoption of handicapped children.

Vocational rehabilitation will place special emphasis on serving 45,000 additional disabled public assistance recipients in 1972.

An expanded program for Retired Senior Volunteers will provide older Americans 29,200 opportunities for meaningful community service.

Veterans programs assist millions of men and women who have provided military service to their country. In 1972, additional education benefits will encourage returning Vietnam veterans to take advantage of education and training opportunities. Special emphasis

Veterans Benefits and Services

Program	Outlays in millions		
	1970 Actual	1971 Estimate	1972 Estimate
Income security for veterans	$6,021	$6,551	$ 6,973
Veterans education, training, and rehabilitation	1,105	1,715	1,981
Veterans housing	54	-147	-334
Hospital and medical care for veterans	1,802	2,056	2,230
Other veterans benefits and services	260	288	301
Deductions for offsetting receipts	-477	-493	-508
Total	8,677	9,969	10,644

will also be placed on improving medical care for veterans disabled in military service by:

- Raising average employment in veterans medical facilities by 4,547; and
- Providing more hospital beds for intensive care and 154 new medical units for specialized treatment.

Income Security for Veterans

Financial help is provided to veterans and their families when the disability or death of a breadwinner reduces their income. Outlays for these benefits will rise by $422 million in 1972 and account for over 65 percent of total outlays for veterans programs.

Monthly *compensation* is paid to veterans or their survivors for disability incurred or aggravated by military service. The amount is based on the severity of disability and impairment of earning power. An estimated 94,000 Vietnam veterans or their survivors are expected to be added to the compensation rolls in 1972, bringing the total from all wars to 2.6 million.

Veterans may qualify for monthly *pensions* on the basis of total disability and financial need. Widows and surviving children may also qualify if their income is below levels set by law. The pension rates were increased substantially in 1970 and 1971. In 1972, $2.5 billion in pensions will be paid to 2.3 million recipients.

A variety of veterans *life insurance* programs protect the families of servicemen and veterans. These programs will cover 8.7 million veterans, and will pay claims or dividends of $1.2 billion.

Veterans Education, Training, and Rehabilitation

To help the returning veteran realize his full potential in civilian life, assistance is provided under the GI bill for education, training, and vocational rehabilitation. Educational benefits are also available to survivors of those who died or dependents of those totally disabled as a result of military service. Outlays for these programs will increase by $267 million, benefiting over 54,000 war orphans or dependent children, 9,000 widows and wives, and 1.8 million veterans.

Veterans Housing

To assist veterans in purchasing homes, the Veterans Administration guarantees private mortgages. This program has been supplemented by direct loans. Special efforts will be made to arrange suitable private financing for veterans living in credit-short areas, thus making possible a termination of the direct loan program in calendar year 1971.

Hospital and Medical Care for Veterans

Medical care is available to veterans in over 200 veterans hospitals and clinics across the country. All veterans with service-connected disabilities are assured of care. When space is available, hospital care is also provided for veterans with disabilities unrelated to service who are unable to pay for care in other hospitals. Patients with non-service-connected ailments occupy about 75 percent of total VA hospital beds.

A record 806,000 veterans will be treated in VA hospitals. On an average day, 79,000 veterans receive such care.

Improvements will continue to be made in the quality of medical care. The 1972 program includes: (1) An average staff increase of 4,547; (2) construction or modernization of five hospitals and activation of three new ones; (3) training for 53,000 medical personnel; (4) addition of specialized medical facilities—primarily for intensive care and treatment of spinal cord injury, heart and kidney diseases, alcoholism, and drug addiction.

Other Veterans Benefits and Services

The 1972 budget provides for continuing improvements in counseling and assistance while servicemen are still in the war zone, in military hospitals, and in separation centers. Special efforts will be made through 71 veterans assistance centers and other VA-supported contact activities to supplement the job counseling and employment activities of the Departments of Defense and Labor.

Veterans Benefits and Services

Fiscal year	Total outlays (in millions)	Percent of total budget outlays
1972 estimate	$10,644	4.6%
1971 estimate	9,969	4.7
1970	8,677	4.4
1969	7,640	4.1
1968	6,882	3.8
1967	6,897	4.4
1966	5,920	4.4
1965	5,722	4.8
1964	5,681	4.8
1963	5,520	5.0
1962	5,625	5.3
1961	5,688	5.8

General Government

Program	Outlays in millions		
	1970 Actual	1971 Estimate	1972 Estimate
Law enforcement and justice	$ 666	$1,116	$1,478
General property and records management . . .	595	643	692
Central fiscal operations.	1,271	1,417	1,570
Central personnel management	166	202	254
National Capital region	226	363	414
Legislative and judicial functions.	362	411	450
Executive direction and other.	309	484	617
Deductions for offsetting receipts	−259	−254	−506
Total	3,336	4,381	4,970

Effective law enforcement, an orderly and fair judicial system, and efficient administration of Government personnel, property, and fiscal management activities are major objectives of general government programs. Federal law enforcement efforts will be upgraded and current programs to achieve a greater degree of intergovernmental law enforcement cooperation will be strengthened. Federal efforts to secure the civil rights of all our citizens will be stepped up significantly. Fiscal and tax operations will be made more efficient.

Law Enforcement and Justice

Major initiatives to provide better law enforcement, more prompt and efficient administration of justice, and more comprehensive rehabilitation of criminal offenders will be undertaken directly by the Federal Government and by State and local governments with Federal financial and technical assistance.

Direct Federal enforcement activities will be intensified. Under recently expanded authority, Federal strike force teams of attorneys and investigators will coordinate efforts to rid our society of organized crime. The FBI will mount a concentrated assault on large-scale gambling operations which are a major source of funds supporting organized crime. Intensified international cooperation and increased inspection at key ports of entry will be employed to destroy major criminal systems that import and distribute narcotics and dangerous drugs.

The Law Enforcement Assistance Administration (LEAA) will have outlays of $603 million in 1972, an increase of $217 million over 1971, to assist State and local governments in improving a wide range of law enforcement functions. LEAA will support comprehensive planning in all 50 States and in many of the Nation's largest cities, and provide funds for major improvements in the operation of State and local police, court, and correctional systems.

To secure equal opportunities for all citizens, the Federal Government will nearly double its efforts against discrimination in Federal and private employment, Federal assistance programs, public education, and housing.

The mechanisms available to the Federal Government for insuring equal employment opportunity will be strengthened. The Office of Federal Contract Compliance in the Department of Labor is responsible for administering the Executive order which prohibits employment discrimination by Federal contractors. It plans to double the number of industrial on-site compliance reviews in 1972.

General Property and Records Management

Economic analysis indicates that Federal leasing of buildings is, in most cases, less costly than Federal ownership and will reflect more accurate annual costs for Federal property. In order to take better advantage of the lease alternative, legislation is being prepared to provide the General Services Administration greater flexibility with respect to planning and contracting for the acquisition of building space. Based on this legislation, a substantial increase in contracts for the acquisition of buildings to house Federal activities is projected for 1972.

To carry out the President's directive that Federal property be used more effectively, more than 115,000 acres of Federal property may be made available during the current year for other Federal use, donations to State and local governments, or sale to the public. Another 3 million acres are to be reviewed by the General Services Administration to determine their availability for other uses. Funds are also provided for screening excess military equipment and supplies in the United States, Southeast Asia, and other overseas locations.

Central Fiscal Operations

The Internal Revenue Service (IRS) accounts for two-thirds of the outlays for central fiscal operations. It will process over 111 million tax returns in 1972, improve the audit of those returns to encourage fuller taxpayer compliance with tax laws, and assume responsibility for the control of explosives through licensing and inspection procedures. Three new IRS service centers will be staffed to process the growing number of tax returns forecast for 1972 and future years.

The Bureau of Customs will expand its operations to accommodate the clearance of increasing arrivals of people and cargo from

General Government

Fiscal year	Total outlays (in millions)	Percent of total budget outlays
1972 estimate	$4,970	2.2%
1971 estimate	4,381	2.1
1970	3,336	1.7
1969	2,866	1.6
1968	2,561	1.4
1967	2,510	1.6
1966	2,292	1.7
1965	2,210	1.9
1964	2,040	1.7
1963	1,810	1.6
1962	1,650	1.5
1961	1,491	1.5

abroad. It will also intensify its antismuggling and narcotics enforcement efforts.

National Capital Region

The 1972 budget proposes that public works of the District of Columbia be financed by the sale of local bonds rather than by direct Treasury borrowing. This is consistent with the objective of greater local autonomy for the District Government. The budget also includes the Federal payment to the District, and funds for continued construction of the long-awaited rapid rail transit system for the Washington metropolitan region.

Interest costs, predominantly interest on the public debt, are expected to rise by $1.1 billion in 1971, and by another $0.2 billion in 1972.

Interest payments for both 1971 and 1972 reflect the recent reduction in interest rates on short-term securities, the sector of the market where the great bulk of Treasury refinancing operations necessarily occurs. Assuming continuance of relatively low market rates of interest, the refinancing of maturing obligations bearing higher rates will provide savings that offset much of the increase that would otherwise occur in 1972 as a result of a larger debt level.

Interest

Program	1970 Actual	1971 Estimate	1972 Estimate
Interest on the public debt.	$19,304	$20,800	$21,150
Interest on refunds of receipts	113	117	117
Interest on uninvested funds.	6	7	6
Deductions for offsetting receipts	-1,110	-1,491	-1,586
Total	18,312	19,433	19,687

Interest

Fiscal year	Total outlays (in millions)	Percent of total budget outlays
1972 estimate	$19,687	8.6%
1971 estimate	19,433	9.1
1970	18,312	9.3
1969	15,791	8.6
1968	13,744	7.7
1967	12,588	8.0
1966	11,285	8.4
1965	10,357	8.7
1964	9,810	8.3
1963	9,215	8.3
1962	8,321	7.8
1961	8,108	8.3

About $1.6 billion of the estimated outlays for interest in 1972 will be offset by collections of interest by the Treasury Department. The interest is on Treasury loans to other Federal agencies to finance their lending and other business-type operations, and to a lesser extent, on loans to foreign governments.

Of the estimated 1972 interest outlays, about 27 percent will be paid to trust funds and other Government investment accounts on the Government securities they hold. More than $3.6 billion of the interest paid on obligations held by the Federal Reserve banks will be returned to the Treasury as miscellaneous receipts through the deposit of excess earnings by such banks. Hence, the net impact on the budget of the interest paid on the Federal debt will be less than $10.8 billion in 1972.

C

Measurement and Problems of Fiscal Policy

The effectiveness of fiscal policy as a stabilization device is open to question. Forecasting is still not sufficiently precise and accurate to indicate the most propitious time to use fiscal policy. Moreover, the time factor is a major problem of fiscal policy. A considerable hiatus exists between the points in time when the need to take action is recognized and actual execution of fiscal policy is taken. There is also the point that inflation can prove to be resistant to both fiscal and monetary policies aimed at curbing it. This inflation can be identified as cost-push and is likely to originate in industries which are relatively concentrated, and in which sellers can exercise control in the formulation of both prices and wages.

The readings are designed to reflect some of the problems of fiscal policy. The first reading, "Economic Forecasting as a Basis for Fiscal Policy Decisions," by Solomon Fabricant, discusses the procedures and problems of forecasting. The second reading, "Scope and Limitations of General Demand Policies," by the Committee for Economic Development, presents some of the limitations of general demand policies. The final reading, "Measures of Changes in Fiscal Policy," by the Council of Economic Advisers, discusses the concept of the full employment budget as a target path for fiscal policy and as a measurement of fiscal impact.

Economic Forecasting as a Basis
for Fiscal Policy Decisions*

Our question is whether forecasting can be of help in making fiscal and other economic policy decisions. I think the answer is in the affirmative. Despite all its limitations—and they are serious—forecasting can help, and in fact is helping, to make economic policy decisions somewhat better than they would be without its assistance.

You will have noticed that I tried to be cautious in wording this conclusion. Nevertheless, it may still seem like a foolhardy statement to make at a time when there are so many differences of opinion on the drift of the economy and concern over the wisdom of current economic policy. Yet I think the statement can be justified. Indeed, the present controversy reflects an awareness and anxiety that might reasonably be viewed as evidence in support of the statement. If it were not for the forecasting going on—mixed though the results are—the country would be less sensitive to the dangers ahead. There might be more serious talk, or more than just talk, about raising taxes. The probability of a recession would be greater.

Let us venture further. Forecasting is helpful, but not as much as it could be even within its present limitations. In many forecasts insufficient use is made of available knowledge. Yet at the same time, more knowledge is implied than anyone now possesses.

I hasten to emphasize, at the cost of repetition, that even at its best forecasting has severe limitations. Forecasts cannot and never will be as helpful as we would like. But they could be, and I believe would be, much more helpful if the current flow of information and the scientific basis of forecasting were to be improved. There is some progress in this respect, but it is not fast enough. A stepped-up rate of investment would yield a high rate of return. It ought to be made.

Patterns and Indicators of Cyclical Change

Let me begin to spell out what I have just put very briefly by assuring the skeptics that economic forecasting is not entirely a matter of hunch. There is plenty of need for hunch in making judgments on the economic outlook, but a responsible judgment will rest also on tested knowledge of how the economy operates. There is such tested knowledge. It is real, and though limited it is not negligible.

*Solomon Fabricant, from *Fiscal Policy and Business Capital Formation* (Washington: American Enterprise Institute, 1967), pp. 85–102.

By subjecting experience to analysis, economists have discovered patterns of long- and short-term change in economic life, and have confirmed that they learned from one sample of experience by analyses of the information for other periods and other countries. We now know—it has become an "obvious" fact—that economic growth proceeds at an uneven pace and that the sequence of events along the path of economic growth is sufficiently repetitive so that we may properly speak of the typical features of a business-cycle expansion or contraction. More specifically, some economic series usually turn down before a peak is reached in general business, and some turn down afterwards. During a business revival there is a similar sequence in which certain economic series turn up before the bottom is reached and some turn up afterwards. The classification of indicators of business expansion and contraction that appears monthly in the Department of Commerce's *Business Cycle Developments*—the leaders, the roughly coincident indicators, and the laggards—is not arbitrary or speculative. The categories are derived from experience. The evidence for the classification is documented in a long series of studies, of which the recently published National Bureau volume by Geoffrey H. Moore and Julius Shiskin is the latest.

These and other systematic patterns of change are useful in formulating expectations about the future. This is so even though the patterns are never perfectly regular, and even when we do not know just why the patterns take the form they do. The knowledge derived from patterns is greater, however, and can be applied more confidently, when there is some understanding of the connections among the events that make up the patterns. Indeed, patterns inevitably stimulate efforts to devise explanations, and economists have long been engaged in this kind of enterprise. They have had some success in learning why one event usually follows another. They know better than before, to refer to an example central to the subject of the present symposium, not only how decisions to invest change during business cycles, but why.

In their analyses further, economists have not neglected to consider systematic and other changes in typical patterns. Study of these changes is an essential step in their tests of the stability of the patterns. In these studies, we have learned something of the extent and manner of variation among business cycles.

To our knowledge of the resemblances that have persisted from one business-cycle generation to another, we are adding an understanding of the kinds of changes that have taken place between generations. The postwar business cycle is different from the prewar, though not as different as some people are prone to assume. And economists are identifying some of the changes in the banking system and our other economic institutions that account for this evolution.

We know something also of the variation caused by the episodic factors that affect business cycles. Each business cycle has its own peculiar characteristics as well as its resemblances to others of its generation and species. These peculiarities are important. To provide information for making sensible policy decisions at any particular time, the forecaster must try to estimate not simply the typical course of events—what may be expected for the species on the average—or even the course of events to be expected in the average postwar business cycle. He must try to estimate the particular course of events that will characterize the business cycle with which he is immediately concerned, the current cycle. Knowledge of the typical course of events and of its evolution is useful for this purpose but it is not sufficient.

"Special" factors are difficult to deal with, almost by definition. Yet even with regard to these, forecasters are not entirely helpless. While the appearance of these factors is usually difficult to predict, economists can often say something about the direction of their effects, should they appear, and sometimes even a bit more. An obvious example is the outbreak of a war, or of a peace. Not all economists failed to see that the pent-up demand for civilian goods, backed by large and highly liquid funds in the hands of buyers, would sustain consumer demand and help to check the recession that followed the severe drop in federal expenditures in 1945.

Interpreting Business Cycle Indicators

I have been saying that "we" know something about the features of business cycles and that this helps "us" to analyze current business conditions. These words need to be qualified. The knowledge is not as widely diffused as it ought to be, even among those who venture to talk publicly about the business situation. Not everyone has the knowledge, or if he has it, does not fully appreciate its significance for evaluating current developments. This is one reason why opinions differ about the business situation today.

A rather common error is to read a decline in the leading indicators as evidence of recession, as some people have been doing for months now. Such a decline does signal the possibility of trouble ahead. The more pervasive, the more persistent, and the steeper the declines among the leading indicators—orders for equipment, profit margins, and industrial material prices, for example—the greater is the probability of trouble. But the threat need not necessarily be followed by a recession and the chances that it will can be reduced if appropriate action is taken by government. The point is that a recession is not defined by a decline in the leading indicators alone. Not until aggregate production, employment, and other roughly coinciding indicators are also falling, can one venture to say that a recession may be under way. And not until these declines—in both leading and coinciding indicators—have persisted long enough to be joined by the lagging indicators can we begin to be sure that it is.

At the present time, which means as of March or even February, because few of the statistics are up to date, all the leading indicators listed in the current *Business Cycle Developments* are below their peaks. Some are down quite sharply. Also, except for housing permits and starts, the stock market, and one or two other series, all seem still to be falling. But most of the roughly coincident series are on a plateau or still rising, with the exception of industrial production. Indeed, with this exception, their levels are at historic highs. And the only lagging indicator not still rising is the series on bank rates charged on short-term business loans. I would judge that we may be very close to being in a recession, but we are not in one yet.

A tendency to see recessions before they have actually appeared stems also from the fact that industrial experience typically becomes rather mixed well before a peak has been reached. Indeed, an expansion is most widely diffused as a rule, some six or 12 months before the highest stage of the business cycle. The proportion of industries experiencing a rise in output, sales, employment, and incomes, then, is typically falling, and the scope of the expansion narrowing as the peak is approached. Industries here and there—still only a minority, to be sure, but a growing minority—stop rising and start to decline. More and more men experience poorer business in their own industries, and they hear complaints of like experience from more and more of their business acquaintances. During the past 14 months, for example, the percentage of nonagricultural industries with rising employment (measured by change over the preceding six-month span) fell pretty steadily from about 95 percent early in 1966 to a level in January, 1967 (the most recent month available) of about 70 percent. A similar measure of change in output for the industries covered by the FRB index of industrial production was 100 percent in February, 1966, 75 percent in July, and under 40 percent in January, 1967.

Profits, Costs, and Investment

Economists will avoid the elementary errors I have just described. But even they may err in their judgment of the business situation when they fail to appreciate or use information supplied by certain cyclical changes to which they should be alert.

My example is again from the sphere of business investment. It is an old story that the incentive to invest in plant and equipment depends on the cost of plant and equipment, the cost of financing investment, and the prospect of profits from investment. More recently, studies of the sort I have mentioned have shown, or at least suggested, how each of these factors behaves during cyclical fluctuations in business, and what their net effect is on decisions to invest at successive stages of the business cycle.

During the course of a business expansion, for example, the costs of acquiring and installing plant and equipment rise, and so do interest rates. To judge from investment commitments, however, profit expectations seem to rise even more rapidly and the expected rate of return to become more and more optimistic. In the late stages of expansion, however, a change takes place in this relation. Costs of plant and equipment continue to rise, it is true, and may even accelerate, and capital funds become more difficult to get at "reasonable" rates of interest. But profit prospects no longer rise more rapidly than construction and equipment and finance costs. The expected rate of return tends to flatten out and then decline, and a powerful brake is applied to plans to expand or even replace capacity.

Expectations of profits need not become dimmer to make the expected rate of return fall. But in fact, they do. What is involved, of course, is a cost-price squeeze, coupled with retardation in the rate of growth of output.

Consider the cost side of the profit margin. Labor productivity, which generally rises throughout the expansion, tends to rise less rapidly as employment becomes fuller. Wage rates, on the other hand, tend to rise more rapidly. Unit labor costs, then, tend to go up. Similar developments raise other costs. Stand-by equipment, brought back into production to meet orders that could not otherwise be filled, tend to raise the costs of fuel, labor, and the other items used in running the equipment. Steady supplies of materials become harder to get in the larger quantities required and their quality tends to deteriorate. Wastage and the proportion of "seconds" increase. Management is stretched beyond the point of optimum efficiency. As a consequence of these various developments, unit costs are pushed up.

In an increasing number of industries, however, prices cannot be raised, or raised sufficiently to offset the effects of higher unit costs. Regulations or custom may keep prices rigid, or prices may be kept down because competing products are benefiting from rapid technological advance, or because demand is no longer buoyant and may even be declining in an increasing proportion of industries, or because new capacity has just been added or is in sight.

With unit costs rising and prices rising less rapidly than these costs, on the average, profit margins begin to decline, or look as if they will decline. If at the same time output rises at a slower rate than before, as in fact often happens at this stage of the cycle, even aggregate profits may stop rising, or look as if they will. But the value of capital assets continues to expand as construction is completed and equipment delivered. The net upshot, as I have said, may be an actual or threatened decline in the average rate of return. Incentives to maintain, let alone expand, the high level of investment commitments are weakened.

These developments are clues to the future course of an important class of expenditures and therefore need to be taken into account in any economic forecast. Yet many economists making their forecasts late last year, or even earlier this year, failed to recognize, or give sufficient weight to, these signs of the emergence of restraints on business investment.

Current Developments

It may be worth taking the time to be specific. Last December the statistics suggested that output per man-hour in nonagricultural industries had stopped rising, and might even have fallen a bit since the first quarter of 1966. Wage rates and other labor costs were rising and could be expected to continue rising more rapidly than in earlier months. It was fair to conclude that unit labor costs, which had been remarkably stable for over four years, were no longer going to remain low. Industrial raw material prices had been falling, but they were still on a fairly high level, and the costs of semi-processed materials and manufactured components were probably still rising. Construction costs were high. Most firms were reporting delays in getting deliveries. The cost of financing investment was extraordinarily high by historical standards.

These developments pointed to a rise in unit costs that might be expected to continue and perhaps accelerate. Had sales been rising vigorously, profit expectations might not have been seriously affected. But in fact retail and wholesale sales were sluggish and little if any higher than nine or 12 months earlier. Manufacturers' shipments and GNP in both real and dollar terms were also showing signs of retardation. Profits per dollar of sales were already falling, and aggregate profits had stopped rising. The liabilities of business failures were up.

It was not surprising, therefore, to come upon evidence that plans to invest were weakening. Orders for machinery and equipment and contracts for commercial and industrial buildings had been sagging for some months. New capital appropriations by manufacturing companies were down from their peak in the second quarter of 1966. Housing permits and starts had been falling drastically for a year or more. In addition, the index of net business formation was down. The McGraw-Hill survey indicated that plans to spend on new plant and equipment in 1967 were only about 5 percent more than in 1966, a rise in expenditures very little different from the probable rise in prices. This meant that a decline was expected in investment volume from the highest level already reached in 1966. In a word, commitments to invest in fixed capital were already showing signs of weakness in the last quarter of 1966, and what could then be seen of the factors that determine these commitments did not justify hope that recovery would soon come in that area.

The inadequate attention paid to these developments may well have accounted for the optimism about 1967 expressed by many forecasters at the time. One may wonder whether this is not also the situation today, and I'll have a word to say about that in a moment.

Information for Forecasting

Because too many people think of economic forecasting as a mysterious process involving supernatural if not divine inspiration, I have been insisting on the existence of a scientific basis for the forecasting. And I have even been saying that forecasting could be better than it is if more use were made of the available knowledge. Yet even at its best, the knowledge needed to make good forecasts is severely limited. These limitations need to be stressed, and we must underscore also the restrictions they impose on what can be said in a forecast and on the confidence with which forecasts can be held.

We would see the limitations most clearly if we were to ask what equations are required for the model, that is, explicitly or implicitly, to be used to make a numerical forecast of the gross national product (GNP), and what information goes into each of the equations. I do not intend to summarize the big book that Professor Duesenberry and his associates put together on the Brookings quarterly model a couple of years ago. It *is* a big book, containing a system of equations that number more than 150. But if one wants an idea of what information is needed, a glance at it would be illuminating.

Let me merely say—I am simplifying drastically—that one needs to estimate the direct and indirect consequences for the future of each major class of expenditures—consumption, investment, government, and net exports—of what has already happened and of what may be expected to happen. We do know a good deal about the factors affecting investment and what has been happening to them, for example, but it is doubtful that we know enough to make, with anything like precision, the numerical estimates that are required. The surveys I have mentioned provide useful information on businessmen's expectations of investment outlays, but expectations may be disappointed. The surveys therefore constitute only one of the items of information to be used in formulating a forecast of investment. And our knowledge of the contribution of each of these items of information—or of the weights to be assigned to them—is rather uncertain. In technical language, the investment function we have is still very primitive. Also, to make a forecast of GNP requires taking account not only of governmental actions already in being or clearly in prospect, but of those that will be induced by what happens—or even by the forecasts of what might happen. And this requires knowing, or guessing, not what governmental authorities say they will do but what they will do. And there are, of course, the difficulties of determining the effects of other "special" or "exogenous" factors. Whether the war will heat up or cool down is usually handled by an explicit assumption, but there are other special factors, less potentially important but not unimportant, the appearance and quantitative effects of which must somehow be estimated or ignored or assumed away.

Uncertainty and Forecasting

I do not want to turn this meeting into a forecasting session, but I should at least illustrate more specifically how some of the difficulties of forecasting make for uncertainties about the outlook. Let us consider the economic situation today.

You will recall my description of the situation as it appeared in December. Since the turn of the year, about three months of information has been added. According to the latest figures, (mostly for February or March, as I have mentioned) unit labor costs in manufacturing industries have risen again and are now about 5 percent above a year ago, and there is no reason to expect payroll costs to rise less rapidly in 1967 than in 1966. Industrial material prices have fallen further, but wholesale prices excluding farm products and foods have risen further. Construction costs are also higher. While interest rates have fallen, they are still high. Profit margins are down still more. With industrial output down, it is likely that aggregate profits in the first quarter will probably also be down. The liabilities of failures and the number of large business failures have increased. The physical volume of retail sales still seems sluggish, despite the jump between

February and March, and the prospects of a strong export demand are not good. Constant-price GNP in the first quarter of 1967 is estimated as no higher than in the last quarter of 1966. Contracts and orders for plant and equipment have fallen further. Plans to put up housing have shown signs of revival, but their level is still very low. Business formation is a bit below the level of three months ago. The McGraw-Hill survey of investment plans has been revised upward a trifle. But the Commerce-SEC survey of expected expenditures on plant and equipment, conducted in late January and February, indicates a rise of only 4 percent between 1966 and 1967. This means that bare maintenance of the fourth quarter 1966 level is expected—and if account is taken of probable price increases, an actual decline in investment volume is anticipated.

The easier monetary policy and the probable restoration of the investment credit may be expected to strengthen investment demand. Housing construction will follow the rise in permits and starts. But this may take some time. The rate of inventory investment has fallen sharply, but with sales still sluggish, it is possible for inventory investment to fall still further and remain negative for a while.

For some months, then, perhaps extending into the fall or even beyond, investment demand can continue weak and even become weaker. This possibility certainly should not be excluded from the range of what seems relevant as one looks ahead, even though no one can express the expected level of investment in anything like a precise quantity.

A further weakening of investment demand and then expenditures could lead to a further reduction in industrial output and construction activity. If this should happen, we could hardly expect employment and payrolls in industry and then also in other branches of the private economy, to remain untouched. And these reductions could, in turn, cause declines in consumption. The so-called built-in stabilizers can be expected to slow down such a cumulation of forces making for recession, but they cannot be expected to stop them.

On the other hand, the economy could start to move up vigorously after the middle of the year, once inventories are in line, and business fixed investment has come down to but not fallen below a "sustainable rate."

What I am getting at is this: At the present time, no one can be sure what the economy will do during the rest of the year. No one, in other words, knows how much stimulus will result from the easing of monetary policy, the release of frozen federal funds, the restoration of the investment credit, and the other actions that are in sight or have already been taken to encourage business. No one can be sure these will do as much as is needed and do it quickly enough to prevent a recession if one is actually in the making. If I am right, neither of the two possibilities I have mentioned can be said to outweigh the other so heavily as to make it unnecessary to give serious attention to both.

If forecasts are to take account also of possible courses of governmental action induced by the unfolding of events, including developments abroad—as the forecasts should—the number of possible futures that need to be considered becomes greater. No private economist can be sure what government will do or what will be the effects of what it does. But the problem confronts also the government economist. One gets the impression that the fiscal authorities are not always sure what the monetary authorities will do and vice versa. Nor can the executive branch be sure what the legislative branch will agree to, nor what the executive branch will want or need to do as circumstances change.

Limitations on Forecasters' Knowledge

The limitations on the knowledge of forecasters have important implications for what can be claimed for forecasting. Too much is claimed by a forecaster, it seems to me, when he comes out with *a* forecast of GNP in the year ahead; when his forecast is expressed in terms of a finite figure—even if it is identified as being at the middle of a range, and even if the range is specified in some way; and when his estimate for the year is distributed over the two halves or four quarters of the year.

The scientific basis of forecasting is such that the case is stronger for indicating the several more likely possibilities than for concentrating on one only; for saying something about the direction of movement, than for stating the amount of change; for saying something about the pressure being built up for a change in direction, than for specifying the date for a change in direction.

To avoid misunderstanding, perhaps I should mention that I do not suppose it would be helpful or even feasible to try to specify *every* possible eventuality. But surely the major—the more probable—futures need to be mentioned. When, as is usually the case, only one forecast is offered, it should be made clear that the forecaster has made up his own mind about the policies that will be followed and their consequences, and also about the other major special factors that will influence events. And what he has assumed should be specified.

If forecasts had no influence on the policy decisions of government and of private citizens, it would not matter what was put into them and what precision was claimed for them. But they do influence these decisions to a significant degree. Forecasts would be more useful or less dangerous if their limitations were admitted and no more were put into them and no more certainty claimed for them than is reasonable in the light of tested knowledge. Perhaps single-valued, unconditional forecasts are made because businessmen and government officials ask for forecasts free of "ifs, ands, and buts." If so, this demand should be resisted. The caveat appended to a forecast of GNP—that it is subject to uncertainty—does not convey a proper sense of the uncertainties if a single estimate is given and it is expressed in units as small as a billion dollars. We live in an uncertain world. It is better to recognize this. And if we do, we will be more alert to change, and quicker to make use of the information that comes into view to revise our forecasts and adjust our policies.

Appraising the Accuracy of Forecasts

The uncertainties surrounding economic forecasting are emphasized by an appraisal by the National Bureau of a sample of short-term forecasts made by a variety of individuals and agencies over the period between 1953-63. The report, by Professor Victor Zarnowitz, appeared only a few weeks ago, and you may not have yet had a chance to digest it. The conclusions of the study that are especially interesting for our present purposes are, first, that forecasts of GNP for the year ahead, or for the next one to three quarters, did better, on the average, than simple mechanical extrapolations of past rates of change. Second, while the mean absolute error of the forecasts for the calendar year ahead (about $10 billion) was no more than 2 percent of the average level of GNP in the period 1953-63, it was about 40 percent of the average year-to-year change in GNP—and it is the latter that constitutes the primary objective of short-term forecasting. Third, the accuracy of the forecasts analyzed diminished as the forecast span increased. The forecasts for four quarters or more ahead were generally not superior to simple extrapolations of the recent average rate of change. Nor, fourth, were the multi-period forecasts able to predict turning points in aggregate output ahead of the turn.

Another National Bureau study by Professor Rendigs Fels covers forecasts published over the period 1948-61. It is described in the annual report of the Bureau, for 1966-67. Fels confirms the findings by Zarnowitz that few forecasts succeed in forecasting cyclical peaks and troughs, and adds that few forecasters were very successful even in quickly recognizing cyclical peaks when they had already occurred. It is only fair to add that because of the lag in current information, forecasts must "in effect predict a little backward in time as well as forward," as Zarnowitz points out.

Forecasting and Government Policies

It is not always easy to decide whether a forecast has been right. Suppose the forecast simply specifies what may be expected if government takes no action to alter the course of events. If the forecast leads to action by government, what happens will differ from what was forecast.

Perhaps the "rolling adjustment" of 1962 provides an example. The narrowing of the scope of the expansion, and the declines in the stock market, in orders for machinery and equipment, and in other leading indicators during the spring—a tendency which the "steel affair" in April may well have reinforced—led economists advising the new administration to set the probability of trouble ahead at an uncomfortably high level. By mid-1962, according to Theodore Sorenson, they were pointing to "the developing recession." But they also argued for a tax cut. While the tax cut did not in fact come until many months later, official talk of it began soon and public confidence that it would come was stimulated. Along with the liberalization of depreciation accounting for tax purposes, the passage of the investment credit, and the steps taken to reassure businessmen that direct price and profit controls were not in the cards, it might well have served to nip the incipient recession in the bud. After some hesitation—and before developments had reached the stage at which a recession could be recorded—the business expansion had resumed its course.

What has been happening in recent months could conceivably turn out to provide another example. The stage of the business cycle is quite different now, of course, and we have to make the best of the mistakes of 1965 and 1966. We should therefore expect—if a recession were in fact avoided—that there would be more rapid price increase and less rapid output increase than in 1962-65.

It goes without saying that we will never have all the information we want. But I think we can make substantial improvements if we try. And we can learn to organize this information better. A few brief observations must suffice to indicate what I have in mind.

First, it is desirable to improve the current flow of information. One of the reasons why the long expansion that began in 1961 developed the symptoms it did in 1966 is because adequate information on the size of the military buildup in 1965 was not available. Had the information been available, it would have been easier to see the inflationary pressures accumulating; and the price and cost developments that became visible in 1966 might have been anticipated. A tax increase or a tightening of monetary policy would have been politically difficult, even with the information available. But its absence made the danger more difficult to recognize and reduced the chances of corrective action to a negligible level. What was needed, and what is still needed, is better and prompter information on the vastly important area of government commitments and expenditures. A reasonably detailed quarterly federal budget, prepared on the several bases now conventional, with projections revised to take account of major changes, would not be easy to prepare. As many economists have been saying, however, it would be worth the trouble.

Second, existing information can be better mobilized. There are grounds for suspecting that the country is more sensitive to the dangers of recession than to the dangers of inflation, for example. An insensitivity to inflationary pressures can lead to the neglect of developments that threaten serious problems for the future. One way to heighten the country's sensitivity to inflation would be to put together a set of "indicators of inflation" and bring it to the attention of the public on occasion or even regularly. Much of the material is already at hand in *Business Cycle Developments* and other government publications. But there are gaps that need to be filled in, especially on wages and other payroll costs. Publication of such information would make it more difficult to ignore a buildup of inflationary pressures.

Third, much needs to be done to improve and deepen understanding of measurements that are widely used in assessing the economic situation—the rate of unemployment, the balance-of-payments deficit, the federal budgetary deficit, GNP, and wages including fringe benefits. The rate of unemployment, for example, is a key indicator to which much attention is rightly paid. Yet this indicator has been changing in meaning and significance over the years. In a study currently underway at the National Bureau, also described in the annual report, Professor Jacob Mincer points to the increase that has taken place in the proportion of "peripheral" workers in the labor force. These persons, married women, retirement-age adults, and school-age youths, tend to move in and out of the labor force according to economic conditions. Their mobility causes them to experience a relatively high rate of transitional unemployment. During an upswing, then, when the expansion is reducing the incidence and duration of unemployment of the "regular" members of the labor force, it is at the same time attracting into the labor force persons who will be looking for jobs. Beyond a certain point, an expansion in aggregate demand may fail to reduce the overall unemployment rate. This has obvious implications for the significance of short- and long-term changes in unemployment and for the guidance of economic policy.

Improving Economic Forecasts

Finally, much more needs to be done to improve methods of forecasting. What forecasters now depend upon is essentially a mixture of chart reading and paper and pencil calculations blended with elements of hunch through an exercise of judgment. What is needed is a practical forecasting procedure that makes use of all the relevant information, organizes this information in a systematic and explicit way that can be followed, and extracts from the information an internally consistent forecast accompanied by a specification of its probable error.

The econometric models to which I referred a few moments ago offer the best promise of eventually providing such a procedure. They are not, in principle, different from the less systematic approaches, since all approaches make or can make use of the same information, and have to deal with the same problems—the problem of interaction among the various elements of the economic system and the problem of estimating the effects of exogenous factors. The so-called indicators approach—when it is not merely mechanical chart reading—uses Mitchell's business cycle theory, which can be translated into a model or system of equations, as Friedman once indicated. The so-called GNP approach by many business economists also in effect uses a model and solves the problem of interaction with an iterative process of approximation rather than by the solution of simultaneous equations. But the approaches do differ in the way in which they organize and use the information, and in the amounts, precision, and formal consistency of the information they aim to provide.

The advantage of the formal econometric model approach is that, being more explicit in the steps taken to make a forecast, it lends itself to improvement more readily than the other approaches. And one way to improve it, I might mention, is to expand it to take more account of the cost-price aspect of economic change than it now does.

At the present time, the econometric model is still in the experimental stage and far from the practical instrument it may become. Its chief defect arises precisely out of the fact that the econometric model, being so explicit and orderly and apparently complete, seems to require less hunch and judgment than the less systematic procedures that are widely followed. When better information becomes available, and in fact less hunch and judgment are required, the comparative advantage of the econometric model will grow and it may eventually displace or absorb the other approaches.

Even when the art or science of forecasting has reached the point at which a single, comprehensive approach is generally used, however, we may expect differences in the results. For whatever the approach, to make an economic forecast requires that estimates be made of the likelihood of various prospective developments abroad as well as in this country, in the political as well as the economic sphere, and also in technology, the weather, and so on. On these, judgments by economists as well as others are bound to vary. But improvements in forecasting should help to narrow the differences among forecasts.

I have said enough, I think, to elicit discussion, Let me add only that the present state of forecasting—the fact that forecasting is neither utterly useless nor really very good—has important implications for policy. The basic question, of course, is that of rules versus authorities. Because forecasting is not very good, we cannot afford to spurn the assistance of general rules or principles as a basis of policy. And this being the case, it would be wise to devote more attention to improving these rules. It would be well also to strengthen our automatic stabilizers.

But we cannot depend on rules and automatic devices only. We are bound to react to what we can see coming, even if we can see it only dimly. This requires flexible policy administered by authorities and, of course, better information to guide them.

Wiser rules, improved automatic stabilizers, and more competent and better informed authorities will not serve to eliminate all cyclical fluctuations in employment and output, however. I do not believe we want to try to do so, since we do not want to sacrifice other national goals to attain complete stability. We must therefore take steps to do more than we now do for those of our citizens who bear the brunt of a decline in economic activity.

*Scope and Limitations of General Demand Policies**

There is wide agreement that appropriate fiscal and monetary policies to restrain over-all demand should constitute the principal weapon against inflation. However, there is far less agreement as to the extent to which policies can be counted on to bring about the simultaneous achievement of reasonable price stability and of steady economic growth at high levels of employment.

Doubts about the degree of reliance that can be placed on general demand policies in an anti-inflationary strategy are principally based on a common observation: unemployment and inflation have in the past typically shown an inverse relationship. In general, the lower the unemployment rate the higher has been the rate of inflation of both wages and prices. Higher unemployment, conversely, has normally been associated with a reduced rate of inflation. This relationship, known technically as the "Phillips Curve," is by no means invariant or very precise. To the extent that it exists, however, it appears to be closely related to the influence of aggregate demand, since this tends to exert a simultaneous impact on both prices and employment.

The observed unemployment-inflation link would pose no particular problem to the policy-maker if it pointed to the existence of some level of aggregate demand at which neither the rate of price increases nor the level of unemployment exceeded socially acceptable limits. It has been widely felt, for example, that at least for an interim period, a rate of increase in consumer prices of less than 2 percent per annum and an over-all unemployment rate of somewhat under 4 percent would fall within such an "acceptable" range.[1] But the record of the past does not provide much reassurance that such a combination can be readily achieved.

*Committee for Economic Development, from *Further Weapons Against Inflation: Measures to Supplement General Fiscal and Monetary Policies*, November 1970, pp. 27–36.

[1] The interim "full" or "high" employment target that has for some time been used by the Council of Economic Advisers is 3.8 percent. This is comparable to the 4 percent target figure used by the Council prior to 1969, when the Census definitions of unemployment were revised. It should be noted that in its policy statement on *Fiscal and Monetary Policies for Steady Economic Growth*, this Committee recommended that "the ultimate objective for high employment should be the maintenance of a level of demand for labor which will provide jobs for those seeking employment at wages which the market places are willing to pay for their capabilities, i.e., their productivity." The statement also indicated, however, that until adequate job vacancy and unemployment data are available to permit calculation of progress toward this objective, continued reliance will have to be placed on the present measure of unemployment as a percent of the labor force.

During seven of the past 20 years, for example, the unemployment rate stood at or below 4 percent. In all except one of these seven years (a year which was affected by the Korean War price controls) consumer prices advanced by more than 2 percent. By contrast, the 12 years when price increases came to 2 percent or less included only one when the unemployment rate was less than 4 percent, and eight years when unemployment exceeded 5 percent. In general, when the economy approached capacity, the upward surge in prices with given increases in employment has tended to be much steeper than at times when the economy was still operating with substantial slack.

While the past existence of an inverse relationship between price increases and unemployment seems well established, there is considerable uncertainty regarding its meaning and its significance for the future.

To some observers, the evidence points to an inevitable and permanent incompatibility between the goals of price stability and high employment. They conclude that a choice has to be made between the two goals, however unpalatable this may be. A lasting decline in unemployment can in this view only be "bought" at the price of substantially more inflation, while reasonable price stability cannot be achieved unless the economy permanently operates substantially below its high employment potential.

There appears to be little doubt that at least for temporary periods some inverse relationship between higher prices and more unemployment cannot be wholly avoided (except perhaps when the economy is operating at relatively low levels of capacity). We firmly believe, however, that over time neither inflation nor excessive unemployment has to be accepted. On the contrary, we are convinced that with proper policies sound growth of the American economy with high levels of employment is indeed achievable with relatively stable prices.

The Inflation-Unemployment Link: Some Major Criticisms

The thesis that observed past relationships point to an inevitable long-term conflict between the high employment and price stability goals is open to a series of possible criticisms. While each of these has some merit, the relative weight that is placed on them makes a considerable difference with regard to the appropriate policy prescriptions, and particularly the extent to which solutions can be based on demand management policies alone.

The Role of Expectations

According to one school of thought, the finding that past data point to a permanent conflict between price stability and high employment rests on a complete misreading of the evidence as well as on a basic lack of understanding of the nature of the inflationary process. What the data really show, in this view, is that employment will only tend to increase (and unemployment decline) when the rate of inflation is not merely *high* but is *rising*. A high rate of inflation as such therefore will not be associated with a *permanent* reduction in unemployment.

The critical element in the inflationary process, according to this view, is the role of *expectations*. Price level increases, it is held, will affect output and employment only to the extent that they are unanticipated—which generally is likely to be true only when inflation is accelerating. In this situation, employees will in effect be temporarily fooled to work for a lower real wage than they would be willing to accept over the longer term. This will lower costs in real (as contrasted with money) terms, and increased profit prospects will lead business firms to offer increased employment. Total activity in the economy will get a temporary stimulus from a wide range of other transactions in which those who are able to anticipate the rising price trend believe they can make temporary gains at the expense of others with less foresight. But this situation cannot last. In time, workers, lenders, suppliers, and others will raise their demands for remuneration to adjust them to the new rate of inflation. When this happens, output and employment as well as unemployment are likely to return to their initial level, even though the rate of price increase will now be substantially higher.

If the mechanism just described holds true, then an expansion in demand that leads to a higher price level cannot permanently add to employment unless demand is further expanded to promote a continuing acceleration of inflation. Once this process gains momentum, however, the opportunities for fooling a large number of people for long about their "real" incomes will rapidly diminish. More and more participants in the economic process will try to adjust their wage and other income demands to the expected future rate of inflation. Virtually every group in society will in effect be asking for an escalator clause. This spreading of inflationary expectations will, in turn, lead to a cumulative upward spiral in wages and prices.

Those who explain the observed inflation-unemployment link exclusively in terms of inflationary expectations have in many cases tended to argue that the link can be broken by appropriate demand management policies alone. If fiscal and monetary policies place a sufficient damper on total demand to end inflationary expectations—which, for a temporary period only, could entail a substantial rise in unemployment—the subsequent rebound of the economy to high employment levels would no longer be accompanied by significant inflation. The breaking of inflationary psychology will in itself be sufficient to produce price stability at high employment.

There is undoubtedly great merit in the view that the role of expectations in the inflationary process has in the past not been adequately appreciated, and that curtailment of inflationary expectations must be a key element in any effective anti-inflationary strategy. This is especially so at times when inflationary psychology is spreading and the rate of inflation is accelerating—as has been the case for a number of years until at least very recently. It may well be the case, too, that the seeming linkage between inflation and unemployment tends to be substantially less over longer periods than during short ones, even in the absence of special measures to affect this linkage.

On the other hand, it is by no means clear that the observed past behavior can be fully explained by expectations. A number of careful recent studies suggest that the facts of U.S. experience do not bear out the hypothesis that inflationary expectations provide the principal explanation of the apparent inflation-unemployment trade-off, or that higher levels of prices induced by demand expansion would not result in some long-term gains in employment. These studies lead to the conclusion that aggregate demand measures designed to break "inflationary psychology" would not necessarily be adequate by themselves to restore the economy to a non-inflationary high employment growth path.

Even those who believe that the linkage between inflation and unemployment is bound to be completely broken in the long run generally hold that the process involved will take a long time—perhaps as much as two decades. There seems to be little question that over shorter periods of a few years, demand measures which help reduce price inflation do tend to have an adverse effect on the level of output and employment. Putting a drastic dent in inflationary expectations by temporary demand restraint alone may require substantially larger increases in unemployment or more prolonged stagnation than are acceptable to the public—and this very fact raises doubts as to whether such a strategy could indeed hope to succeed in overcoming the inflationary psychology.

The Influence of More Balanced Growth in Demand

A second line of objection to any mechanical extrapolation of the observed unemployment-inflation link rests on the fact that most studies of past linkages have tended to depend on averages combining periods of expansion in demand that have been fundamentally different in character. This ignores, however, that the degree of inflation tends to be associated not merely with the *level* of demand and employment but is also significantly affected by the *speed of increase* in such demand and the *degree of balance* among different economic sectors. Thus, the extent of price increases at a given level of unemployment has been much more substantial during periods of sudden and rapid military buildup, such as the Vietnam escalation of 1965-68—or of periods like the concentrated capital boom of the mid-1950's—than at times of more orderly and balanced growth to total demand.

All this is readily understandable. A sudden and unbalanced forward spurt in demand connected with a wartime boom is bound to produce numerous kinds of bottlenecks in supplies, materials, and labor that tend to lead to exceptional price and wage increases as efforts are made to redirect resources rapidly into new fields. It is also a matter of common observation that the industries and areas that lose demand in such a spurt rarely if every reduce their prices long enough or fast enough to offset the price increases occuring elsewhere. When more time is allowed for the shifting of resources and the extent of resource reallocation is more modest, the economy can adjust far more readily to higher levels of employment without sharp upward price movements.

To use the average experience of past periods of balanced as well as unbalanced expansion as a basis for predicting future behavior can be expected, therefore, to lead to an exaggerated view of the degree of potential conflict between price stability and high employment. Analyses of both British and U.S. experience that were conducted some years ago suggested that with more balanced demand expansion, a slower rate of increase in wages and prices should be expected than would otherwise occur. A recent preliminary analysis of U.S. experience since the Korean War lends support to the hypothesis that balanced growth in over-all demand should improve the "trade-off" between unemployment and price changes by close to one percentage point. In other words, at relatively high levels of demand utilization and employment the rate of price increase that might be expected on the basis of average past experience would be reduced by approximately one percentage point. About one-quarter of the improvement can be attributed to a dampened rate of wage increases, while the remainder reflects the beneficial effect of more balanced expansion of productivity. These figures, moreover, may not manifest the full beneficial price impact of gradual and orderly expansion, as contrasted with a sudden boom. In the latter situation, there is not only a direct tendency for prices and wages to rise more abruptly, but if the imbalances cumulate, they have a significant potential for triggering a continuing wage-price spiral.

These analyses, unlike the "expectations" thesis previously discussed, do not suggest that demand policies alone could eliminate the presumed conflict between inflation and unemployment entirely. But they do indicate that orderly and gradual growth of total demand can have a significantly greater effect in reducing the extent of the conflict than has been suggested by many past studies of the so-called Phillips Curve.

Structural Impediments and Cost-Push

A third line of criticism of the presumed "irreconcilability" of high employment and price stability—and one that is not necessarily in conflict with the arguments cited above—stresses the fact that not *all* observed price and unemployment behavior ought to be attributed to the influence of total demand. Even when aggregate demand and supply appear to be in satisfactory balance and the economy is at high employment, substantial upward price pressures tend to exist as a result of imperfections in the structure of our markets and institutions and of the possession of discretionary market power by sellers of both goods and labor. These pressures—some of which are manifested in supply bottleneck situations in particular sectors of the economy—reflect some basic inflationary bias in the economy and cannot be corrected by demand measures alone.

This does not mean, however, that there is little future possibility of achieving a satisfactory level of employment and price stability simultaneously. What it does signify, in this view, is a need to supplement appropriate general demand policies with more direct measures to cope with structural impediments to price stability and other "cost-push" pressures. Moreover, at any given level of total demand the volume of unemployment, too, can be reduced by a variety of structural measures.

The prescriptions for attaining high employment without inflation that are outlined in the following sections draw in some measure on each of the lines of argument presented here. Thus, these prescriptions (a) recognize the importance of breaking the vicious spiral of inflationary expectations; (b) stress that appropriately stabilizing fiscal and monetary policies along lines long advocated by this Committee can have a major impact in containing inflation—not merely by preventing excessive levels of demand but also by providing for an orderly rate of change in demand and for balanced growth of different sectors of the economy; and (c) place special stress on the need for a wide range of anti-inflationary measures that supplement over-all demand management policy.

Fiscal-Monetary Policy for Next Year and Beyond

Over the past quarter century, this Committee has evolved a set of broad principles to assist in the development of stabilizing fiscal and monetary policies.[2] Applying these principles in the setting then prevailing, our Program Committee in December 1969 recommended that

* In view of the continuing severity of inflationary forces, fiscal and monetary policies in 1970 should not merely aim at preventing an excess of aggregate demand over aggregate supply but should for a limited period be designed to produce an average growth of real GNP that would fall short of the growth in potential output.

* Federal expenditure programs and tax rates should be so set as to yield a substantial "high employment" budget surplus of about $6–$9 billion, representing approximately the same "high employment" surplus then existing.

* With the expected moderate slackening of underlying demand pressures, monetary policy should be gradually eased to produce a much-needed improvement in the fiscal-monetary mix.

* To assure an appropriate high employment budget surplus, while at the same time providing sufficient scope for monetary easing and for adequate federal expenditures on urgent domestic needs as well as essential defense and international requirements, the 5 percent surtax should be continued for *all* of 1970, and possibly longer.

[2] Last stated in the January 1969 statement, *Fiscal and Monetary Policies for Steady Economic Growth*. The main elements of these principles can be summarized as follows:

a) The impact of the budget should vary with the condition of the economy as a whole, being more expensive when the economy is depressed and more restrictive when the economy is booming or inflationary.

b) The over-all impact that the budget exerts upon the economy should not, when combined with appropriate monetary and other policies, be so restrictive as to make attainment of high employment ordinarily unlikely to be so expansive as to lead to persistent inflation.

c) To achieve these objectives, the federal government should normally set its expenditure programs and tax rates at levels that would yield a moderate budget surplus on a National Income and Product Account (NIA) basis under conditions of high employment and price stability.

d) The "high" employment budget position attained in this manner should be one which permits an adequate flow of funds to the private credit markets and to the markets for state and local securities, avoiding excessive tightness of monetary policy and helping to promote sound economic growth.

e) If demand conditions deviate significantly from those on which the stabilizing budget is based, flexible adjustments should be made in monetary policy and, if need be, in tax rates and some types of expenditures.

The Committee also indicated the need for flexible adjustments in demand policies if events were to deviate significantly from forecasts.

Since then, demand has on balance slackened further than generally expected. This has resulted in a growing gap between actual and potential GNP, as shown in Chart IV. The rate of rise in consumer prices initially was even larger than anticipated but has subsequently receded. Monetary policy has eased, particularly following a period of severe liquidity strains for corporations and major financial institutions. Contrary to expectations, the actual budget position has moved from surplus to deficit as a result, on the one hand, of lagging receipts induced by lower over-all activity and declining profits and, on the other, of larger federal outlays than anticipated in the January budget. By mid-1970, the amount of budget surplus estimated to exist under assumed high employment conditions had declined to less than $5 billion.

A resumption of economic expansion during the remainder of 1970 and in 1971 is widely expected, partly because of the stimulus provided by the lapse of the 5 percent surtax at mid-year. But there is much uncertainty as to whether such an upswing might not prove quite slow and will thus still leave the economy well below high employment levels, or whether strong pressures for higher government expenditures and a renewed splurge of private spending might provide major new forward momentum to the economy.

In light of the fact that demand restraints have held down the growth of the economy to less than its long-term optimum rate for some time, and assuming that appropriate supplementary policies will be pursued, we recommend the following guidelines for general fiscal and monetary policies for the next year and beyond:

The basic aim of fiscal and monetary policies should now be to restore an orderly resumption of real economic growth to levels at which aggregate demand and supply will be generally in balance.

Budgetary policy over the next year should seek to achieve a "high employment" budget surplus in the neighborhood of $6–$10 billion. No attempt should be made, however, to resist deficits in the actual budget to the extent that they are needed to counter the current weakness in the economy. This is particularly true of portions of the deficit that reflect the effects of the economic slowdown on tax receipts, and thus serve as automatic stabilizers for the economy. **A principal share of the stimulus that the economy currently requires to resume its forward movement should be provided by monetary policy.**

CHART 4. ACTUAL AND POTENTIAL GNP

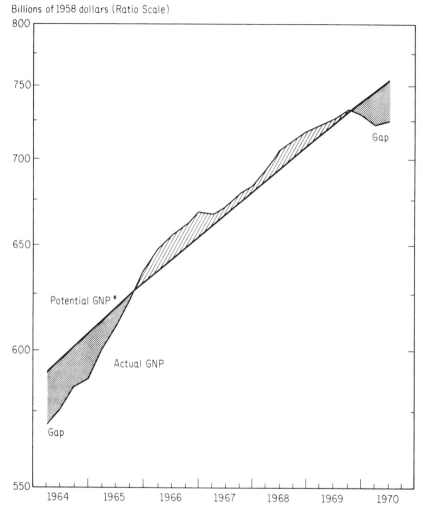

Billions of 1958 dollars (Ratio Scale)

* The potential GNP is a measure of the economy's total output under conditions of "full employment," defined by the Council of Economic Advisers until 1969 as 4 per cent unemployment of the labor force, and since then as 3.8 per cent.

The growth in potential GNP, estimated on the basis of potentially available man-hours and expected rise in productivity, is represented here by a trendline of 3.75 per cent per year through 1965–IV; 4 per cent from 1965–IV to 1969–IV; and 4.3 per cent thereafter.

Source: U.S. Department of Commerce, Bureau of the Census.
        Business Conditions Digest; and Council of Economic Advisers.

For the longer run, we believe it is vitally important that fiscal policy be designed to (a) permit a definite shift in the fiscal-monetary mix that will lead to a significant easing in the pressure on financial markets and to lower interest rates and (b) allow adequate room for critically needed federal expenditures in support of domestic programs to deal with the urgent problems of our cities, education, poverty and welfare, health care, and the environment.

To achieve these ends, every effort will have to be made to secure the needed additional fiscal resources through prudent budgetary management and reduction or elimination of programs of lesser essentiality. Current endeavors to achieve further significant savings in the defense budget are to be commended. We are also encouraged by the reductions the Administration has made in the space program; in our view, however, additional cuts should be made in this program. Furthermore, we reiterate our previous recommendations for sizable cuts in the present large-scale agricultural subsidies, and urge that proposals for new subsidy programs—such as those for the supersonic transport and the maritime fleet—be subjected to the closest possible scrutiny. If budgetary savings do not, however, prove adequate over the longer run to provide the added fiscal resources needed, we believe it is essential that taxes be increased sufficiently to produce the required extra revenue.

To assure that flexible tax adjustments can be made promptly in case of need, we again recommend that the Congress grant the President discretion to raise or lower personal and corporate income tax payments by up to 10 percent, in a form to be decided by Congress and subject to its veto.

Measures of Changes in Fiscal Policy*

When the effects of budget policy on the overall economy first came to general attention 35 years ago, the expansiveness of the budget was commonly measured by changes in the actual deficit or surplus. This measure can be grossly misleading, however. Even if existing tax and spending legislation remains unchanged, the actual budget balance will rise and fall, as changes in incomes influence tax

*Council of Economic Advisers, from *Economic Report of the President* together with the *Annual Report of the Council of Economic Advisers*, February 1971, pp. 70-74.

receipts and call for different unemployment and welfare payments. In fact, the actual deficit can rise in the face of restrictive policy actions of Government. For example, a fall in tax revenues can coincide with an increase in tax rates if incomes decline sufficiently. A given change in the actual deficit (or surplus) between two years has a very different significance if economic activity is rising between those two years than if it is falling.

Clearly, a need has existed for a better measure of Government budget policy and its effects—one that would show what effects were the result of tax and expenditure decisions and what effects the economy itself had exerted on the budget. There are a number of possible solutions to the problem. Econometric models, for example, can be used to estimate the impact of various combinations of tax rate and expenditure changes on the level of economic activity. Different models utilize different assumptions regarding the nature and relative importance of various determinants of economic behavior, and therefore they provide different estimates of the economic impact of various fiscal policy changes. Consequently, fiscal policy analysts cannot place too much reliance on the results of a particular model, although the distribution of estimates provided by a variety of available models is a useful guide.

For the purposes of public discussion, it is convenient to use simple measures of the stance of fiscal policy which summarize the more complicated policy changes used in the complex models. As noted below, however, considerable care must be exercised in using simple measures of changes in fiscal policy to estimate the effects of these policies on economic activity.

One simple measure of changes in policy can be obtained by calculating the effect of changes in revenue and expenditure legislation at a particular level of economic activity. This technique abstracts from the effect of changes in economic activity on the budget and provides a clearer view of purely discretionary policy changes. For example, at the level of economic activity prevailing in 1970, changes in tax rates occurring during 1970 reduced revenues by roughly $9 billion while expenditures increased by about $15 billion. In other words, exogenous policy actions during 1970 provided a fiscal stimulus of $24 billion.

While changes in the surplus or deficit at a given level of money GNP provide a convenient measure of discretionary policy changes, fiscal policy planning requires a measure containing somewhat more information. Because the labor force and productivity normally rise and prices rarely fall, money GNP normally grows. Consequently revenues also rise and over time the budget surplus would tend to grow rapidly if spending and tax rates remained unchanged. Spending and tax programs that would yield an unchanged surplus in an economy with a constant GNP would thus tend to hold down growth at the normal rate by generating larger and larger surpluses.

It has been found of interest to ask how the surplus or deficit would change if the economy moved along a specific path. Conceptually, any number of growth paths could be selected for this purpose; it is the change in the budget position along the assumed path that will indicate whether the budget policy has been or will be restrictive relative to that path—that is, whether the budget is tending to push the economy above or below the assumed path.

In order to give the measure more relevance it is common to select a growth path that has some normative significance. The full employment growth path has been used most frequently since the concept of a full employment budget was developed and publicized by the Committee for Economic Development in 1947. Changes in the full employment surplus measure changes in spending and tax legislation as well as the effect of full employment growth on revenues. The difference between the full employment budget balance and the actual balance reveals the effects of short-run variations in economic activity around the full employment growth path.

A particular target growth path could serve as an alternative to the full employment path. Sometimes this path is identical to the full employment path, but in 1970 it was necessary to be below full employment temporarily in order to moderate the inflationary pressures which had become excessive in 1969 and early 1970. In other circumstances the desired path may be steeper than the full employment growth path, if it is necessary to regain full employment from a less than full employment position. The target path budget would reveal the effect of discretionary tax and spending changes and the effect of target growth on tax revenues, but would abstract from the effect on the budget of deviations of economic activity away from the target.

Method of Computation

The figures for the full employment budget provided in Tables 1 and 25 are computed in the following manner: First, the full employment growth path is estimated in terms of the real value of production. Second, the real growth path is converted into current dollar terms using the actual rate of price inflation. This step suffers from the difficulty that a revenue change resulting from price changes would alter the estimate in discretionary tax and expenditure policies. One way out of this difficulty might be to convert real output to money income using the inflation rate that would have occurred if the economy had actually been at full employment. But this figure is so difficult to estimate, if indeed there is any unique rate, that the actual inflation rate despite its shortcomings is used as a convenient approximation.

Next, full employment income must be distributed into various tax bases, such as corporate profits, personal income, and other categories. The calculations used in this chapter are based on an estimate of the distribution which would emerge if the economy were actually operating continuously at full employment. For the purposes of comparing full employment budgets at different points of time it is important that a constant distribution pattern be used. Otherwise the estimates would shift with distributional changes that are unrelated to fiscal policies.

Average tax rates are then estimated for different types of income under current legislation. On the basis of these estimates full employment revenues can then be calculated. Full employment expenditures are estimated by adjusting actual expenditures to allow for the difference between actual outlays on unemployment compensation and those that would occur at full employment.

It is clear that the full employment estimate depends on numerous assumptions and that these create the possibility of error. This problem should not, however, be exaggerated. For most purposes interest focuses on changes between years, and if the assumptions are consistent between years the errors in the estimated changes in the budget position are likely to be small. Moreover, estimates of the full employment budget for the future are probably subject to less error than estimates of the actual budget, because the actual future path of the economy is more variable and uncertain than the full employment path.

The Full Employment Budget as a Measure of Fiscal Impact

The absolute level of the full employment surplus or deficit is of limited significance for indicating how much restraint or stimulus the budget would exert on the economy if it followed the full employment path, or indeed for indicating which of these directions its influence would take. Changes in the full employment surplus from period to period are much more important indicators of how much fiscal policy is moving toward contraction or expansion. The fact that the full employment budget has a surplus does not imply that the budget is not having an expansionary impact on the economy;

the effects may be expansionary if the surplus is declining. Similarly a budget with a deficit may be restrictive if the deficit is declining.

Although changes in the full employment budget balance provide a convenient summary measure of changes in fiscal policy, they do not tell the whole story. A given change in the balance may exert a different force, depending on whether the change stems from a change in transfer payments, purchases of goods and services, corporate taxes, personal taxes, or other instruments of fiscal policy. Results vary because different policy changes affect economic behavior differently, even though the same amounts of money are involved. Some of the most important differences can be considered in complex models of the economy, but no model can capture all of the subtle effects of fiscal policy. For example, virtually identical policy changes may have different results depending on circumstances. A long-anticipated increase in Social Security benefits may have a different consequence from that of an unexpected increase. Similarly, a permanent cut in income taxes probably has a more powerful impact than an equivalent reduction that is known to be temporary. Conceptually models could be constructed to take account of such differences, but they would be extremely difficult to manage.

Recent Changes in the Full Employment Budget

Table 25 illustrates changes in the full employment budget during the last decade. If fiscal policy changes are measured by the

TABLE 25

The Full Employment Receipts and Expenditure Estimates, National
Income Accounts Basis, 1960–70

| Calendar year | Billions of dollars | | | | Change as a percent of full employment GNP |
	Receipts	Expenditures	Surplus or deficit (−)	Change in surplus from preceding year	
1960	105.0	92.0	13.0	8.3	1.5
1961	109.2	100.4	8.8	−4.2	−.7
1962	113.8	109.4	4.4	−4.4	−.7
1963	121.8	112.8	9.0	4.6	.7
1964	119.2	117.5	1.8	−7.2	−1.1
1965	124.2	123.2	1.0	−.8	−.1
1966	139.3	142.9	−3.6	−4.6	−.6
1967	153.1	163.6	−10.5	−6.9	−.9
1968	175.7	181.7	−6.0	4.5	.5
1969	203.3	191.7	11.7	17.7	1.9
1970	212.0	205.3	6.7	−5.0	−.5

Note.—Detail will not necessarily add to totals because of rounding.
Source: Council of Economic Advisers.

annual change in the surplus relative to full employment GNP, the largest stimulus of the decade came with the tax cut of 1964. The largest shift toward restraint came in 1969, or, on a 2-year basis, in 1968 and 1969.

The full employment budget can be computed by using either national income accounting concepts or the concepts applied in deriving the unified budget, which appears in the President's annual budget statement. Economists generally favor the national income accounting approach in the belief that on balance it provides a more accurate measure of fiscal effects; but both concepts have advantages and disadvantages.

On both the expenditure and revenue sides these concepts embody important differences of timing. In the national accounts budget, purchases of goods and services are recorded when delivery is made. The unified budget records them when checks are issued for payment; this might occur before or after delivery. It is sometimes argued that neither method of timing truly captures the fiscal impact and that for such a purpose the timing of orders should be used.

On the revenue side the unified budget again uses cash receipts. In the national income accounts budget most receipts, such as corporate income and excise taxes, are recorded on an accrual basis, but personal income taxes are recorded when paid by individuals. Steps are now being taken to put the unified budget more on an accrual basis.

The national accounts budget omits the direct lending activities of Government except for Commodity Credit Corporation (CCC) "nonrecourse" commodity loans, which are treated as expenditures rather than loans. The unified budget also treats as expenditures CCC loans as well as foreign loans made on noncommercial terms and domestic loans where repayment may be waived. A unified budget deficit can be computed for the expenditure account alone, or it can be defined to include the net lending not already considered in the expenditure account. In fiscal 1970 such lending amounted to $2.1 billion.

Neither budget considers the loan guarantee and insurance programs of Government, and besides these there are a number of Government-sponsored lending institutions which operate outside of the budget. During fiscal 1971 it is expected that Government net guaranteed and insured loans will increase by about $13 billion, while the increase in the net lending of Government-sponsored institutions will be about $8 billion.

D

Fiscal Experiments in the 1960's

To a considerable extent, the 1960's represented a period in which the federal government made active use of fiscal policy measures to provide the economy with a stimulus or a restraint. In 1962 the investment tax credit was passed for the purpose of stimulating new investment, and thus promoting a more rapid rate of economic growth. In 1964 personal and corporate income tax rates were reduced for the purpose of stimulating aggregate demand. In subsequent years, fiscal restraints were utilized. In 1967 the investment credit was temporarily repealed in order to dampen the level of investment. In 1968, a surtax on incomes was levied as an anti-inflationary measure.

The readings reflect the experiments and fiscal issues of the 1960's. The first reading, "Federal Fiscal Policy in the 1960's," by the Board of Governors of the Federal Reserve System, presents a chronological review of fiscal policy measures which were taken during the decade of the 1960's. The last article, "Measuring the Impact of the 1964 Tax Reduction," by Arthur M. Okun, a member of the Council of Economic Advisers during the Johnson Administration, analyzes the effectiveness of the 1964 income tax cuts in terms of their impact on the economy.

*Federal Fiscal Policy in the 1960's**

A major shift in the budgetary stance of the Federal Government from fiscal stimulus toward fiscal restraint began with the revenue and expenditure control law enacted in late June. While the Federal budget in the fiscal year ending June 1968 showed the largest deficit since World War II, the administration is now projecting that the move toward restraint will reduce the deficit by more than $20 billion in the current fiscal year.

The June legislation is the latest in a series of fiscal actions taken during the 1960's to influence the state of domestic economic activity. During the first half of the decade, such actions focused on the need to encourage more rapid expansion in private sectors of the economy through various forms of tax incentives. After mid-1965, however, total Federal outlays grew rapidly—chiefly because of the unexpected upsurge in defense spending needed to support expanded U.S. participation in the Vietnamese conflict. With expenditures in

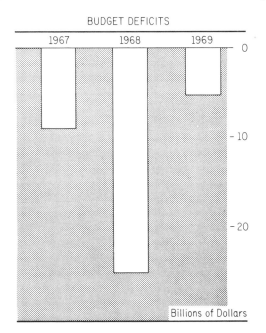

Fiscal year 1969 Federal budget deficit as estimated in *Summer Review of the 1969 Budget.*

*Board of Governors of the Federal Reserve System, *Federal Reserve Bulletin*, September 1968, pp. 701–708.

private sectors also large—due partly to the tax incentives legislated earlier—over-all demands for the nation's resources became excessively strong and upward pressures on prices persistent. Therefore, the direction of compensatory fiscal policy was reversed in early 1966, as several steps were taken to augment receipts. A more extensive proposal to raise taxes, initiated in 1967, was ultimately embodied in the June 1968 law.

A review of the record of contrasting fiscal actions before and after escalation of U.S. involvement in Vietnam leaves little doubt that compensatory fiscal policy can exert a powerful influence on the economy. But the record also suggests that under present institutional arrangements the flexibility of such policy is sometimes limited.

Time is required for the administration to recognize a need for fiscal action and to formulate a specific policy proposal. Further time then ensues while Congress considers, debates, and acts upon the proposal. These lags may be prolonged, if the action recommended heightens continuing differences of opinion as to the appropriate scope and functions of Federal spending; even a proposal to raise or lower taxes temporarily tends to be viewed not just in terms of its immediate fiscal policy objective but also in light of its potential long-run effects on the level of Federal spending.

Moreover, particular policy requests are difficult to evaluate be-

CHART 1. FEDERAL DEFICIT DEEPENS SUBSTANTIALLY AFTER 1966

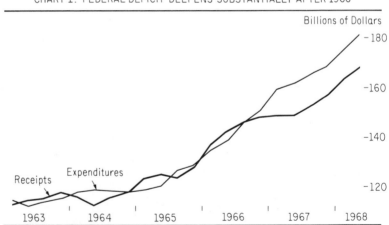

Federal receipts and expenditures as recorded in the national income accounts. Receipts for the first two quarters of 1968 measure corporate tax accruals before the imposition of the surcharge on June 28; after that date corporate tax accruals were revised upward for each of these two quarters by $3.4 billion due to the retroactive feature of the surcharge.

cause the actual deficit (or surplus) may not reflect the true economic effect of the budget. A particular deficit (or surplus) may be either too stimulative or too restrictive, depending on the extent to which resources in private sectors are employed. Finally, even after a given fiscal policy change has been adopted, there is typically some further lag as its effects work their way through the economy. Here, full implementation of a decision to change Federal spending often takes longer than for the economy to respond to a change in taxes. In the face of these lags, responsible proposals for fiscal action must obviously be based in large measure on a forecast of the expected course of future events. This need too makes the policy task more difficult.

Period of Tax Reductions

The first major tax change of the 1960's—the investment tax credit passed in 1962—permitted a credit against business income tax liabilities amounting to as much as 7 percent of outlays for new investment in machinery and equipment. Its purpose was to promote more rapid economic growth through the encouragement of private investment spending, which had been sluggish since 1957. To achieve the same end, the Treasury also announced new guidelines liberalizing the computation of depreciation and shortening (for tax purposes) the useful life of depreciable assets.

Although these tax incentives were expected to have a significant cumulative impact on economic activity over time, the domestic economy in late 1962 and early 1963 was still operating well below its potential. In assessing the need for possible further fiscal action to overcome this persistent underutilization of resources, the administration made use of the concept of a "high-employment budget." The high-employment budget is an estimate of the Federal surplus or deficit in the national income accounts at some target level of gross national product representing a high, but noninflationary level of economic activity. This estimate assumes the same level of Federal spending as that already projected in the regular budget (except that unemployment compensation is at a different rate), but it bases receipts on levels of income and profits that would prevail at the target level of GNP rather than the one assumed in the official budget.

Estimates derived for the high-employment budget in 1963 showed that with Federal receipts computed to allow for the full potential level of national income as well as for the existing progressive tax rate structure, the Federal sector was showing a tendency toward a very large high-employment surplus at a time when spending in other sectors of the economy was not sufficient to offset the restrictive influence of this surplus. In other words, if the economy moved toward higher levels of employment, tax receipts would tend to grow more rapidly than either GNP or Federal spending, so that in effect the budget would exercise a "fiscal drag" and prevent full realization of the high-employment goal.

HIGH EMPLOYMENT SURPLUS

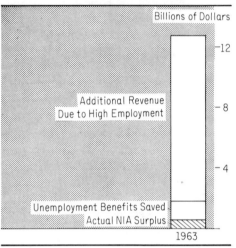

Data are retrospective computations for calendar year 1963.

Admittedly the high-employment budget does not give a complete measure of the fiscal impact of the Federal sector—partly because the private economy reacts with various lag patterns to Federal fiscal activities and partly because fiscal policy includes indirect incentives and penalties in addition to the flow of taxes and spending. Moreover, the concept runs into difficulty when the economy is operating at high employment because no allowance is made for inflation. Nevertheless, in circumstances such as those prevailing in the early 1960's when the economy was underemployed and price increases were not inflating Federal outlays, the concept does provide a more meaningful measure of the Federal budgetary impact than the published measures of actual Federal surplus or deficit taken by themselves.

Based on the evidence of fiscal drag in the early 1960's, the administration in early 1963 proposed a major reduction in income tax rates. This recommendation, in effect, called for compensatory fiscal

Revenue Actions Taken to Influence Economic Activity

Measure	Date recommended	Date enacted	Remarks
Period of tax reductions			
Investment tax credit	April 1961	October 1962	Provided a sizable incentive for new investment in depreciable equipment for domestic use. A 7 per cent credit against income tax liabilities is allowed on such investment with a service life of 8 years of more. For assets with service lives of 6–8 years, two-thirds of the full credit is allowed; for those with lives of 4–6 years, one-third is allowed. For certain public utilities the amount is 3 per cent. An over-all ceiling was set on the tax credit amounting to $25,000 plus 25 per cent of the remaining tax liability.
Liberalized depreciation guidelines	Promulgated in July 1962 by Treasury Department decision—no new legislation required.		New guidelines (1) allowed a faster rate of charge-off of costs for investment outlays and (2) shortened the useful lives of equipment for purpose of computing depreciation.
Revenue Act of 1964	January 1963	February 1964	A permanent cut in income tax rates for all individual and corporate taxpayers. Personal taxes were cut by more than 20 per cent and corporate taxes by about 8 per cent. Before the cut the marginal personal tax rates ranged from 20 to 91 per cent; afterwards the range was 14 to 70 per cent. For most corporations rates fell from 52 to 48 per cent.
			For calendar year liabilities, tax rates were cut in two stages with part of the cut postponed until 1965. Personal withholding rates were reduced by the full amount as early as March 1964.
			The Act also provided for a gradual acceleration of income tax payments by large corporations to a pay-as-you-go basis. Prior to the 1964 change, taxes on a corporation's estimated liability in excess of $100,000 were due in equal quarterly instalments with a 6-month lag

Revenue Actions Taken to Influence Economic Activity, *Continued*

Measure	Date recommended	Date enacted	Remarks
Period of tax reductions			
			between liability and payment. The 1964 change provided for an acceleration of payments from this old basis over a 7-year period, at the end of which the full amount of estimated tax liability in excess of $100,000 would be due within the year of liability. On both the old and the new bases penalties were assessed if current payments totaled less than 70 per cent of the tax liability due; however, in lieu of the 70 per cent requirement, a corporation could elect to pay quarterly taxes on the basis of its preceding year's profits. The Act also increased allowable depreciation through an amendment to the investment tax credit (the Long Amendment) providing that the tax credit need not be deducted from the depreciable value of affected assets.
Excise Tax Reduction Act of 1965	January 1965	June 1965	Provided repeal of Federal excise taxes on appliances, radios, television sets, jewelry, furs, toilet preparations, luggage and other items; and systematic reductions in rates on passenger automobiles and parts, and telephone and other communication services. The law set up a schedule of reductions, the first one of which became effective July 1965 and the second January 1966. The Act did not change Federal excises for alcoholic beverages, tobacco, gasoline, tires, trucks, trailers, and some other items.
Period of tax increases			
Tax Adjustment Act of 1966	January 1966	March 1966	Main features: (1) Restored excise tax rates on automobiles and telephone service to levels preceding the second-stage reduction in January 1966. Second-stage reductions were rescheduled effective April 1, 1968.

Revenue Actions Taken to Influence Economic Activity *Continued*

Measure	Date recommended	Date enacted	Remarks
Period of tax increases			
			(2) Introduced graduated tax rates on withheld personal taxes—to speed up collections of tax receipts.
			(3) An additional speed-up of corporate income tax payments telescoped the time period over which the acceleration provided for in the 1964 Act would occur, from a total of 7 years to a total of 4 years.
			(4) Quarterly (rather than annual) payments required for social security taxes for the self-employed.
Suspension of investment tax credit	September 1966	November 1966	Investment tax credit, along with accelerated depreciation options as they apply to buildings, were suspended on items acquired or ordered beginning October 10, 1966, with a scheduled date for restoration of January 1968.
			The suspension law carried an amendment that would liberalize the tax credit as of the time of restoration by increasing the permissible ceilings on the tax credit from 25 per cent to 50 per cent of the tax liability in excess of $25,000.
Restoration of investment tax credit[1]	March 1967	June 1967	Investment tax credit restored, effective March 10, 1967. This restoration immediately provided for the more liberal ceilings scheduled for the anticipated 1968 restoration.
Surcharge on individual and corporate income taxes	January 1967	June 1968	Enacted as Revenue and Expenditure Control Act of 1968. Chief features are a 10 per cent surcharge on income taxes paid by individuals, effective April 1, 1968, and by corporations, effective January 1, 1968; surtax expires June 30, 1969.[2] These rates had been recommended by the President in August 1967. Individuals whose taxes fall only within the lowest two rate brackets were exempted from the surtax.
			In addition excise tax rates on automobiles and telephone ser-

Revenue Actions Taken to Influence Economic Activity *Continued*

Measure	Date recommended	Date enacted	Remarks
Period of tax increases			

<table>
<tr><td></td><td></td><td></td><td>vice were kept unchanged, with the cut previously scheduled for April 1968 postponed until January 1, 1970.
The Act further accelerated corporate income taxes by increasing the 70 per cent estimating requirement to 80 per cent. Act also provides for virtual elimination of the $100,000 exemption of tax liability, regarding acceleration, to occur in gradual stages over the next 10 years.
Law also provides for a ceiling on fiscal year 1969 expenditures, cuts in requested appropriations, rescissions of some unobligated balances, and gradual reduction in the size of Federal civilian employment.</td></tr>
</table>

[1] This action was stimulative rather than restrictive in its effect on the economy and was taken at a time when the rate of economic expansion had temporarily slowed.
[2] Amount of surtax due is computed prior to any investment tax credit deduction.

action at a time when the economy, while sluggish, was not in a recession and when the actual Federal budget was in deficit. The purpose of the request was to boost private spending and bring total output to its high-employment potential. In the process the tax cut was expected to reduce the high-employment budget surplus—which was averaging over $10.0 billion annually and tending higher.

After considerable delay, the essentials of the administration's 1963 request were embodied in the Revenue Act of 1964, passed in February. The Act provided for a cut in income tax rates to become effective in two stages, one in 1964 and the other in 1965. Altogether, marginal tax rates for individuals were reduced to a 14 to 70 percent range from the 20 to 91 percent range previously prevailing, and corporate income tax liabilities were reduced for most corporations from 52 percent to 48 percent. When originally enacted, the cut in tax liabilities amounted to $13 billion at an annual rate, with some $10.6 billion accruing to individuals. In terms of the higher income and price levels of 1967, the annual tax saving had grown to more than $18 billion.

Cuts in withholding rates for individuals—from 18 to 14 percent —became effective in March 1964, ensuring that the tax reduction would have an immediate impact on after-tax incomes and hence would have a rapid, and eventually multiple, feedback on spending and output. Because the withholding rate was cut at the outset to reflect both stages of the reduction, taxes withheld in 1964 left a larger than usual share of total liabilities to be paid up in April 1965.

The anticipated effect of the 1964–65 tax cut on aggregate spending was not long in materializing. By the first half of 1965 the shortfall between actual and potential GNP had narrowed by more than one-half from the $25 billion to $30 billion gap that had prevailed earlier in the 1960's. Of course, the over-all stimulus to economic expansion provided by tax incentives in this period was not confined to the cut in income taxes. It also included the very significant lagged effects of the investment tax credit and liberalized depreciation allowances, as well as an additional liberalization of the investment tax credit enacted in 1964 (the Long Amendment), which eliminated the 1962 provision that actual tax credits had to be deducted from the base used in computing depreciation.

Even so, there was still some concern in early 1965 about the tendency for actual GNP to fall short of its potential. To help offset this continuing fiscal drag and at the same time make good on a long-deferred promise to reduce indirect taxes levied in World War II, a multiple-stage cut in Federal excise taxes was enacted in the spring of 1965. This provided for a lowering or elimination of excise taxes on consumer durable goods, telephone service, and certain other items. The first stage—amounting to a $1.7 billion cut at an annual rate—became effective in mid-June 1965; the second stage—of an equal amount—was scheduled to become effective at the start of 1966.

By mid-1965, just prior to the escalation of fighting in Vietnam, the economy had, nevertheless, made fairly good progress toward full employment. Real GNP had grown some 13 percent in the 2 1/2 years from the end of 1962. While the unemployment rate of 4.7 percent in June of 1965 was still above the target level of 4 percent, it was a full percentage point below the 1962–63 average. Wholesale and retail prices of commodities had remained quite steady through 1963 and had advanced only slightly by early 1965. Clearly the fiscal program to stimulate aggregate demand and business investment, along with a relatively easy monetary policy, had played a primary role in the nation's steady and largely noninflationary growth in this period.

Spending Increases

The upsurge in total Federal spending that developed following the escalation of fighting in Vietnam, coming as it did at a time when the economy was already moving toward high employment, tipped the balance of economic pressures toward inflation. While the ultimate cost of U.S. involvement in the Vietnamese war was underestimated during the build-up in 1965 and 1966, the decision to expand U.S. participation had an early impact on business expectations and through this on business spending. Prior to the escalation of U.S. involvement many business analysts had begun to expect a slackening in the private investment boom, together with some moderation of inventory accumulation and consumer spending. Realization that Federal contracts and defense spending would instead be accelerating rapidly during the fiscal year 1966 suddenly shifted the outlook to concern about inflation. In the face of these changed expectations, inventories were rapidly accumulated, consumer spending spurted, business plans for investment were revised upward, and price increases became widespread.

Defense Spending

From a low of $52 billion reached in the first quarter of 1965, defense obligations (contracts and payrolls) rose steadily by almost $20 billion in the following four quarters. After the first quarter of 1966 obligations rose more gradually, increasing by $8 billion in the next four quarters and by only $3.5 billion from early 1967 to the latest available reports, which show a total of $82.5 billion for the 5 months ending in May 1968.

Defense purchases at first rose much more slowly than contracts, increasing by only $6.8 billion from the first quarter of 1965 to the first quarter of 1966. But in the following four quarters, the rise amounted to nearly $15 billion. While defense purchases continued to increase at an average annual rate of $6 billion through mid-1968, the much more moderate recent rise in obligations would seem to indicate some leveling off of defense outlays in the period immediately ahead. During the third quarter of 1968, however, special allowance has to be made for the recent pay raises to military and civilian defense employees, which totaled $1.2 billion at annual rates.

Nondefense Spending

Major increases have also occurred over the past 3 years in Federal nondefense spending. In particular, payments for education grants to public schools and colleges, and transfer payments for social security benefits, including medicare, have both risen at a faster rate—though of course by much smaller dollar amounts—than defense outlays. Also, with output expanding and prices of many farm commodities declining from the high levels reached in 1966, enlarged

CHART 2. MOVEMENTS IN DEFENSE OBLIGATIONS LEAD PURCHASES

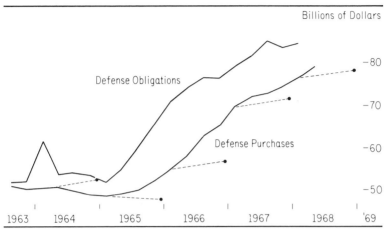

Billions of Dollars

"Defense obligations" covers gross obligations incurred outside the Government for national defense functions; source: Defense Indicators, Dept. of Commerce; latest data: 1st quarter 1968. "Defense purchases" is the national income account series on national defense purchases of goods and services; latest data: 2nd quarter 1968. • indicates initial Budget Bureau fiscal year estimates of national defense spending plotted at the midpoint of the fiscal year. Adjustments were made to the Budget Bureau estimates to improve comparability with data on national defense purchases of goods and services. Dashed lines begin in the month when the budget estimates were published.

stabilization operations by the Commodity Credit Corporation were required; expenditures for agricultural programs have therefore risen, particularly in recent months.

On the other hand, spending increases have moderated significantly in some other program areas where expansion was particularly large during earlier years. In space programs, for example, the level of spending actually declined, and in highway grants—where increases were so large in the 1950's—the more recent pattern of growth has been moderate. Welfare grants have continued to increase, partly as a result of developments in programs for medicaid and aid to dependent children.

All other nondefense programs showed a sizable advance in expenditures, but this change was spread rather widely over a number of areas, including the new programs to combat poverty. Altogether the general pattern in the 1965-68 period has clearly been for more rapid growth in both defense and nondefense Federal spending than in the first 5 years of the decade.

Social Security Benefits Versus Tax Rates

Changes in both social security receipts and payments have had sizable temporary effects on total purchasing power in the 1960's as the table on the following page suggests. Transfer payments to beneficiaries under old age insurance rose from an annual rate of $16.6 billion in the first half of 1965 to $29.2 billion in the first half of 1968 (Chart 3). One-third of this increase was accounted for by the

CHART 3. MOST TYPES OF FEDERAL EXPENDITURES ACCELERATE SINCE EARLY 1965

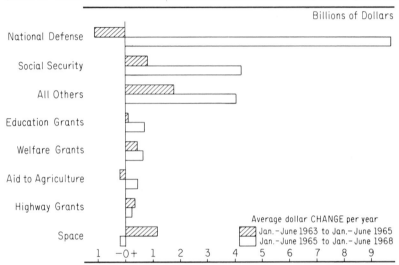

"Social security" covers benefits from old age, survivors, and disability insurance trust funds, railroad retirement insurance trust fund, and after mid-1966 medicare.
"Welfare grants" covers grants to States for public assistance and relief programs, such as aid to dependent children; medicare grants are included beginning 1966.
"All other" represents those Federal expenditures, as recorded in the national income accounts, that are not shown separately in the other categories of the chart.
Source: Estimates by National Income Division of Dept. of Commerce and Federal Reserve.

medicare program, which had not been legislated 3 years earlier; most of the remainder resulted from two sizable upward revisions in old age benefit schedules effective September 1965 and March 1968. Increases in benefit payments were introduced partly in an effort to maintain the real purchasing power of benefits received as consumer prices rose and partly to provide liberalized benefits.

To offset these increased benefit payments there were several increases in payroll taxes and in the salary base on which such taxes are paid. While these changes were intended to help match social security receipts with the level of expanded benefit payments, the timing of changes in revenues and in benefit payments was not completely synchronized.

Federal Lending

A significant part of total Federal outlays takes the form of Federal lending to private sectors and affects spending only indirectly; hence, like financial transactions generally, it is excluded from the national income accounts. Lending programs too have added significantly to total Federal outlays over the past 3 years, largely in response to developments in housing markets.

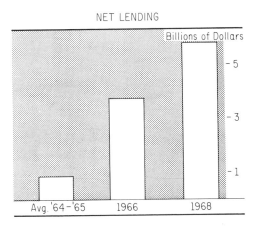

NET LENDING

Net lending for selected fiscal years as defined in new Federal budget. Excludes lending by privately-owned Federally-sponsored agencies, such as Federal home loan banks; also excludes foreign loans made on noncommercial terms.

The new unified Federal budget provides a measure of total Federal outlays, including those for Federal lending programs as well as expenditures recorded in the national income accounts. Thus, this budget measures the need for Federal cash borrowing, although it no longer includes borrowing by several Government-sponsored, but privately-owned, lending agencies. In fiscal 1968, the unified budget showed a deficit of $25.4 billion, some $12 billion more than the Federal deficit in the national income accounts. Nearly half of this difference reflected a record $6 billion of Federal lending; most of the rest was attributable to differences in accounting for corporate income tax receipts and defense purchases. These items presently are included on a cash basis in the unified budget and on an accrual and delivery basis, respectively, in the national income accounts.

Major Changes in Benefit Schedules of, and Tax Rates for,
Social Security Trust Funds, January 1962 to January 1969

Effective	Increased benefits	Increased tax rates	Dollar amount[1]
January 1962		Combined rate for employer and employee increased from 6.00 to 6.25 per cent . .	.4
January 1963		Combined rate increased to 7.25 per cent	2.0
September 1965	Benefits increased	[2] 1.3
January 1966		Combined rate increased to 8.40 per cent. Maximum earnings subject to tax lifted from $4,800 to $6,600. The latter change affects cash flows of taxes mainly in the second half of the year	6.0
July 1966	Medicare health benefits begin		[3] 3.1
July 1966		Supplementary medical insurance premiums ($3.00 per month) initiated on a voluntary basis	.6
January 1967		Combined rate increased to 8.80 per cent	1.1
January 1968		Maximum earnings subject to tax lifted to $7,800. Mainly affects cash flow of taxes in the second half of the year	2.2
March 1968	Scale of benefits substantially increased		3.5
April 1968		Voluntary supplementary medical insurance premiums increased to $4.00 . .	.2
January 1969		Combined rate scheduled to increase to 9.60 per cent . .	3.0

[1] Billions of dollars for first full year of operation.
[2] This amount shows the increase in regular payments beginning October at an annual rate. In addition, a lump sum retroactive payment was disbursed in September in the amount of $0.9 billion.
[3] Medicare benefit payments did not reach a normal level of operation until after the first quarter of 1967—due to start-up problems. Benefit payments for full year beginning April 1967 amounted to $4.9 billion.

Shift to Tax Increases

As a consequence of the trends in total Federal outlays and receipts that began to emerge with the escalation of fighting in Vietnam, the administration in early 1966 began to shift its previous approach and recommended various measures for increasing revenues. In 1966, these proposals were relatively modest, since it was assumed that the increase in defense outlays would be of short duration. But as the ultimate costs of the war and its unfavorable influence on domestic prices and the U.S. balance of payments became clearer, the administration responded by proposing more restrictive measures.

Tax Changes in 1966

In early 1966, the Federal sector in the national income accounts was still showing a surplus of $2 billion, and Federal receipts had remained in fairly close balance with expenditures since 1963, as Chart 1 shows. Temporary shortfalls in receipts below expenditures in 1964 and the latter half of 1965 reflected the stimulative cuts in income and excise taxes already noted. But as growth in over-all economic activity responded to these stimuli, total receipts quickly moved back to and above their levels before the tax cut. Moreover, receipts were increased sharply at the beginning of 1966 by the $6 billion (annual rate) increase in social security taxes.

With inflationary pressures already evident, however, and with the outlook for very large future increases in Federal outlays, the administration in early 1966 recommended several compensatory fiscal actions designed to increase revenues. Corporate payments were accelerated to move collections of taxes on profits closer to a pay-as-you-earn basis and to provide for faster depositing of taxes withheld by businesses. A graduated withholding tax was introduced to speed up collections of withheld personal income taxes still further, and social security taxes for the self-employed were placed on a more current basis by requiring quarterly declarations. At the same time, the second stage of the excise tax cut—which had already gone into effect at the start of 1966—was rescinded but rescheduled for April 1968.

While all of these recommendations were enacted promptly, except for the postponement of the excise tax cut, they merely shifted the timing of cash payments of taxes rather than increasing their total magnitude. Nevertheless, in the regular budget accounts, receipts in fiscal years 1966 and 1967 were enlarged because the corporate tax acceleration caused collections to exceed current accruals of tax liabilities. Once the acceleration program was completed, however, corporate tax payments fell by $5.3 billion in fiscal year 1968 due partly to the fact that corporate profits had declined in 1967.

As 1966 progressed, it became clear that Federal spending and borrowing would be much larger than initially projected and that strong inflationary pressures would persist. To help counter these pressures, monetary policy was tightened substantially. With demands for funds from private sectors very large—reflecting to some extent the unexpected acceleration of corporate income tax payments—interest rates rose steeply. Credit rationing by lending institutions became severe, particularly in markets for the financing of housing; and by the late summer of 1966, these pressures were creating signs of disorder in financial markets that threatened to brake the pace of economic activity much too sharply.

In these circumstances the administration announced additional proposals for fiscal restraint, designed in part to permit some easing of monetary policy and a resultant measure of relief in credit and housing markets. To slow the pace of business investment spending, which had been accounting for a major part of the continuing excess demands in resource and financial markets, Congress suspended for 15 months the investment tax credit, along with accelerated depreciation options as they applied to buildings. These actions applied to items acquired or ordered on or after October 10, 1966. In addition, the administration announced plans for moderate cutbacks in Federal spending. The announcement effect of these proposals for fiscal action helped to correct the deep general deterioration of psychology prevalent in credit markets. At the same time, it became evident that over-all credit demands had slackened in response to the monetary and fiscal restraints introduced earlier in the year.

Request for Surtax

In early 1967, while the pace of the economic expansion was continuing to slow, the administration requested Congress to enact a temporary 6 percent surcharge on both corporate and individual income taxes, to become effective in July 1967 and to run for 2 years or until commitments in Vietnam tapered off. This request reflected an assumption that the rate of economic expansion would accelerate sharply again after mid-1967 and thus would require more fiscal restraint if inflationary developments were to be checked without risking an overly abrupt return to credit restraint, particularly in markets for home financing. With economic activity slowing in the first half of 1967, Congress showed little willingness to accept the administration proposal for a 6 percent surtax; nor did the administration press its case very strongly. In fact the administration called for and obtained a quick restoration of the investment tax credit.

By the late summer of 1967, however, the economy was again showing signs of overheating. Federal budget receipts were not increasing correspondingly partly because the various tax-speed-up measures of 1966 had already been completed, as noted, but also because receipts were still reacting to the slowdown in economic activity of early 1967. With deficit financing of the Federal Government expected to reach a new peacetime record, private borrowers scrambled aggressively to cover, through anticipatory financing, the bulk of their own expected needs. Consequently, even though monetary policy remained relatively easy, interest rates rose sharply to levels above the previous post-World War II peaks reached in the 1966 period of credit restraint.

Since much of this renewed pressure on credit markets reflected expectations of developments likely to result from an overly stimulative fiscal policy, the administration in early August strongly reiterated its request for the enactment of a surtax. Because it seemed likely that any final action on the request would come well after the July 1967 effective date originally proposed, the requested surtax rate was raised from 6 to 10 percent. This proposal was also greeted with considerable opposition, notwithstanding the massive budgetary deficit that loomed ahead for the fiscal year 1968. Evidence of renewed business expansion was still not wholly conclusive, and so the principal basis for action was still a forecast. Furthermore, the on-again-off-again experience with the tax-credit suspension had tended to create resistance to fine-tuning through fiscal action.

Finally, many people who were prepared to admit the need for some fiscal action to minimize the budget deficit and to avoid a credit crunch similar to the one that had occurred in 1966, preferred a reduction in spending as a means of achieving this goal rather than an increase in taxation. Opposition to the enlarged size of Federal spending in some cases was focused on social programs and in other cases on the high cost of the war in Vietnam. Reflecting this deep division of opinion, on both the over-all need for fiscal action and the means of implementing it, action on the proposed legislation was deadlocked until spring 1968.

Revenue and Expenditure Control Act of 1968

The deadlock was resolved only when it became evident that the U.S. economy was experiencing renewed inflationary pressures. In addition to their effects on domestic economic activity, these pressures—by weakening the U.S. balance of payments—aggravated the uncertainties in foreign exchange and gold markets that had followed the devaluation of sterling in November 1967. The implications of these domestic and foreign developments for U.S. monetary policy led to a further sharp general advance of interest rates in domestic financial markets. Under pressure for some positive fiscal action to reverse these unfavorable developments, a compromise was reached that involved both a surtax and a cut in spending. As a result, the total fiscal restraint package finally legislated in June 1968 was more restrictive than many had expected.

As finally passed, the Revenue and Expenditure Control Act of 1968 imposed a temporary 10 percent surcharge on personal and corporate income taxes and at the same time set a ceiling on Federal lays for fiscal year 1969. This ceiling was $6 billion below the $186.1 billion level of outlays that had been projected for this period in the January 1968 budget. Certain categories, including Vietnam-related spending, interest, veterans affairs, and social security payments, were exempted from the ceiling so the total of actual outlays for the fiscal year is generally expected to exceed $180.1 billion. Apart from these specific exemptions, however, the law reinforced the ceiling on total outlays by providing for cuts of $10 billion in requested appropriations, by requiring gradual reductions in the number of Federal civilian employees, and by calling for rescissions of $8 billion in such unobligated balances as remain available after June 30, 1969.

Prospects for Expenditures

The administration in its summer budget review gave a revised projection of fiscal year 1969 outlays. Spending for programs exempted from expenditure control has been revised upward relative to the January budget and some nonexempt programs—such as farm

Estimated Outlays for Fiscal Year 1969 Based on Summer Budget Review

(In billions of dollars)

Total Federal outlays—January 1968 budget estimate		186.1
Plus: Estimated increases for programs exempt from expenditure control		4.4
Vietnam-support operations	2.3	
Interest	.9	
Veterans benefits and social security trust funds	1.1	
Tennessee Valley Authority.	*	
Plus: Selected increases in programs not exempt.		1.2
Farm price support purchases	.7	
Welfare grants (including medicaid).	.5	
Less: Budget cuts and other reestimates[1]		−7.2
Department of Defense, military and military assistance . . .	−2.8	
Net lending	−1.2	
All other expenditures	−3.2	
Equals: Federal outlays—Summer budget review.		184.4

*Less than $50 million.
[1] Net budget cuts exceed $6.0 billion because the estimated increases in nonexempt programs have been absorbed by other offsetting reductions.
Note.—Components may not add to totals due to rounding.

price supports and medicaid, in which outlays reflect conditions not subject to executive control—are also indicated to rise above earlier projections, as shown in the table. Details on planned spending cuts and reestimates by individual Federal agencies are shown in the review.

Prospects for Receipts

In addition to being affected by legislative constraints on spending, the Federal budget deficit for fiscal year 1969 will be significantly affected by a number of influences on receipts. Among these, the surtax is most important—its full-year liability at 1968 income levels is estimated at $10.2 billion in the Ways and Means Committee conference report. Economic growth is also expected to increase Federal receipts, although the amount of increase depends on the degree to which the new fiscal package restrains expansion in current dollar GNP.

Beyond these influences, several other factors will also help to bolster receipts in fiscal 1969 relative to fiscal 1968.

(1) The increase in social security payroll tax ceilings from $6,600 to $7,800, which became effective in January 1968, will have most of its positive effect on revenues only beginning with the third quarter of 1968 because calendar year wages and salaries of most employees will not exceed $6,600 before that time. Moreover, payroll taxes for social security programs are scheduled to increase, for employees and their employers combined, from 8.8 to 9.6 percent, effective January 1, 1969. Together these two changes are expected to add about $5 billion to total receipts at an annual rate.

(2) The retroactive feature of the surcharge legislation will result in Federal surtax collections during fiscal year 1969 in excess of 12 months' worth of tax accruals under the surcharge rates because the surtax—which became effective on July 15—is retroactive to January 1, 1968, for corporations and to April 1, 1968, for individuals. Moreover, 15 months' worth of corporate tax payments under the further speed-up provisions of the new law will occur in fiscal 1969. These provisions speed up tax payments of corporations by gradually eliminating most of the previous exemption of the first $100,000 of tax liability from pay-as-you-go. In addition they raise from 70 to 80 percent the percentage of tax liability that must be paid annually to avoid penalty.

(3) Finally, the Federal Government has provided for a more abrupt change in personal withholdings than in calendar-year tax liabilities. Withholding rates (except for the lowest two income tax brackets, to which the surtax is not applicable) were increased by 10

percent effective July 15 and are scheduled to drop by 10 percent next July 1, whereas calendar-year personal tax liabilities (again excepting the lowest two brackets) increase by 7.5 percent for calendar year 1968 and 5 percent for calendar year 1969.

Measuring the Impact of the 1964 Tax Reduction*

This paper was written during the summer of 1965. It reported on the way the Revenue Act of 1964 had served as a major stimulus to economic activity in the preceding year and a half. Just about the time that this paper was completed, we entered a new chapter in our economic history in which the key fiscal impact on the economy came from the extra defense expenditures required to fulfill our commitments in Southeast Asia. Any analysis of fiscal impact that covered the more recent period could no longer treat monetary policy as a passive supporting force, nor could it continue to ignore the influence of higher levels of aggregate demand on prices. Moreover, an updated version of this paper would revise the quantitative estimates associated with the tax reduction. Both revisions in earlier data and more recent experience would influence the point estimates. But neither the consideration of the most recent period nor the statistical refinement would change the basic conclusion that the tax cut of 1964 carried us a giant step toward full employment.

In the process of doing so, it also had important consequences for economic growth, which justify the inclusion of this topic in a volume of essays dealing with the subject of growth. To be sure, the Revenue Act of 1964 was aimed at the demand, rather than the supply, side of the nation's economy. Its objective and achievement was primarily to put productive capacity to work by raising private demand. Effects on the productive capability of the nation were largely incidental but nonetheless important.

By promoting fuller use of capacity, the tax cut created powerful incentives for growth-oriented activity by business. This was most apparent in the subsequent investment boom with its important widening, deepening, and updating of our capital stock. Fuller employment of labor, meanwhile, encouraged greater efforts in the private

*Arthur M. Okun, *Perspectives on Economic Growth*, Walter Heller (ed.), New York: Random House, 1968, pp. 27–49.
This paper was made possible by the able assistance of Allen Lerman.

training of manpower and improved the mobility and upgrading of our human resources.

Finally, the tax cut set the stage for a heightened interest in public policy to stimulate growth. When the nation was failing to make full use of its existing productive capacity, there were good reasons for policy-makers to be unenthusiastic about measures that promised an accelerated growth of supply capabilities. Indeed, there was even a powerful attraction to proposals that sought deliberately to curtail growth, such as by enforcing artificially a marked shortening of the workweek or earlier retirement of senior workers. The realization of full employment was a prerequisite for the serious consideration of policies to stimulate economic growth. Once we can enjoy an environment of peacetime prosperity, growth policy will come to the fore. And it will owe much to the demonstration through the 1964 Revenue Act that we can make full use of rapidly growing productive capacity.

Introduction

The best-known fact about the Revenue Act of 1964 is that, in the year and a half since it took effect, economic activity has expanded briskly. But such *post hoc, propter hoc* reasoning will never do. Many things happened early in 1964, and, by reference only to the course of events, one could attribute the buoyant performance of the economy to Illinois' victory in the Rose Bowl or to Goldwater's decision to stand in the New Hampshire primary. *Post hoc, propter hoc* somehow always seems to be on the other guy's side. If the economy had slipped into recession in 1964, it would have been viewed as a refutation of the efficacy of the tax cut. It would have been awfully difficult to get a serious discussion of whether an even worse setback might have occurred if not for the tax cut. At least now one can attract an audience to consider more analytical types of reasoning.

The analytical principles of macro-economics argue that rises in the incomes of individuals stimulate their consumer spending, while some combination of profit rates, cash flow, and sales is important as a determinant of business investment. The Revenue Act of 1964 affected these variables directly by adding to personal disposable income and to corporate profits after taxes. To the extent that the tax cut raised spending by consumers and businessmen through this direct route, it should also be credited with additional effects through the familiar multiplier process, whereby the spending of one individual or firm adds to the incomes and hence to the spending of others.

In the area of consumer spending, just a casual observation of the recent aggregative data suggests that there must be some validity to this story. By the second quarter of 1965, consumption expenditures had registered a remarkable rise of $45 billion from their rate in the last quarter of 1963—the quarter immediately preceding the tax cut. Such an increase over six quarters is unmatched in our peacetime history. If one ignores the tax cut, that surge is an insoluble mystery. On the other hand, the expansion of consumer purchases is easily accounted for by the income gains associated with the tax cut and the hypothesis that consumers have treated the increase in take-home pay from the tax reduction in the same way they treat increases in take-home pay from other sources.

By definition, individuals do something with income gains—they cannot ignore them and, according to the principles of utility maximization, they will not throw income away. Hence, the issue is how they allocate the proceeds between consumption and saving.[1] Both on the average and on the margin, the bulk of disposable income is consumed. If tax-cut gains are treated like other increases in income, most will be consumed and only a little will be added to saving.

The premise that tax-cut dollars are treated like other dollars of additional income is the foundation of the analysis. It is only fair to give warning that once this premise is accepted, the rest of the story follows readily. For our historical time-series data yield consumption-income relationships in which the marginal propensity to consume is very close to the average. Similarly, the quantitative record on investment tells us statistically that profits and sales have substantial effects on capital outlays. Indeed, this fundamental premise is the reason that so many economists expected so much from the 1964 Revenue Act. This premise can be subjected to some empirical check, although it cannot be supported by any refined verification from aggregative time-series data. If relationships established in the past hold up reasonably well after the tax cut, when tax-cut gains are added to other dollars of income, that supports the premise. But the real appeal is analytical: It is hard to see why people should want to segregate tax-cut dollars and treat them or think of them differently from other gains in their pay-checks or their corporate tills.

Given the fundamental premise, the analysis of the effects of the tax cut is an exercise in the dynamics of income-expenditure relationships. But that does not mean it is a simple exercise. Virtually

---

[1] The Department of Commerce's recently amended conceptual framework introduces a new third option for consumers. They are now free to engage in personal transfers to businesses or to foreigners by paying interest on personal debt or making gifts to persons overseas. All empirical work in this paper is based on the revised national accounts data shown in the *Survey of Current Business*, August 1965.

every issue in aggregative econometrics bears on the result. The answer ought to be based on a fully articulated set of economic relationships that takes proper account of all the ways that everything depends on everything else in the economy. You will not be surprised to learn that the estimates developed below do not rest on such a complete analysis of the economy. Instead, they depend on a few key estimated functions and a liberal sprinkling of assumptions (which I note along the way) that other possible effects can be ignored.

In fact, I will temporarily assume that the only effects that need to be considered are those on consumption and personal disposable income. This gives us the familiar case of the pure consumption multiplier, where any and all effects on investment are ignored, and where the increment in Gross National Product is taken to consist entirely of consumption. The consumption gain can be divided into two parts. One reflects the direct result of tax reduction in raising personal disposable income, and the second stems from the extra incomes generated by additions to consumer spending. The first of these is logically prior to the second. Nevertheless, because consumers do not adjust spending fully and immediately to the increases in their incomes, the two parts will overlap chronologically, and both will contribute to the growing increment in GNP over time.

The pure consumption case is interesting and instructive, and its dynamics are challenging. But it is certainly misleading. Nobody can really believe that a surge in consumer spending and a major rise in corporate profits and sales would have no impact on outlays for plant, equipment, and additional inventory. We must move on into the world of the accelerator or supermultiplier, as difficult as it is to quantify that world. Hence, I will emphasize quantitative estimates of the effects of tax reduction when both consumption and investment outlays are taken into account. But first I must back up and start at the beginning.

The Size of the Tax Cut

The first question in evaluating the impact of the 1964 tax cut is how big was it? And the answer is not as easy as one would wish. We can estimate that the tax reduction for individuals lowered liabilities on Federal individual income taxes by $6.7 billion for 1964 and by $11.5 billion for 1965. But the reduced liability is not the way the tax cut shows up in personal disposable income.

Our national income accounting takes the view that the spending of individuals (unlike that of corporations) is influenced by income taxes when these are paid rather than when the liabilities accrue. Actual payments were affected when the withholding rate declined from 18 percent to 14 percent in March 1964. The corresponding reduction in withheld taxes during 1964 amounted to a good deal more than $6.7 billion; indeed, it was above $8 billion. During the year, people were getting increases in take-home pay that exceeded the reductions in their tax liabilities. In part, this was associated with a reduced claim on the Federal Government for tax refunds early in 1965—any nontaxable dollar to which withholding had been applied generated a fourteen-cent refund rather than the eighteen-cent refund associated with the old withholding rate. Moreover, it was no secret that the 14 percent rate applied to ten months of the year would leave many people on less of a pay-as-you-go basis than they had been under the previous regime. In principle, anyone who changed his withholding voluntarily to maintain his degree of "pay-as-you-go" should have this adjustment subtracted from the dollar value of the tax cut for 1964.

There obviously were some such adjustments of withholding on a voluntary basis. Quantitatively, however, the best guess today is that they did not amount to much. Similarly, some of the self-employed reduced their estimated tax payments in June and September of 1964 in light of the lower tax rates. But, again, the adjustment does not seem to have been quantitatively significant and it would have operated in the other direction. Hence, we get a good approximation to the effect of the tax cut on disposable income through 1964 if we take actual withheld taxes after March, collected at a 14 percent rate, and apply a 2/7 ratio to them, so as to allow for the decline of four percentage points. For the first half of 1965, we must allow for the reduced refunds and the somewhat larger "clean-up payments" on the 1964 liabilities, which reduce the magnitude of the tax cut.

In principle, we should calculate the dollar value of the tax cut by applying the lower rates to incomes as they would have been in the absence of the tax cut and not to incomes as they actually turned out. But this difference is minor, and there are enough big problems to justify compromises on the little ones. I have rounded down the dollar estimates to make a rough allowance for this difference. The resulting estimates in billions of dollars (seasonally adjusted at annual rates) run as follows:

1964-I	3.2
-II	10.0
-III	10.0
-IV	10.0
1965-I	9.0
-II	9.5
-III	10.0
-IV	10.0

For corporations, the calculation is easier, simply because we treat taxes on a liability basis. The two-point reduction in the corporate tax rate for 1964, augmented by a switch between normal and surtax rates and by a liberalization of the investment credit, added up to $1.8 billion for the year. Another rate cut of two points took effect in 1965, and brought the 1965 total to $3 billion. The really important question about the corporate tax cut is whether it was shifted (either forward to consumers or backward to workers) or whether its benefits remained in the corporate sector. Without great conviction, I assume that there was no shifting in the short-run period covered by this paper.

The Pure Consumption Multiplier

The case of the pure consumption multiplier assumes away many of the difficult issues. To deal with it, all we need to know is (a) how much the tax cut adds directly to disposable income, (b) how much each dollar increase in disposable income adds to consumption, and (c) how much a dollar of additional consumption, in turn, adds further to disposable income.

The basic ingredient is the consumption-disposable income relationship. This is the most famous of all quantitative economic relationships, and it has appeared in all shapes, sizes, degrees of disaggregation, and other variations on the Keynesian theme. I shall use a simple form which treats consumer spending as a single total. It makes aggregate consumption in the current quarter depend only on aggregate consumption of the preceding quarter and on the personal disposable income of the current quarter. The presence of lagged consumption does, however, introduce a cumulative influence of the whole history of consumption and income on current consumption. The lagged consumption variable implies the presence of habit persistence or inertia in living standards. The equation has a respectable genealogy, going back (at least) to an article by T. M. Brown in *Econometrica* of July 1952.

The equation is spelled out in Table 1, as are its implications. According to it, an additional dollar of disposable income in the current quarter raises current consumption by 37.1 cents. If the income gain is maintained, consumption in the next period will be above its base level by 59.7 cents—the sum of 37.1 cents and .609 of 37.1 cents. Ultimately, the effect on consumption reaches 94.9 cents, as can be seen by solving the equation for $C_t = C_{t-1}$.

The intercept of this equation is a small negative number, surprisingly suggesting that the marginal propensity to consume is larger than the average propensity. But the difference is very small and has

TABLE 1

Incremental Consumption Associated with a
Maintained $1 Increase in Disposable Income

Quarter	Incremental consumption
0	0
1	.371
2	.597
3	.735
4	.819
5	.870
6	.901
.	.
.	.
∞	.949

$$C_t = -1.40 + .371\, Y_t + .609\, C_{t-1}$$

(billions of current dollars; fitted to period from
1954-I to 1964-IV)*

$$\bar{R}^2 = .999 \qquad \bar{S}_E = 1.71$$

*A homogeneous form $C_t/Y_t = .343 + .635$
C_{t-1}/Y_t gives virtually identical results.

no economic significance despite the statistical significance of the intercept. If the consumption function is forced through the origin and fitted homogeneously, one obtains a very similar equation which yields essentially the same results over time. These equations were also fitted with lagged income as well as lagged consumption, but the results were not improved. Asset variables deserve an opportunity to help explain consumption, but they did not get their chance in this analysis. Nor was there any attempt to disaggregate consumption, such as by separating out expenditures for durable goods.

The consumption function alone would enable us to estimate the consumption gains associated with the direct income gains of the tax cut. But those direct income gains do not account for the full increase in personal disposable income. Part of the gain in disposable income results from the addition to consumption. Hence, we need to know how much each extra dollar of consumption (or, equivalently, of GNP) adds to disposable income. The best way I know to deal with the marginal share of disposable income in GNP is to subtract the other leakages that do not go into disposable income. It turns out that the marginal share of disposable income in GNP is considerably less than the average ratio of disposable income to GNP.[2] One major reason for this is that, in the short run, when GNP increases, Government transfer payments do not keep pace; in fact they are actually

[2] I have discussed this elsewhere. See "Short-Term Forecasting by the President's Council of Economic Advisers" in O.E.C.D., *Techniques of Economic Forecasting*, Paris, 1965, pp. 163–65.

reduced through a decline in unemployment insurance benefits. The other and even more important reason is that corporate profits get a very large marginal share of GNP, particularly when the increase is sudden. Since dividends adjust very slowly through time, the bulk of the marginal share of profits is a withdrawal from disposable income.

As noted in Table 2, I have explained the sum of profits and corporate capital consumption allowances, using as independent variables the level of GNP, the change in GNP from the preceding quarter, and a utilization variable which multiplies GNP by the excess of the unemployment rate over 4 percent. On the basis of this equation, the marginal corporate share is a strikingly large 67 percent when GNP rises in a quarter, and it remains at 34 percent in succeeding quarters if the gain in GNP is maintained. The importance of fixed costs supplies good analytical reasons for a large marginal corporate share. Still, the quantitative estimates of the marginal share derived from equations are always surprisingly large to me. After investigating the effect of alternative variables on the magnitude of the corporate marginal share, I bow to the persistence of the empirical results.

The other leakages in Table 2 are based on elasticity estimates which have a variety of underpinnings. They are nowhere nearly so troublesome as profits in the probable error they introduce in the marginal disposable income calculation. Taking account of the various leakages, we conclude that a dollar increase in GNP raises disposable income in the current quarter by 21.5 cents; if the GNP gain is maintained, the disposable income gain reaches about 50 cents in the second quarter. It keeps creeping up slightly because dividends keep rising very gradually in response to the increase in corporate profits. The whole process can be simplified and summarized adequately by assuming that, in the second and succeeding quarters, the marginal share of disposable income in GNP levels off at .505. In the pure consumption case, there is one further influence to take into account: The corporate tax reduction generates extra dividends through time. Quantitatively, this does not amount to much; but it is registered in the results shown in Table 3.

Now we have, in effect, a two-equation system. The marginal consumption tells us how much added consumption is generated by extra disposable incomes; while the marginal disposable income-GNP relationship tells us what further gains in disposal income are produced by added consumption. Tables 3 and 4 show the numerical solutions of this system. By the fourth quarter of 1964, through the pure consumption route, disposable income is estimated to have been $15.1 billion higher as a result of the tax cut and consumption to have been $10.5 billion higher. These gains continue to expand in the

TABLE 2

Marginal Shares of Receipts from a
Maintained $1 Increase in Gross National Product

		\multicolumn{5}{c}{Quarter}
		0	1	2	\multicolumn{2}{c}{3 · · · 6}
1.	*Gross National Product*	0	1.000	1.000	1.000	1.000
2.	Corporate Profits before Taxes	0	.667	.340	.340	.340
3.	Corporate Taxes	0	.264	.134	.134	.134
3a.	Federal	0	.248	.127	.127	.127
3b.	State and Local	0	.015	.008	.008	.008
4.	Corporate Profits after Taxes	0	.404	.206	.206	.206
5.	Corporate Dividend Payments	0	.020	.029	.037	.058
6.	Undistributed Corporate Profits	0	.384	.177	.169	.148
7.	Indirect Business Taxes	0	.056	.056	.056	.056
7a.	Federal	0	.023	.023	.023	.023
7b.	State and Local	0	.033	.033	.033	.033
8.	Social Insurance Taxes	0	.011	.025	.025	.026
8a.	Federal	0	.009	.021	.021	.022
8b.	State and Local	0	.002	.004	.004	.004
9.	Transfer Payments	0	−.035	−.035	−.035	−.035
9a.	Federal	0	−.035	−.035	−.035	−.035
9b.	State and Local	0	0	0	0	0
10.	*Personal Income*	0	.251	.572	.580	.600
11.	Personal Taxes	0	.036	.082	.083	.086
11a.	Federal	0	.030	.068	.068	.071
11b.	State and Local	0	.006	.015	.015	.015
12.	*Disposable Personal Income*	0	.215	.490	.497	.514
Addendum: Net Government	Receipts	0	.402	.333	.334	.338
	Federal	0	.345	.273	.274	.277
	State and Local	0	.057	.060	.060	.061

Details may not add to totals due to rounding.

$$(10) = (1) - (3) - (6) - (7) - (8) + (9)$$
$$(12) = (10) - (11)$$

Corporate profits were estimated marginally from:

$$(P + CCA)_t = {}^-6.4229 + .1686\, Y_t + .3267\, \Delta Y_t {}^- .5502\, X_t$$

$$\overline{R}^2 = .961 \qquad \overline{S}_E = 1.403 \qquad \text{d.w.} = .846$$

where $(P + CCA)$ is Corporate Profits before Taxes including Inventory Valuation Adjustment plus Corporate Capital Consumption Allowances

Y is Gross National Product

and X is a measure of excess capacity associated with unemployment.

$$(U - .0400) \times \text{GNP},$$

where U is the unemployment rate.

The equation was fitted to quarterly data (seasonally adjusted at annual rates) for the period 1954-I to 1964-IV, and variables were measured in billions of current dollars.

The incremental calculation estimates that the unemployment rate is reduced by one percentage point by a 3.2 percent increment in GNP.

Throughout, capital consumption allowances are taken to be unaffected by changes in GNP.

Dividend payments were determined quarterly on the margin from:

$$D_t = .92\, D_{t-1} + .05\, AP_t$$

where AP is Corporate Profits after Taxes.

Corporate profits taxes were estimated at 39.5 percent of corporate profits.
Other taxes were estimated by taking the actual 1964 ratio to either GNP (Y) or Personal Income (Y_p), as appropriate, and using the following elasticities:

Federal Indirect Taxes	0.9	on Y
State and Local Indirect Taxes	0.5	on Y
Federal Social Insurance Taxes	0.75	on Y_p
State and Local Insurance Taxes	0.75	on Y_p
Federal Personal Taxes	1.2	on Y_p
State and Local Personal Taxes	1.2	on Y_p

TABLE 3

Sources of Gains in Disposable Income
(Pure Consumption Multiplier)

(in billions of current dollars)

	1964				1965	
	I	II	III	IV	I	II
Direct gain from personal tax reduction	3.2	10.0	10.0	10.0	9.0	9.5
Dividends attributable to corporate tax reduction	0.1	0.2	0.3	0.3	0.4	0.6
Induced gains: a) Due to GNP gain of preceding quarter	—	0.8	2.6	4.1	5.3	6.0
b) Due to additional GNP gain in current quarter	0.3	0.7	0.6	0.5	0.3	0.3
Total increment in personal disposable income	3.6	11.7	13.5	14.9	15.1	16.4

Details may not add to total because of rounding.
The results of Table 2 are used here in a simplified form, which assumes that the
marginal share of disposable income is constant at .505 after a lag of one quarter. The
simultaneous share is taken at .215 as shown in Table 2. Accordingly, the *induced* gain in
disposable income consists of:
a) .505 of the preceding quarter's gain for GNP plus
b) .215 of the *increase* in the GNP gain in the current quarter.
The induced gains in disposable income shown here are calculated from the bottom
line of Table 4. "Gain" or "increment" for a given quarter refers to the amount over and
above the hypothetical no-tax-cut situation; it does not decide the quarter-to-quarter
change.

first half of 1965 but at a slower rate. In part, the leveling off reflects
the downward bump in the size of the tax cut for the first half of
1965; in part, it suggests that the process was, by that time, beginning to approach its full effect.

But the ultimate full effect is considerably larger than the $13.4
billion gain in consumption shown for the second quarter of 1965.
Holding the personal tax cut at $10 billion and the corporate reduction at $3 billion, we would ultimately reach a consumption gain of
more than $21.2 billion.

The corporate tax reduction would be credited with a $3 billion
contribution to consumption after the very long wait required for
dividends to be fully adjusted. This is not a great performance as a

TABLE 4

Consumption and GNP Gains Related to Disposable Income Gains
(Pure Consumption Multiplier)

Quarter	Gain in disposable income	Resulting gain in consumption in:					
		1964-I	1964-II	1964-III	1964-IV	1965-I	1965-II
1964:							
I	3.6	1.3	0.8	0.5	0.3	0.2	0.1
II	11.7		4.3	2.6	1.6	1.0	0.6
III	13.5			5.0	3.0	1.9	1.1
IV	14.9				5.6	3.4	2.1
1965:							
I	15.1					5.6	3.4
II	16.4						6.1
Total consumption (or GNP) gain in given quarter		1.3	5.1	8.1	10.5	12.0	13.4

Details may not add to totals because of rounding.
The cells above show the "phasing-out" of income gains into consumption gains in accordance with the consumption equation set forth in Table 1. That consumption equation and the disposable income relationship summarized in the note to Table 3 form a two-equation system in consumption and disposable income.
In the "pure consumption multiplier" case, the GNP gain is set equal to the consumption gain.

consumption stimulus, but corporate tax cuts have never been expected to star in that respect.

The bulk of the ultimate consumption gain—$18.2 billion—would be attributable to the personal tax reduction. Based on a .949 marginal propensity to consume and a .505 marginal share of disposable income, the steady-state multiplier is 1.82. Given the nature of this calculation, "close to two" remains a good familiar approximation to the pure consumption multiplier for a tax cut.

Induced Investment

Now I move to the more difficult but more realistic situation in which induced investment is recognized. We will continue to assume that neither net exports nor residential construction is affected by the tax cut or by the subsequent increases in incomes. These simplifying assumptions are not likely to be quantitatively important and at least they are offsetting in direction: Net exports would be lowered by higher GNP, while residential construction would be favorably affected, given the state of credit conditions. The induced effects we deal with are those on business fixed investment and inventory investment.

The choice of an equation for explaining business fixed investment is exceedingly difficult. Here, we cannot take advantage of the survey data and other barometric indicators that are so helpful in forecasting plant and equipment. Sales, utilization measures, and cash flow variables all have excellent claims for appearing in the equation. But when all of these are allowed to compete in equations fitted from time-series data, chaos results. The coefficients are highly unstable with respect to the choice of lags and the specification of variables. I trust that the econometric conflict between cash flow and accelerator models will be settled some day, but I am convinced that the decisive battle will not be fought with aggregative time-series data.

Many time-series equations with a few lags and a few variables perform about equally well. A cash flow equation with four quarterly lags in that single variable gave good results and reasonable coefficients. That is what I am using, as shown in Table 5. To the ex-

TABLE 5

Increments in Business Fixed and Inventory Investment from
a Maintained $1 Increase in Final Sales of GNP

Quarter	Business fixed investment	Inventory investment
0	0	0
1	0	.041
2	.118	.163
3	.134	.207
4	.163	.197
5	.176	.157
6	.154	.105

Business fixed investment was calculated marginally from:

$$I_t = 9.02 + .293 F_{t-1} + .182 F_{t-2} + .162 F_{t-3} + .110 F_{t-4}$$
$$\overline{R}^2 = .968 \qquad \overline{S}_E = 1.30 \qquad d.w. = .609$$

F is corporate cash flow (corporate profits after tax, including inventory valuation adjustment, plus corporate capital consumption allowances).

The equation is fitted to quarterly data for 1954-I through 1964-IV and all variables are quarterly totals at seasonally adjusted annual rates expressed in billions of current dollars.

F was estimated marginally using the profits function set forth in Table 2 and an estimated profits tax share of 39.5 percent, as noted in Table 2.

Inventory investment was calculated from:

$$V_t = -45.56 - .1715 H_{t-1} + .5842 V_{t-1} + .0428 S_t + .1099 S_{t-1}$$
$$\overline{R}^2 = .733 \qquad \overline{S}_E = 1.908 \qquad d.w. = 1.886$$

where   *V* is the change in Business Inventories;
           H is *V* cumulated from 1947-I;
and   *S* is GNP Final Sales.

Variables are quarterly totals, seasonally adjusted at annual rates in billions of 1958 dollars. The equation was fitted to 1954-I to 1964-IV but omitting the period from 1959-II to 1960-I.

tent that cash flow really serves here as a proxy for other influences, such as sales and utilization, this should not be disturbing. The reliance on cash flow does credit the corporate tax cut with direct influence, but the omission of after-tax profits in the investment equation would assume that it had no direct effect. According to this equation, a dollar of extra after-tax corporate profits ultimately raises investment by seventy-five cents, working out its effects over the succeeding four quarters, as shown in Table 5.

The results of the inventory equation are also shown in Table 5. Inventory investment is explained using lagged stocks, lagged inventory investment, and current and last quarter's final sales of GNP. This equation and other inventory equations was a terrible estimator for the period from the second quarter of 1959 to the first quarter of 1960, when inventory investment was dominated by first the expectation, then the realization, and finally the recovery from the steel strike. Nevertheless, other periods of steel-dominated inventory activity did not show unreasonable results. Hence, the four misbehaving quarters were thrown out of the sample from which the equation was calculated. Because of the presence of the stock variable, there is no ultimate maintained level of inventory investment. As Table 5 shows, the induced inventory investment associated with a $1 maintained increase in GNP begins to decline after three quarters. It would eventually turn negative and oscillate, ultimately converging to zero.

The fixed investment and inventory equations do not include any monetary variables. In principle, they belong here. I would certainly expect a significant change in the costs or availability of credit to have an important influence on business investment. In practice, dealing with the period from early 1964 through mid-1965, I cannot believe that the omission of monetary variables can make a serious difference. By any measure of interest rates or credit conditions I know, there were no significant monetary changes that would have either stimulated or restrained investment to a major degree. Obviously, the rising incomes and investment of this period generated increased demands for financial assets and for loans. In this environment, the maintenance of stable interest rates and stable credit conditions required action by the monetary authorities to expand the reserve base more rapidly so as to accommodate expansion.

In this sense, monetary policies made a major contribution to the advance, but that contribution can be appropriately viewed as permissive rather than casual. The monetary authorities supplied a good sound set of tires for the economy to roll on, but they did not contribute the engine. That came from fiscal policies. If monetary policy had been the driving force, that would have shown up—at least initially—in a decline of interest rates and a relaxation of credit conditions.

It is reasonable to ask how much slower the overall economic advance might have been and how much less expansionary the tax cut would have been if monetary policy had not been accommodating. One could hypothesize an alternative monetary policy which held down the growth of bank reserves or the money supply (or other liquidity variables) to some stated degree. And one could then try to assess what difference this tighter monetary policy would have made in the pace of economic advance. That would be an interesting statistical exercise. It just does not happen to be the particular statistical exercise which this paper attempts to perform.

We can now put the whole process in motion, using the inventory and the investment equations along with the disposable income relationship and the consumption function discussed earlier. The results are shown in Table 6. The gains in GNP are, of course, larger than

TABLE 6

GNP Gains by Components Allowing for Induced Investment

(in billions of current dollars)

	1964				1965	
	I	II	III	IV	I	II
Gains in:						
Corporate Cash Flow	2.4	4.1	5.2	6.1	8.0	8.8
Direct from profits tax reduction	1.8	1.8	1.8	1.8	3.0	3.0
Induced profits before tax	1.0	3.8	5.6	7.2	8.3	9.6
Less: Induced profits taxes	-0.4	-1.5	-2.2	-2.8	-3.3	-3.8
Disposable Income	3.6	11.9	14.5	17.1	18.5	21.2
Direct from personal tax reduction	3.2	10.0	10.0	10.0	9.0	9.5
Dividends attributed to corporate tax reduction	0.1	0.1	0.2	0.3	0.4	0.5
Induced	0.3	1.8	4.2	6.8	9.1	11.2
Consumption	1.3	5.2	8.6	11.6	13.9	16.3
Business Fixed Investment	—	0.7	1.6	2.6	3.7	4.8
Inventory Investment	0.1	0.4	1.2	2.1	2.8	3.2
Total GNP	1.4	6.3	11.4	16.3	20.5	24.4

those estimated in the pure consumption case, Indeed, consumption itself rises more strongly because of the greater induced gains in disposable income. And, after a slow start, the investment components are contributing about one-third of the estimated total gain in GNP after the fourth quarter of 1964. The total gain in GNP reaches $17.1

billion in the final quarter of 1964 and goes on to $24.4 billion in the second quarter of 1965. If we continue the process for another two quarters, the GNP increase would exceed $30 billion in the fourth quarter of 1965.

And it will be rising. With a $10 billion personal tax cut and a $3 billion corporate reduction, the GNP gain would ultimately be $36.2 billion, $7.8 billion in business fixed investment and $28.4 billion in consumption. In this final situation, inventory investment would no longer contribute to the gain.

Of this "final" $36.2 billion gain in GNP, $25.9 billion results from the personal tax reduction and $10.3 billion from the corporate tax cut. The "steady state" multiplier for personal taxes is 2.59. The ultimate multiplier for the corporate tax cut is estimated at 3.4. But the corporate cut takes a much longer time to approach its full effects, because dividends creep up so slowly and gradually. Throughout the first two years following a tax cut, the estimated impact per dollar of the personal tax reduction is substantially greater than that of the cut for corporations. Moreover, we should recognize the possibility that the cash flow character of the investment equation may be too generous to the corporate tax cut.

According to these results, the Federal Government received $7 billion of extra net receipts in the second quarter of 1965 (on a national income accounts basis) as a result of the gains attributable to the tax cut. By this Federal budgetary criterion, the tax cut had paid for more than half of itself by then, and the fraction was rising. In addition, state and local governments were the beneficiaries of an estimated $1.5 billion increase in net receipts in the second quarter. In the ultimate situation, the induced gain in Federal net receipts would be $10 billion, and the state and local gain $2.2 billion, adding to a total that nearly matches the $13 billion of tax reduction.

Conclusion

This is not the first quantitative estimate that has been made for the Revenue Act of 1964; and it will not be the last. I trust also that it will not be the best. At the Council of Economic Advisers, we hope to improve the tools needed in this analysis and to remedy some of the limitations I have noted above.

Nevertheless, the results shown in Table 6 looks sensible and plausible to me. One way of viewing the conclusions is to consider what they imply about the hypothetical world in which no tax reduction had taken place. The hypothetical no-tax-cut world is constructed by subtracting from actual national accounts variables the

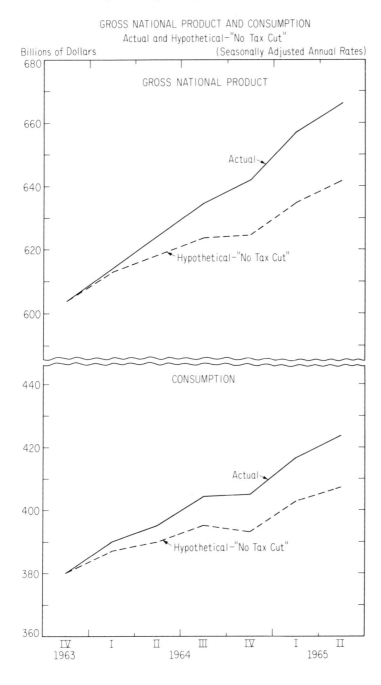

GROSS NATIONAL PRODUCT AND CONSUMPTION
Actual and Hypothetical—"No Tax Cut"
(Seasonally Adjusted Annual Rates)

estimated gains from the tax cut over the six quarters from the beginning of 1964 to mid-1965. Instead of a rapid growth in GNP of more than $10 billion a quarter in that period, the world without a tax cut has an average quarterly increase of $6.3 billion, as shown in the accompanying chart. When the same thing is done for the other key variables, the results form a consistent pattern—slow growth in disposable income, small advances in consumption, and a leveling off in fixed investment in the first half of 1965 following some slippage in corporate profits during 1964. This no-tax-cut world would have shown rising unemployment and sagging operating rates.

I suggested at the outset one possible check on the fundamental premise that tax cut dollars are treated like other dollars: It consists of looking at empirical relationships established in the past to see whether they went haywire in the period following the tax cut. I can report that the equations held up quite well. Of course, they do not fit perfectly during the last year and a half, but neither did they fit perfectly in the years prior to the tax cut.

In the consumption function, there were sizable errors for two quarters, a $4.5 billion overestimate in the fourth quarter of 1964 and an offsetting $3.5 billion underestimate in the first quarter of 1965. In view of the slow deliveries of new cars during the auto strikes of the autumn of 1964 and the subsequent extraordinary catch-up, this pattern seems perfectly sensible. The profits equation fits unusually well during 1964 and the first half of 1965. Its largest error is in the second quarter of 1965, when it understates the level of profits by $1.7 billion; during the sample period, its standard error of estimate was $1.4 billion. The root-mean-square error in the inventory equation for the six quarters was identical to its $1.9 billion standard error of estimate over the sample period. Fixed investment is exceedingly well estimated for the first half of 1964; but it is underestimated consistently thereafter by amounts ranging from $1.2 to $3.5 billion and averaging $2 billion per quarter. There are grounds for suspicion that the investment equation we have used may have been conservative in its estimate of the induced effects stemming from personal tax reduction.

According to the estimates cited above, the tax cuts of 1964 are credited with a $25 billion contribution to our GNP by mid-1965, a $30 billion effect by the end of 1965, and an ultimate $36 billion increment. I have mentioned many reasons why these point estimates should be viewed as the center of a sizable range. Even with all the appropriate qualifications, these results provide important analytical confirmation that the Revenue Act of 1964 lived up to the intentions and expectations of its advocates, and that it has delivered a powerful stimulus to economic expansion.

III

Resource Allocation in the Federal Sector

A

The Planning-Programing Budget

The purpose of cost-benefit analysis is to improve the allocation of public resources. There is concern that the federal government may utilize national resources for relatively low-priority programs in terms of national needs, while more worthwhile projects are deferred for lack of funds. Thus, what is required is the development of some methodology to allocate resources on a more rational basis than exists at the present. There must be a systematic attempt to appraise the desirability of the choices implicitly made in the allocation of government resources among major alternative uses.

The two readings are designed to explain the development and objectives of the Planning-Programing Budget. The first reading, "Origin and History of Program Budgeting," by David Novick, explains how the need for some sort of cost-benefit analysis developed. The second article, "PPB in Brief," by Charles L. Schultz, explains the actual mechanics of the Planning-Programing Budget.

*Origin and History of Program Budgeting**

For the next half-hour, I shall be talking about the origin and history of program budgeting as part of the Civil Service Commis-

*David Novick, Subcommittee on National Security and International Operations of the Committee on Government Operations, United States Senate, 90th Congress, 1st Session, 1967, pp. 28–34.

Any views expressed in this paper are those of the author. They should not be interpreted as reflecting the views of The RAND Corporation or the official

sion's orientation and training courses for the Planning-Programming-Budgeting System (PPBS) which was introduced by the Federal Government in August 1965. The occasion for this can be viewed from two angles: First, the intellectual or scholastic one that claims people do a task better when given an understanding of the background and roots of the process in which they are engaged. The other, and probably the more appropriate one, is to try to deal with comments that have been made from time to time about the Planning-Programming-Budgeting System either as something brand new or something that is specifically designed for application to the military or Defense Department activities.

As I hope to indicate over the next half-hour, the program budget has a rather ancient and hoary origin and it did not start in the Department of Defense. There are two roots of this concept and method: one in the Federal Government itself where program budgeting was introduced as part of the wartime control system by the War Production Board in 1942; the other root—an even longer and older one—is in industry. To be honest with you, I don't really know precisely when or how the program budget was introduced in business.

In 1959, after I had been writing about PPBS for more than five years, I had a visitor who said he had only recently become familiar with my proposals, and on reading the material he thought I'd be interested in his experience along the same lines. He gave me a set of written documents—General Motors Budget and Finance Procedures for the Year 1924.

The visitor was Donaldson Brown, who had retired as chief financial officer of General Motors and who was until his death a member of the board of directors of DuPont. According to Mr. Brown, by the time that DuPont made its investment in General Motors, DuPont was already using something very much like a program budget system. And, this way of planning and budgeting was one of the major innovations in General Motors after the takeover.

Let me start by talking about the part of the origin that identifies to the Federal Government because this is the one in which I was closely involved and with which I therefore have a greater familiarity.

In the early summer of 1940, President Roosevelt created the National Defense Advisory Commission which was to assist our

opinion or policy of any of its governmental or private research sponsors. Papers are reproduced by The RAND Corporation as a courtesy to members of its staff.

This is a transcription of a talk filmed on August 11, 1966, for the courses sponsored by the U.S. Bureau of the Budget and the U.S. Civil Service Commission for oreintation and training in the Planning Programming Budgeting System.

friends or "allies-to-be" in facilitating their war efforts. To do this, we undertook a variety of new or expanded production efforts and a number of new construction projects. In all of this, the building of ships and shipyards and the construction of new factories, one item of demand was common—overhead cranes.

As a result, by late 1940 the first of what was to become our World War II controls was introduced—a limitation order controlling the schedule of distribution and use of overhead cranes. This was followed over the next year and a half by a series of orders that copied the pattern of control of industrial production and distribution that had been used in World War I.

There was a limitation order dealing with aluminum as the aircraft demands made this metal in short supply. There were orders dealing with various alloying materials, as hard steel demands for military equipment increased. There were orders stopping the production of pleasure automobiles to cut back the use of materials like chromium and components such as ball bearings, and so on. The result was that even before the war had started, by the summer of 1941 we had a real traffic jam in our control system.

The military was using authority that had been given them to place priorities for deliveries of finished products such as tanks, aircraft, ships, and the like. The civilian supply agency also was authorized to place priorities on steel, copper, aluminum, and other materials for milk pails, medical and hospital supplies, and other essentials.

There were a great many priorities and these priorities soon started to outstrip the available supply. As a consequence, it became apparent that this way of doing business—separate controls for each situation—was not likely to work. In the early fall of 1941, a scheme which I developed—the Production Requirements Plan—attempted to deal with the priority and allocation problem on an across-the-board basis. Shortly after Pearl Harbor, this was made a mandatory nationwide system.

However, the Production Requirements Plan had been designed as a stopgap measure. That is, recognizing that the military did not know what was required to build their ships and planes and tanks, and did not have a schedule that could identify delivery in appropriate time periods, and did not have a way of effectively controlling the dollar volume of contracts placed, there was one essential need—to identify these fundamentals.

The Production Requirements Plan was designed to identify the material and component requirements for contracts that were being placed by the military, and probably more importantly, to measure the inventories and capacities of America's producing industry. It was an interim step on the road to a program budget in that it provided the first overall picture of the United States needs and resources for war.

From this we learned that we could not look at one thing at a time, be it airplanes, ships, or stainless steel milk pails on the demand side; or steel, aluminum, overhead cranes, and ball bearings on the supply side. As a consequence, by early 1942, the War Production Board was looking at the total of military requirements and the total of war-essential civilian requirements in terms of a series of identifiable groupings; and, perhaps more significantly, these groups were being studied by the analytical tools then available.

The essential features of the situation can be made rather simple. Although we needed all the airplanes that we could get, all of the airplanes were not that important. At some point, roller bearings for the 2,000th B-17 were less important than the roller bearings for a refrigerator in a municipal hospital. At some point, the 1,000th tank of a certain type was less important than the stainless steel milk pails essential for milk to be supplied to either soldiers or civilians. As a consequence, the War Production Board learned the need for weighing and evaluating, and this led to the introduction in late 1942 of the Controlled Materials Plan.

The Controlled Materials Plan is to my mind the first program budget used in the Federal Government. It usually is not so identified because the budgeting was done in terms of copper, steel, aluminum, and other critical material rather than dollars, and for most people budget is associated with dollars. However, in choosing the media of exchange—copper, steel, and other critical items—we were recognizing that in 1942, dollars were less meaningful than physical resources. Currency could be created by fiat and without restraint, whereas materials of the type labelled as controlling were limited in quantity and their supply could only be increased by a slow, and usually resource-demanding, expansion.

As a consequence, for the balance of World War II—that is, from 1943 through 1945—we effectively controlled the system of production in the United States and the distribution of output from that system through the Controlled Materials Plan, which was the first Federal program budget. I call it a program budget because it had the following characteristics:

I. Identification of major goals.
   United States or allied combat needs
   Essential civilian requirements
   Other essential military or civilian demands

Aid to friendly nations
Economic warfare
II. Each major goal was identified in program objectives; for example:
    A. United States Military
       1. Combat theater equipment and supplies
       2. Combat support
       3. Zone of interior activities
III. Program objectives were further defined in program elements, for
    1. Combat theater equipment and supplies
      (a) aircraft
         (1) (further defined by type and model)
      (b) tanks
         (1) (broken down into size and purpose categories)
      (c) automobiles
         (1) (identified as trucks, jeeps, personnel vehicles, etc., and trucks further refined into size and use categories)
IV. Programs crossed service lines so as to identify land, sea, and air forces as well as essential nonmilitary contributions to identified objectives.
V. There was an extended time horizon. A budget was prepared every three months or quarter and it was projected for 16 periods, that is, the next quarter and the 15 succeeding ones.
VI. Alternatives were examined and systematic analysis was made of both supply and requirements. Sometimes this meant resources were augmented by stopping production; the outstanding example: gold mining. This provided additional labor and equipment for other mining activities. In other cases, essential needs were met by "freezing" inventories and controlling distribution as was done in the case of passenger automobiles. In every case, the action was the result of analysis.

Our systematic analysis was not necessarily systems analysis in the breadth and depth we now identify to such studies; but under the Controlled Materials Plan we did cost-effectiveness analysis even if it did not have the sophistication which we expect today. However, in terms of the state-of-the-art of the time, I think the analytical and related methodology used in our World War II Controlled Materials Plan can be properly identified as a program budget.

The next steps in the federal development of a program budget took place in the Bureau of Reclamation, the Coast Guard, and some few other government agencies, and at RAND. I shall detail the RAND activities.

Early in its history, RAND decided that the traditional standards for choosing among preferred means of warfare of the future—for example, for aircraft, higher, faster, more payload—were not the only ones and so expanded the criteria into what is now known as *weapons systems analysis.* The first of these studies was completed in 1949 and in it a number of new factors were introduced—e.g., social, political, and economic—so that the study aims went beyond what the specific piece of equipment would do, and added considerations such as demands on the U.S. economy, and impact on the economy of the enemy. With the wide range of considerations in systems analysis, it was determined that there was only one way to bring this heterogeneous group together, and that was with the common denominator of the dollar.

At that time, RAND looked to the Air Staff for its data, and the dollar data were made available in the traditional form; that is, budget and financial information in terms of equipment, construction, personnel, and the like. Although there had already been some efforts in the Air Staff to develop a means for looking at weapon systems, these had not proceeded very far and as a consequence the traditional budget and financial data were something less than satisfactory for weapons systems analysis as developed at RAND.

If one wanted to do a systems analysis in which there would be a comparison between various types of bombers—for example, the proposed B-17 and B-52 and the existing B-36, B-29, and B-50—the data just were not available. When RAND decided that it would have to engage in a more detailed analysis of the economic requirements of the proposed weapons systems, it became necessary to examine in considerable detail the available sources of information.

After several years, it became apparent that these would not provide the answers if they were maintained in the existing and traditional form. As a consequence, in 1953 there was a RAND publication[1] proposing the first program budget to be applied to the Air Force. It also suggested that the methodology could be extended to the total of military activities.

The Air Force accepted this document with something less than complete enthusiasm, and as a consequence the idea was kicked around for many years. Let me say as an aside that although the Air

[1] Novick, D. *Efficiency and Economy in Government Through New Budgeting and Accounting Procedures,* The RAND Corporation, R-254, December 3, 1953.

Force did not endorse the idea, is also did not prohibit, or in any way interfere with, RAND continuing to expose the concept. The consequence was continued study and publication at RAND of ideas which we now associate with the program budget. This led to a culmination in 1960 in two documents—one, *The Economics of Defense in the Nuclear Age*;[2] the other, *New Tools for Planners and Programmers*[3]—which were brought to the attention of persons in the incoming Kennedy Administration who generally agreed that this might be one way of facilitating the treatment, analysis, and study of one large segment of the United States budget, namely, the military components.

And, as you know, in 1961 the initial effort was launched in the Defense Department and it has continued since that time. Program budgeting in the Department of Defense has been the subject of various types of criticism. Maybe I'm prejudiced, but to me most of it sounds very complimentary.

Turning again to the historical stream, as indicated at the outset, I really don't know when the DuPont Company came up with the idea of a program budget. However, as indicated earlier, they introduced their concept into General Motors in the very early 1920s. The important thing, I think, from our point of view, is that whether we're thinking of the application in industry or in government, we all have one common objective in the Planning-Programming-Budgeting process. That is not just to identify resources for administrative purposes *per se* in terms like real estate, equipment, personnel, supplies, and so on.

The PPBS method is to set forth certain major objectives, to define programs essential to these goals, to identify resources to the specific types of objectives and to systematically analyze the alternatives available. I think this may be made more simply by illustrating it in automobile industry terms. For example, at General Motors it means not only dividing up between Chevrolet and Cadillac divisions and the other major lines that General Motors produces. It also means within the Chevrolet line, identification of objectives in terms of price classes, categories of cars that they are trying to sell, and setting up specific programs for each of them. Then they calculate the resources required and the potential profits and losses under various conditions.

Now the word "potential" immediately introduces one of the

[2] Hitch, Charles J., and Roland N. McKean, *The Economics of Defense in the Nuclear Age*, A RAND Corporation Research Study, Harvard University Press, Cambridge 38, Massachusetts, 1960.

[3] Novick, D., *New Tools for Planners and Programmers*, The RAND Corporation, P-2222. December 1960.

major factors in the program budgeting system. That is, that we are dealing with uncertainty. In the typical budget proposal, we usually look at a relatively short period of time—that is, one year—and in handling that, we assume that we have complete confidence and knowledge about what will transpire.

As all of you know, the truth of the matter is that even within as short a span of time as a year, things happen and events do not work out exactly as planned. As a consequence, even then there is an element of uncertainty. One of the major features of the system that was introduced in Detroit was the fact that they were not planning just for next year's automobile, and had to deal with uncertainty in terms of four, five, or more years in the future.

In the current time period, next year's model or the automobile for year I is a fixed thing with only a little possibility of change. The article for the year after that or year II, is almost a fixed thing because commitments must be made to long lead-time items as much as 18 months in advance. Even the automobile for year III is fairly well developed at this point in time and they are also planning for automobiles for years IV and V.

In other words, Detroit continuously has five model years in planning, as well as one model in production. And, they look at all of these in terms of all of the possible alternatives with respect to market conditions, the kinds of competition that they will be facing, the changes in income for their customers that can be projected, and the like. And this leads to a broad range of studies or systematic analyses. In addition and on top of this, they are at the same time treating of the capital investment program, because by and large they cannot make capital investments for an automobile more close at hand than year VI. In fact, if a change requiring investment in a new plant is to be made for an earlier period of time, they must take into account the tremendous upset and additional costs that will be involved.

I hope that this rather generalized illustration of the way in which automotive planning, programming, and budgeting is done, gives you a better feel for just what is done in the system developed and used in Detroit.

Let me digress a moment, because although I didn't identify it, the concept of systems analysis, which again is closely identified with program budgeting, did not really originate in program budgeting *per se*. Systems analysis always has been a part of the work of competent engineers and engineering firms. Probably the greatest innovations in systems analysis were initiated in the 1920s in the Bell Laboratories.

Actually, in many respects the Bell Lab's method of analysis then and today bears a close resemblance to what we called "weapons systems analysis" in the Defense Department or in other organizations such as RAND.

There is one major distinction and I think it is worth noting. That is, that the engineers (and this includes the Bell Laboratories) oriented their thinking largely, and sometimes exclusively, to the hardware or the equipment considerations.

Although they sometimes introduced economic, social, and political aspects, they treated these in a very primitive way. And I think the great significance of the change that we call weapons systems analysis today is the broadening of both the nature and content of the analysis.

In all of this, quantitative aids are of great importance, and we want to quantify as much as we can. But as has been stated repeatedly by Mr. McNamara; by Mr. Hitch, when he was Assistant Secretary of Defense (Comptroller); by Mr. Enthoven, the first Assistant Secretary of Defense (Systems Analysis); computers and quantitative methods are not decisionmakers. They are, instead, aids to the decisionmaking process. They are aids in illuminating the issues. Today, I think most of us realize that we are not talking about computers as the decisionmakers in the PPB process. In fact, I think we realize it is "Anything But."

In fact, it is recognized that as important as, and in many cases more important than quantitative considerations, are problems of a qualitative nature for which we do not have numbers. This does not mean that analysis is not possible just because we cannot quantify. On the contrary, there are many ways of analyzing qualitative problems and it is an essential ingredient of this process that we undertake to do a substantial amount of qualitative analysis in addition to the quantitative work.

As you all know, and the reason that we are here is that in August of 1965, President Johnson said that this system which has been so successful in the Defense Department was now to be applied to all the executive offices and agencies of the United States Government. Even though there is a long history of program budgeting, even though it originates outside of the federal establishment, even though there are some 25 years or more of history that we can identify to the activity within the federal establishment, the truth of the matter is that the problem that we are now facing—that is, the application of the PPB concept to new areas of interest—is a new and very difficult one. And, one of the major problems is that of identifying the missions, the objectives, or the goals, not only of the federal establishment as such, but of each of the offices and agencies which make up the total of the executive department.

I think our Planning-Programming-Budgeting System offers all the advantages that President Johnson set forth in his 1965 announcement. It will be up to you and the others who are working on the problem in the federal establishment to give us as a nation the benefit of this new way of doing business.

*PPB in Brief**

Chapters 2 and 3 lay the groundwork for a later evaluation of PPB in the political process. Chapter 2 provides a brief description of PPB as a system for aiding the decision maker while Chapter 3 describes the political framework within which the public decision maker operates. The subsequent chapter then analyzes and compares these two aspects of decision making.

The Goals of PPB

PPB can be viewed as both a set of goals and objectives and as a system for achieving those goals. It seeks to accomplish the following ends.

First, PPB calls for careful identification and examination of goals and objectives in each major area of governmental activity. It attempts to force governmental agencies to step back and reflect on the fundamental aims of their current programs. For example, what are the goals of federal manpower programs? To reduce structural unemployment and inflationary pressure by retraining programs that increase the number of workers with skills in short supply? To raise the income of hard-core disadvantaged by upgrading their skills and improving their work habits? To create more job opportunities for the unskilled? While they are not wholly incompatible, they are different and the design and composition of public manpower programs will depend upon the particular combination of objectives sought.

Intercity highway programs provide another example. The objective of the intercity highway program ought not to be simply

*Charles L. Schultz, from *The Politics and Economics of Public Spending* (Washington: The Brookings Institution, 1968), pp. 19–34.

building highways. Highways are useful only to transport people and goods efficiently and safely. Once this objective is recognized, it becomes possible to analyze alternative transportation investments as means to these ends. So long as the ultimate goal of the highway program is considered the laying of x miles of concrete, comparison of the effectiveness of various investments is impossible.

At the same time, we cannot expect the perspectives of any given level in the decision hierarchy to be as broad as those of the next higher level. The federal highway administrator will not, and should not, have the same range of objectives as the secretary of transportation nor will the secretary deal with as broad a range of alternatives as the President. Each level in the decision-making process has its own role to play. In seeking to specify program objectives, PPB aims at a realistic broadening of perspective, not at making the objectives of every participant coextensive with the President's. An attempt to force too wide a span of objectives on a participant in the process may well render the whole effort fruitless. In short, PPB seeks to encourage an analysis of program objectives in order to widen but not homogenize the perspective with which agency heads view their programs, thereby broadening the range of alternatives considered for policy and program design.

The second task of PPB is to analyze the *output* of a given program in terms of its objectives. For example, the effectiveness of various manpower training programs can only be determined in relation to a particular set of objectives. "Creaming off" the manpower pool by concentrating training resources on unemployed white high school graduates may prove highly effective when measured by the proportion of trainees subsequently employed at steady jobs and higher wages. But if the objective is to improve the lot of the hardcore unemployed or underemployed in the ghetto, comparing alternative programs on the basis of such measures of effectiveness would be inappropriate and misleading. Similarly in evaluating the highway program, it is not sufficient to ask how many miles of concrete are laid, but what the program produces in terms of safer, less-congested travel—how many hours of travel time are eliminated and how many accidents are prevented.

The third objective of PPB is the measurement of total program costs, not for just one year but for at least several years ahead. Two kinds of costs are involved. The first relates to the future budgetary consequences of current decisions. The 1968 budget, for example, requested $10 million to design a 200 billion electron volt research accelerator for the Atomic Energy Commission at an estimated construction cost of $240 million. But over a longer time period—say ten years—the total system's cost of this decision may exceed $1 billion, since operating costs, once the machine is built, will run between $60 and $100 million per year. In terms of overall budget policy it is necessary to know the extent to which future budgetary commitments are being made by current decisions. Moreover, in comparing alternative programs designed to accomplish a given objective, the comparison should be made on the basis of all the relevant costs, not just the immediate costs.

In addition to budgetary costs, there are often other costs associated with a proposed program which should be taken into account in making a decision. The costs of urban freeways, for example, are not merely the construction costs of the freeway itself but include the cost of relocating displaced residents. Even where these costs are not reflected in the budget, they are still costs to society and should be identified in the statement of program costs.

PPB, then, seeks to provide the decision maker with all the relevant costs that his decision would entail. This sounds so sensible that to belabor the point seems unnecessary. Yet too often large federal investment decisions have been made in the annual budget on the basis of only the next year's cost—or made without taking into account any of the indirectly associated costs.

A fourth and closely related goal of PPB is the formulation of objectives and programs extending beyond the single year of the annual budget submission. Most federal programs cannot achieve their intended objectives in one year. Many, like the collection of taxes, are a continuing activity some of whose components, such as the computerization of returns, have discrete time-phased objectives spread over a number of years. Others seek goals that only make sense in terms of a multiyear effort, for example, the gradual expansion of medical schools in order to bring the size of the annual graduating class to a particular level. One of the major problems of budgeting has been and remains the limited period of time covered by annual budgetary decisions. PPB seeks to relate annual budget allocations to longer-term plans.

The long-term nature of most public programs calls for long-range planning. In practice, an equally important *tactical* aspect of multiyear planning has become evident. In the short run, and in particular in the annual budget process, federal agencies are captives of the past. Prior commitments, inertia, promises to an appropriations subcommittee chairman, the need to "educate" interest-group constituents about program changes, and the like, often cause rigid constraints on yearly budget decisions. In any one year, therefore, the impact that an agency head can have on his operating bureaus is limited. By concentrating solely on what can be done in each annual budget, he can achieve very little. Major changes in objectives, operating practices, and budget allocations must be accomplished in the light of longer-range goals. By requiring subordinate bureaus to prepare the annual budget within the framework of broad, long-range budget allocations, however, the agency head can exert more influence on the general course of programs in his department than he could by fighting annual budget battles under severe constraints. Long-range budget allocations will, and should, be modified from year to year. Their value is not in their immutability, but in their use as a tool of secretarial influence over his own department. However, the role and meaning of long-range planning have been among the most troublesome aspects of PPB in civilian agencies. This problem will be discussed in Chapter 5.

The fifth and crucial aim of the PPB system is the analysis of alternatives to find the most effective means of reaching basic program objectives, and to achieve these objectives for the least cost. The goal is to force federal agencies to consider particular programs not as ends in themselves—to be perpetuated without challenge or question—but as means to objectives, subject to the competition of alternative and perhaps more effective or efficient programs. Looked at another way, PPB seeks to replace, at least in part, the pernicious practice of incremental budgeting, under which the budget allocation process does not involve a review of the basic structure of programs but primarily consists in making decisions about how much each existing program is to be increased or, much less frequently, decreased. Each program cannot, of course, be reviewed from the ground up each year. But the analytic steps of PPB call for a periodic review of fundamental program objectives, accomplishments, and costs while considering the effectiveness and efficiency of alternatives.

The sixth and final goal of PPB is to establish these analytic procedures as a systematic part of budget review. PPB seeks to subject policies and programs to analysis and to integrate the decisions into the budgetary process. Two considerations encourage this integration.

First, the allocation of limited budgetary resources among competing claims can be more intelligently made if fuller information and analysis of program objectives, effectiveness, and costs are available. When relatively narrow choices are involved—such as the allocation of funds among various alternative manpower training programs—analysis can contribute directly to program decisions. But even when broader questions are being considered—such as the allocation between education and housing—analyses that present the payoffs or consequences of each program can assist the decision maker in weighing the alternatives.

Second, if it is to be more than an academic exercise, program analysis must be built into the decision-making process at each level of the decision hierarchy. By its very nature, the budget, more than any other process in the federal system, forces action. The need to formulate budget requests each year compels program decisions to be made, by the President, agency heads, bureau chiefs, and their subordinates.

These then are the aims of PPB: the specification of objectives, the evaluation of program output as it relates to objectives, the measurement of total systems costs, multiyear program planning, the evaluation of alternative program designs, and the integration of policy and program decisions with the budgetary process.

PPB as a System

The formal structure of the PPB system as it has been established in civilian agencies consists of four elements.

Program Budgeting

The activities and budgetary costs of federal programs are grouped into program categories. The literature on the desirability of these output-oriented classifications as an aid to analysis is abundant.[1] The nature of the output produced by federal agencies is the key discriminant in defining program categories and assigning individual federal activities to them. Programs whose outputs are closely related, and therefore either close substitutes or necessary complements to each other, are grouped together. Broad categories such as "health," are subdivided into subcategories, such as "development of health resources" and "prevention and control of health problems." Each of the subcategories is, in turn, further subdivided into program elements. The subcategory "prevention and control of health programs," for example, contains such program elements as "mental retardation," "radiological health," and "air pollution control."

There is nothing sacred about these program classifications. They can and should be changed as analytical need dictates. Several dif-

[1] See, for example, Charles J. Hitch, "On the Choice of Objectives in Systems Studies," P-1955 (processed; Santa Monica, Calif.: RAND Corporation, 1960), and Arthur Smithies, "Conceptual Framework for the Program Budget," in David Novick (ed.), *Program Budgeting: Program Analysis and the Federal Budget* (Harvard University Press, 1965), pp. 24–60.

ferent kinds of classifications may be needed for different analytical purposes. Their main function is to emphasize that government programs have an output, and that they should be analyzed and evaluated on the basis of how effectively and efficiently that output meets program objectives.

The set of categories appropriate to strategic planning and analysis is often quite different from the categories appropriate to the control or management efficiency functions of budgeting. A good example is found in the various classifications of the Coast Guard budget.

Appropriation categories (objects of expenditure): operating expenses; acquisition, construction, and improvements; retired pay; reserve training.

Activity schedule (types of operational processes): vessel operations; aviation operations; shore stations and aids operations; repair and supply facilities; training and recruiting facilities; administration and operational control; other military personnel expense; supporting programs.

Program budget (program outputs and objectives): search and rescue; aids to navigation; law enforcement; military readiness; merchant marine safety; oceanography and other operations; supporting services.

Since appropriations are made to the Coast Guard by type of expenditure, the budget system must provide controls to insure that obligations and expenditures stay within appropriation limits. The activity schedule is a good example of performance budgeting. It groups budgetary data by the type of operational activity and is primarily a tool of operating managers who must carry out these activities. The program budget, on the other hand, is designed to focus attention on the outputs and objectives of the Coast Guard— those objectives it seeks, and the kinds and levels of output it produces.

Program and Financial Plan

Each agency is required to submit as part of the annual budget process a multiyear (usually five years) program and financial plan according to program categories, subdivided into subcategories and program elements. Both financial costs and, wherever possible, measures of proposed program outputs are provided. In most cases the simple output measures contained in the plan are only indicators of more complicated outputs. Since the President must recommend his budget to Congress in terms of the congressionally established appropriation structure, the plan also provides a "crosswalk" that translates program costs classified by output category into individual appropriation requests.

In effect, the program and financial plan is a tabular record of an agency's proposed activities, measured in both physical and financial terms and grouped by output-oriented categories. Originally the program and financial plan was conceived as a five-year planning document, incorporating proposals for program decisions over that five-year period. In early 1967 the program and financial plan was modified for most agencies so that future financial and output data reflected only the consequences of decisions proposed for the subsequent budget.

As a hypothetical case, let us assume that the Federal Aviation Administration proposes in the 1969 budget to initiate procurement of long lead-time equipment for traffic control systems at air terminals (radars, computers, display equipment, and the like). The five-year, time-phased costs of procuring, installing, and operating the system would be included in the agency's program and financial plan. These would be the future costs of current decisions. But if the agency also believed that in 1970 a series of improvements in air navigation facilities would be desirable, the costs and outputs of this project would not be included in the current program and financial plan since a decision need not be made on the matter until the next year's budget. Thus, the program and financial plan is not a planning document in the true sense of the word since the plan does not fully reflect the agency's proposed course of action over the period covered by the plan. There are, in effect, two types of forward plans: The first covers the future budgetary consequences of current decisions—it provides an information system whereby built-in budgetary increases can be estimated, in the aggregate and by individual programs; the second projects the composition of agency programs over an extended period, including the consequences of decisions which will not be taken for several years. Such plans are, by nature, highly tentative and change periodically. But they can be an important, internal management tool through which an agency head may influence the long-range course of his department. The ambiguities and difficulties that accompany the pursuit of long-term planning will be discussed in Chapter 5.

The program and financial plan, as I mentioned earlier, includes a bridge between the program budget and the appropriation structure. From a technical standpoint this is necessary because program decisions have to be translated into specific appropriation requests. But more importantly, it turns out that it is impossible for the department head, the budget director, or the President to make decisions solely on the basis of program categories. In most civilian agencies the individual appropriations have lives of their own. The problems that arise in integrating the PPB system into the political process can be seen from the following example. In the Department of Agriculture there is a program subcategory called "agricultural production capacity," which covers those programs aimed at increasing farm efficiency and productivity.[2] Some of the activities in this subcategory are research efforts, such as control of crop-destroying pests and research into better seed strains. Most of this research is carried on by the Agricultural Research Service, which also conducts equally important research affecting other programs—nutrition and agricultural marketing and distribution, to mention a few.

Appropriations are made directly to the Agricultural Research Service—the administering agency. There is one appropriation for operating expenses and another for facilities construction. The Appropriations Committees are vitally interested in what happens to the Agricultural Research Service as an organizational entity. The committees are particularly concerned with the dispensing of operating funds to the hundreds of small agricultural research stations judiciously scattered throughout the country—stations which are often too small to be efficient. They are also interested in the facilities appropriation, both the overall size and the particular location of proposed facilities. Other research in the production capacity program category is carried out through formula grants to university agricultural experiment stations. These grants are administered by the Cooperative State Research Service, a separate organization with a separate appropriation. This service also makes grants for research in program categories other than production capacity. Here, again, a whole new set of interests—well-organized interests—affects the appropriation to the Cooperative State Research Service. It determines the fate of a particular set of institutions across the country.

The agricultural Extension Service provides another example. The service administers the federal grants-in-aid to the state agricultural extension programs. Agricultural extension activities are quite diverse, and in the program or output-oriented budget these activities are assigned to various categories, depending on the particular objective. The appropriations for all of these programs, however, are made to a single organization—the Extension Service. The size and language of that appropriation is again a matter of vital concern to the Appropriations Committees and to the well-organized agricultural extension interests, whose influence was felt by the administration several years ago when it tried to substitute direct project grants—determined on "merit"—for a small fraction of the formula grants.

[2] As a sidelight on the problems involved, a companion subcategory in the same program is labeled "farm income." This subcategory includes most of the price support programs—whose major objective is to *limit* farm production as a means of raising prices and income.

The goal of the administration was precisely to direct the extension grants toward specific program objectives, and in particular toward the alleviation of rural poverty. This attempt was defeated on grounds that the administration was seeking to seize control of program content.

Because organizations have a political importance in their own right, it has been impossible to make budget decisions solely on the basis of program categories. The allocation of budget resources cannot be decided solely on the basis of how those resources contribute to program objectives. The implicit effect of budgetary decisions on organizations remains an essential element in the decision process.

These same problems occur in almost every civilian agency. I am not simply making the point that consideration of political values must enter into major decisions on program strategy—that fact is too obvious to need comment. What is significant here is that even at the lowest level of detail, decisions about the effectiveness and efficiency of programs impinge upon the political values—and indeed the very future—of particular groups in society. This aspect of PPB is much more pervasive in most civilian agencies than in the Department of Defense. This is exemplified by the broad general structure of the Department of Defense appropriations compared to the detailed structure of appropriations for the Department of Health, Education, and Welfare.

As a consequence of this fact, PPB has not been characterized by the making of program decisions that are mechanically translated into appropriation requests. Rather, the installation of PPB has led to a parallel and interacting process under which decisions have been based on a joint consideration of program structure and appropriation structure. This should not be considered a downgrading of PPB. It simply reflects that PPB and all it entails can be an important part, but not the whole, of the decision process, no matter what level of detail is being examined.

The Program Memorandum

While the program and financial plan is a tabular record of cost and output consequences of proposed budgetary decisions, the program memorandum provides the strategic and analytical justification for these decisions. Each major program is covered by a program memorandum. Ideally, it summarizes the analytic basis for important policy and budget choices. Since every program area encompasses a multitude of individual program elements, each of which requires some budgetary decisions, the program memorandum is designed to cover only the major issues. Indeed, the number of major issues requiring analysis far exceeds the capacity of existing staffs. In areas where no analytical work has been done, the program memorandum simply identifies major decision proposals and provides a statement of why particular choices are recommended. Thus, the PPB system tries from the start to force an *explicit* statement of broad program strategy as the basis for detailed budget decisions, even where limitations on staff resources make detailed analysis impossible. This is part of the constant attempt to integrate broad policy and program decisions into the budgetary process rather than having the two proceed on separate tracks, with a forced reconciliation at the end.

Special Issues

The program memorandum, to be a useful tool of decision making, cannot incorporate the in-depth analytical studies of program issues, but can only summarize the basic program strategy, and, where relevant, the analysis on which it is based. Each year the Bureau of the Budget and the individual federal agencies jointly agree on a number of program issues for which detailed analytic studies are to be carried out. The results of these studies are themselves the subject of discussion and debate, and form the basis for program memoranda. Often these studies relate to issues that cut across many program categories—federal policy in distributing research grants among various kinds of institutions, the role of federal hospitals in improving hospital design and management, criteria for setting user charges in federal recreation areas, and so forth.

Misconceptions about PPB

Several misconceptions surround PPB and its objectives. To many people, the use of program or output-oriented categories in the budgetary process is the chief element and distinguishing characteristic of PPB. The program grouping of budgetary data is, indeed, a most important aid in the analytic decision-making process, since program budgets, when properly conceived, almost force the decision maker to think in output terms. But other elements of PPB are equally, if not more, important.

Another misconception is that there is a single "ideal" program structure. Program structures are not immutable and should be changed as circumstances change. Moreover, for the analysis of certain problems several crosscutting sets of program categories are needed. A program structure that provides across-the-board information on federal support for basic research, or on all federal funds flowing to universities, is quite useful for some purposes. But the components of these programs are also included in the mission-oriented programs of different agencies. For some purposes veterans' housing programs are viewed as veterans' benefits; for others this program must be combined with other housing programs. Program structures, therefore, need be neither unidimensional nor immutable. While the program structure is an important part of PPB, it is by no means the be-all and end-all of the system.

The effectiveness of PPB does not depend on reorganizing operating units to conform to program categories, as is often claimed. In fact, this would be harmful in some cases and impossible in others. Organizations are characterized, chiefly, by the type of operations they carry out. For efficient management this is an appropriate organizational criterion. But each organization usually contributes to several different kinds of output. To split the Agricultural Research Service into five or six components and to recombine one of those components with parts of the Soil Conservation Service just because they both contribute to raising farm productivity makes little managerial sense.

One of the most important aspects of the whole PPB system—and the one that still causes a good deal of trouble—is its relationship to the annual budget cycle within the executive. Budgetary decisions are crowded into the months of October through December. There is literally no time for extended analysis of program proposals. More important, the detailed preparation of budget requests in the thousands of bureaus, offices, and field establishments of the federal government must begin much earlier than the October–December period. Analytic studies, initial drafts of program memoranda, and basic outlines of proposed financial plans should be available by midsummer if they are to have a meaningful impact on subsequent budget formulation. Ideally, a series of major decisions would be ready in midsummer, on the basis of which detailed budgetary requests could be written. Realistically, this is impossible. No President, budget director, or agency head is likely to make decisions about the size of the poverty budget, the new housing program, or the pace of the postlunar landing effort until the overall size of the budget and the expected shape of future economic conditions are known. This information is not available in midsummer. But the availability of the results of special studies and of draft program memoranda earlier in the budget cycle are critical to the success of the system. These documents, even in draft form, can be a vehicle for isolating differences in major issues, for discovering what additional information is required, and, most important, for putting the agency head's perspective on the detailed budget requests that his subordinates send to him. For numerous reasons, however, a proper time cycle has not yet been established. In too many cases, program memoranda and special studies are available only *after* the subordinate units of the agency have submitted their budget requests to the secretary. As a consequence, they often come too late to have any impact on those requests and lose some of their effectiveness as a vehicle for critical discussion of alternative courses of action and for decisions on overall program strategy.

This, then, is the basic nature of the planning, programming, and budgeting system as it is being developed and applied in the civilian agencies of the federal government. In one sense, it is a systematic organization of the third step in the budgetary reform which began more than fifty years ago: financial control, managerial efficiency, and, now, strategic planning. But its basic aims are substantially different from those of the preceding steps. It brings both the budgetary process and the analytic problem-solving approach into the specification of objectives and the selection of alternatives among programs, and these are the very essence of the political process. Although PPB does not seek to replace the political decision-making process, it will—if successful—modify that process. And, equally, it must adapt itself to the essentially political nature of program decision making.

B

Developing a Program Budget and Tax Expenditure Budget for the Federal Government

In establishing specific objectives, the efficiency and equity rationale of various kinds of government programs should be clearly recognized. The objectives of programs which are designed to correct resource misallocation generated by the private economy should be framed in terms of the economic benefits which are to be produced. There is a need to pinpoint areas of waste and inefficiency in federal government policy and to focus attention on the potential contribution of improved budgetary procedures and policy analysis. The federal budget is the fulcrum through which national economic policies are carried out, but functional classifications of outlays contained in the budget can present a distorted picture of national priorities. The budget can be changed to provide a mechanism for making better choices of national priorities.

The readings are designed to discuss various ideas for improvement in budgetary procedures with respect to more efficient resource allocation. The first reading, "The Federal Budget Document Has Serious Deficiencies as an Instrument of Economic Policy and the Rational Allocation of Public Expenditures," by the Joint Economic Committee, discusses shortcomings in the federal budget and makes suggestions for achieving increased efficiency. The second article, "Federal Priorities and Public Sector Decision-Making," by Murray L. Weidenbaum, discusses the application of the Planning-Programming Budget technique to the entire operations of the federal government. The reading, "The Tax Expenditure Budget," by Stanley Surrey, presents the use of what is called a tax expenditure

270

budget which would provide information on the effectiveness of government expenditures.

The Federal Budget Document Has Serious Deficiencies as an Instrument of Economic Policy and the Rational Allocation of Public Expenditures*

The 5-volume Federal Budget document is the basic economic document of the Federal Government. It is virtually the only source of information concerning the cost implications of Government choices among alternative expenditure programs.

On several occasions over the past decade, the Joint Economic Committee has studied the structure and composition of the budget document. Numerous recommendations designed to improve the quality, accessibility, and usefulness of the budget as an economic document have been made.[1] In the past few years, a number of these recommendations have been implemented, resulting in an improved budget document.

The publication of the budget in several forms, with different levels of detail, has improved its usefulness to the Congress and has increased its accessibility to a wider range of interested citizens. The development of the unified budget concept, based on the report of the President's Commission on Budget Concepts, has reduced the previous confusion among the "cash," "administrative," and "national income accounts" budgets and has encouraged use of the budget as an economic as opposed to an accounting document. Further, the increased use of appendices for "special analyses" pertinent to budgetary control represents a significant improvement.

These developments notwithstanding, there are still major shortcomings in the budgetary document. Most of the committee's recommendations have not been followed. The Bureau of the Budget

---

*Joint Economic Committee, from Economic Analysis and the Efficiency of Government, Report of the Subcommittee on Economy in Government, Joint Economic Committee, 91st Congress, 2d Session, 1970, pp. 17–23.

[1] See especially, U.S. Congress, Joint Economic Committee, "Federal Expenditure Policies for Economic Growth and Stability," report of the Subcommittee on Fiscal Policy, 1958: "The Federal Budget as an Economic Document," staff study prepared for the Subcommittee on Economic Statistics, 1962; "The Federal Budget as an Economic Document," report of the Subcommittee on Economic Statistics, 1963.

appears reluctant to open up to public scrutiny any budgetary information save that directly related to either the annual budget proposal or past years' expenditures allocated to agencies and functions in "line-item" fashion. The scope of the budget document is still far too limited to enable rational consideration of economic policy alternatives by the Congress.

The primary purpose of the budgetary document is to assist Congress in allocating expenditures among alternative programs and in making decisions on other economic policy matters, such as the tax reform effort recently undertaken by the Congress. The basic characteristic of all of these decisions is that they have economic consequences. They benefit some people while imposing costs on others: they stimulate some regions of the Nation often at the expense of economic growth in others. While some of these decisions are efficient, others entail costs in excess of benefits. While some of them make the distribution of income more equitable, others do quite the opposite. If the Congress is to choose wisely among the many policy and budgetary options, it requires more comprehensive information on the economic consequences of decisions than is now available. While the current budget document itemizes Federal expenditures by agency and by functional categories, there is a great deal of necessary economic information which is either excluded from the budget document or hopelessly buried in a welter of detail.

A Program Budget

Each of the major objectives of the Federal Government is served by several programs administered by a number of executive departments. Nowhere in the budget document have the major program objectives of the Federal Government been stipulated along with the direct expenditures contributing to the attainment of these objectives, irrespective of the administering agency. Sound and rational decisions cannot be made if major elements of cost are charged to budgets which give no indication of the objective being served.[2]

While we recognize the difficulties of establishing meaningful, comprehensive, and consistent program structures, the potential improvements in economic expenditure policy from such a full pro-

---

[2] The allocation of Defense Department requirements for atomic warheads to the budget of the Atomic Energy Commission was cited in the subcommittee hearings as an example of the difficulties of sound budget policy without program budget information. Similarly, the fact that the bulk of Federal support for police training is hidden in the budget of the Veterans' Administration hinders the development of sound and rational Federal law enforcement policy.

gram budget warrant the expenditure of substantial effort toward developing such a structure. It should be emphasized that budgeting on a program basis does not require elimination of the agency line item budgets or the functional budgets. All of these budgetary formats can be linked by an appropriate "crosswalk."

Comprehensive Budget Projections

Budgetary information in the current budget document is backward looking. The budget requests of the Executive are presented to the Congress with only the past level of appropriations and expenditures as background. The effect of this form of presentation is to induce excessive emphasis on the question: "Is the budget for agency (item, function) x being increased or decreased from last year?"

Because of the absence of prospective data the Congress possesses no indication of the future expenditure consequences of policy decisions which it has already made. There is, for example, no reflection in the budget document of the enormous future expenditure commitments made by a congressional decision to appropriate the first 1 or 2 percent of the cost of new procurement and construction projects. Surely a responsible decisionmaking process requires that, at a minimum, the future budgetary implications of the decisions already taken be displayed in the basic budget document.

The subcommittee takes special note of existing legislation which requires the executive branch to present to the Congress 5-year budget projections on new programs and additional or expanded program functions involving more than a $1 million annual expenditure. Public Law 84-801, which requires such annual projections, is shown as appendix 2 to this report. While the executive has responded to the few congressional requests for such projections, it has not generally met the requirements of this law. The subcommittee reminds the administration of its responsibilities in this regard. We, in addition, urge that such 5-year projections be prepared for all programs and submitted to the Congress.

Program Overview Information

Each member of the Congress should be able to clearly discern the characteristics of the programs on which he is being asked to spend taxpayers' money. He must be able to readily determine the objectives of the program, the character of program outputs, the value of these outputs, the method by which program benefits are distributed to the people, and the characteristics of the people who are benefited or hurt by the program.

An important start toward providing this overview type information has been made by the Bureau of the Budget in its program overview study. Through this study, benefit-cost ratios are estimated for each Federal program, as well as a breakdown of the program benefits by income class, geographic region, race, and so on. In appendix 3 to this report, a sample format of a program overview sheet is presented, along with data on five individual programs.

We commend the Bureau for initiating the preparation of this data. It is long overdue. The calculations necessary to complete these tables should be made as soon as possible and for all Federal programs, and a complete display should be presented in the budget document.

A Regional Budget

The current budget document provides no information on the regional impacts of Federal spending. Without such, the Congress is seriously hindered in developing consistent national policy for regional objectives.

Moreover, because program expenditures are not broken down regionally, the priorities of localities and regions cannot influence the mix of Federal appropriations. Insofar as many Federal budgets—including those for hospital construction, pollution control, and highways, for example—are decided nationally the choice offered the locality or region is a take-the-gift-or-leave-it choice. The region is given no chance to say: "Highway project X is of relatively low priority to us, while hospital project Y is far more important." Consequently, the ability of the Federal Government to respond to the needs of localities and regions, *as the people there see these needs*, is decreased. Substantial gains would result from the formation of a regional breakdown for major portions of the budget.[3]

---

[3] In a statement presented to the subcommittee, former Director of the Bureau of the Budget Charles L. Schultze described the desirability of regional budgets combined with some grant of allocation authority to local and regional officials as follows:

"Experimentation with a limited form of regional budgeting could be very worthwhile. Tentative functional budgets could be drawn up on a national basis, just as they are now. But in each locality, Governors and mayors could be given the right, up to some limit, to propose reallocations among particular Federal aid funds flowing into their jurisdictions. They might propose, for example, an increase in funds for education and a decrease in highway grants. In effect, the final allocation of Federal budgetary funds would arise out of a joint set of considerations—national allocations based on nationwide objectives, modified by

"Tax Expenditure" Analysis

Currently, special provisions in the Federal tax structure—referred to as tax expenditures—provide $45 billion in subsidies to specific groups or activities. It is increasingly recognized that these special provisions in the tax structure entail a loss of Federal revenue and, hence, represent an expenditure of tax dollars in the same way as Federal spending. Consequently, dollars of tax expenditures have resource allocation effects similar in nature to and fully as significant as those stemming from dollars of direct spending. For example, tax expenditures in the form of the oil depletion allowance cause reallocations of labor and capital from one firm to another, from one region to another, from the production of one kind of output to another, in the same way that a Federal spending program say, the highway program, reallocates resources. Similarly, it is increasingly recognized that substantial redistributions of income can be accomplished by either mechanism.[4]

While the current budget document does classify direct expenditures by agency and function, it does not even mention tax expenditures. Needless to say, the budget provides no information on the resource allocation and income redistributive impacts of these special tax provisions.

Because of the failure of the Executive to present the detail of these tax expenditures to the Congress on a regular basis, either through the budget document or some other vehicle, congressional efforts to develop coordinated and efficient public policy are severely impeded. The difficulty of forming appropriate expenditure decisions with little direct knowledge of the costs and gains of alternatives is complicated severalfold by the nearly complete lack of knowledge on the existence, size, and economic impacts of tax expenditures. Indeed, without this information, the Congress cannot know if the economic effect of the direct spending which it is undertaking duplicates, offsets, or complements the economic effects of tax expenditures.

---

reallocations based on conditions and preferences in particular communities. Functional budgeting would be supplemented where appropriate and feasible by regional budgeting."

[4] In the hearings of the subcommittee, Budget Bureau Director Mayo quoted President Nixon as follows:

"Tax dollars the Government deliberately waives should be viewed as a form of expenditure, and weighed against the priority of other expenditures. When the preference device provides more social benefit than Government collection and spending, that 'incentive' should be expanded; when the preference is inefficient or subject to abuse, it should be ended."

In the subcommittee hearings, Stanley S. Surrey, former Assistant Secretary of the Treasury, described the need for knowledge of the economic and equity effects of tax expenditures in the following terms:

The total of these expenditures is over $45 billion. Now, $45 billion of expenditures is a large amount to be lost or misplaced. * * * Yet, these $45 billion are in a real sense lost in our Government accounts. * * * One suspects there is much waste and water in the tax expenditure budget. [They] are * * * to be classified among the uncontrollable expenditures of government. * * * When [, for example,] the government spends nearly $1 billion on buildings through * * * [tax expenditures], what is it obtaining? * * * Clearly, we are in need of applying the techniques of cost-benefit analysis and program planning to these tax expenditures, many of which have not been studied at all.

He noted that in some functional categories of the budget, tax expenditures exceed the volume of direct budget outlays—"for example, in community development and housing, the tax expenditures are nearly 200 percent of the budget outlays."

Arguments made with respect to tax expenditures apply with equal force to Federal programs which involve lending or loan guarantees and public enterprises. All of these activities involve resource allocation effects of a magnitude several times that implied by the direct appropriation or expenditure recorded in the Federal budget.

For example, a Federal program which pays a portion of the interest cost on private loans for some purpose is likely to be a relatively inexpensive program in budgetary terms. However, it is likely to induce increased borrowing and economic costs by several times the budgetary outlay of the Government. To the extent that this borrowing would not have taken place in the absence of the Government program, resources are being reallocated from their alternative uses. Much this same sort of "resource swinging" leverage is present in Federal Government loan guarantee programs. Again, rational and consistent policymaking requires that the Bureau of the Budget substantially increase the amount of economic information on the resource allocation effects of these forms of public expenditure policy in the budget document.

Subsidy Program Information

About $10 billion of annual direct Federal expenditures provide subsidy to special groups or individuals. The fact that these expendi-

tures are labelled subsidies does not argue that they are either inefficient, inequitable, or inappropriate instruments of public policy.
While some of these subsidy programs are designed to give incentive
to individuals and businesses to pursue social objectives, others
represent outright gifts or grants with no implied private response.
While some of these programs grant subsidy by directly transferring
income to the selected individuals, other subsidy programs aid the
beneficiary groups by given them valuable goods and services either
free of charge or at a price which is below cost. As we noted in the
previous section, still other Government subsidies are awarded
through special allowances in the tax system—"tax expenditures"—or
loans provided at preferential terms.

As the 1965 study of subsidy programs published by the Joint
Economic Committee noted, many of the largest and most
prominent Federal programs are providing subsidies to selected
individuals.[5] These include—

- Agricultural subsidies;
- Airport construction and navigation aids;
- Direct loan programs of several varieties;
- Insurance programs of several types;
- Navigation and irrigation facilities construction;
- Pollution control grants;
- Shipbuilding and ship operating subsidies; and
- Welfare programs.

Often as a side effect of their primary purpose, these programs
provide implicit subsidy to particular groups at the expense of taxpayers in general. For this reason, they should come under particularly close scrutiny by the Congress and the administration. As
circumstances change, the relative priority given many of these programs may be reduced and the program cut back or eliminated.
Indeed, it should be presumed that the necessity for all of these
subsidy programs should be eliminated with the passage of time.
Whatever their initial justification, these programs should be structured so as to eliminate the need for their existence in as short a time
as possible. If we fail to adapt the scope and character of each of
these subsidy programs in response to changing economic circumstances, higher priority objectives will be neglected and taxpayers
will bear an unnecessary burden.

Although considerations of efficiency in Government demand
that particularly careful and regular scrutiny be given these subsidy

[5] U.S. Congress, Joint Economic Committee, "Subsidy and Subsidy-Effect
Programs of the U.S. Government," study prepared by the Legislative Reference
Service of the Library of Congress, Mar. 31, 1965.

programs, the budget document provides no assistance whatsoever. There is no special analysis of these subsidy programs and their budgetary costs, nor is there any analysis of their future budgetary requirements, the characteristics of the people being subsidized, and the amount of subsidy which they are receiving. In fact, there are no regular reports from the Budget Bureau or any other executive agency on the economic and equity impacts of subsidy and subsidy-like programs. The executive branch and especially the Bureau of the Budget should, in the course of the budgetary process, recognize their responsibility to provide the Congress with the data and analysis necessary for informed decisions on these public subsidy programs. Improved public policy in these areas requires the clearest possible exposition of their purpose and economic effects.

Recommendations

The Bureau of the Budget, in consultation with appropriate congressional committees, should immediately undertake a major effort to expand the comprehensiveness of the budgetary document. This effort should be directed at providing, in an open and explicit form, information on economic and equity impacts of all Federal programs. This revised budget document should include, where feasible—

(*a*) A breakdown of the Federal budget by detailed, Government-wide program categories;

(*b*) Five-year budget projections for each major Federal expenditure program, describing the future implications of commitments or decisions made and proposed, of the sort required by Public Law 84–801 for new programs;

(*c*) An experimental regional budget covering those Federal programs of a grant, construction, investment, or project-type nature:

(*d*) A detailed analysis of "tax expenditures" including a functional and agency breakdown of these "expenditures"; and

(*e*) A detailed analysis of the full economic and distributive impact of subsidy and subsidylike programs, including those involving loans and guarantees.

The Bureau of the Budget should accelerate its efforts to develop a full *Program Overview* study with a view to releasing it to the Congress. When developed, this study should be updated annually and submitted to the Congress as a separate report. This study should have the general format shown in appendix 3 and include estimates of benefits, costs, and income redistributive impacts of all Federal Government programs. All new legislative proposals forthcoming from the Executive should be accompanied by the information and data shown in the format in appendix 3.

The Joint Economic Committee should, as part of its annual hearings, explicitly consider those sections in a revised budget document displaying 5-year budget projections of Federal programs, analyses of "tax expenditures" and Federal subsidy programs and, when prepared, the Budget Bureau's *Program Overview* study.

Federal Priorities and Public Sector Decision-Making*

We hear so much talk these days about priorities and the need to change them. I would like to indicate a course of action that could provide the mechanism for making more enlightened choices on national priorities. The mechanism can be developed from existing budget information.

Functional classifications of outlays as now presented in the budget contain serious limitations that can result in a distorted picture of national priorities. Also, failure to consider in conjunction with regular outlays the fast growing Federal credit programs financed outside of the budget and the numerous "tax aids" can lead to further distortions of priorities. Because of these deficiencies, the scope and magnitude of future claims on economic resources can easily be misconstrued.

Developing a Program Budget for the U.S. Government

In order to assess and compare alternative programs for fulfilling national goals, we need to consider a program budget for the entire Government. This approach builds on the Planning-Programming-Budgeting (PPB) System and attempts to fill a major remaining gap. Despite its accomplishments to date, the PPB approach is not coming to grips with the larger choices in allocating Federal funds among different agencies and programs.

"Would a dollar be more wisely spent for education or for public works?" This fundamental question is not raised (and probably cannot be answered) in the budgetary process at the present time. The current emphasis is on choosing among more specific alternatives

*Murray L. Weidenbaum, from *Remarks of the Honorable Murray L. Weidenbaum, Assistant Secretary of the Treasury for Economic Policy, Before the Economics and Allied Social Science Associations*, December 1970, pp. 1-13.

The author is indebted to Dr. Panos Konstas of the U.S. Treasury Department for assistance in the preparation of this paper.

within the education and public works categories. The choices are restricted usually to those which can be made within each of the many agencies involved in education or public works.

We also need to distinguish between the immediate purpose for which budget outlays originate and the final objective that such outlays serve. Educational allotments under the G.I. Bill owe their origin to national defense considerations; but in the end, it is the field of education to which the benefits from these expenditures should be assigned. To be sure, numerous borderline cases exist. Housing for the military, for example, serves no doubt national housing needs but at the same time contributes to the current posture of the Nation's defense capabilities.

Nevertheless, the need for another examination of budget outlays for the entire Government is there, and a classification of budget outlays according to the purpose they in effect serve will show a different picture of national priorities from that in the current budget. Moreover, an analysis of this kind makes it possible to evaluate the various items in each priority category and thus to assess the relative efficiency of each item.

From available material we can develop a hypothetical Government-wide budget wherein each expenditure is classified according to the end purpose, or final goal, of that expenditure. This is in contrast to present budget practices whereby expenditures of different types are grouped usually according to the broad functions of the receiving agency or program.

Table 1 presents such a Government-wide budget for the fiscal year 1971.[1] The total budget is divided into four broad categories. In a world of critical international tensions, the initial purpose that comes to mind is the protection of the Nation against external aggression—to maintain the national security. A variety of Federal programs exists in this category, ranging from our own military establishment, to bolstering the armed forces of other nations, and to negotiating arms control agreements.

A second basic national purpose, one also going back to the Constitution, is the promotion of the public welfare. Here, we find the Federal Government operating in the fields of unemployment compensation, social security, veterans' pensions, and many other such activities.

---

[1] The procedure for calculating Table 1 was to classify each appropriation in Part 5 of *The Federal Budget for the Fiscal Year 1971* (Federal Program by Agency and Account, pp. 191–523) according to its end purpose. The data are on a budget authority basis which includes both new obligational authority and loan authority.

TABLE 1
Hypothetical Government-Wide Program Budget
Fiscal Year 1971

Category	Total Amount (Billions of Dollars)	Percent of Total
National Security		
U. S. Military Forces	68.2	29.3%
U. S. Passive Defense	.1	*
Foreign Military Aid.	.5	0.2
Foreign Non-Military Aid	1.9	0.8
Scientific Competition	3.3	1.4
Psychological Competition	.3	0.1
Arms Control	—	—
Total	74.3	31.8%
Public Welfare		
Insurance and Retirement	60.8	26.1%
Unemployment Benefits	4.0	1.7
Public Assistance	9.0	3.9
Veterans Benefits.	7.4	3.2
Aid to Farmers and Rural Areas	8.0	3.4
Urban Housing and Facilities	3.7	1.6
Specialized Welfare	1.2	0.5
Anti-Poverty Programs	1.5	0.6
Total	95.6	41.0%
Economic Development		
Natural Resources and		
Regional Development	10.1	4.3%
Manpower Development	1.7	0.7
Transportation Facilities	13.1	5.6
Education and Research	4.2	1.8
Health Research.	5.3	2.3
Business Subsidies	.9	0.4
Total	35.3	15.1%
Operations		
Interest	19.0	8.2%
Legislative Function	.4	0.2
Judicial and Law Enforcement	1.3	0.6
Economic Regulation	.3	0.1
Housekeeping	2.5	1.2
Foreign Relations.	1.2	0.5
General Aid to States and Localities	.3	0.1
Total	25.0	10.9%
Allowances	2.6	1.1%
GRAND TOTAL	232.8	1C0.0%

*Less than $50 million
Source: Developed from data in *The Budget of the U.S. Government—Fiscal Year 1971*

A third major purpose of Government programs has received an increasing amount of attention in recent years—the continued development of the American economy. This area covers the various programs to develop our natural resources and transportation facilities, as well as support of education, health, research and development, and other attempts to increase economic growth. A comparatively small portion is devoted to the economic development items, about 15 percent of the total budget.

Finally, there is the routine day-to-day operation of the Government, such as the functioning of the Congress and the Federal courts and the collection of revenue.

When we examine the budget and congressional appropriation hearings over the years, we find little, if any, systematic attempt to appraise the wisdom or desirability of these overall choices implicitly made in the allocation of Government resources. It may be mere conjecture to conclude that the allocation of funds would possibly have been different if the appropriation requests had been reviewed with an eye on the total picture, as shown in Table 1, instead of examined as individual appropriation items in isolation.

National Security

The greater part of the national security budget is devoted to the U.S. military forces. However, one-tenth of the total is comprised of programs that would promote the national security through more indirect means, such as conducting nonmilitary forms of competition (NASA and USIA) or increasing the military capabilities of friendly nations.

This programmatic approach lends itself to raising and answering questions such as the following:

(a) Would national security be improved by shifting some or all of the $5.7 billion for foreign aid and nonmilitary competition to the U.S. military establishment itself?

(b) Conversely, would the national security be strengthened by moving a relatively small share of the direct military budget, say $500 million, to the USIA or arms control effort and thereby obtaining proportionately large increases in these latter programs?

(c) Are we putting too much into foreign economic aid and not enough into the space program? Or vice versa?

(d) Would the Nation be better off if we shifted some of the funds now going to passive (civil) defense to the Arms Control and Disarmament Agency? Or vice versa?

The very existence of the type of information presented here may lead not only to attempts to answer questions such as these but, more fundamentally, to widen the horizons of budget reviewers.

Public Welfare

It may come as a surprise to many people to learn that public welfare, rather than national security, receives the largest single share of the budget. Over two-fifths of the 1971 budget is devoted to programs in this general area. Most of the funds in this category consist of appropriations to the Department of Health, Education, and Welfare. The rest are brought together from activities of other agencies such as the Defense Department (retired military pay and family housing for the military), the Labor Department (unemployment trust funds), the Veterans Administration (veterans' pensions), and Agriculture (farm price supports).

The various life insurance, unemployment compensation, and retirement programs receive the great bulk of the funds for public welfare—over three-fifths. However, this is hardly a conscious decision. The level of expenditure for these programs—such as the old-age, survivors and disability insurance system—is predetermined by basic, continuing statutes; they are financed by permanent, indefinite appropriations which are not subject to review during the budget process because they do not even appear in the annual appropriation bills.

The expenditures under the various agricultural price support programs (which dominate the category of "Assistance to Farmers and Rural Areas") exceed all of the outlays for the programs of urban housing, antipoverty, and other specialized welfare activities combined. Again, the farm subsidy program is generally set by the substantive laws on price supports and farm aid, rather than through annual appropriations.

This level of detail permits some cross-comparisons of Government programs which are not currently made. For example, the $1.5 billion for formal efforts to reduce poverty in the United States is less than the $1.9 billion for foreign economic aid. Would some trade-off between the public welfare and national security areas result in a net advantage?

Economic Development

In this exploratory categorication of Government programs, a number of activities are listed under the heading, "Economic Development." Transportation facilities account for the largest single share and when combined with natural resource and regional development account for almost two-thirds of the total. Most of these activities will no doubt contribute to the more rapid growth of the U.S. economy. The contribution to economic development of certain others such as subsidies to business may be less certain.

At any rate, a Government-wide program budget can be useful for questions such as these: "Would a shift of funds between transportation and education be advisable? Between natural resources and research?" Raising these questions need not be taken as expressing value judgments, but rather as indicating a new pattern for governmental decison-making.

Government Operations

The final category of Government programs represents the general costs of operating the Government, the relatively day-to-day functions. More than three-quarters of the funds in this category cover the payment of interest on the public debt. The bulk of the remaining outlays for Government operations is devoted to collecting internal revenue and the housekeeping activities of the General Services Administration.

Further Applications

If this sort of analysis were incorporated in the annual budget document, it could result in growing congressional and public concern and awareness of the problems of choosing among alternative uses of Government funds. In the absence of an automatic market mechanism, such an approach might introduce a healthy degree of competition in governmental resource allocation.

Alternatively, a congressional staff could rework the existing budget submissions within this framework for use by the entire Appropriations Committee prior to its detailed examination of individual appropriation requests. This would permit the appropriation committees to set general guidelines and ground rules for its detailed budgetary review. It would also permit some improvement over the current situation, in which overall Government policy often seems to be the accidental byproduct of budget decisions on the various departmental requests—rather than the guiding hand behind those decisions.

The underlying theme of this program approach to government budgeting is the need to array the alternatives so that deliberate choices may be made among them. It has its counterpart in the private sector. Many families might rush out and spend the Christmas bonus for a new car; a more prudent family may carefully, although subjectively, consider the relative benefits of a new car, a long summer vacation, or remodeling the basement. Similarly, a well-managed company would not impulsively decide to devote an increase in earnings to raising dividends, but would consider in detail the alternative uses of the funds—embarking on a new research program, rebuilding an obsolescent manufacturing plant, or developing a new overseas operation.

Still another application of this approach is to detect and evaluate changes in priorities. Although data prior to fiscal 1971 are not provided here, it can be established that between the fiscal years 1969 and 1971 public welfare has been the major area of expansion; it received 38 percent of the total appropriations in 1969, and it is expected to receive 41 percent of the total in 1971. Economic development and Government operations show significant but lesser expansions between 1969 and 1971. In contrast, the portion for national security declined from 40 percent to 32 percent in the two-year period.

Accounting for Government-Related Activities

Thus far, the analysis of governmental priorities has been limited to items contained in the budget. The analysis can be further refined and improved by taking into account two other types of Government-related programs that at present are not included in the budget proper. These programs, nevertheless, represent large claims on economic resources and therefore have considerable impact on the question of priorities.

Governmental Credit Programs

The first category of such items consists primarily of Federal credit assistance programs which currently are funded outside of the budget. This financing is accomplished by means of various loan guarantee techniques and loans made by Federally-sponsored but ostensibly privately-owned agencies.

Of the $22 billion increase in Federal loans outstanding for the fiscal year 1971, only $1 1/2 billion are direct loans which show up in the budget. For the $20 billion of Federally-assisted credit programs which are not contained in the budget, there is little overall consideration given to their impact on financial markets and on the economy.

The largest single category of Federally-assisted private credit is to the home mortgage market. This is accomplished through a variety of mechanisms—such as mortgages insured by the Federal Housing Administration, the Veterans Administration, and the secondary market for FHA mortgage lenders operated by the Federal National Mortgage Association (Fanny Mae).

So long as Federally-assisted loans and loan guarantees are excluded from the budget and thus are not subject to effective control, there are strong incentives to convert from direct loans to these more indirect techniques.

However, any comprehensive analysis of governmental priorities needs to take account of the operation of these Federally-assisted credit programs. They can strongly influence the allocation of credit and hence the distribution of real resources, thus adding to the economic impact implied from an examination limited to the budget proper.

One way of providing some control over these credit programs would be to impose a ceiling on the total borrowing of Federal and Federally-sponsored credit agencies, both those "in" and those "out" of the budget. Also, a ceiling could be enacted on the overall volume of debt created under Federal loan guarantees.

Tax Aids

The second type of governmentally-related activities (also excluded from the budget) includes special exemptions, deductions, and credits in our tax system. These items affect the economy in ways that could be accomplished by direct Government spending. For example, the expenditure side of the budget properly records items for medical assistance. However, nowhere in the budget is account taken of the $105 million a year foregone in fiscal 1971 by the tax system by reason of the special exemption for sick pay.

The natural resource agencies of the Federal department, such as the Interior Department, dutifully record outlays for programs in those areas. However, no mention is made of the $1.3 billion in assistance to natural resource industries through depletion allowances and other special tax provisions. It may be useful, therefore, to quantify the expenditure equivalents of at least the more obvious benefit provisions. To be sure, this is a difficult undertaking involving many arbitrary categorizations.

It is difficult to decide which tax rules are integral to a tax system in order to provide a proper measure of net income—as opposed to those provisions which provide relief or assistance to a particular group or activity. Tax aids have the outward appearance of involving no Government costs. They are, in effect, netted out of receipts by the taxpayers themselves so that taxes paid by taxpayers, and hence taxes collected by the Government, are net after adjustment for tax concessions. However, there is a very real cost to the Government in terms of foregone revenue and to the economy as a whole in terms of the increased share of current national output available to the beneficiary of the particular tax aid.

A tax aid for our purposes will be defined as the difference between the tax actually paid and the tax that would be paid in the absence of the tax aid. It must be made clear, however, that the mere tabulation of tax aids should not be labeled a listing of "loopholes." The purpose of the tabulation is to illuminate the cost of these provisions rather than to raise a question about tax equity. As a general matter, I find the case rather persuasive for using tax incentives as a means of solving certain national problems through the private sector rather than through direct Federal expenditures.

Clearly, however, tax aids are one among alternative uses of potential Federal revenues, and any comprehensive analysis needs to take account of them.

Table 2 shows the impact of Federal credit programs and tax aids on national priorities.[2] In 1971 housing is the largest beneficiary of Government-assisted credit. Agriculture and rural development is also a major recipient of Federally-assisted credit from the Government-owned agency Farmers Home Administration and three Government-sponsored agencies, the Banks for Cooperatives, the Federal Intermediate Credit Banks, and the Federal Land Banks. Both credit aid to housing and to farmers are in the area of public welfare in our hypothetical Government-wide budget layout.

Smaller but significant amounts of Federal credit aid are also directed toward export credit and education, the latter in the form of student loans and loans for college housing.

On the question of tax aids, we find that over half of such aids are related to public welfare activities (see Table 2). These include a whole series of deductions from taxable incomes such as interest on home mortgages, state and local taxes, charitable contributions, as well as payments relating to retirement and pension plans.

Tax provisions benefiting business in general—such as the since-repealed investment credit and the continuing surtax exemption—are another large type of tax aid. The estimated cost of these provisions in terms of foregone revenue is $9 billion in the fiscal year 1971.

Benefits directed to state and local governments in the form of deductibility of state and local taxes, interest on municipal debt, and related provisions come to an estimated revenue cost of $7.9 billion in 1971.

The variations in governmental priorities can be perceived by bringing together the direct outlays of the Federal Government, the tax aids, and the various credit programs as shown in Table 2. There are, of course, pitfalls in adding the proverbial apples and oranges—although those do add up to pieces or pounds of fruit. At least in this

---

[2] Amounts on Government-assisted credit are on net basis, i.e., intra-agency holdings of loans are not included in the data.

TABLE 2

Hypothetical Government-Wide Program Budget and Related Activities
Fiscal Year 1971
(In billions of dollars)

Category	Direct Outlays	Government Assisted Credit	Selected Tax Aids	Total
National Security				
U. S. Military Forces.	68.2		0.5	68.7
U. S. Passive Defense	.1			.1
Foreign Military Aid	.5	*		.5
Foreign Non-Military Aid	1.9	1.8	0.4	4.1
Scientific Competition	3.3			3.3
Psychological Competition.	.3			.3
Arms Control				
Total	74.3	1.8	0.9	77.0
Public Welfare				
Insurance and Retirement	60.8		6.6	67.4
Unemployment Benefits	4.0		0.4	4.4
Public Assistance	9.0		0.1	9.1
Veterans Benefits.	7.4	1.9	0.6	9.9
Aid to Farmers and Rural Areas . . .	8.0	3.4	1.0	12.4
Urban Housing and Facilities	3.7	11.9	6.0	21.6
Specialized Welfare	1.2		9.9	11.1
Anti-Poverty Programs	1.5			1.5
Total	95.6	17.2	24.6	137.4
Economic Development				
Natural Resources and Regional Development	10.1	*	1.3	11.4
Manpower Development	1.7			1.7
Transportation Facilities	13.1	0.1	0.1	13.3
Education and Research	4.2	1.1	1.4	6.7
Health Research	5.3	0.1	3.2	8.6
Business Subsidies	.9	0.5	6.2	7.6
Total	35.3	1.8	12.2	49.3
Operations				
Interest	19.0			19.0
Legislative Function	.4			.4
Judicial and Law Enforcement	1.3			1.3
Economic Regulation	.3	*		.3
Housekeeping	2.5	0.1		2.6
Foreign Relations	1.2			1.2
General Aid to States and Localities.	.3		7.9	8.2
Total	25.0	0.1	7.9	33.0
Allowances	2.6			2.6
GRAND TOTAL.	232.8	20.9	45.6	299.3

*Less than $50 million

Sources: For Direct Outlays, *The Budget of the U.S. Government—Fiscal Year 1971;* for Government Assisted Credit, *Special Analyses—Budget of the United States* (Analysis E); for Tax Aids, Treasury Department—Office of Tax Analysis

case they all add up in terms of dollars—although not necessarily in terms of total economic impact. There are undoubtedly different effects on resource allocation among direct Federal purchases, transfer payments, loans, tax aids, and credit-backing. Nevertheless, "summing up" for the purpose of understanding better the nature of governmental priorities is well justified.

In a number of cases, Federal outlays constitute a relatively small proportion of the total volume of governmentally-related financial activity affecting a given program area. A prime example of this is urban housing and facilities where, in fiscal year 1971, $3.7 billion of Federal funds are appropriated. But the assistance through $6 billion of tax aids and $12 billion of Federally-assisted credit boosts the total in this area to nearly five times the budget amount. Other program areas where the extra-budget activities are very substantial

TABLE 3

The Changing Order of Government Priorities
(Fiscal Year 1971)

Individual Program	Budget appropriations only	Budget plus credit aids	Budget plus credit & tax aids
U. S. Military Forces	1	1	1
Insurance and Retirement	2	2	2
Interest	3	4	4
Transportation	4	5	5
Natural Resources	5	7	7
Public Assistance	6	9	10
Aid to Farmers and Rural Areas	7	6	6
Veterans Benefits	8	8	9
Health	9	10	11
Education and Research	10	11	14
Unemployment Benefits	11	12	15
Urban Housing and Facilities	12	3	3
Scientific Competition	13	14	17
Allowances	14	15	18
Housekeeping	15	16	19
Foreign Non-Military Aid	16	13	16
Manpower Development	17	17	20
Anti-Poverty	18	18	21
Judicial and Law Enforcement	19	20	22
Specialized Welfare	20	21	8
Foreign Relations	21	22	23
Business Subsidies	22	19	13
Foreign Military Aid	23	23	24
Legislative Function	24	24	25
Psychological Competition	25	25	26
Economic Regulation	26	26	27
General Aid to States and Localities	27	27	12
U. S. Passive Defense	28	28	28

Source: Table 2

include agriculture, business, and state and local governments. However, in the case of national defense, the direct outlays account for virtually all of the program area.

Another way of looking at priority changes is to examine relative standings of individual programs after taking account of Government-related activities not in the budget. The changes are significant but not drastic. Table 3 ranks (in terms of dollar amounts) the individual programs before and after the introduction of credit and tax aids. The most conspicuous move appears to be in the housing category which goes from 12th to 3rd place. General aid to state and local governments rises from next to last place to 12th, and specialized welfare moves from 20th to 8th. In contrast, several major categories experience some diminution in implicit priority. Health drops from 9th to 11th, education from 10th to 14th, and natural resources from 5th to 7th.

However, the two largest categories—national defense and insurance and retirement—remain securely in first and second places with or without the credit and tax aids.

Concluding Comments

This presentation offers several analytical techniques for improving the quality of Federal decision-making. As we look at the decade ahead, it seems clear that many difficult and important decisions and choices will face national policy-makers. Even in an economy as rich and productive as ours, resources are limited. Claims on output must be balanced against the economy's capacity to produce. As always, there will be a satisfaction of some demands over others. Hopefully, these choices will reflect national priorities and changes in priorities. However, any enlightened attempt to reorder and establish priorities cannot take place until we possess a clear understanding both of the existing general ordering of priorities and the nature of the possible choices to be made.

Our inferences regarding the nature of underlying priorities changes significantly as credit and tax aids are taken into account. In particular, the area of public welfare appears to be preempting a much larger share of Government outlays, direct or indirect, than may be generally appreciated. Moreover, the analysis of a Government-wide program budget points to certain implications about changes in national priorities in the years ahead. The budget document for fiscal 1971 goes at some length to discuss the budget controllability problem. But Federal credit programs and certain tax aids are capable of preempting future economic resources as well and thus, perhaps inadvertently, commit the Nation to specific priorities.

In some future reformulation, it might be desirable to give different dollar weights to transactions such as Government-sponsored credit activities compared to expenditures within the budget. However, even within the budget, purchases and transfers would not be expected to register the same economic impact, dollar for dollar.

Development of a Government-wide program budget, enabling us to evaluate choices which cut across existing agency and program lines, would be a valuable asset to our decision-making efforts. In addition, bringing such "extra-budgetary" items as Federal credit assistance and Federal tax aids into the analytical framework would enable us to have a more complete accounting of the existing order of Federal priorities.

The pressure of competing demands and the need for exercising hard choices makes this process difficult enough without further complicating matters by the absence of adequate information. Hopefully, improvement in the quality of our information can lead to improvement in the quality of our decisions.

The Tax Expenditure Budget*

Just what is the tax expenditure budget? The annual report of the Secretary of the Treasury, for the fiscal year 1968, contained for the first time an exhibit entitled "the tax expenditure budget." This exhibit provided a conceptual analysis of tax expenditures, followed by a classification of existing tax expenditures and the revenue amounts involved. The tax expenditures so analyzed, simply stated, are expenditures of Government funds that are made through the special provisions contained in the income tax laws.

I believe some quotations from the Treasury report will serve to describe both tax expenditures and the Treasury analysis:

> As every taxpayer knows, income tax laws and regulations are complex. Much of the complexity derives from the numerous deductions, exemptions, credits, and exclusions allowed taxpayers in stipulated circumstances. Many, probably most, of these provisions exist because of the belief that they are directly related to the measurement of net income appropriate to an income tax.
>
> But others appear in the tax code because of the belief that

---

*Stanley Surrey, from *Economic Analysis and the Efficiency of Government*, Hearings Before the Subcommittee on Economy in Government, Joint Economic Committee, 91st Congress, 1st Session, 1970, pp. 82–91.

while not required to measure net income, the provisions promotes some other objective, such as economic growth or a desirable expenditure pattern by taxpayers.

In many areas the influence of the tax code on private economic behavior through these special tax provisions is of an amount which approaches and, in some instances, surpasses that of direct Government expenditures directed to the same objective.

Each of these special tax provisions reduces Government revenues available for other purposes, much as do increases in direct Government expenditures. In most cases, direct expenditures or loan programs exist as alternatives for achieving the same purpose that the special tax provisions are designed to accomplish. Our Federal budget as presently constituted, however, does not report those tax revenues which the Government does not collect because income subject to tax is reduced by these special provisions and the various special credits, deductions, exclusions, and exemptions which they provide. The budget in its present form thus understates the role of Federal Government financial influences on the behavior of individuals and businesses and on income distribution.

As a consequence of these special provisions in the tax system (some provisions are in the statutory tax law and others appear in regulations and rulings), the personal and corporate income tax bases deviate in numerous ways from widely accepted definitions of net income. Numerous kinds of income are excluded from taxation altogether while others are included only in part. Various types of expenditures by households give rise to deductions which are subtracted from income.

These special tax provisions and adjustments have been controversial in varying degree at varying times. In many cases, differences of opinion persist as to whether or not the effects of these deviations on income distribution and resource allocation are desirable. This special analysis is not concerned with the desirability of these provisions. Rather, it lists the major respects in which the current income tax bases deviate from widely accepted definitions of income and standards of business accounting and from the generally accepted structure of an income tax, together with estimates of the amount by which each of these deviations reduces revenues. It also arrays these tax provisions in the functional categories under which direct expenditures are classified in the Federal budget.

The purpose of this analysis is to present information on the basis of which each of these special tax provisions and their revenue cost can be compared with other such provisions which entail a reduction in revenues, and with direct expenditures or loan programs which result in outlays of a similar magnitude. The inclusion of such information, in addition to the ordinary budget accounts, can clarify and present more fully the role of the Federal Government in various functional areas. This information cannot presently be obtained from either the budget documents or the Statistics of Income published by the Internal Revenue Service . . .

. . . The special tax provisions take many forms. Under some, certain types of incomes are excluded from taxation, a few examples being interest on State and local government bonds, half of realized long-term capital gains, social security benefits to the aged, and employer payments for fringe benefits, such as hospitalization, surgical, and group life insurance premiums. Other special tax provisions are in the form of deductions for certain personal expenses, such as charitable contributions, medical expenses, and interest payments.

Other special deduction provisions allow business expenditures in excess of actual cost (percentage depletion, certain bad debt reserves) or earlier in time than the cost would become an expense under business accounting (agriculture, research and development, exploration and discovery of natural resources). Other special provisions provide a lower effective tax rate than is generally applicable, such as the lower statutory rate on Western Hemisphere trade corporations and the lower ceilings rate on long-term capital gains. Still other provisions take the form of tax credits (retirement income credit, investment credit).

Most of these special tax provisions are designed expressly to achieve objectives similar in nature to those of direct Government expenditures or loan programs. In each functional area, the Federal budget includes direct Government expenditures, direct Government loans, loans insured by the Government, and loan subsidies which have similar though perhaps not identical objectives. In each of these areas, such direct spending or loan programs would be an alternative method to accomplish the purpose which the special tax provision seeks to achieve or encourage.

We can examine several of these tax provisions to indicate how "tax expenditures" are alternatives to direct expenditures or Government lending programs. As a first illustration, consider the provisions which benefit the aged. The Federal budget lists under the functional category of "health, labor and welfare" large direct expenditures including the social security and medicare trust funds for the aged. But the budget contains no item to show the $2.3 billion expended through the tax system to aid the elderly through the retirement income credit, the additional $600 exemption, and the exclusion of social security retirement benefits. The same assistance could be achieved by additional transfer payments to the aged rather than by tax provisions ...

... Direct expenditures for natural resources, as another example, are itemized in the budget but no items are presented to cost out the assistance the tax system provides these industries by permitting the expensing of certain capital costs, the use of percentage depletion in excess of cost depletion, and special capital gains treatment for timber and for iron ore and coal royalties. Direct expenditures could be tailored to achieve the same purpose as these expenditures through the tax system. For example, subsidies might be paid to encourage exploration and development of selected minerals or good forest management. (Annual Report of the Secretary of the Treasury, Fiscal Year 1968, pp. 326–328.)

This Treasury analysis, which related to the fiscal year 1968, was updated in a special submission made by the Secretary of the Treasury to the Joint Economic Committee on January 17, 1969 in its hearings on the Economic Report of the President. It was there stated:

> Tax expenditures are not disclosed in the budget and therefore are not subject to careful annual scrutiny in the budget and appropriation process. Budget outlay decisions, on the other hand, involve the departments and agencies, the Bureau of the Budget, the House and Senate program committees which are competent and experienced in their specialized fields, and the appropriation committees. Tax expenditures are not generally considered by the program departments and congressional committees concerned, and are not reviewed annually or periodically to measure the benefits they achieve against the amounts expended.
>
> The purpose of this analysis is to present information which compares tax expenditures with direct expenditures or loan programs in various functional areas and thus to clarify and present more fully the role of the Federal Government in these areas. Such a comparison should be helpful in the allocation of public resources. (Hearings before the Joint Economic Committee on the Economic Report of the President, 91st Cong., first sess. [Jan. 17, 1969], p. 32.)

The Treasury analysis presented for the various budget categories—national defense, agriculture, natural resources, commerce and transportation, community development and housing, and so on, and for a special category not listed as such in the budget—though included in a special analysis—aid to State and local government financing—the amounts expended through the regular budget for these categories and the amounts expended through the tax system. The comparisons are interesting and revealing. In some categories, the tax expenditures exceed the budget items; for example, in community development and housing, the tax expenditures are nearly 200 percent of budget outlays; in commerce and transportation, 110 percent. In other categories, the tax expenditures are also significant; in natural resources, about 90 percent; health and welfare, about 36 percent. In only two categories, national defense and veterans, is the figure less than 10 percent.

I have attached to this statement copies of the material in the Treasury report and the submission to the Joint Economic Committee.

This then, is the concept of tax expenditures and the Treasury analysis of existing tax expenditures in the form of a tax expenditure budget. (The substance of my testimony today is that a tax expenditure budget is feasible and useful.) I, therefore, believe it should be a continuing task of the Treasury Department to prepare this tax expenditure budget annually.

The tax expenditure budget should be included as a regular item in the Annual Report of the Secretary of the Treasury and in the budget document, perhaps as a special analysis. I believe that the tax expenditure budget and such regular public presentation will contribute to economic and other analysis of tax expenditures and these in turn will contribute to efficiency and economy in Government.

Feasibility of Preparing a Tax Expenditure Budget

Let me first consider the feasibility of preparing a tax expenditure budget. As stated above, this Treasury analysis is the first presentation that has been made of this category of Government expenditures. Since it has been made public, I have heard no basic criticism of the presentation or the data.

To be sure, there are conceptual aspects involved, as the analysis itself describes. It is necessary to separate the special tax provisions— the "tax expenditures"—from the basic structure of the income tax. Here the analysis uses the standard of "the generally accepted measure of net income"—or, phrased another way, "widely accepted definitions of income and standards of business accounting and . . . the generally accepted structure of an income tax"—as the guidelines to separate the customary structural provisions from the special tax provisions.

Thus, matters such as personal exemptions, rates, and income splitting allowed for married couples filing joint returns are considered as part of the structure of an income tax based on ability to pay and therefore do not involve tax expenditures. Similarly, deductions necessary to the computation of business or investment net income are part of the structure of an income tax. But exemptions, deductions or credits that lie beyond the customary determination of net income—for example, excessive depreciation, percentage depletion, expensing of capital costs, exemption of State and local bond interest—are special provisions and thus involve tax expenditures.

These standards enable us readily to classify most of the income tax provisions. There are some residual items on which there can be difficulty or disagreement in the classification, but this aspect is minor in comparison to the large body of information made available by the tax expenditure budget.

There are also some problems associated with the estimates required. These problems largely stem from the incompleteness of the underlying data, and the continued task of analysis and estimate would serve to produce more complete data. The estimates, parenthetically, are "first level" figures, that is, they involve the revenue that would be obtained from a change in the tax provisions involved without anything else being changed. Hence, the estimates do not involve predictions of what taxpayers would have done in the light of change. Budget estimates of direct expenditures also do not involve the second-level effects of the expenditure itself, or its absence.

Continued refinement of the tax expenditure analysis would develop useful explanatory material to indicate this difference between first- and second-level effects.

Further analysis would also develop a more refined allocation of some tax expenditure items among the budget classifications. Thus, individual capital gains in the Treasury analysis are placed in a separate heading, since the existing data did not permit an appropriate allocation of the large amount involved—$5 1/2 billion to $8 1/2 billion—among the activities in the various expenditure categories, such as agriculture, natural resources, commerce and transportation, housing and community development, and health and welfare. The capital gains special provisions cut across all these fields. While the use of a special heading avoids the task of allocation, it also results in an understatement of tax expenditures in those categories in which capital gains are significant, such as commerce and transportation.

Continued attention to the analysis of tax expenditures would improve that analysis, just as continued attention to the budget has improved the concepts and data underlying that document. The important fact for the present is that the Treasury analysis demonstrates that present data and analysis do make feasible a helpful classification and estimate of tax expenditures in the form of a tax expenditure budget.

Given the feasibility of a tax expenditure budget, what is its utility?

Information on Tax—and Government—Expenditures

The first aspect to be stressed in considering the utility of the tax expenditure budget is that of information. The total of these tax expenditures is over $45 billion. Now, $45 billion of expenditures is a large amount to be lost or misplaced in Government accounts. Yet, this $45 billion are in a real sense lost in our Government accounts—they do not show in the budget and they do not appear, for the most part, in Treasury Statistics of Income. Until the Treasury analysis was published, the data were not available to the public—and not comprehended within Government. No one really knew what was being spent through the tax system and for what purposes.

The fact that Government expenditures are actually over 20 percent higher than the current budget figures of $190 billion—and revenues also higher—is highly important. So also is the fact that the Government is actually spending three times the budget figures to assist community development and housing and twice the budget figures on commerce and transportation and national resources. If direct expenditures of these amounts had been omitted or mislaid, the budget would certainly be discredited. Yet, tax expenditures are a form of Government expenditures and their existence is as important as direct expenditures for budgetary purposes. But until now, these tax expenditures have in effect been the hidden expenditures of Government.

It seems obvious that we should have current and detailed information on these tax expenditures. The tax expenditure budget would provide this information.

Economic Analyses of Tax Expenditures

Once we have the information on tax expenditures—the activities affected and the amounts involved—we can proceed to a wide variety of studies. Essentially, these studies would relate to the efficiency of Government. We should be finding out just what the Government is obtaining in return for the $45 billion or more spent through the tax system.

When Government spends nearly a billion dollars on buildings through excessive tax depreciation and capital gains, what is it obtaining—how many additional buildings, of what types, in what areas? Are these buildings—which include office buildings, hotels, motels, shopping centers and the like—the types of buildings on which we should be spending Government funds?

When Government spends over $1 1/2 billion through the tax system on natural resources, what is it obtaining in the way of additional exploration and reserves; what kinds of minerals are involved and in what places are they located?

When Government spends over $1 1/2 billion through the tax system on agriculture, what activities and what areas are being aided? And are they in need of that aid?

When Government spends nearly $2 1/2 billion through the tax system for relief of the aged, just which of the aged are receiving these funds and how much in need are they?

We really know very little about the answers to questions such as these, questions which can be asked about each of our tax expenditures. Clearly, we are in need of applying the techniques of cost-benefit analysis and program planning in these tax expenditures, many of which have never been studied at all. Examples of relevant studies are the recent CONSAD cost-benefit study of tax expenditures for oil and gas and the econometric studies of the investment credit, which were done for the Treasury Department.

It is to be expected that the tax expenditure budget, by providing information on the activities and amounts involved, will prompt the necessary studies. It is also to be hoped that the various Government departments and agencies involved would themselves become more curious about these matters and seek to raise the relevant questions and then to answer them. At present, the department generally take the view that since it is not in "our budget," we needn't think about the expenditure or seek to ascertain whether it is in the public interest.

This, of course, is the real question—are these expenditures in the public interest? In many cases the question has barely been raised or debated, let alone answered. Some of these tax expenditures came quietly into the tax law decades ago through administrative rulings where the focus was on the exigencies of tax administration and not on expenditure policy.

Moreover, the amounts involved were small and the resource allocation aspects not perceived or then significant. Others were adopted by Congress years ago in much the same fashion. Only infrequently was there a deliberate desire to achieve a given public purpose through the allocation of resources. Yet today, many of these provisions are now defended in public policy expenditure terms, but unfortunately without any accompanying analysis and evaluation. The need for such analysis and evaluation is obvious.

Promotion of Efficiency of Government

The Treasury analysis calls attention to the consequences for efficiency of Government that are involved in a tax expenditure budget. It points to this statement in the 1966 Economic Report of the President:

> In a fully employed economy, special tax benefits to stimulate some activities or investments mean that we will have less of other activities. Benefits that the Government extends through direct expenditures are periodically reviewed and often altered in the budget-appropriation process, but too little attention is given to reviewing particular tax benefits. These benefits, like all other activities of Government, must stand up to the tests of efficiency and fairness. (Treasury Report, p. 327.)

It then goes on to state:

It is clear, however, that more efficient use of resources by the Federal Government is advanced if explicit account is taken of all calls upon budget resources, so that the importance of different budgetary objectives and the effectiveness of alternative uses, whether through direct expenditures, loan subsidies, or tax expenditures, may be fully understood, examined, and reevaluated periodically. (Treasury Report, p. 328.)

One aspect of increased efficiency would lie in the basic re-examination of the amounts now being spent through tax expenditures—a total that is over 50 percent of the Defense Budget. One suspects there is much waste and water in the Tax Expenditure Budget. It must be remembered that these tax expenditures are generally open-ended, in that the total to be spent is not predetermined, but instead depends on the degree of taxpayer activity. These tax expenditures are thus to be classified among the uncontrollable expenditures of Government, along with such items as interest on the public debt. But they need not be uncontrollable; they are simply presently just structured that way.

One also suspects that many of these tax expenditures would be framed much differently if cast as direct expenditures. Government would then be far more interested in what it is receiving for its outlays. The traditions respecting scrutiny, review, and skepticism are different for direct expenditures than for tax expenditures.

Another aspect of increased efficiency would lie in greater co-ordination between direct expenditure policy and tax expenditure outlays. At present, the various legislative committees of Congress and the Appropriations Committees legislate, determine, and co-ordinate our spending programs. But they have no jurisdiction over the tax expenditures.

In turn, the tax committees largely formulate the tax expenditures without any coordination with the legislative committee having jurisdiction in the areas involved or the Appropriations Committees. The tax expenditure really operate as back-door financing of the activities involved.

This lack of coordination can only make for inefficiency and waste. The priorities in our regular budget programs do not appear to be reflected in our tax expenditures. The priorities—if that term can be applied to what has developed largely by happenstance—of our tax expenditures are not the priorities of our regular Budget. Nor has the expertise regarding substantive programs that lies within Government, legislative and executive, really been applied to tax expenditures.

A third aspect of increased efficiency would lie in the coordination of tax expenditures with overall Government expenditure policy. When the Congress or the President, or both, determine overall expenditure limits, those limits are applied to the regular budget programs. But the tax expenditures are immune from these limits. Hence, regular programs must often be cut back when a rational view of overall priorities and programs would have produced instead a reduction or slowdown in some of the tax expenditure programs.

Yet, had these tax programs been structured as direct expenditures, they would have no such immunity. In substantive terms, they do not merit that immunity any more than direct expenditures, yet their tax clothing serves to shield them. We have learned as respects the more traditional expenditure techniques that as long as any form of Government assistance is out side the purview of the Budget—be it a loan an interest subsidy, or a guaranty—that the absence of periodic review inevitably makes for waste and inefficiency and misdirection of resources. We now have to apply that learning to tax expenditures.

Alternative Methods of Government Assistance

I would like to relate tax expenditures and the above comments to the subject of tax incentives and tax credits. We recognize that Government can allocate resources and assist activities through a variety of monetary techniques. It can use direct grants of money; it can lend money; it can guarantee loans; it can subsidize interest rates; it can purchase assets.

The Tax Expenditure Budget points to another alternative—the reduction of the tax liabilities of particular taxpayers through special tax provisions. In a given area, Government thus may use the traditional methods of assistance, or it may use a tax expenditure. The reverse is even more important—where the Government is giving assistance through a tax expenditure, it could give that assistance directly and need not resort to the tax system.

Therefore, once it is decided that Government assistance is to be given—and this decision is, of course, a basic prerequisite—then the question arises, how should that assistance be structured? Should it be framed as a direct expenditure, using one or more of the techniques available for that purpose? Or should it be framed as a tax expenditure?

In recent years it has been the fashion to suggest the use of tax incentives or tax credits as solutions to many of our urban and social problems—pollution control, manpower training of the unskilled and semiskilled, the establishment of new businesses in the inner cities and depressed rural areas, and so on. These tax incentives or credits involve additional tax expenditures. They thus give rise to the difficulties I have described regarding existing tax expenditures. These difficulties, to say the least, would appear to be persuasive reasons militating against the use of tax incentives and credits for such purposes.

Much more could be said on this subject. My only purpose here is to relate current policy problems and issues to the tax expenditure budget.

Recent examples of tax incentives underscore the need for caution and analysis before adding additional tax expenditures. Thus, the legislative committees have struggled long and hard to find the most efficient ways to expend Government resources in the battle against pollution.

There are many claimants for Government dollars, and those concerned about combating pollution have found it difficult to secure the funds they desire. Interested legislators speak of scrounging a few more millions here or there to add to an inadequate budget figure. Yet now, at one stroke, the Ways and Means Committee decides to spend $400 million (by 1974) in the pollution control area by allowing 5-year tax amortization of the cost of installing pollution control facilities. But the committee does not refer to any study which indicates that—if the Government is to allocate an additional $400 million to pollution control—the particular device and particular approach chosen by the Ways and Means Committee would have top priority. Instead, $400 million is allocated to this purpose without any coordination with other planning or expenditures in the pollution control area and without regard to what are the priority needs once it is decided to add $400 million to pollution control expenditures.

There are other examples in the current tax bill, for example, assistance to housing and to production of railroad cars. Here also many millions of dollars are to be spent through the tax system, again without study, without coordination with other programs, without any determination of the competing priorities for Government funds. This back door, almost haphazard financing, is totally antithetical to efficient and orderly program planning.

Conclusion

The tax expenditure budget is a necessary part of the Government's fiscal accounts. It should be published on an annual basis by the Treasury Department and included in the general budget, perhaps as a special analysis. The items in the tax expenditure budget should be carefully studied and cost-benefit analyses made in appropriate cases. Such an approach to the tax expenditure budget and its components is bound to promote greater efficiency in Government and stronger control over expenditures.

IV

Federal Expenditures and National Priorities

A

The Public Welfare System

There is widespread agreement that there is a need to reform the welfare system in the United States. Basically, criticism of the welfare system centers around two main points: first, there are too many programs in existence, some of which duplicate each other. Secondly, there is a need to reach many needy persons who are not touched by the existing welfare programs. There is also concern over the lack of uniformity in welfare payments among states, and the increase in the cost and the number of persons on welfare.

The two readings are designed to present the characteristics of the welfare system and also proposals for welfare reform. The first reading, "Development of the Current Welfare System," has two purposes. The first purpose is to present a chronological description of how the welfare system developed and expanded over the years, and the second purpose is to present a description of the various programs which are in use. The second reading, "Summary of Provisions of the Social Security Amendments of 1971," represents the welfare reforms which have been developed by the House Ways and Means Committee. These reforms, which include the Nixon Family Assistance Plan, represent primarily the work of Chairman Wilbur D. Mills.

Development of Current Welfare System*

In general terms, governmental assistance programs in the United States can be divided into two types of programs. One type limits benefits to those who can establish need by satisfying a means test. The other type is broader in purpose and more general in coverage. It includes, for example, programs such as social security, medicare, unemployment compensation, various education programs and subsidies, all of which distribute their benefits broadly to many who are not poor as well as many who are. The administration's welfare reform proposal is concerned with the first type of program.

The largest of the need-related welfare programs is categorical public assistance for the blind, disabled, needy aged, and families with dependent children. Other programs that distribute benefits on the basis of need are (1) medicaid for the indigent and "medically indigent," (2) certain food and nutrition programs, (3) nonservice-connected pensions for wartime veterans, and (4) low-rent public housing and rent supplements. Benefits under these programs take the form of direct cash payments or benefits-in-kind (e.g., indirect or vendor payments for services, merchandise payments, and direct provision of commodities).

Categorical Public Assistance

America's system of federally-aided public assistance originated with the Social Security Act of 1935. Prior to that time, the needs of the poor had been met by private charities or by state and local governments (which included requirements that relatives, who were able, must provide assistance) and federal concern with welfare problems had been limited to specific emergencies or major disasters.

The public assistance titles of the 1935 act established a federal-state partnership in welfare wherein federal matching grants, financed from general revenues, are made available to states on a matching basis for cash payments to specified categories of the needy. The original act authorized grants for three categorical programs, old age assistance (OAA, Title I), aid to dependent children (ADC, Title IV), and aid to the blind (AB, Title X). It also established a related program of grants for maternal and child health and welfare services (Title V).

---

*American Enterprise Institute, from Welfare Reform Proposals (Washington: American Enterprise Institute, 1971), pp. 3-13.

Those poor who did not meet the criteria for any of the federal categorical programs received assistance, if any, from state or local general assistance programs (e.g., "home relief" in New York). Benefits varied not only from jurisdiction to jurisdiction but within jurisdictions depending on the availability of funds and the attitude of the controlling body at the time (e.g., city councils, county commissioners).

Although the new public assistance program violated the long standing principle of state responsibility for welfare, it generated little opposition at the time. It was adopted as an emergency or stop-gap measure to meet the immediate needs of specific categories of indigents (elderly, blind or children deprived of support due to the death, continued absence, or incapacity of a parent) at a time when the states were unable to do so. Later, it was viewed as a residual program that would tend to wither away as the contributory social insurance programs established by the Social Security Act took hold and eliminated certain causes of indigency. Old age insurance, the predecessor of OASDI (Old Age Survivors Disability Insurance), was expected eventually to assume much of the burden of supplying a floor of retirement income for the aged. Unemployment insurance was intended to provide a measure of income support during periods of short-term unemployment. The latter two programs were the controversial parts of the 1935 act. Neither required indigency as a condition of eligibility.

Program Expansion

At the outset federal matching was limited to 50 percent of cash assistance payments of up to $30 monthly for the aged and the blind, and to one-third of payments for dependent children of up to $18 monthly for the first child in a family and $12 for each additional child. In December 1936, at the end of the first year of operation, there were 1,107,649 recipients in old age assistance, 43,608 in aid to the blind, and 52,716 in aid to dependent children.

Since then, public assistance has been expanded in various ways. Up until the early 1960s congressional action concentrated primarily on liberalizing the federal matching formula in an effort to raise the level of cash benefits paid by the states. Thus the 1939 Social Security amendments increased federal matching for ADC from one-third to one-half, thereby bringing it into line with the formula applicable to benefits for the aged and the blind. Subsequently, in 1946, 1948, 1952, 1958, 1961, 1962, and finally in 1965, the level of federal sharing and the reimbursable limits were progressively increased for all three programs (and for the aid to the disabled program from 1952 on). Also the 1958 amendments introduced a variable matching scale of 50 to 65 percent for the federal share, under which states whose per capita income is below the national average receive more favorable matching than states with above average per capita income.

In addition, the 1950 amendments established a new categorical program of grants for the permanently and totally disabled (APTD, Title XIV), sometimes called AND. Secondly, they inaugurated federal sharing in vendor payments for medical services to the indigent.

The 1950 amendments also authorized an optional earnings exemption for aid to the blind, an exemption that was made mandatory for all states in 1952. Subsequently, optional earnings exemptions were authorized for the needy aged (1962) and for the disabled and dependent children under 18 (1965).

Beginning in the early 1960s, congressional emphasis in public assistance shifted to efforts designed to decrease caseloads by increasing the self-sufficiency of recipients. More specifically, it shifted to ADC. By this time, old age assistance had indeed begun to wither away as more of the aged population came under the coverage of OASDI. The number of OAA recipients had declined from a 1950 high of 2.8 million, despite a steady increase in the number of aged persons. The aid to the blind caseload was down slightly from a peak of 109,800 in 1958, and the year-by-year increases in recipients of aid for the permanently and totally disabled were moderate. But the ADC program had grown from 1.2 million recipients in 1949 to 2.2 million in 1950 and 3.1 million in 1960. Moreover, the nature of the ADC caseload had changed. What had begun as a "widows' and orphans' program" had become largely a program for families whose father was absent due to desertion, separation, divorce, illegitimacy, or imprisonment.

The new emphasis was foreshadowed in 1956 when provision was made for 50 percent federal matching for rehabilitation services. However, the real turning point occurred with the Social Security amendments of 1962. Those amendments (1) changed the name of the program from Aid to Dependent Children to Aid to Families with Dependent Children, (2) authorized 75 percent federal matching for prescribed services and rehabilitation programs, (3) provided for the development of community work and training programs, optional with the states, that included child care services and earnings exemptions to cover work expenses, and (4) extended to 1967 the optional program of aid to families with an unemployed parent (i.e., AFDC-UF, sometimes called AFDC-U) that had been enacted on a temporary basis in 1961. States using the unemployed parents option had to require participants to register with public employment offices and to accept bona fide job offers from employment offices or employers.

At the time of the 1962 amendments the number of AFDC recipients had grown to 3.7 million. By 1967 the number was approaching 5 million.

In the 1967 public welfare amendments to the Social Security Act, Congress fashioned a combination of incentives, services, and penalties designed to move as many AFDC recipients as possible into training or work.

1. It made the AFDC-UF program permanent, though still optional with the states, and defined unemployment more precisely so that the program would not become a catchall.

2. As a work incentive, it replaced the dollar-for-dollar offset of earnings against benefits in AFDC with a system that exempts the first $30 of earnings plus one-third of additional earnings for the purposes of determining eligibility and payments. This change lowered the marginal tax rate for AFDC from 100 percent to 66 2/3 percent.

3. It authorized the Work Incentive Program (WIN) under the Department of Labor to replace previous work and training programs operated under provisions of the Social Security Act (Title IV) and the Economic Opportunity Act (Title V). WIN entailed expanded work training (with 80 percent federal matching), mandatory referral for training or work of "appropriate" AFDC adults (including the mothers of preschool children not needed at home), training incentive payments of $30 a month, and more funds for day care facilities (with 75 percent federal matching).

4. It ordered the so-called "AFDC freeze" which limited further federal financial matching after June 1968 to payments only for the number of children receiving aid as of January 1968.

5. It authorized federal grants for emergency assistance to families with needy children and for a voluntary birth control program.

The provisions of the 1967 amendments went into effect at various times up to July 1, 1969—except for the "AFDC freeze," which was repealed in 1969 by the 91st Congress.

Program Characteristics

Policy outlines set forth in the Social Security Act of 1935 have survived, with only minor modification, to the present day. First, public assistance is a categorical program—it makes no provision for general relief to needy people who do not fit its categories. In the

1930s, general relief was handled as an emergency matter directly from Washington through the Federal Emergency Relief Administration and the Works Progress Administration. Later, in 1943, when the federal government got out of the business of direct relief, the combination of economic recovery, wartime manpower demands, and growing state-local revenues made it unnecessary to develop a federal-state program for general assistance. Thus, general noncategorical assistance had remained a state responsibility, and coverage varies.

Second, the public assistance titles are enabling legislation. The decision to operate a program lies with the states—and, to a degree, so does the determination of who is eligible for benefits, how much can be granted, and under what conditions. Third, the programs are administered by local governments or the states (under the authority of state laws)—with the proviso, however, that administrative responsibility be lodged in a single state agency operating under a federally-approved statewide plan. Fourth, the authorization is open-ended and thus expands automatically to cover the federal matching obligation resulting from the increase in eligible applicants, rising benefit levels, and program additions.

In recent years, the areas of state discretion have been greatly reduced as a result of HEW regulations and court decisions. Nevertheless there continues to be wide disparity from state to state in program coverage, administrative practices, and benefit levels. For example, out of 54 jurisdictions, only 25 operate the optional AFDC-UF program and only 17 have emergency assistance programs as authorized in the law. Nevada has no program of aid to the disabled. Many states have adopted the optional earnings exemptions for old age assistance, aid to the disabled, and AFDC children under 18, but others have not. Under the WIN program, there are great state-to-state differences in work referral procedures for "appropriate" AFDC adults and in-training program availability. As to the latter the "special work" project provision in WIN has only been implemented in a meaningful way in one state.

With respect to eligibility (assets and status), some states put no restriction on the value of a recipient's home while others restrict it to $3,000 or less; some exempt $1,000 worth of personal property and others less than $500; and some have made payments where there is cohabitation with a man who is not a lawful spouse, others in practice have tended to ignore it, and some have made it an automatic ground for ineligibility. Moving from the state down to the local level of administration, local officials and caseworkers have considerable discretion in applying regulations governing eligibility, benefits, and services. The report of the Heineman Commission quotes as follows from a 1968 study of welfare administrations in Los Angeles:

> Depending upon where the recipient lived, and the office he or she was served by, he would have anything from a 15 to 92.3 percent chance of obtaining funds for a needed refrigerator. The greatest range appears to be in providing supplementary funds for child care should the mother be working. There the gap is 81.3 percentage points, from a low of 10 percent to a high of 91.3 percent. Chance and statistical error cannot account for such a variation in practice, nor for the routine spreads of from 60 to 70 percentage points in most items.

Benefit levels also vary substantially from program to program and state to state. In November 1970, the average monthly payment under the adult program was $75 per recipient for OAA, $102.55 for the blind, and $94.25 for the disabled. Under AFDC it was $48.35 per recipient and $183.40 per family. In OAA, average payments per recipient ranged from $169.55 in New Hampshire down to $48.55 in Mississippi. In AFDC they ranged from roughly $71 per recipient and $235 per family in Alaska, Massachusetts, New Jersey, and New York to $12.10 per recipient and $46.50 per family in Mississippi.

Currently, federal assistance grants for the aged, blind, and disabled (and those adult categories as combined under Title XVI) are distributed under a complex formula providing a federal share equal to $31 of the first $37 in monthly payments per recipient, plus 50 to 65 percent of the remaining state payment (with the percentage depending on state per capita income) up to a $75 statewide average. Comparably, the basic matching formula for AFDC provides for federal shares amounting to $15 of the first $18 for each recipient, plus the variable percentage share of the balance up to a limit of $32, multiplied by the number of recipients.

Public assistance distributed cash benefits to an average monthly caseload of 10.2 million in 1970, up from 8.9 million in 1969. Federal outlays in 1970 were $6.6 billion, up from $5.7 billion. (Table 1 gives actual figures for outlays, beneficiaries, and average payments in fiscal 1970 and estimated figures for fiscal 1971 and 1972.)

The caseload continued to grow throughout 1970. On March 11, 1971 Secretary of HEW Elliot Richardson decried "the rise of some two million persons on the nation's welfare rolls over the past year—from 11.6 million in February 1970 to 13.5 million last November." (His figures include the federal categorical programs and general assistance.) Table 2 shows the increase in recipients, outlays and average payments from November 1969 to November 1970.

TABLE 1
Outlays, Recipients, and Average Payments for Public Assistance FYs 1970-72

	Outlays (millions)			Number of recipients (thousands)			Monthly payments per recipient[a]		
	1970 actual	1971 est.	1972 est.	1970 actual	1971 est.	1972 est.	1970 est.	1971 est.	1972 est.
Public assistance payments —federal share									
Old age assistance	$1,242	$1,509	$ 1,666	2,048	2,098	2,169	$51	$60	$64
Aid to the blind	56	60	62	80	83	84	58	60	62
Aid to disabled	528	662	797	798	940	1,070	55	59	62
AFDC	2,034	3,002	3,719	7,270	9,119	10,837	23	27	29
Emergency assistance	8	10	12	11	11	12	60	81	85
Total payments	$3,868	$5,243	$ 6,257	10,207	12,250	14,172			
Federal share									
Add: state and local share	2,777	3,797	4,720						
Total	$6,645	$9,040	$10,977						

[a] Averages based on total payments, including state and local contributions.

Source: Special Analyses; Budget of the United States, 1972 (Washington: U.S. Government Printing Office), Table L-14.

TABLE 2

Changes in Public Assistance: Recipients, outlays, and payments[a] per recipient, November 1970 and November 1969

Program	November 1970	November 1969
RECIPIENTS OF MONEY PAYMENTS:		
Old-age assistance	2,073,000	2,067,000
Aid to the blind.	80,600	80,400
Aid to the permanently and totally disabled . .	918,000	794,000
Aid to families with dependent children:		
Families	2,475,000	1,826,000
Recipients	9,390,000	7,124,000
Children	6,849,000	5,288,000
General assistance:		
Cases	521,000	408,000
Recipients	1,014,000	824,000
ASSISTANCE PAYMENTS (In 000's):		
Total	$1,296,172	$1,019,454
Money payments, total	761,408	589,740
Old-age assistance	155,573	151,582
Aid to the blind	8,269	7,898
Aid to the permanently and totally disabled.	86,500	70,640
Aid to families with dependent children . . .	453,916	318,697
General assistance	57,150	40,923
Medical assistance, total	493,448	406,224
Federally aided	485,513	400,777
General assistance	7,935	5,447
Emergency assistance	1,110	1,239
Payments to intermediate care facilities	40,206	22,251
MONEY PAYMENTS PER RECIPIENT:		
Old-age assistance	$ 75.05	$ 73.35
Aid to the blind.	102.55	98.25
Aid to the permanently and totally disabled . .	94.25	89.00
Aid to families with dependent children:		
Average per family	183.40	174.50
Average per recipient	48.35	44.75
General assistance:		
Average per case	109.60	100.25
Average per recipient	56.35	49.65

[a]Payments are averages based on total payments including state and local contributions less deduction for income, etc.

Source: Public Assistance Statistics, November 1970 (National Center for Social Studies, NCSS A2, HEW), p. 8.

Other Need-Related Assistance Programs

The largest of the benefit-in-kind programs that is related to need began 20 years ago. The 1950 amendments to the Social Security Act authorized, for the first time, federal sharing in vendor payments made to doctors, nurses, and health care institutions for the treatment of persons receiving public assistance. In 1960, in an attempt to increase state spending for the medical care of the aged, the Kerr-

Mills amendments liberalized federal matching for vendor payments under OAA (Title I, amended) and established a separate grant program of medical assistance for the aged (MAA, Title XVI) to provide for the "medically indigent." The Kerr-Mills program has now been replaced by parts of both medicaid (for the medically indigent) and medicare (for the elderly), enacted in 1965.

Nonservice-connected cash pensions are paid to wartime veterans and their survivors on the basis of established need, the amount depending on income from other sources and the number of dependents. In addition, the federal government provides cash assistance to Cuban refugees and to Indians.

Food and nutrition programs whose benefits are need-related include surplus commodity distribution (authorized by Section 416 of the Agricultural Act of 1949), the food stamp program (begun on a permanent basis with the Food Stamp Act of 1964), as well as smaller programs for school lunches, special milk, and OEO emergency food assistance. Federal efforts to subsidize low-income households by providing public housing whose rent is below its economic rent began during the depression of the 1930s and evolved into their present form through a succession of housing acts, and last one in 1968. Rent supplements to enable low-income families to afford private housing were begun in 1966 under the Housing and Urban Development Act of 1965. The families pay 25 percent of their income toward the rental rate. Approximately 1/4 of the families also receive welfare.

For these programs, as for federally-aided public assistance, accessibility and benefit levels tend to vary widely from program to program, state to state, and person to person. For example, food stamps, public housing, and rent supplements do not independently serve the most destitute because they require the recipient to pay cash. Medicaid does—but in 22 states, only if applicants are eligible for public assistance. In general, the poor veteran is permitted to have greater resources and earnings without jeopardizing his relief status than the non-poor veteran. Similarly, a poor child in the core city has less chance of receiving a free school lunch than an equally poor child outside the core city, and the probabilities of poor families receiving housing relief differ considerably from state to state.

Federal outlays for these need-related programs were $13.9 billion in 1970 and are estimated to be $17.2 billion in 1971 and $19.1 billion in 1973. (For detailed figures, see Table 3.)

As indicated at the outset of this section, a number of other federal programs provide services and aid to poor or low-income persons and families. Among them are welfare services, legal services,

TABLE 3

Outlays and Beneficiaries for Selected Need-Related Programs

	Benefit outlays (millions)			Number of beneficiaries (thousands)		
	1970 actual	1971 estimate	1972 estimate	1970 actual	1971 estimate	1972 estimate
Benefits-in-kind						
Food and nutrition:						
Food stamps	$ 551	$ 1,490	$ 1,941	4,300	9,000	11,000
Child nutrition	379	673	667	20,594	26,055	26,055
Special milk	102	102	14	16,700	16,700	0
Removal of surplus commodities	519	487	527	29,853	32,278	31,919
OEO emergency assistance	39	31	22	1,200	950	650
Health care:						
Medicare	6,783	7,868	8,597	20,000	20,300	20,600
Medicaid (federal outlays)	2,612	3,072	3,216	11,658	13,787	15,747
Medicaid (state and local payments)	(2,460)	(2,912)	(3,081)	...	...	...
Housing:						
Public housing	433	616	752	2,780	3,100	3,453
Rent supplements	19	44	88	79	162	297
Home ownership and rental housing assistance	22	152	448	339	1,390	2,736
Other programs	181	203	213	800	858	920
Proposed legislation included above	...	(13)	(−801)	...	...	...
Subtotal	11,641	14,738	16,485			
Cash benefits						
Veterans pensions:						
Veterans	1,351	1,391	1,439	1,105	1,075	1,050
Survivors	903	1,001	1,087	1,744	1,829	1,896
Total, veterans pensions	2,255	2,392	2,526	2,929	2,904	2,946
Assistance to refugees	50	64	90	76	93	115
General assistance to Indians	16	34	37	36	64	70
Subtotal other cash benefits	2,321	2,490	2,653			
Total benefits, cash and in kind	13,962	17,228	19,138			

Source: Special Analyses, Budget of the United States, 1972 (Washington: U.S. Government Printing Office).

TABLE 4

Federal Aid to the Poor by Activities

(in billions of dollars)

Category	1968 actual	1969 actual	1970 actual	1971 estimate	1972 estimate
Income security	10.2	11.3	13.2	17.1	19.2
Cash benefits	(9.6)	(10.4)	(11.8)	(14.3)	(15.7)
In-kind benefits	(.6)	(.8)	(1.4)	(2.8)	(3.4)
Education	1.5	1.5	1.8	2.1	2.2
Health	3.8	4.7	5.7	6.3	6.8
Manpower	1.4	1.4	1.6	1.9	2.0
Other	.6	.6	.7	.9	.9
Total	17.6	19.5	23.0	28.3	31.1

medical services, special education programs, and manpower training. Programs of this type are excluded here because their purpose is not income support for the needy and/or because their means limitations are less exacting than those of the need-related programs. Nevertheless they are an important part of overall federal aid to the poor. Tables 4 and 5 set forth the aggregate amounts of federal resources that are estimated to be directed to the needs of the poor. Table 6 shows the combined benefits available to a female-headed family in Chicago.

TABLE 5

Federal Aid to the Poor by Analytical Categories[a]

(in billions of dollars)

Category	1968 actual	1969 actual	1970 actual	1971 estimate	1972 estimate
Poverty entitlement	8.1	9.2	11.3	15.1	17.4
Human investment	(2.9)	(2.8)	(3.1)	(3.8)	(4.1)
Maintenance	(5.2)	(6.4)	(8.2)	(11.2)	(13.2)
Normal entitlement	9.5	10.4	11.6	13.2	13.8
Human investment	(.7)	(.8)	(.9)	(1.0)	(1.0)
Maintenance	(8.8)	(9.6)	(10.7)	(12.2)	(12.8)
Total	17.6	19.5	23.0	28.3	31.1

[a]This table distributes federal outlays for the poor by eligibility criteria. Poverty entitlements include programs such as Medicaid, food stamps, and public housing directed to the poor specifically by reason of their poverty. Normal entitlements include programs from which the poor receive benefits for reasons other than poverty, such as social security benefits which the poor receive because they have an earnings history. Human investment programs include all federal activities that actively promote the development of work skills, education, economic development, and similar activities to assist the poor to break out of poverty. Maintenance programs comprise both cash and in-kind payments such as public assistance and food stamps.

Source: (Tables 4 and 5) Special Analyses, Budget of the United States, 1972 (Washington: U.S. Government Printing Office).

TABLE 6

Benefits Available to 4-Person Female-Headed Families in Chicago, Ill. under Current Law

Earnings	AFDC[a]	Benefits potentially available to 82 percent of AFDC recipients in Chicago					Benefits potentially available to 18 percent of AFDC recipients in Chicago			Total
		Total gross cash income	Total Federal, State, and social security taxes[bcd]	Net cash income	Current schedule[e] food stamp bonus*	Total net cash and food	Current public housing bonus[f]	Total net cash, food and public housing	Average vendor payment to health services** for AFDC families[g]	
$0	$2,976	$2,976		$2,976	$480	$3,456	$840	$4,296	$790	$5,086
$720	2,976	3,696	$ 35	3,661	360	4,021	840	4,861	790	5,651
$1,000	2,976	3,976	48	3,928	312	4,240	840	5,080	790	5,870
$2,000	2,590	4,590	96	4,494	288	4,782	840	5,622	790	6,412
$3,000	1,923	4,923	144	4,779	288	5,067	840	5,907	790	6,697
$4,000	1,256	5,256	332	4,924	288	5,212	840	6,052	790	6,842
$5,000	589	5,589	567	5,022	288	5,310	840	6,150	790	6,940
$6,000		6,000	837	5,163	…	5,163	960[h]	6,123	…	6,123
$7,000		7,000	1,074	5,926	…	5,926	(i)	5,926	…	5,926
$8,000		8,000	1,318	6,682	…	6,682	(i)	6,682	…	6,682
$9,000		9,000	1,527	7,473	…	7,473	…	7,473	…	7,473

*Less than 40 percent of the poor nationwide currently receive some form of food benefits.
**Medical vendor payments do not represent cash income available to families and should not be counted as part of total family income. Such payments are made on behalf of families with medical needs only. The AFDC maximum payment level for a 4-person family ($3,156) is adjusted here to $2,976 because public housing rent is less than the maximum AFDC rent allowance.
aState supplement is based on the following maximum payments: New York City, $3,756 (adjusted to $3,576 for rent as paid to public housing); Chicago, $3,156 (adjusted to $2,976 for rent as paid to public housing). Work-related expenses were based on estimated state averages of $708 in Illinois, $900 in New York.
bFederal tax based on current schedule, including surcharge.
cState tax based on current schedule.
dSocial security tax based on 4.8 percent of earnings up to $7,800.
eFood-stamp bonus based on value of food-stamp allotment less purchase price.
fPublic housing bonus calculated on the basis of the value of equivalent private market rentals less the maximum rent allotment for AFDC recipients ($90 in Chicago and $105 in New York).
gMedicaid benefit shown is the average benefit for all AFDC families in state. Individual families may receive more or less depending upon medical needs. State eligibility standards apply.
hBonus in areas above AFDC breakeven as families move from welfare to nonwelfare rent schedules.
iAbove continued occupancy limits, but families may be allowed to stay until other housing is located.

Source: Information provided by HEW to Senate Finance Committee, Finance Committee Hearings, 1970, p. 1031.

Summary of Provisions of H.R. 1,
*The Social Security Amendments of 1971**

Chairman Wilbur D. Mills (D., Ark.), Committee on Ways and Means, Announces Action of Committee on H. R. 1, "The Social Security Amendments of 1971"

Chairman Wilbur D. Mills (D., Ark.), Committee on Ways and Means, House of Representatives, today announced that the Committee has completed decisions on H.R. 1, the Social Security and welfare reform bill which has been under consideration, and that the Committee today ordered the bill reported to the House with an amendment which strikes all the original language and substitutes new language on all titles of the bill. It is expected that the Committee report will be filed May 26, 1971.

A summary of the major provisions of H.R. 1 as ordered reported to the House follows:

I. Provisions Relating to the Social Security Cash Benefits Program

[omitted]

II. Provisions Relating to Medicare, Medicaid, and Maternal and Child Health

[omitted]

III. Provisions Relating to Assistance for the Aged, Blind, and Disabled

The existing Federal-State programs of aid to the aged, blind, and permanently and totally disabled would be repealed, effective July 1, 1972, and a new, totally Federal program would be effective on that date. The new national program is designed to provide financial assistance to needy people who have reached age 65 or are blind or disabled and would be established by a new Title XX of the Social Security Act. The program would be administered by the Social

*Committee on Ways and Means, from H.R. 1, "The Social Security Amendments of 1971," May 1971, pp. 87-101.

Potential Fiscal Year 1973 Costs of H.R. 1
(In billions of dollars, negative amounts indicate decreases)

	Federal			State and local			Net cost to all governments
	Current law	H.R. 1	Net cost	Current law	H.R. 1	Net saving	
Payments to families.	$3.9	[1]$5.8	$1.9	$3.3	$3.1	-$.2	$1.7
Less savings from public service jobs	. . .	-.3	-.3	. . .	. . .	. . .	-.3
Subtotal	3.9	5.5	1.6	3.3	3.1	-.2	1.4
Payments to adult categories	2.2	4.1	1.9	1.4	1.4	. . .	2.0
Cost of cash assistance	6.1	9.6	3.5	4.7	[2]4.5	-.2	3.3
Federal cost of Hold Harmless provision .	. . .	1.0	1.0	. . .	-1.0	-1.0	. . .
Food programs	2.3	.7	-1.6	. . .	. . .	. . .	-1.6
Cost of maintenance payments.	8.4	11.3	2.9	4.7	3.5	-1.2	[4]1.7
Day care.	.4	.9	.5	. . .	. . .	. . .	.5
Training.	.2	.5	.3	. . .	. . .	. . .	.3
Public service jobs	. . .	.8	.8	. . .	. . .	. . .	.8
Supportive services	. . .	.1	.1	. . .	. . .	. . .	.1
Administration	.4	[3]1.1	.7	.4	. . .	-.4	.3
Cost of related and support activities. . .	1.0	3.4	2.4	.4	. . .	-.4	2.0
Total cost of program	9.4	14.7	5.3	5.1	3.5	-1.6	3.7
Impact on medicaid	. . .	.1	.1	. . .	.1	.1	.2
Grand total	9.4	14.8	5.4	5.1	3.6	-1.5	3.9

[1] Includes only 6 months of payments to families in which both parents are present, neither is incapacitated and in which the male parent is not unemployed. The effective date for this provision is Jan. 1, 1973.
[2] Assumes that the States, through optional supplemental programs, maintain benefit levels including the value of food stamp bonuses.
[3] Allows for the extra expense of start-up costs in the 1st year of the program.
[4] Represents increased payments to recipients.

Security Administration through its present administrative framework and facilities.

The eligibility requirements and other legislative elements of the new program are as follows:

Eligibility for and amount of benefits. Individuals or couples could be eligible for assistance when their monthly income is less than the amount of the full monthly payment.

Full monthly benefits for a single individual would be $130 for fiscal year 1973; $140 for fiscal year 1974, and $150 thereafter. Full monthly benefits for an individual with an eligible spouse would be $195 for fiscal year 1973, and $200 for fiscal year 1974 and thereafter. Benefits would not be paid for any full month the individual is outside the U.S.

The Secretary would establish the circumstances under which gross income from a trade or business, including farming, is large enough to preclude eligibility (net income notwithstanding). In addition, people who are in certain public institutions, or in hospitals or nursing homes getting medicaid funds, would be eligible for benefits of up to $25 a month. People who fail to apply for annuities, pensions, workmen's compensation, and other such payments to which they may be entitled would not be eligible.

Definition of income. In determining an individual's eligibility and the amount of his benefits, both his earned and unearned income would have to be taken into consideration. The definition of earned income would follow generally the definition of earnings used in applying the earnings limitation of the social security program. Unearned income would mean all other forms of income, among which are benefits from other public and private programs, prizes and awards, proceeds of life insurance not needed for expenses of last illness and burial (with a maximum of $1,500), gifts, support, inheritances, rents, dividends, interest, and so forth. For people who live as members of another person's household, the value of their room and board would be deemed to be 33 1/3 percent of the full monthly payment.

The following items would be excluded from income:

1. Earnings of a student regularly attending school, with reasonable limits.

2. Irregular earned income of an individual of $30 or less in a quarter and irregular unearned income of $60 or less in a quarter.

3. The first $85 of earnings per month and one-half above that for the blind and disabled (plus work expenses for the blind). The first $60 of earnings per month and one-third above that for the aged.

4. The tuition part of scholarships and fellowships.

5. Home produce.

6. One-third of child-support payments from an absent parent.

7. Foster care payments for a child placed in the household by a child-placement agency.

8. Assistance based on need received from certain public or private agencies.

9. Vocational rehabilitation allowances.

Exclusions from resources. Individuals or couples cannot be eligible for payments if they have resources in excess of $1,500. The following items would be excluded from resources:

1. The home to the extent that its value does not exceed a reasonable amount.

2. Household goods and personal effects not in excess of a reasonable amount.

3. Other property which is essential to the individual's support (within reasonable value limitations).

4. Life insurance policies (if their total face value is $1,500 or less). Other insurance policies would be counted only to the extent of their cash surrender value.

The Secretary would prescribe periods of time and manners in which excess property must be disposed of in order that it not be included as resources.

Meaning of terms. An eligible individual must be a resident of the United States, Puerto Rico, the Virgin Islands, or Guam and a citizen or an alien admitted for permanent residence, and be aged, blind, or disabled.

Aged individual: One 65 years of age or older.

Blind individual: An individual who has central visual acuity of 20/200 or less in the better eye with the use of a correcting lens, or equivalent impairment in the fields of vision.

Disabled individual: An individual who is unable to engage in any substantial gainful activity by reason of a medically determinable physical or mental impairment which is expected to last, or has lasted, for 12 months or can be expected to end in death. (This definition is now used for social security disability benefits.)

Eligible spouse: An aged, blind, or disabled individual who is the husband or wife of an individual who is aged, blind, or disabled.

Child: An unmarried person who is not the head of a household and who is either under the age of 18, or under the age of 22 and attending school regularly.

Determination of marital relationship: Appropriate State law will apply except that, if two people were determined to be married for purposes of receiving social security cash benefits, they will be considered to be married, and two persons holding themselves out as married in the community in which they live would be considered married for purposes of this program.

Income and resources of a spouse living with an eligible individual will be taken into account in determining the benefit amount of the individual, whether or not the income and resources are available to him. Income and resources of a parent may count as income of a disabled or blind child.

Rehabilitation services. Disabled and blind beneficiaries would be referred to State agencies for vocational rehabilitation services. A beneficiary who refused without good cause any vocational rehabilitation services offered would not be eligible for benefits.

Optional State supplementation. A State which provides for a State supplement to the Federal payment could agree to have the Federal Government make the supplemental payments on behalf of the State. If a State agrees to have the Federal Government make its supplemental payments, the Federal Government would pay the full administrative costs of making such payments, but if it makes its own payments, the State would pay all of such costs.

States could but would not be required to cover under medicaid persons who are made newly eligible for cash benefits under the bill.

The Federal government, in administering supplemental benefits on behalf of a State, would be required to recognize a residency requirement if the State decided to impose such a requirement.

Payments and procedures. Benefits could be paid monthly, or otherwise, as determined by the Secretary of Health, Education, and Welfare. Benefits could be paid to an individual, an eligible spouse, partly to each, or to another interested party on behalf of the individual. The Secretary could determine ranges of incomes to which a single benefit amount may be applied.

Cash advances of up to $100 could be paid if an applicant appears to meet all the eligibility requirements and is faced with a financial emergency. Applicants apparently eligible for benefits on the basis of disability could be paid benefits for up to three months while their disability claim was in process.

The Secretary may arrange for adjustment and recovery in the event of overpayments or underpayments, and could waive overpayments to achieve equity and avoid penalizing people who were without fault.

People who are, or claim to be, eligible for benefits and who disagree with determinations of the Secretary, could obtain hearings if they request them within 30 days. Final determinations would be subject to judicial review in Federal district courts, but the Secretary's decisions as to any fact would be conclusive and not subject to review by the courts.

The right of any person to any future benefit would not be transferable or assignable, and no money payable under the program would be subject to execution, levy, attachment, garnishment, or other legal process.

If an individual fails to report events and changes relevant to his eligibility without good cause, benefits which may be payable to the individual would be terminated or reduced.

The heads of other Federal agencies would be required to provide such information as the Secretary of HEW needs to determine eligibility for benefits.

Penalties for fraud. A penalty of up to $1,000 or up to one year imprisonment, or both, would be provided in case of fraud under the program.

Administration. The Secretary of HEW may make administrative and other arrangements as necessary to carry out the purposes of the program and the States could enter into agreements to administer the Federal benefits during a transitional period.

Evaluation and research. The Secretary of HEW would continually evaluate the program, including its effectiveness in achieving its goals and its impact on related programs. He could conduct research and contract for independent evaluations of the program. Up to $5 million a year would be appropriated to carry out the evaluation and research. Annual reports to the President and the Congress on the operation and administration of the program would be required.

IV. Provisions Relating to Family Programs

The present program of aid to families with dependent children (AFDC) would be repealed effective July 1, 1972, and two new totally Federal programs would take effect on that day. The new programs would be adopted for a period of five years (through fiscal year 1977) in order to give Congress an opportunity to review their operation before continuing them in subsequent years. The new programs would be established by a new Title XXI in the Social Security Act. A description of the two new programs follows:

Families in which at least one person is employable would be enrolled in the Opportunities for Families Program, administered by the Department of Labor. Families with no employable person would be enrolled in the Family Assistance Plan administered by the Department of Health, Education, and Welfare.

A—Opportunities for Families Program

Registration for employment and training. Every member of a family who is found to be available for work by the Secretary of Health, Education, and Welfare would be required to register for manpower services, training and employment.

An individual would be considered available for work unless such person—

(1) Is unable to work or be trained because of illness, incapacity, or age;

(2) Is a mother or other relative caring for a child under age 6 (age 3 beginning July 1974);

(3) Is the mother or other female caretaker of a child, if the father or another adult male relative is in the home and is registered.

(4) Is a child under the age of 16 (or a student up to age 22);

(5) Is needed in the home on a continuous basis because of illness or incapacity of another family member.

Nevertheless, any person (except one who is ill, incapacitated, or aged) who would be exempted from registering by the above provisions could voluntarily register.

Every person who registered (other than a volunteer) would be required to participate in manpower services or training and to accept available employment. An individual could not be required to accept employment however—

(1) If the position offered is vacant due to a strike, lockout, or other labor dispute;

(2) If the wages and other employment conditions are contrary to those prescribed by applicable Federal, State, or local law, or less favorable than those prevailing for similar work in the locality, or the wages are less than an hourly rate of 3/4 of the highest Federal minimum wage ($1.20 per hour under present law);

(3) If membership in a company union or non-membership in a bona fide union is required;

(4) If he has demonstrated the capacity to obtain work that would better enable him to achieve self-sufficiency, and such work is available.

Child care and other supportive services. The Secretary of Labor directly or by using child care projects under the jurisdiction of the Department of Health, Education, and Welfare, would provide for child care services for registrants who require them in order to accept or continue to participate in manpower services, training, employment, or vocational rehabilitation.

The Secretary of Labor would be authorized funds to provide child care by grant or contract. Families receiving such services might also be required to pay all or part of the costs involved. A total of $488 million would be authorized for child care services in the first full year.

Health, vocational rehabilitation, family planning, counseling, social, and other supportive services (including physical examinations and minor medical services) would also be made available by the Secretary of Labor to registrants as needed.

Operation of manpower services, training and employment programs. The Secretary of Labor would develop an employability plan designed to prepare recipients to be self-supporting. The Secretary would then provide the necessary services, training, counseling, testing coaching, program orientation, job training, and followup services to assist the registrant in securing employment, retraining employment, and obtaining opportunities for advancement.

Provision would also be made for voluntary relocation assistance to enable a registrant and his family to be self-supporting.

Public service employment programs would also be used to provide needed jobs. Public service projects would be related to the fields of health, social service, environmental protection, education, urban and rural development and redevelopment, welfare, recreation, public facility and similar activities. The Secretary of Labor would establish these programs through grants or by contract with public or nonprofit agencies or organizations. The law would provide safeguards for workers on such jobs and wages could not be less than the higher of the prevailing or applicable minimum wage or the Federal minimum wage.

Federal participation in the costs of an individual's participation in a public service employment program would be 100 percent for the first year of his employment, 75 percent for the second year, and 50 percent for the third year.

States and their subdivisions that receive Federal grants would be required to provide the Secretary of Labor with up-to-date listings of job vacancies. The Secretary would also agree with certain Federal agencies to establish annual or other goals for employment of members of families receiving assistance.

Allowances of individuals participating in training. An incentive allowance of $30 per month would be paid to each registrant who participates in manpower training (States would have the option of providing an additional allowance of up to $30). Necessary costs for transportation and similar expenses would also be paid.

Utilization of other programs. The Secretary of Labor would be required to integrate this program as needed with all other manpower training programs involving all sectors of the economy and all levels of government.

Rehabilitation services for incapacitated family members. Family members who are incapacitated would be referred to the state vocational rehabilitation service. A quarterly review of their incapacities would usually be made.

Each such incapacitated individual would be required to accept rehabilitation services that are made available to him, and an allowance of $30 would be paid him while he receives such services. (States would have the option of providing an additional allowance of up to $30.) Necessary costs for transportation and similar expenses would also be paid.

Evaluation and research; reports. The Secretary of Labor would be authorized to conduct research and demonstrations of the program and directed to make annual evaluation reports to the President and the Congress. An appropriation of $10,000,000 would be authorized for these purposes.

B—Family Assistance Plan

Payment of benefits. All eligible families with no member available for employment would be enrolled and paid benefits by the Secretary of Health, Education, and Welfare.

Rehabilitation services and child care for incapacitated family members. Family members who are unemployable because of incapacity would be referred to State vocational rehabilitation agencies for services. A quarterly review of their incapacities would usually be made. Such persons would be required to accept services made available, and would be paid a $30 per month incentive allowance plus transportation and other related costs. (States would have the option of providing an additional allowance of up to $30.)

Child care services would also be provided if needed to enable individuals to take vocational rehabilitation services.

Evaluation and research; reports. The Secretary of Health, Education, and Welfare would be authorized to conduct research and demonstrations of the family assistance plan and directed to make annual evaluation reports to the President and the Congress. An appropriation of $10,000,000 would be authorized for this purpose.

C—Determination of Benefits

Uniform determinations. Both Secretaries would be required to apply the same interpretations and applications of fact to arrive at uniform determinations of eligibility and assistance payment amounts under the two family programs.

Eligibility for and amount of benefits. Family benefits would be computed at the rate of $800 per year for the first two members, $400 for the next three members, $300 for the next two members and $200 for the next member. This would provide $2,400 for a family of four, and the maximum amount which any family could receive would be $3,600. A family would not be eligible unless it had countable resources of $1,500 or less.

If any member of the family fails to register, take required employment or training, or accept vocational rehabilitation services, the family benefits would be reduced by $800 per year.

Benefits would be determined on the basis of the family's income for the current quarter and the three preceding quarters.

After a family has been paid benefits for 24 consecutive months, a new application would be required which would be processed as if it were a new application.

The Secretary could determine that a family is not eligible if it has very large gross income from a trade or business.

Families would have to apply for all other benefits available to them in order to be eligible.

Definition of income. Earned income would follow generally the definition of earnings used in applying the earnings limitation of the social security program. Unearned income means all other forms of income among which are benefits from other public and private programs, prizes and awards, proceeds of life insurance not needed for last illness and burial (with a maximum of $1,500), gifts, support, inheritances, grants, dividends, interests and so forth.

The following items would be excluded from the income of a family:

1. Earnings of a student regularly attending school, with limits set by the Secretary.

2. Irregular earned income of an individual of $30 or less in a quarter and irregular unearned income of $60 or less in a quarter.

3. Earned income used to pay the cost of child care under a schedule prescribed by the Secretary.

4. The first $720 per year of other earned income plus one-third of the remainder.

5. Assistance based on need received from public or private agencies, except veterans' pensions.

6. Training allowances.

7. The tuition part of scholarships and fellowships.

8. Home produce.

9. One-third of child support and alimony.

10. Foster care payments for a child placed in the family by a child placement agency.

The total of the exclusions under (1), (2), and (3) above could not exceed $2,000 for a family of four rising by $200 for each additional member to an overall maximum of $3,000.

Exclusions from resources. A family cannot be eligible for payments if it has resources in excess of $1,500. In determining what is included in the $1,500 amount, the following items are excluded:

1. The home to the extent that its value does not exceed a reasonable amount.

2. Household goods and personal effects not in excess of a reasonable amount.

3. Other property which is essential to the family's self-support.

An insurance policy would be counted only to the extent of its cash surrender value except that if the total face value of all such policies with respect to an individual is $1,500 or less, no cash surrender value will be counted.

The Secretary would prescribe periods of time, and manners in which, property must be disposed of in order that it would not be included as resources.

Meaning of family and child. A family would be defined as two or more related people living together in the United States where at least one of the members is a citizen or a lawfully admitted alien and where at least one of them is a child dependent on someone else in the family.

No family will be eligible if the head of the household is an undergraduate or graduate student regularly attending a college or university. Benefits would not be payable to an individual for any month in which he is outside the United States.

The term "child" means an unmarried person who is not the head of the household, and who is either under the age of 18 or under the age of 22 if attending school regularly.

Appropriate State law would be used in determining relationships.

The income and resources of an adult (other than a parent or the spouse of a parent) living with the family but not contributing to the family would be disregarded.

If an individual takes benefits under adult assistance, he could not be eligible for family benefits.

Optional State supplementation. If a State decides to supplement the basic Federal payment, it would be required to provide benefit amounts that do not undermine the earnings disregard provision. A State could agree to have the Federal Government make the supplementary payments on behalf of the State. If a State agrees to have the Federal Government make its supplemental payments, the Federal Government would pay the full administrative costs of making such payments, but if it makes its own payments the State would pay all of such costs.

States could but would not be required to cover under medicaid persons who are made newly eligible for cash benefits under the bill.

The Federal Government, in administering supplemental benefits on behalf of a State, would be required to recognize a residency requirement if the State decided to impose such a requirement.

D—Procedural and General Provisions

Payments and procedures. The Secretary would be permitted to pay the benefits at such times as best carry out the purposes of the title and could make payments to a person other than a member of the family or to an agency where he finds inability to manage funds. The Secretary's decision would be subject to hearing and review.

The family benefits could not be paid to an individual who failed to register, or take work, training or vocational rehabilitation.

Cash advances of $100 or less could be paid if an applicant appears to meet all the eligibility requirements and is faced with a financial emergency.

The Secretary may arrange for adjustment and recovery in the event of overpayments or underpayments, with a view toward equity and avoiding penalizing people who were without fault.

People who are, or claim to be, eligible for assistance payments, and who disagree with determinations of the Secretary, could obtain hearings if they request them within 30 days. Final determinations would be subject to judicial review in Federal district courts, but the Secretary's decisions as to any fact would be conclusive and not subject to review by the courts. The Secretary would also be given authority to appoint qualified people to serve as hearing examiners without their having to meet the specific standards prescribed under the Administrative Procedure Act for hearing examiners.

The right of any person to any future benefit would not be transferable or assignable, and no money payable under this title would be subject to execution, levy, attachment, garnishment, or other legal process.

In addition, the Secretary would establish necessary rules and regulations dealing with proofs and evidence, and the method of taking and furnishing the same, in order to establish the right to benefits.

Each family would be required to submit a report of income within 30 days after the end of a quarter and benefits would be cut off if the report was not filed. If a family failed, without good cause, to report income or changes in circumstances as required by the Secretary, it would be subject to a penalty of $25 the first time, $50 the second time and $100 for later times.

The head of any Federal agency would be required to provide such information as the Secretary of HEW needs to determine eligibility for benefits under this title.

Penalties for fraud. A penalty of $1,000 or 1 year imprisonment, or both, would be provided in the case of fraud under the program.

Administration. Both the Secretary of Health, Education, and Welfare and the Secretary of Labor could perform their functions directly, through other Federal agencies, or by contract. An additional Assistant Secretary is authorized in the Department of Labor to head up the new program in that Department.

Child care. The Secretaries of Labor and Health, Education, and Welfare are each given the authority and responsibility for arranging day care for their respective recipients under the Opportunities for Families Program and the Family Assistance Plan who need such day care in order to participate in training, employment, or vocational rehabilitation. Where such care can be obtained in facilities developed by the Secretary of Health, Education, and Welfare, these would be utilized.

Insofar as possible, arrangements would be made for after school care with local educational agencies. All day care would be subject to standards developed by the Secretary of Health, Education, and Welfare, with the concurrence of the Secretary of Labor. Both Secretaries would have authority to make grants and contracts for payment of up to 100 percent of the cost of care. The Secretary of Health, Education, and Welfare would have total responsibility for construction of facilities. $700 million would be authorized for the provision of child care services in the first fiscal year, and such sums as Congress may appropriate in subsequent years. In addition, $50 million would be authorized for construction and renovation of child care facilities for each fiscal year.

Obligations of parents. A deserting parent would be obligated to the United States for the amount of any Federal payments made to his family less any amount that he actually contributes by court order or otherwise to the family.

Any parent of a child receiving benefits who travels in interstate commerce to avoid supporting his child would be guilty of a misdemeanor and subject to a fine of $1,000, imprisonment for 1 year, or both.

The Secretary would report to appropriate officials cases of child neglect or abuse which came to his attention while administering the program.

Local committees to evaluate program. Local advisory committees would be set up throughout the country, with a minimum of one in each State, which would evaluate and report on the effectiveness of the elements of the program designed to help people become self-supporting. Each committee would be composed of representatives from labor, business, and the public, as well as public officials not directly involved in the administration of the programs.

V. Other Related Assistance Provisions

Adoption and Foster Care Services Under Child Welfare

Authorizations of $150 million for fiscal year 1972 and higher amounts for subsequent years would be provided for payments to the States to support foster care and related services.

Provisions Related to New Assistance Programs

Effective date for adult assistance and family programs. Major changes made in the assistance programs would be effective July 1, 1972 The child care provisions would become effective upon enactment of the bill. The amendments which provide benefits to families where the father and mother are both present, neither is incapacitated, and the father is not unemployed (the "working poor") would become effective January 1, 1973.

Prohibition against participation in food stamp program by recipients of payments under family and adult assistance programs. The bill would amend the Food Stamp Act of 1964 by providing that families and adults eligible for benefits under the assistance programs in this bill would be excluded from participation in the food stamp program.

Special provisions for Puerto Rico, the Virgin Islands, and Guam. There would be special provisions for Puerto Rico, the Virgin Islands, and Guam. The amounts used in the family assistance plan and the aid to the aged, blind, and disabled (other than the $720 amount of annual earnings to be disregarded and the $30 per month incentive allowances) would be adjusted by the ratio of the per capita income of each of these jurisdictions to the per capita income of the lowest of the 50 States.

Determination of medicaid eligibility. The Secretary would be able to enter into agreements with States under which the Secretary would determine eligibility for medicaid both for those eligible for Federal payments and the medically needy in cases where the State covered the medically needy. The State would pay half of the Secretary's additional administrative costs arising from carrying out the agreement.

Effective date.—July 1, 1972

Transitional administration of public assistance. The Secretary of Health, Education, and Welfare could enter into agreements with States under which a State would administer the Federal assistance program for a period of up to one year from the beginning of the program.

Limitations on increases in State welfare expenditures. States would be guaranteed that, if they make payments supplementary to the Federal adult or family programs, it would cost them no more to do so than the amount of their total expenditures for cash public assistance payments during calendar year 1971, to the extent that the Federal payments and the State supplementary payments to recipients do not exceed the payment levels in effect under the public assistance programs in the State for January 1971. The value of food stamps would be taken into account in computing whether the guarantee would go into effect if the State pays in cash the value of food stamps. Most States would save money under the provisions of the bill; this provision would guarantee that no State would lose money.

Limitation on Federal expenditures for social services. The Federal Government would continue to provide 75 percent matching funds to the States for child care and family planning services on an open-end appropriation basis. Federal matching for other specified social services would be limited to the amounts appropriated by the Congress.

Public Assistance Amendments Effective Immediately

Additional remedies for State noncompliance with provisions of assistance titles. The Secretary would be able to require States to make payments to people who did not receive all money due them because the State failed to comply with a Federal requirement.

The Secretary could require a State which is in noncompliance with a Federal requirement to set up a timetable and method for assuring compliance, or could request the Attorney General to bring suit to enforce the Federal requirements.

Effective date.—Enactment.

Statewideness not required for services. A State would be permitted to furnish social services in one area of a State without being required to furnish such services in all geographic areas of the State.

Effective date.—Enactment.

Optional modification in disregarding income under AFDC. States would be permitted, between enactment and July 1, 1972, to modify their present AFDC programs so as to substitute the earnings disregard provisions in the family assistance provisions (cost of child care, plus $720, plus one-third of the remainder) for provisions of present law (the first $30 and one-third of the remainder after which actual work expenses are deducted).

A State could also apply the maximum dollar limits in the family programs on child care and student earnings ($2,000 for a family of four rising to $3,000 for a family of nine or more) to its present AFDC program.

Effective date.—Enactment.

Individual programs for family services not required. States would no longer be required to prepare a separate plan of services for each individual who is eligible for AFDC.

Effective date.—July 1, 1972, or earlier if the State so chooses.

Enforcement of support orders. States would be required to secure support for a spouse of a parent from the other parent (of children receiving assistance payments) where he has deserted or abandoned his spouse, utilizing reciprocal arrangements with other States to obtain or enforce court orders for support.

Effective date.—July 1, 1972, or earlier, if the State plan so provides.

Separation of social services and cash assistance payments. Each State would be required to submit a proposal to the Secretary by January 1, 1972 providing for the administrative separation of handling eligibility for cash payments and the provision of social services by July 1, 1972.

Increase in Federal matching to States for costs of establishing paternity and collecting child support payments. Federal matching would be increased from 50 percent to 75 percent for State costs incurred in establishing the paternity of AFDC children and locating and collective support from their absent parents.

Effective date.—Enactment.

Vendor payments for special needs. States would be permitted to provide for non-recurring items of special need by means of vendor payments.

Increase in Federal matching—WIN program. Effective immediately, the Federal matching under the WIN program would be increased from 80 to 90 percent. This provision expires June 30, 1972.

B

The Environment

The quality of the environment has emerged as one of the major issues of the 1970's. In the United States, concern over pollution expressed for years by scientists and conservationists spread to the general public in the late 1960's. In addition to each citizen's personal experience with foul air, bad water, excessive noise, overcrowding, and disappearing landscapes, the impetus behind the rising concern over the environment has also come from the Malthusian warnings on population. There is the question of whether or not man will complete the destruction of his planet or learn to live in harmony with it.

The readings in Section B are designed to present the issues involved in the control of the environment. The first reading, "The Economy and the Environment," by Hendrik S. Houthakker is a general statement on the relationship of environmental problems to the national economy. The readings, "The Complex Nature of Pollution Control," and "Government Role in Aiding Pollution Control," by the Tax Foundation calls attention to some of the problems involved in isolating the causes of pollution and discussed the role of the government in providing solutions to pollution. The final article, "Tax Assistance and Environmental Pollution," by Douglas B. Wilson discusses the possible use of tax incentives as one device to assist industry in solving the pollution problem.

The Economy and the Environment*

Some people may feel that to link the environment with the economy is to pollute the sacred with the profane. The environment, we are sometimes told, is a subject that economists should stay away from; it belongs to the domain of human ecology. Unfortunately it does not seem that human ecology has as yet progressed beyond the embryonic stage. While human ecology does not seem to have developed either the conceptual framework or the empirical evidence that would make it into a science, the literature makes up for this by a liberal supply of horror stories that make the description of economics as the dismal science obsolete. It took economics two thousands years to progress from Aristotle, who gave economics its name, to Adam Smith, who gave it some substance. We must hope it will not take human ecology equally long, especially since according to some ecologists the remaining time span of humanity is very much shorter than that. While the prophets of doom do not always agree whether the human race will starve to death, boil to death, freeze to death, or merely blow itself up, they do seem to agree that things cannot go on much longer. This feeling is due in part to the widespread abuse of trend extrapolations. There used to be a popular pastime of imagining some large sum of money to be divided into dollar bills, and then to see how far the bills would stretch if they were laid end to end. Thus it can be shown that if the Gross National Product were treated in this fashion it would carry us a long way toward the moon. With the advent of space travel this particular exercise seems to have lost most of its popular appeal, but equally meaningless trend extrapolations have taken its place. Thanks to the marvels of exponential growth, anything that increases at a constant percentage rate will surpass any given number after a sufficiently long period of time, and a large variety of calamities can thus be prophesied with seemingly mathematical precision. It takes only a sliderule and a quick look at the World Almanac, for instance, to predict when the world will run out of food. What these calculations ignore, of course, is that nature and society have all sorts of built-in checks and balances, which prevent these trends from continuing indefinitely. And these checks and balances are just what economics is about.

The fact that in the field of human ecology it is sometimes

*Hendrik S. Houthakker, Remarks of Hendrik S. Houthakker, Member, Council of Economic Advisers, before the Cleveland Business Economics Club, April 19, 1971, pp. 1–15.

difficult to distinguish between science and science fiction should not lead us to the conclusion that environmental problems are not serious. On the contrary, it is precisely because they are serious that economists can make a major contribution in this area. We may leave it to others to decide whether the future of humanity is at stake; Pollyanish though it may seem, the economist may reasonably start out from the assumption that mankind will be with us for some time to come.

Like most economic problems, the problem of the environment is primarily one of choice. Certain commodities, such as air and water, were free because until recently the supply vastly exceeded the demand. Since they were free, or virtually free, there was no need to establish property rights or other procedures for deciding on their use. As demand has grown, however, the supply has become inadequate and we therefore have to find ways of allocating these scarce commodities among different uses, that is to say of using them efficiently. This is by no means a new problem. Land also was free in many parts of the world during much of recorded history. In the United States we don't have to go back very far to find a period when the value of land was virtually zero. But when land did become valuable, we already had some mechanisms, brought from more densely populated countries, for allocating its use. In the case of air and water we have much less experience to draw upon. Because of their mobility, it is much more difficult to attach property rights to air and water than to land. Indeed even in the case of land the mere establishment of property rights is not necessarily sufficient to obtain the best use; I shall speak a little later about the problem of forests, where this question comes up.

In the absence of property rights we are led to other types of control on the use of air and water by individuals, firms and municipalities. The form of these controls determines their effectiveness, and also has a major influence on the operations of firms and municipalities. The main purpose of these controls, of course, is to keep air and water reasonably clean, so that nobody will be adversely affected either by being exposed to harmful substances, or by having to incur unreasonable costs to render air and water sufficiently clean for his consumption. The mere use of words like "unreasonable" and "undue" indicates that there is room for compromise here and the economics of pollution control consists largely in helping find this compromise. The purist may say that air and water have to remain as clean as they were prior to the emergence of mankind, but in many cases this would put a greater burden on society than the citizens are willing to bear.

The question then arises how clean is clean. In the absence of a price mechanism, this can only be settled through the political process, and it is therefore appropriate that standards for clean air and water are set by legislation. Thus the Clean Air Act, as amended in 1970, provides for standards on air quality; there is similar legislation for water, but for simplicity I shall confine myself to air pollution, especially from industrial sources. The standards provided by the Act are ambient air standards, that is to say they refer to the average quality of the air in an area rather than to the composition of the atmosphere in the neighborhood of some source of pollution. To achieve the ambient air standards it is necessary to control these emissions, which, together with meteorological and topographical factors, determine the quality of air in any particular area. The control of emissions can be achieved in two different ways, by emission standards or by taxes; much of the current debate centers on the relative importance that should be given to these two methods.

In the case of air pollution the emission standards are usually formulated in terms of a percentage reduction of the pollutants originally generated by some production process. Thus in the case of copper smelting sulfur oxides are among the principal pollutants produced, and a number of states now require that 90 percent of the sulfur oxides be removed before the stackgases are released into the atmosphere. In principle, the emission standards can be chosen in such a way that the ambient air standard is satisfied, though we have to realize that the technical knowledge in this area is still far from perfect. Moreover, the formulation of ambient air standards and emission standards implies a value judgment about the degree of control that can be reasonably achieved, and such a judgment is inevitably subject to controversy. The dispute usually turns on the cost of achieving a given emission standard, and it is distressing to see how widely the estimates of pollution control costs can vary. In the case of copper smelters, an area with which I happen to be somewhat familiar, the estimates range from 1¢ per pound of copper to 5 or 6¢ per pound of copper, depending on whether one believes the pollution controllers or the copper industry. Because of the implied value judgment I just mentioned, it is of course very important to know what the cost of pollution control is, especially when this cost is borne by the polluters. That the cost should be borne by the polluters, and hence ultimately by the people who consume the products affected, is fortunately much less controversial.

It may well be that as more experience is gained there will be greater unanimity about the cost of pollution control. Nevertheless this disagreement is one of the arguments in favor of another method of controlling emissions, namely by levying emission charges. Rather than requiring copper smelters to reduce the sulfur oxide by a given percentage, they could be taxed according to the sulfur oxide they do release into the atmosphere. Each polluter could then decide for himself how much control it is worth his while to provide. A firm that, for one reason or another, has higher costs of control would presumably release relatively more pollutants than a firm with low control costs. Nevertheless by appropriately choosing the level of the tax it would be possible to achieve the ambient air standard, which remains the ultimate criterion. Since emission charges would take advantage of differences in control costs among polluters (who are not necessarily in the same industry) it is possible to reach the ambient air standards at a lower cost to society than by applying a uniform emission standard. Another advantage of emission charges is that there is less need for giving variances, a practice that is almost inevitable under emission standards. Emission charges also provide some revenue.

It is important to realize that emission charges and emission standards do not necessarily exclude each other. A combination of both may well be the most effective way of attaining ambient air standards. This could be done, for instance, by setting a uniform emission standard for all polluters and in addition a tax on pollutants. There would consequently be some minimum level of control, but it would not be so high as to cause serious difficulties for firms with high control costs. The ambient air standard would then be reached by correspondingly greater efforts on the part of firms with low control costs, and variances may not be needed at all.

This combination of the two methods, incidentally, does not mean a trade-off between emission charges and the *enforcement* of emission standards, as has recently been suggested. There is no question that the Clean Air Act will be enforced, irrespective of whether the ambient air standards it provides for will be achieved by standards or by charges. The only question is how these goals can be reached most efficiently, that is to say at the lowest cost to society, and it is primarily in this respect that emission charges merit consideration.

Another problem in this general area that has given rise to some misunderstanding is whether ambient air standards should be uniform all over the country. As I have pointed out before, any ambient air standard implies a value judgment on the social importance of clean air relative to the social cost of achieving it. There is no obvious reason why this value judgment should lead to the same conclusion everywhere. It is conceivable that a depressed area may want to attract industry at the expense of a less stringent ambient air standard; the citizens of that area should be able to have some influence on the choice involved, even though it is also appropriate for the Federal Government to set minimum standards for the entire country, as the Clean Air Act provides. The matter of local choice becomes especially important in the case of an attempt to set uniform emission standards for the country as a whole (which is not required by the Clean Air Act), since the costs of control may vary depending on local geographical factors as well as on the preferences of the local population. The idea that some areas may want to have lower standards in order to attract industry has been described as "a Magna Carta for polluters," but this is a misconception. Just as the social cost of a given degree of pollution control can be reduced by allowing for differences among polluters, so the social cost can also be minimized by recognizing that there are geographic differences. The increased emphasis on pollution control will in any case lead to some shifts in the geographical distribution of industry. Some firms, for instance, obtain sulfuric acid as a by-product of the removal of sulfur oxides from smoke, and they may not be able to find a market for this sulfuric acid at any positive price. They may therefore be compelled either to close down or to move to an area where sulfuric acid can be disposed of; the only alternative would be to switch to the production of elemental sulfur, which unlike sulfuric acid can be stored. There are many other reasons why efficient pollution control will require a change in the location of industry.

The efficient control of air pollution is only one of the many problems that are raised by the increased concern for the environment. Let us now turn to another one where the requirements of the economy and of the environment are seemingly in conflict, and where some compromise therefore has to be found. I am referring to the Alaska pipeline, which is being held up by an understandable concern with its environmental implications. It is proper that these implications be thoroughly investigated, but at the same time we have to realize that the country has an urgent need for the large oil reserves that have been discovered on the North Slope. Although there is still some surplus crude capacity in Texas and Louisiana it has long been impossible for the "lower forty-eight" to satisfy the nation's demand for petroleum. Since for national security reasons we should not be unduly dependent on overseas supplies, the discovery in Alaska has been particularly valuable.

As far as we can tell at the moment, there is no satisfactory alternative to a pipeline for transporting this oil to the West Coast, where it is most needed. A pipeline to Canada is also a possibility, but it would be much longer and more expensive, and could not easily serve the West Coast. The difficult climate and terrain in Alaska pose unusual problems for the pipeline builders, but there is no reason to think that these problems are insuperable. The owners of the pipeline, presumably, have no interest in seeing it break or sink into the mud, although it is true that the standards of safety they would apply on their own might be less stringent than those required by the public interest. On the other hand, it is clearly extreme to suggest that we cannot take any chances at all with the permafrost. Even in the highly unlikely event that some of the permafrost would be melted, the area involved could hardly be more than a fraction of one percent of the total permafrost in Alaska. There is also some danger that a few of the tankers that will transport the oil from the South Coast of Alaska to other Pacific ports will spill oil. Here again we should perhaps remember that it is not the business of oil companies to pour oil on troubled waters, as it used to be quaintly called.

It must be hoped, therefore, that the environmental problems will be quickly resolved and that a start can soon be made with the construction of this much needed pipeline. In view of the many uncertainties now besetting the world petroleum market, the alternative to Alaskan oil would probably be greater use of coal, which raises plenty of environmental problems of its own, such as a sometimes high sulfur content and the landscape damage from strip mining. As in many other affairs, the search for perfection is not likely to serve us well; instead, the rule of reason should prevail.

Much the same can be said about another area where the conflict between the needs of the economy and the needs of the environment has not been resolved. This is the case of timber production, especially from the National Forests. Even though our housing production has been at rather low levels for the last two years, we have already been pressed to find enough lumber and plywood. As housing starts are increasing, the problem becomes more severe, and a sizable jump in lumber and plywood prices occurred in the early months of 1971. At the same time conservationist groups are attempting to reduce the cut in the National Forests by lawsuits and other means. They have been especially aroused by the practice of clearcutting, which inflicts very visible scars on the landscape. The search for less damaging ways of cutting timber should be actively pursued, but at the same time we should be careful not to impair our ability to supply the nation with the housing it needs while at the same time satisfying the legitimate demands for a better physical environment. Some of the more extreme conservationists come close to arguing that there should be no cutting on the National Forests at all; indeed one would not be surprised to learn that they apply the same argument to private lands, which incidentally would show that private ownership of land does not necessarily take account of all uses. Conceivably we could save on lumber in housing construction by using more cement and steel, but the environmental consequences might be on balance even less desirable than relying on forest products, which in any case are renewable.

It should perhaps also be mentioned that the clearing of forests does not necessarily lead to a deterioration of the environment. Most people who have been there consider Vermont, with its typical pattern of wooded hillsides and open valleys, to be one of our most beautiful states. Yet they often do not realize that this pleasing landscape is partly manmade. The early settlers cut down the woods that covered nearly all the land; later on they were allowed to grow again on the steeper slopes that were not suitable for crops or grazing, but even in the valleys trees would take over if left to themselves. Many people probably like Vermont better as it is now.

What we may need is a more clear-cut division of the national forests into recreational and other uses. At the moment the management of these forests is based on the concept of multiple use, which has worked well until recently, but apparently no longer satisfies present conservationists demands. The Administration and the Congress have already spent much time on establishing the relative priorities, and will no doubt be spending more time in the coming years. Perhaps some of the more scenic and accessible National Forests should be reassigned as national parks, while intensive management of the remaining National Forests could help to meet our lumber needs. Or perhaps the solution lies in institutions such as the Nature Conservancy, which buys up tracts of land for the enjoyment of future generations. In any case we have to be sure that no single interest group, no matter how highly motivated, be allowed to dictate an extreme solution that is not in the general interest.

In the preceding remarks I may have occasionally sounded critical of the environmentalist movement. Let me make it clear therefore that personally I share many of their concerns, and hope that they will be realized to the extent that our various other national concerns permit. It will be a great challenge for economists in the coming years to work out procedures by which this reconcilation can be effected.

*The Complex Nature of Pollution Control**

Few domestic matters have galvanized public attention as strikingly as problems of pollution have in recent times. The stream of information which has poured forth since pollution became a popular issue has left no doubt that better control is essential if mankind is to enjoy a tolerable future—or, in the view of some, any future at all. Although there may be scope for dispute on the degree of urgency, virtually all agree that current pollution controls are inadequate and that improvement is mandatory.

Those who are most alarmed about pollution feel anxiety on two points: The probability that pollution creates health hazards, some of which may be life-endangering, and the possibility that pollution may in time upset the balance of nature to such an extent that earth can no longer support human life on its surface. Others, unwilling to accept an extreme viewpoint, nonetheless object to increasing annoyances and assaults on health and aesthetic sense resulting from various types of pollution.

Dangers to Health and Life

When an issue becomes tangled with emotion, the ascertaining of fact becomes difficult; no attempt will be made in this study to evaluate just how dangerous pollution may be now and in the future. That pollution *sometimes* is exceedingly dangerous no one can deny; indisputable evidence exists that on several occasions, air pollution has resulted in fairly rapid deaths for large numbers of victims.[1]

Less dramatic, but perhaps more important, some medical authorities believe that deleterious effects are not confined to acute episodes in which pollution levels temporarily rise very high. A former surgeon general of the U.S. Public Health Service has observed that a relationship exists between a community's level of air

---

*Tax Foundation, from *Pollution Control: Perspectives on the Government Role* (New York, Tax Foundation, 1971), pp. 11–18 and pp. 19–25.

[1] More than two decades ago during the infamous Donora (Pennsylvania) air pollution episode, 6,000 people—nearly half the town's population—became ill, and 20 of these died. In New York City in the winter of 1963, 15 days of smog resulted in approximately 400 deaths in excess of the norms for that period. Health officials identified smog as the villain in London during a two-week period of 1952, when some 4,000 excess deaths occurred, and again a month later, when during January and February deaths shot up to 8,000 over the average.

pollution and residents' death rate from lung cancer, cancer of the esophagus and stomach, and arteriosclerotic disease.[2] Other researchers contend there is strong evidence that air pollution is associated with various respiratory ailments, such as emphysema, asthma, bronchitis, and others. Even the common cold, it is held, strikes with more frequency in high pollution communities. Moreover, it has been estimated that the direct costs of medical care plus the indirect costs of earnings lost because of illness and premature death could be cut by more than $2 billion annually if there were a 50 percent reduction in air pollution levels in major urban areas.[3]

Health hazards do not stem from pollution in the air alone, of course. Discussions of the effect of dangerous trace elements in food even now occupy congressional committees. Occasional epidemics flare up from polluted water.[4]

Fears that mankind may permanently damage the balance of nature raise controversial issues. The degeneration of Lake Erie from a sparkling, productive lake to a malignant body of water resulted when its life-cycle was forced out of balance by excessive municipal and industrial wastes, and does provide a dramatic example of what can happen. Other balance-of-nature theories are concerned with irretrievably poisoning the soil, or eliminating some species of insect or animal crucial to nature's balance, through excessive use of pesticides or radioactive accidents. Another terrifying speculation concerns the increasing use of fossil fuels, which gradually add to the carbon dioxide cloud cover over the world. Not harmful in itself, this cloud is thought to interfere with the radiation back out into space of some of the energy which the earth absorbs from the sun. An increase in the cloud conceivably could cause temperatures to rise enough to melt polar icecaps, flooding many major cities, and changing ecology in unknown ways.

Aside from the dramatic and controversial aspects of pollution, there remain the workaday irritations and costs visible to all. Problems of solid waste disposal and noise pollution add to the harassments in large cities. Beaches closed, fishing prohibited, ugly thin mists enveloping cities, smelly eye-irritants permeating the atmosphere, blackened buildings—any city dweller knows these and other hallmarks of pollution well.

[2] Orris C. Herfindahl and Allen V. Kneese, *Quality of the Environment: An Economic Approach to Some Problems in Using Land, Water, and Air.* Baltimore, Maryland: Johns Hopkins Press, 1965, p. 29.
[3] Lester B. Lave and Eugene P. Seskin, "Air Pollution and Human Health," *Science*, Vol. 169, No. 3947 (August 1970), p. 730.
[4] For example, in 1965 some 18,000 people suffered gastroenteritis and three died from polluted water wells in Riverside, California.

Underlying Factors

Today more than half the people in the United States live in urban places which, taken together, account for only one percent of the total area of the country; two-thirds live in 9 percent of the space. Such clustering of population greatly intensifies pollution problems. The very process of living generates wastes—wastes which, for the most part, nature can cope with efficiently until population density becomes quite high. Thus at least part of the pollution problem stems from the concentration of large populations into relatively small areas.

Ironical though it may seem, widespread affluence also has aggravated pollution.[5] Great numbers of people living in one tiny spot create serious amounts of waste even if they live at a simple level. If they have the wealth to demand many goods and services, all the while retaining an indifferent attitude toward worn and broken items and packaging materials, the situation can become acute. One has only to visit a Mexican import shop, and see shelves of high-priced glassware made from melted-down bottles poured into discarded American forms, to realize that at low income levels almost nothing usable is thrown away, while at high income levels consumption patterns can be profligate. Moreover, life styles have changed as wealth has increased, and many of these changes act to increase pollution in one way or another. Endless paper towels replace the reused "dish rag" of yesteryear. Parents who themselves walked to school obligingly transport their children by auto day after day. And what church today would expect its congregation to keep cool with paper fans from local funeral parlors, even though the generation of electricity to operate air conditioning may add to pollution problems?

Concentrated population, affluence, changes in life styles and demand patterns—all contribute to pollution problems. But solutions based on attempts to alter these underlying causes might extract a higher price than most would be willing to pay. In any case, only an autocratic government would consider any direct attack on variables so closely related to individual rights, and no indirect methods seem likely to work rapidly enough to do the job.

---

[5] Pollution problems are by no means confined to the wealthier nations. It is only the relatively prosperous nation, however, which can spare the resources to do something about it. It also should be noted that socialist countries suffer just as serious pollution problems as those of the capitalist countries; see Marshall I. Goldman (ed.), *Controlling Pollution*, Englewood Cliffs, N.J., Prentice Hall, 1967, pp. 153–170, for articles from *Izvestia*, *Pravda*, etc., concerned with pollution in the U.S.S.R.

Major Sources of Pollution

Four sources bear responsibility for the major part of pollution today: municipalities, agriculture, industry, and automobiles. Although some overlapping exists, the special problems of each differ markedly from those encountered by the others.

In today's social climate, critics have often singled out industry as the prime generator of pollution. Undeniably, dramatic instances of industrial pollution can be found quite readily, in part because much industrial pollution tends to be painfully visible. For instance, untreated effluent from a large sulphate pulp mill ("large" defined as production of 600 tons daily) can equal the sewage from a city about the size of Sacramento, California, or Richmond, Virginia. Moreover, today's rapidly advancing technology constantly creates new problems of pollution; the very processes which improve the ordinary man's lot as a consumer may act against him as an individual concerned about ecological balances. As an example, when steelmakers generally changed over from open hearth methods to the more efficient oxygen process, the demand for scrap metal dropped, since the oxygen process mainly uses iron ore and taconite pellets. Consequently, the incentives for junk dealers to salvage old cars became so low that demand dropped until some dealers succeeded in insisting upon actually being paid for accepting old vehicles. The inevitable result followed that cities began to face the expensive chore of disposing of automobiles abandoned in all sorts of ingenious places and ways.[6] Modern detergents, without question far better cleansing agents than old-fashioned soaps, have brought pollution problems which have been widely reported in the daily press. Modern packaging techniques—i.e., cans and non-returnable bottles—taken together with human indolence have created mountains of trash and headaches for those charged with keeping ahead of litter.

Industry, along with the general public and perhaps in response to it, has grown increasingly alert to pollution problems in recent years. One indication of industry involvement—admittedly an imperfect one—appears in Table 1, which shows the percentage of total capital expenditures devoted to pollution control devices for a number of major industry divisions over the period 1966–1968. These figures, based on data gathered by the Conference Board as a special part of its regular annual survey of capital expenditures, admittedly

---

[6] The case raises subtle questions as to who is the polluter: the steelmaker who changed his process? the auto manufacturer who builds a car which fails to disintegrate readily once the moving parts fail? the auto owner who behaves in an indisputably antisocial way?

TABLE 1

Ratio of Pollution Control Expenditures to Total Capital
Expenditures, by Industry
1966-1968

Industry	Total			Air		Water	
	1968	1967	1966	1968	1967	1968	1967
Durable goods industries							
Primary iron and steel	5.83%	4.76%	3.23%	3.02%	2.81%	2.81%	1.95%
Primary nonferrous metal	2.37	—	3.76	2.18	—	0.19	—
Electrical machinery & equipment	1.08	1.21	0.35	0.32	0.34	0.76	0.87
Machinery, except electrical	1.51	1.31	0.35	0.83	0.85	0.68	0.46
Motor vehicles & equipment	2.08	3.39	2.38	1.92	2.09	0.16	1.30
Transportation eqt., except motor vehicle	1.65	1.03	1.49	0.98	0.83	0.67	0.20
Stone, clay & glass	2.35	2.68	1.91	1.42	1.99	0.93	0.69
Fabricated metal products	1.02	1.49	0.40	0.73	0.81	0.29	0.68
Instruments & photographic eqt.	1.36	0.93	0.25	0.56	0.66	0.80	0.27
Other durable	1.49	—	0.49	0.77	—	0.72	—
Nondurable goods industries							
Food and beverages	1.36	3.68	1.33	0.65	1.27	0.71	2.41
Textile mill products	2.24	5.70	0.49	0.85	0.45	1.39	5.25
Paper & allied products	9.45	4.51	2.42	2.73	1.40	6.72	3.11
Chemical & allied products	2.41	2.33	1.56	1.41	1.02	1.00	1.31
Petroleum & coal products	4.38	4.71	1.41	2.16	2.19	2.22	2.52
Rubber products	1.18	0.63	0.18	0.31	0.16	0.87	0.47
Other nondurable goods	0.50	—	0.20	—	—	0.50	—

Source: The Conference Board Record, February 1970, p. 55; September 1968, p. 28, September 1967, p. 28.

not only are subject to the usual shortcomings associated with sample survey data, but are further weakened in the case of many of the firms because accounting procedures create difficulties in segregation of pollution-related outlays from ordinary capital expenditures. For instance, one iron and steel producer commented in response to the survey.[7]

> Our experience in recent years is that at any given point in time we have about 1,000 projects in various stages of design and construction. Many of these involve some kind of pollution control equipment or higher cost equipment chosen because of built-in or inherent pollution control characteristics, and it is very difficult to distinguish or identify and track the status of costs so related.

The interesting point brought out by Table 1, however, does not

[7] The Conference Board Record, February 1970, p. 56.

rely on the accuracy of the figures in any particular year. Presumably the same sorts of errors would reappear in the absolute figures year after year, so that any *trends* toward increased or decreased investment could be accepted, despite doubts about the actual levels of the figures. Thus, the table shows that the primary iron and steel industry devoted 3.2 percent of total capital expenditures in 1966, the first year of the survey, to pollution control equipment, gradually increasing to 5.8 percent in the latest year reported, 1968. While one might consider the actual percentages as no more than rough indicators, the quite rapid upward trend cannot be missed. Similarly, comparing 1966 with 1968, a number of other industries appear to be increasing their relative investment in pollution control equipment.

The table also indicates that most of those industries which have received the brunt of criticism are putting comparatively high percentages of investment into pollution equipment. Paper and allied products, iron and steel, and petroleum and coal reported the highest 1968 investment percentages. Other high investors in pollution equipment are chemical and allied products, primary nonferrous metals, textile mill products, and motor vehicles and equipment.[8]

Municipal pollution raises quite different problems from the industrial case, despite some overlapping. Localities must contend with two major kinds of potential pollutants, sewerage and solid wastes such as garbage, sometimes on an incredibly large scale. In addition, cities which operate their own public utilities, maintain public housing, and conduct other quasi-business activity meet the same difficulties as their counterparts in private business. In seeking solutions, however, the management of the city is constrained not only by available resources, technology, and the other limitations encountered by industry, but also by complex political forces.

Automobiles generate a large part of air pollution, according to recent estimates accounting for 60 percent of total air pollution in the United States and as much as 85 percent in some urban concentrations.[9] And yet even so apparently simple a matter as the identity of the polluter cannot be established with definiteness. Blame cannot be placed on "the automobile"—a mere machine, powerless to do anything about its condition. So then responsibility must fasten on

[8] In evaluating these figures the reader should bear in mind that they represent only an isolated period in time. Industries with an apparently poor showing may have made substantial investments in pollution control equipment in the past.

[9] U.S. Congress, Senate Committee on Commerce. *The Search for a Low-Emission Vehicle.* (Government Printing Office, 1969, 91st Congress, 1st Session), p. 2.

the auto's owner; but perhaps the owner also is powerless. In any event, he would seem to have no practical option, given his need or wish for a vehicle of mobility, to use anything other than a polluting apparatus. This then raises the allegation that perhaps the manufacturer is somehow responsible. But the manufacturer can contend, with considerable validity, that he can hardly be criticized for failing to produce that for which there has been no market—namely, a vehicle with low emissions. He might add that even if he did develop such a car, it would require fuel of a type which other industries could not supply (and they in turn would point out that they would supply special fuel if the market existed).

Agriculture adds to pollution in several ways: wastes from feed-lots, fertilizers containing nutrients which nourish algae in water, pesticides, and sediments carried by erosion. Unfortunately, very little is known about the extent and possible methods for control of agricultural pollution.

Pollution does, of course, originate in sources other than those mentioned. Drainage from mines accounts for significant amounts of the water pollution in many parts of the country. Watercraft wastes and oil spills contaminate beaches and harbors. Solid wastes originate from many sources: forms arousing particular concern include beverage containers, paper, and virtually indestructible plastics.

The preceding discussion has implied that pollution problems are confined to air and water. In fact, other types of pollution occur—such as noise and radiation—but, in some ways, are of less immediate concern. This study, while acknowledging the importance of all sources and types, will concentrate on pollution of air and water which originates in industry, municipalities, and automobiles.

Externalities and Pollution Control

By and large, people live in a world of self-regulating mechanisms, and therefore unconsciously assume that most processes will be subject to natural controls acting for the general good. Natural controls work everywhere automatically, beginning with one's own body. Nature offers endless examples of self-regulation, and the marketplace depends on it for the balancing of myriads of forces. Thus, it comes as something of a surprise the first time a person notices an area in which lack of automatic self-regulation does not lead to self-destruction. One tends to assume, especially in connection with productive processes, that the effects of any action eventually will be felt, for good or bad, by the initiator of that action.

But sometimes a producer induces side effects from which he is totally immune. As an example, jet airplanes may fill the air with noxious substances, yet few of the persons affected would boycott air travel as a consequence. Economists have long been aware of such special cases, and have given them a name which, in this day of concern about pollution, is beginning to fall into the common man's vocabulary: technical external diseconomies, also known simply as externalities or external costs.

Externalities explain to a large degree why reliance on autonomous control generally will lead to results short of desirable. Even with the best good will in the world, even with a highly evolved social conscience, in many industries externalities render reliance on the producers' decisions all but impossible. If pollution controls add appreciably to costs, any businessman who installs them either must be assured that his competitors will follow suit, or he must be in the unusual position of possessing some cost advantage over others. If his competitors can undersell him, the socially conscious producer will probably find himself forced out of business. Moreover, under autonomous control each producer must make his own judgment on the level of control which is adequate; inevitably, the resulting standards will range from excessively low to excessively high.

Exceptions can be found, however, to this generally discouraging picture. Although the usual market forces do not operate to limit the imposition of polluting byproducts on society, other forces can exert pressure. The two most important of these are: (1) the need to maintain good will, and (2) the possibility of developing profitable uses for wastes. The first, one might predict, will become increasingly significant as public awareness and concern about the consequences of pollution grow. As for the second, many industries have taken an active interest in the possibilities, and are devoting considerable portions of their research budgets to the conversion of wastes to useful products.

The pressure of public relations may become an even more significant factor then in the past, now that pollution has turned into an issue of general concern. But even some years ago, many firms showed awareness of the possibility of adverse effects on good will. In the 1967 Conference Board survey, for instance, 70 percent of the 37 reporting chemical companies indicated that they considered pollution reduction at least as important as other community relations programs and sometimes more so. One firm even corrected, for purely psychological reasons, a harmless but colored air emission.

An interesting recognition of the importance of public relations took place in Chicago several years ago. In 1965 and 1966, municipal and industrial effluents made it necessary to close several South Side beaches, two or three of which were used primarily by minority races. The firms involved accepted the additional expenses of an accelerated cleanup when Federal authorities pointed out the danger that failure to reopen the beaches might lead to race riots which would be blamed on the polluters.

The danger of damage to good will rarely operates, however, in the case of city governments. After all, who would take offense at the pollution?—generally speaking, residents and downstream or downwind communities. Residents are also taxpayers, who themselves will bear the cost of any controls introduced. The reaction, either favorable or antagonistic, of other communities usually will have little financial meaning to the city, although recent attempts to initiate law suits may change the picture.[10]

The possibility of converting wastes into valuable byproducts preoccupies many who discuss pollution problems. Sometimes one senses a feeling that only industry's indifference and failure to assign sufficient research facilities stand between present practices and an idealized world in which manufacturing operates as a closed cycle, efficiently transforming wastes into useful products and using for raw materials either its own worn-out products or those from some other industry. To some degree, of course, this sort of thing has been happening for years—waste paper into paperboard, sawdust into fiberboard, etc. Unhappily, there would seem to exist very definite technological limits. Some utility companies sell precipitated fly ash for use in masonry block, but for comparatively small additions to revenue; a petroleum company managed to reclaim carbon black, but discovered the value did not justify the investment and operating costs involved; one paper company manufactures yeast with waste sulphite liquor and another paper company is experimenting with the conversion of some of its waste to an animal-feed supplement. Thus far, for most firms the returns from marketable reclaimed wastes amount to sums which rarely offset the cost of installation, operation, and maintenance of the control equipment, although there are exceptions.

The possibility of profitable byproducts from waste appears to have been rarely considered by local governments, although excep-

---

[10] In a recent historic case, reported in *All Clear*, Vol. 2, No. 2 (March/April 1970), p. 9, the mayor and six council members of West Elizabeth, Pennsylvania, were fined $500 each (but given suspended sentences) for failing to halt the discharge of raw sewage into the Monongehela River.

tions prove that the possibility exists. For instance, some cities (Las Vegas and Amarillo among others), realizing that sludge makes excellent fertilizer, now solve a disposal problem by selling the sludge which accumulates in their sanitary processing plants. St. Petersburg, Florida, has made an arrangement with a private firm to handle its garbage, at a price about half the usual cost; the firm then processes the garbage to make a compost which it sells to truck farmers and home gardeners. Other cities have experimented with sanitary landfill. Government grants have underwritten the transformation of a dump in Washington, D.C., into a park, and the building of a hill for recreation in Virginia Beach, Virginia. In general, however, very few cities have undertaken such experiments.

Recent events will force considerable changes in auto design to lessen polluting characteristics. Manufacturers, already disposed to risk incorporating pollution control devices on vehicles, despite the unwelcome increase in price which must follow, now must produce a virtually pollution-free car by 1975 in order to comply with the latest Clean Air Act. Major petroleum firms seem willing to undertake expensive conversions necessary to produce less damaging gasoline. The prospects for cooperation from auto users, however, seem less hopeful. The possibility that a sizable minority of drivers will not feel any concern about the exhaust from their particular car vastly complicates the producer's problem. Manufacturing representatives have pointed out that control devices which rely on regular maintenance—i.e., monetary outlay by the consumer—probably would not sufficiently reduce auto pollution over the long run unless the owner is compelled to maintain certain standards.

Other Approaches to Pollution Control

In view of the relative unreliability of autonomous control on the part of potential polluters, what remains? Two major additional approaches might be applied to the problem. Government might encourage control by offering appropriate tax devices, subsidies, and other economic inducements. Government also might exercise direct control by establishing pertinent regulations, which would be enforced through the use of fees and/or penalties. In varying degree, both these approaches have been brought into action already by various levels of government. The following sections will outline the steps which government has already taken, and will consider in some detail the relative merits of financial incentives and of a regulatory approach to pollution control.

*Government Role in Aiding Pollution Control**

Government activity in connection with pollution control involves several major dimensions. Government units have acted as regulators, establishing law, setting standards, monitoring and supervising compliance. Government also has offered a helping hand by providing special tax assistance and subsidies, and by underwriting or directly engaging in appropriate research. In addition, certain operations require government to turn attention to ways of coping with its own harmful byproducts.

Federal Legislation

Federal action dates back as far as the turn of the century, when the Refuse Act of 1899 prohibited the discharge of waste material into navigable waters. A 1912 act assigned responsibility for pollution, previously under the Secretary of the Army, to the Public Health Service. The Oil Pollution Act of 1924 forbade discharge of oil into coastal waters.

In 1948 Senators Barkley and Taft sponsored the Water Pollution Control Act of 1948. Asserting that pollution problems are better handled at the local level, the act nonetheless authorized the Public Health Service to coordinate research, provide technical information, and, on request from the states involved, provide limited enforcement over interstate waterways. Congress's failure to make suitable appropriations rendered largely ineffective a provision for individual project loans (up to $250,000 at 2 percent interest). The appropriations reached a high of $3 million in 1950 and declined to less than $1 million by 1955.

The Water Pollution Control Act of 1956, along with amendments in 1961, 1965, 1966 and 1970, considerably extended Federal involvement, both regulatory and financial, in water pollution control. The Water Quality Act of 1965 created the Water Pollution Control Administration. Almost as soon as this body was set up, it was transferred to the Department of the Interior. Responsibility for air pollution, however, remained with the Department of Health, Education, and Welfare.

Federal laws concerned with air pollution were instituted in 1955, when Congress authorized technical assistance to states and

*Tax Foundation, *Pollution Control: Perspectives on the Government Role* (New York, Tax Foundation, 1971), pp. 11–18 and pp. 19–25.

localities, as well as a research program. In 1963, the Clean Air Act established direct grants to states and localities for the purpose of developing, establishing, or improving control programs, as well as Federal enforcement action in interstate pollution cases. The 1963 act also provided for expanded Federal research, particularly in connection with pollution from motor vehicles and from the burning of coal and fuel oil, called for development of data on the effects of air pollution on both health and property, and emphasized the need for controlling pollution from facilities operated by the Federal government. A 1965 amendment authorized Federal regulation of motor vehicles, through standards to become effective in the 1968 model year. In 1966, another amendment expanded the Federal aid program, making grants available for maintenance of state and local control programs.

The Air Quality Act of 1967 directed HEW to delineate broad atmospheric areas for the entire country, as well as air quality control regions.[1] The 1967 act continued and strengthened most of the provisions of the earlier legislation, and provided for special studies of jet aircraft emissions, the need for national emission standards, and manpower and training problems. The 1967 law also established the Presidential Air Quality Advisory Board.

The Clean Air Act of 1970 requires that by 1975 new cars be virtually pollution-free, specifying that emissions of hydrocarbons and carbon monoxide gases must be 90 percent less than levels permissible in 1970. The Act requires manufacturers to provide a 50,000-mile warranty on auto emission control devices. It also establishes strict standards for fuel additives and permits a ban on the sale or manufacture of fuels containing additives deemed dangerous to health.

The 1970 act also provides for national standards for air pollution, with the states required to establish and enforce programs which meet national standards within the next four to six years. Wilful polluters will be subject to fines of up to $50,000 a day and jail sentences of up to two years. The Act gives all citizens and groups the right to sue in Federal court to force polluters, the U.S. government included, to cease and desist. The act also authorizes $1.1 billion for state agencies to use over the next three years for air pollution research, establishes a one-year study of noise pollution, and sets up a Federal Office of Noise Abatement and Control.

The National Environmental Policy Act of 1970 created a permanent Council on Environmental Quality, consisting of three members and a small professional staff, whose functions are to advise and

[1] See p. 29 for description of areas and regions.

assist the President in environmental matters. The act also requires all Federal agencies to consider the environmental effect of all contemplated actions.

Legislators introduced more than 600 proposals related to pollution problems during the 91st Congress, and of these a dozen or so mostly concerned with relatively limited matters (such as the extension of particular research programs, effluents from navigable vessels, etc.), have been passed.

State Legislation

States have enacted air and water pollution control regulations at an accelerated pace in recent years. Virtually all states now have enacted legislation which establishes a legal basis for control of sources of pollution. Much of this legislation, particularly in the case of air pollution, has appeared very recently. For instance, 23 states enacted their initial law concerned with air pollution during 1967–1968, and by 1968 only 30 states had adopted air pollution regulations.

Many states now offer financial assistance in the construction and operation of local waste treatment plants; 21 of the 31 states which have authorized assistance programs have funded their programs. A few states (for instance, Nebraska, New Hampshire, and New York) underwrite local bond issues for local treatment plants. Ohio has authorized the Ohio Water Development Authority, with power to construct, operate, and assess charges for treatment plants within the state. Maryland has established a Waste Acceptance Service with similar functions.

States also have improved supervision of local waste disposal operations by expanding monitoring and inspection of plants, and upgrading operators' qualifications and skills through mandatory certification requirements and training programs. At present, some 46 states require permits for industrial and municipal discharges; in six states plants are inspected monthly, in five quarterly, and in 13 annually. Certification of waste plant operators is mandatory in 16 states, and monthly operating reports must be submitted in 43 states. Unfortunately, it is reported that in many states these regulations do not work as well as they might.

Control of Pollution from Federal Facilities

As a consequence of the provisions in the Air Quality Act and the Clean Air Act, considerable action has taken place to abate pollution from Federal facilities. During fiscal 1968, remedial steps were taken at 387 installations located throughout the nation. In 126 cases, open burning or poor incineration was discontinued, and in 140 cases the Federal facility switched to fuel oil or coal with a lower sulfur content or converted to gas. Chemical or vapor emissions were reduced at 31 installations. Other action included installation of new or upgraded incinerators, replacement or improvement of heating plants, installation of improved particulate collectors, and introduction of monitor systems.

In 90 cases, however, "action" consisted merely of studies, project cost estimates, and the like. Moreover, a number of important exemptions were granted, primarily on grounds that the large capital expenditures required would make it impossible to meet Federal regulations established for its own facilities. Exceptions included installations of the Department of Defense in New York City and Philadelphia, Atomic Energy Commission in New York and Chicago, Department of Transportation in New York, and Department of Agriculture in New York.[2]

Tax Devices

Increasingly in recent years, Federal and state governments have turned to the use of tax and fiscal devices to encourage the introduction of pollution control facilities. These have taken the form of subsidies under the Federal grant-in-aid program and a variety of tax credits and exemptions in 31 states.

The Federal government offers some inducement to investment in pollution control equipment by allowing accelerated depreciation of such equipment. A profitable company thus gets whatever advantage there is from early as against later deduction in computing taxable income.[3] Seven states also provide for rapid amortization—in all cases, over a 60-month period—of new pollution control facilities (Table 2).

At the state level, however, the most favored tax approach appears to be an exemption of pollution control facilities from the property tax, with 24 states specifying such exemption in 1970. In

---

[2] Secretary of Health, Education, and Welfare. *Air Pollution Abatement by Federal Facilities* (Sen. Doc. 91-10, 91st Congress, 1st Session.), Government Printing Office: March 1969, 27 pp.

[3] Under provisions of the Tax Reform Act of 1969, a 60-month write-off is allowed for pollution control equipment added to plants which were in operation before January 1, 1969, if the equipment is placed in service before January 1, 1975.

TABLE 2

Special Tax Provisions for Installation of Pollution
Control Facilities, by State, June 1970

State	Property tax exemp-tion	Sales and use tax exemp-tion	Income tax credit	Rapid amor-tization
Alabama	x			
Arizona				x
Arkansas		x		
California				x
Connecticut	x	x	x	
Florida[a]	x			
Georgia	x	x		
Hawaii	x			
Idaho	x			
Illinois	x	x		
Indiana	x			
Maine		x		
Massachusetts	x			
Michigan	x	x		
Minnesota	x		x	
Missouri		x		
Montana	x			
New Hampshire	x			
New Jersey	x			
New York	x		x	
North Carolina	x			x
Ohio[b]	x	x		
Oklahoma			x	
Oregon	x		x	
Pennsylvania		x		
Rhode Island	x	x		x
South Carolina	x			
Tennessee	x			
Vermont	x			
Virginia				x
Washington		x		
West Virginia		x	x	
Wisconsin	x			x
Wyoming	x			

a. Sales tax exemption repealed at time property tax exemption introduced in July 1969.

b. Also provides pollution facilities not to be considered assets in determining value of stock on which Ohio's franchise tax is levied.

Source: Based on data from Commerce Clearing House and state pollution control laws.

many states, the exemption is carefully restricted to that portion of a facility which can be demonstrated to be utilized in pollution control, with any portion producing a marketable byproduct subject to tax.

Twelve states specifically exempt pollution control equipment from sales and use taxes. Six states provide income tax credits. Connecticut, Minnesota, and Oregon allow a credit amounting to 5 percent of outlay for qualified equipment (restricted in Minnesota to $50,000 annually with provisions for carryback and carryover); Oklahoma permits a 20 percent credit. In New York, the taxpayer has the option of taking either the usual 1 percent tax credit allowed for new equipment of any kind, or deducting the entire cost of the pollution control equipment from taxable income.

In Louisiana, plants which utilize principally waste materials in their production processes are valued for property tax purposes at only 25 percent. The law mentions specifically such waste materials as water hyacinths, rice hulls and straws, sugar cane stalks, bagasse, waste rags and clippings, waste paper, oyster shells, and other items, but does not appear to confine the exemption to the materials listed.

Subsidies and Other Direct Expenditures

Federal expenditures for air pollution control began in 1956, when less than $1 million was spent on a research program in the Public Health Service and technical assistance to state and local agencies. Expenditures have risen steadily since that time, totaling more that $4 million in 1959 and more than $67 million in 1969 (Table 3). Federal expenditures have been divided among a number of functions. Direct operations include such activities as abatement and control, manpower training, various management services, research, development, and demonstration projects. The grant program, begun

TABLE 3
Federal Expenditures for Air Pollution Control
Selected Fiscal Years, 1959-1971
(Millions of dollars)

Year	Total expenditures	Direct operations	Grants
1971	$111.0[a]	NA	NA
1969	67.6	NA	NA
1968	49.6	22.2	27.4
1967	32.9	15.3	17.6
1966	25.4	11.6	13.8
1965	20.6	9.8	10.8
1964	12.8	8.0	4.8
1963	10.4	7.0	3.4
1962	8.4	6.3	2.1
1961	7.0	5.1	1.9
1960	5.2	NA	NA
1959	4.4	NA	NA

a. Estimate by Bureau of the Budget.
Source: Bureau of the Budget.

in 1961, has expanded rapidly, from an initial outlay of $1.9 million up to $27.4 million in the latest year for which details are available, 1968.

Fairly substantial portions of these grants have gone to state and local governments directly since 1965. The amounts have varied considerably from state to state, both in terms of totals and per capita amounts (Table 4). Five states (Alaska, Delaware, Maine, South Dakota, and Vermont) received no grants for air pollution control at all during 1965-1968, while four others (California, Illinois, New Jersey, and Pennsylvania) each received a cumulative total in excess of $1 million over that same period. At first glance it would seem that population explains the variance among states, since the zero-grant group consists of generally small states, while those getting most have large populations. But per capita figures suggest otherwise. Per capita grants range from zero to 27 cents; the five highest states on a per capita basis (Kentucky, Connecticut, Colorado, Arizona, and Washington, in that order) seem to have no relevant traits in common, such as population density, geographic location, prevalence of large metropolitan centers, or unusual pollution problems.

Very little information is available with respect to state and local expenditures for air pollution control. HEW estimates that 85 local air pollution control agencies operated with total expenditures of about $8 million, and 17 state agencies with total outlay of about $2 million, for a state and local total of approximately $10 million in 1961. By contrast, in 1969 an estimated 142 local agencies spent $29.7 million and agencies in nearly all of the states spent $17.6 million, for a state and local total of $47.5—close to a fivefold increase over the 1961 total.[4]

The U.S. Budget for 1971 provides information on Federal expenditures for water pollution control in urban areas, giving some impression of the rapid expansion in such programs. In 1961 water pollution control outlays came to $24 million, and by 1969 had increased fourfold, to $104 million. Expenditures for water and sewer facilities also had increased, from $36 million in 1964 (the earliest year data are available) to $52 million in 1969.

Federal grants to state and local governmental units for water pollution problems fall under many different categories and agencies, and consequently are quite difficult to identify in total. While air pollution has been in the domain of the Department of Health, Education and Welfare throughout, an assortment of departments and

---

[4] U.S. Secretary of Health, Education and Welfare, *The Cost of Clean Air* (91st Congress, 1st sess. Sen. Doc. No. 91-40; Washington, D.C.: Government Printing Office, 1969), p. 11.

TABLE 4

Federal Grants to State and Local Governments for Air and Water Pollution Control, by State
Fiscal 1965-1968 and 1968

State	Grants for air pollution control, 1965-1968		Grants for water pollution control, 1968	
	Total (millions)	Per capita	Total (millions)	Per capita
TOTAL	$13.8	$.07	$264.9	$ 1.33
Alabama	.3	.07	4.4	1.24
Alaska	—	—	.6	2.18
Arizona	.3	.16	3.9	2.36
Arkansas	(a)	.02	6.3	3.11
California	1.2	.06	21.6	1.12
Colorado	.4	.19	4.5	2.22
Connecticut	.6	.20	3.1	1.05
Delaware	—	—	1.8	3.37
Florida	.2	.03	9.9	1.61
Georgia	.2	.05	6.9	1.51
Hawaii	(a)	.05	2.3	3.02
Idaho	(a)	.02	2.4	3.42
Illinois	1.4	.12	11.4	1.04
Indiana	.3	.06	5.9	1.16
Iowa	(a)	.01	4.6	1.68
Kansas	(a)	.01	5.5	2.40
Kentucky	.9	.27	3.3	1.03
Louisiana	.1	.03	3.9	1.04
Maine	. . .	. . .	3.0	3.02
Maryland	.6	.15	5.0	1.32
Massachusetts	.3	.06	2.6	.49
Michigan	.4	.05	8.6	.99
Minnesota	.1	.04	5.9	1.62
Mississippi	(a)	(b)	3.4	1.45
Missouri	.3	.06	6.3	1.35
Montana	.1	.11	1.6	2.36
Nebraska	(a)	.01	2.1	1.49
Nevada	(a)	.06	4.6	10.11
New Hampshire	(a)	.08	1.4	2.00
New Jersey	1.0	.14	6.8	.96
New Mexico	.1	.12	3.3	3.23
New York	.9	.05	16.3	.90
North Carolina	.2	.04	7.9	1.55
North Dakota	(a)	.04	1.6	2.63
Ohio	.3	.02	10.7	1.01
Oklahoma	.1	.02	2.9	1.15
Oregon	.2	.13	2.8	1.42
Pennsylvania	1.2	.10	9.1	.77
Rhode Island	.1	.06	1.7	1.87
South Carolina	.1	.03	3.6	1.32
South Dakota	—	—	2.4	3.71
Tennessee	.1	.03	5.8	1.46
Texas	.6	.05	12.2	1.11
Utah	.1	.06	1.8	1.77
Vermont	—	—	2.6	6.10
Virginia	.1	.02	6.6	1.43
Washington	.5	.16	6.0	1.83
West Virginia	.1	.05	3.6	2.01
Wisconsin	(a)	.01	6.9	1.63
Wyoming	(a)	.01	.7	2.19

a. Less than 0.1 million.
b. Less than 1 cent.
Source: Computations based on data from U. S. Treasury.

agencies concern themselves with water. These include a program in the Department of Agriculture concerned with rural water and waste disposal; in the Department of Housing and Urban Development concerned with water and sewer facilities; several programs in the Department of Interior dealing with such problems as waste treatment works construction, water resources research, and pollution control directly.

The Federal government expends considerably more on water pollution than on air pollution, if judgments may be made from the comparative size of grants-in-aid to state and local units for the two purposes. In 1968, for example, total grants for air pollution amounted to $13.8 million, whereas all the grants concerned with water pollution in that year totaled $264.9 million. Per capita amounts to states in 1968 ranged from $10.11 in Nevada down to 49 cents in Massachusetts (Table 4).

Regulation and Fees

Late in 1970, President Nixon announced a mandatory industrial waste permit system, to be administered by the Army Corps of Engineers under the 1899 Refuse Act. An estimated 40,000 industrial dischargers into navigable waters or their tributaries have until July 1, 1971, to submit an application for a permit, but the President has warned that violators of standards will not be exempt from legal action during the period preceding the permit deadline. The Environmental Protection Agency is developing guidelines for 22 industrial groups. The Refuse Act provides criminal and injunctive measures against noncompliance, and the administration has stated these will be actively utilized. The Refuse Act, because it specifically exempts refuse flowing from streets and sewers, generally does not apply to municipalities, but the President has indicated he will seek other regulatory devices to reduce municipal water pollution.

Some states take a straightforward regulatory approach, with no financial concessions offered. One such, Mississippi, levies annual inspection fees ranging from $50 to $200 for firms, depending on their employee-size, and from $50 to $1,000 for municipalities, depending on population.

Vermont has embarked upon a new approach which will require every individual or firm discharging waste into a watercourse to obtain a permit from the state. Fees will be charged for permits, the amounts presumably so designed as to induce polluters to install suitable processing equipment. The law, which was passed in mid-1970 and becomes effective July 1971, provides broad scope to the

Department of Water Resources in establishing fee levels, which must be set by the beginning of 1971. An economic-engineering study will provide the basis on which fees will be determined.

Tax Assistance and Environmental Pollution*

Excessive air and water pollution is the result of the use of our rivers and atmosphere as free and inexhaustible resources. Clearly, they are not. If these two resources are limited, how then should they be rationed? Does tax assistance aid in this rationing? To discern answers to these questions, it is necessary to examine various forms of federal assistance now rendered as well as the merits of additional federal tax assistance.

Present Federal Assistance

The most significant form of aid to industry is the substantial sharing of pollution abatement costs already being undertaken by the federal government through the current corporate tax laws. The net impact on industry profits of expenditures on pollution abatement equipment is much less than the dollar amount spent. This is because a firm is allowed a depreciation write-off for investment in pollution abatement facilities that will result in a lower tax liability than would have occurred without the abatement investment. For every dollar of depreciable capital investment undertaken for pollution control pur-

EDITOR'S NOTE: This issue of *Tax Policy* is extracted from the paper presented by Mr. Wilson at the Tax Institute of America symposium on "Tax Incentives" on November 21, 1969. The complete paper will appear in the symposium volume, which will be published by Heath Lexington Books early in 1971. This abridged version is being printed with the permission of the publisher.

This paper draws largely on work which the author did with Dr. Jack Carlson, et al., in *Cost Sharing with Industry?* Summary Report of the Working Committee on Economic Incentives (Revised), November 20, 1967. A second source was *Incentives to Industry for Water Pollution Control: Policy Considerations*, Cambridge: Abt Associates, Inc., 1967 (Prepared for the Federal Water Pollution Control Administration, Department of the Interior).

*Douglas B. Wilson, from Tax Assistance and Environmental Pollution from *Tax Policy*, Vol. XXXVII, published by Tax Institute of America, July–August 1970, pp. 3–11.

poses, the government pays from 33 to 43 percent of the firm's costs in the form of a reduction in corporate tax revenues.[1]

The federal government also offers assistance on the expenditure side to states, municipalities, and interstate agencies through its federal water pollution program which is currently about $390 million. Elements of this program include research and development, training and planning grants, and municipal sewage treatment construction grants. Manufacturing firms benefit from federally aided municipal treatment facilities and gain economies of scale of area-wide pollution control. For air, budgeted federal assistance is currently $87 million. These funds are spent for research, training, technical assistance, and grants and aids to state, local, and regional government agencies.

Additional Tax Assistance as a Form of Federal Assistance

The usual argument for additional tax assistance, beyond the current levels of aid, is based on the belief that needed pollution control will be relatively expensive. However, this does not seem to be the case. Although the additional annual costs of air and water pollution control are difficult to measure because they are a function of local water and air quality standards, plant location, topography, stream capacity, meteorology, production processes, and pollutants, it is estimated that they will be less than .4 per cent of value added by manufacturers.[2] This assumes a hypothetical standard requiring 85 per cent removal of biochemical oxygen-demanding waste and suspended solids. The air pollution standard is assumed to be a reduction of sulphur oxide gases (SO_x) and particulate exposure by 60 to 75 percent below present levels.

For particular industries and firms, the burden, of course, will vary from the average. The chemical industry is likely to spend nearly four times this average for water pollution control while the machinery industry is likely to spend less than one-fourth. It is not clear, of course, that pollution abatement need affect the firm's rate

[1] The exact amount of aid depends upon the tax accounting methods and discount rate of the firm involved. The more rapidly the investment is depreciated for tax purposes, the sooner tax savings accrue to the firm, and hence the more valuable they are. The higher a firm's discount rate, the less value money has if it accrues later as opposed to earlier. The range of values reflects discount rates from between 4 and 10 percent, approximately 15-year depreciation lives for the assets, and the sum-of-the-years-digits depreciation method. In short, the government may be viewed as participating in unproductive investments to the extent of the present worth of future income taxes foregone.

[2] *Cost Sharing with Industry?* Summary Report of the Working Committee on Economic Incentives (Revised), November 20, 1967, pp. 12-25.

of profit in so far as individual established firms may have considerable flexibility to shift the small increase in costs to the purchasers of their products.[3] It is with this note on expected additional costs of abatements and its incidence in mind that possible additional tax assistance will be examined.

Numerous proposals in Congress have been made for offering greater assistance to industry through increased investment tax credits or accelerated amortization of capital expenditures for pollution abatement. Proposals range from increasing the investment tax credit for pollution devices of 14 or 20 percent and/or allowing amortization normally scheduled over fifteen years to be scheduled over five years, three years, or even one year. The capital subsidy would range from 18 percent for an investment tax credit of 14 percent to 46 percent for implementing a 20 percent tax credit and a one-year accelerated amortization schedule. The subsidy would total roughly $315 million for water and $80 million for air for the three-year accelerated amortization allowance if applied to the estimate of the additional capital required to meet the standards mentioned earlier. (See Table 1.)

Additional abatement assistance in this manner has, however, a number of shortcomings. It should be noted first that additional tax assistance does not provide an incentive to undertake further abatement. When tax credits or accelerated amortization is allowed for profitable investments, the effect is to enhance the rate of return. However, tax assistance for abatement devices excludes profitable investments. An unprofitable investment remains a loss to the firm regardless of whether tax assistance exists. Moreover, it is not clear that tax assistance generally aids a firm to raise capital for pollution

---

[3] The degree to which a firm in the short run can pass forward to the consumer the increased costs of manufacturing resulting from abatement depends upon the elasticity of the supply and demand for the output. If demand is absolutely inelastic, then consumers will purchase the same quantity at a higher price. If, on the other hand, demand is fairly elastic (quantity purchased is responsive to price changes), then the firm and the consumer will share the cost of control; a somewhat smaller quantity will be purchased at a slightly higher price. Firms with sharp increments in costs associated with small increases in output will be less likely to shift pollution costs forward because of the larger margin of profit gained on incremental amounts sold compared to firms experiencing less rise in their incremental costs. The firm with steeper incremental costs has more to lose by sacrificing its marginal units of production than other firms. In so far as not all firms within a competitive market are required to abate, then the abating firm may not be able to pass forward the cost of the abatement. In this case, the abatement cost may result in a reduction in employment and output in the firm's effort to maintain normal profits. This, however, is not a case of backward shifting because it is not suggested that temporarily unemployed resources would receive less remuneration to gain employment in other firms or industries.

TABLE 1

Comparison of the Additional Subsidy to Industry Through Alternative Forms of Federal Assistance[a]

Type of Assistance	Subsidy as a Per Cent of Capital Cost	Subsidy as a Per Cent of Annual Cost[c]		Rough Estimate of Likely Assistance to Industry for Capital Expenditures to Meet Hypothetical Standards in 5 Years: 1969-1973[d] (In Millions)	
		Water	Air	Water[e]	Air[f]
Accelerated amortization: 5 years	13%	5%	2%	$241	$ 61
3 years	17	6	3	315	80
1 year.	21	9	4	389	99
Tax credits: 14%	18	7	4	333	85
20%	25	10	5	463	118
Accelerated amortization and tax credit combined:					
14% tax credit and 3-year accelerated amortization	35	14	7	648	165
20% tax credit and 1-year accelerated amortization	46	21	10	851	216
Reduced interest loans:[b]					
6% (3% below discount rate)	11	4	2	204	52
4% (5% below discount rate)	17	7	3	315	80

[a]Assume 52.8 per cent effective tax rate, 15-year functional life (straight line) for pollution abatement facilities and 10 per cent discount rate. Excluding accelerated depreciation now available in existing tax laws—e.g., sum of digits or double declining balance.

[b]15 years, straight reduction loan, 9 per cent discount rate for industry (if assume 6 per cent, then zero gain for 6 per cent interest loan and 7 per cent or $71 million interest loan).

[c]Includes annual capital cost (amortized) and operation and maintenance expenditures, increase in total cost of abatement because of excessive use of artificially cheaper capital costs.

[d]Assuming all capital expenditures are subsidized whether to industry or households. Capital costs would undoubtedly drop after the initial investments are made to achieve standards.

[e]Based on industrial profiles: $1.15 billion additional investment plus $.7 billion replacement investment which equals $1.85 billion for BOD and suspended solids for hypothetical standard of 85 per cent treatment of industrial wastes.

[f]Assuming 20 years of additional capital investment is made in 5 years. The total capital as indicated by the "Typical City" Study should be $470 million to achieve a hypothetical standard of reducing human exposure by 60-75 per cent of SOx and particulates.

abatement. A firm which has difficulty raising capital for abatement probably has difficulty raising capital for profitable investment as well and is in no frame of mind to consider the use of its scarce resources on pollution abatement. These are tentative hardship cases about which more will be said later.

The subsidy supplied by tax assistance is partly illusory in so far as a higher level of expenditure results from the incentive to overuse capital to the neglect of operating and maintenance expenditure. This arises because capital costs are made artificially cheaper by virtue of the tax write-off. Tax write-offs are handicapped because they are incapable of providing assistance to all the costs of abatement. Capital costs, it is estimated, account for roughly one-third of the total cost for water pollution abatement and one-eighth for air pollution abatement. When subsidies are given to capital alone, the capital cost proportion will tend to rise and unnecessarily consume resources. Alternative means of pollution control are often less costly than building additional capacity in order to treat larger waste loads. Fuel substitution, for example, is estimated to be the least costly alternative in over half of the cases involving sulphur oxide air pollution abatement.

A related shortcoming is that tax write-offs are difficult to apply to many changes in the production process which reduce not only the generation of waste loads but also add to plant output. In water pollution control, it has been shown that some industries find over 50 percent of the least-cost opportunities for reducing waste load discharges in such process changes. Moreover, the Treasury Department would be faced with the difficult task of certifying the proportion of the cost attributable to pollution abatement or disallowing assistance for production improvements. In many such cases, the final decision may have to be made after lengthy debate in the courts. To the extent that the proportion is disallowed, plants would be given an incentive to ignore many improvements which have been shown to be least costly. Also, the implementation of selective write-offs for pollution abatement opens the door for other programs to receive similar treatment. Proposals for tax write-offs for training, education, mining, transportation, housing, and others have already been made. The cumulative effect for industry could be, conceivably, an increase in the corporate tax structure or a lag in the long-run reduction of tax rates and thus no net benefit to firms facing pollution abatement expenditure.[4]

---

[4] The reader may be concerned with the apparent inconsistency between the argument that the corporate income tax is a vehicle through which the government aids pollution abatement and the present contention. The discussion in the paper simply recognizes that the government shares in the results of a firm's productive as well as unproductive efforts.

Moreover, public accountability of such subsidies is difficult and would probably create an annoying problem in its removal when social policy dictated a change. Even in the year-to-year operation of the program, the amount of abatement assistance would not be controllable as in the case of an annual appropriation where a mix of air and water pollution abatement assistance would be provided. The task of putting together an air and water pollution strategy should be thought of in unitary terms in which there is a consideration not only of the range of pollution problems, but also of the range of techniques needed to ameliorate them. A successful pollution control program must work on a broad front rather than concentrate on limited solutions.

There are a significant number of ways to combat environmental pollution. There is recovery and reuse of materials and of the pollutants themselves. Through waste treatment, there may be both modification of contaminates in waste and their removal and disposition. Products may be modified by introducing pollution-reducing properties into potentially contaminating materials. Contaminate-using processes can be altered to prevent or reduce release of pollutants. The development of nonconventional power sources for automobiles and improved internal combustion engines are examples of this. The waste discharge can be dispersed over a larger area or through a greater volume. The use of high smoke stacks or regulating discharge to coincide with stream flows illustrate dispersion. Pollutants can be held in detention for gradual or later release. There can be diversion by transporting the waste to another location for discharge. There can be environmental treatment to remove pollutants or diminish their effects. There can be desensitization of pollutant recepters. The screening of junkyards is an example with regard to the land environment. Vaccination against waterborne diseases exemplifies desensitization in the water area.

It is clear that any pollution control system will require the development and deployment of a combination of these methods. They complement each other. Well-planned and administered public expenditure programs are needed to effectively encourage suitable abatement procedures and techniques. Tax assistance provides no incentive to efficiently develop or use these various solutions.

One of the chief difficulties in using tax incentives to control environmental pollution is that they cannot be readily targeted to meet priority areas. For example, in air it is transportation, not manufacturing, that is the chief source of pollution. Transportation produces 60 percent of the emissions, manufacturing 20 percent, and electric power generation 12 percent. Also, it would not be possible to use the federal tax system to target incentives toward particular cities or regions in the country. Los Angeles, New York, and Chicago are far more polluted than Charlottesville or Grand Rapids. An increment of pollution in these latter cities is equally less worth while than in the larger cities. Our resources are scarce; they need to be targeted well.

In a similar fashion, tax assistance does not encourage firms to take account of some of the potentially important economies in pollution control which come from regional cooperation. Among the economies which may result are those associated in water pollution abatement with large-scale treatment plants or the manipulation of waste loads to respond to river characteristics. If anything, tax assistance encourages firms to construct individual and therefore inefficient abatement facilities. If regional authority is seen as a long range solution, tax incentives offered today will help create exactly the kinds of inefficient individual facilities which such an authority is designed to avoid. To put it alternatively, the initiation of additional tax assistance does not alleviate the need for regional abatement. Significant reductions in cost may be achieved in this manner. It was found, for example, in a simulation exercise that the cost of air pollution abatement of sulphur oxides would be decreased by 50 percent if selective abatement were used as opposed to across-the-board emission reductions.[5] Thus, anything which inhibits the formation of regional abatement solutions will result in both excessive delay in amelioration of the pollution as well as in excessive costs.

Alternative Policies for Additional Assistance

It might be argued that tax assistance, although ineffective, forms a second-best solution. There are, however, a number of other alternatives which would be more effective than rapid tax write-offs. One possibility is grants and loans for firms issued through regional pollution control agencies. These agencies could dispense funds to industrial plants which requested assistance for studies to determine the feasible way to achieve quality standards. The plants which are likely to face the largest abatement could easily be identified and feasibility studies could help identify least-costly expenditures in order that these plants achieve the desired standards. Information of a nonproprietary nature could be shared to help other plants facing similar problems. A subsidy of this kind would tend to increase the flow of

---

[5] *Cost-Sharing with Industry? op. cit.*, pp. 19–25. See also United States Department of Health, Education, and Welfare, *An Economic Analysis of the Control of Sulphur Oxides Air Pollution*, Program Analysis No. 1967-9, Washington, 1967, p. V-8.

human and physical resources into pollution abatement and create demand pressures for technological advances. Although this alternative is not without precedence, it does tread close to the presently perceived separation between government and industry in the American economy.

From an equity standpoint, assistance could be considered for "hardship" plants. Such assistance could be in the form of low interest loans, loan guarantees, lease guarantees, preferential government purchase arrangements, and other programs which already exist. The Small Business Administration (SBA) and the Economic Development Administration (EDA) may assist in such hardship cases. The most useful SBA programs for hardship cases are Section 7a loans or loan guarantees, and the lease guarantee program. Under Section 7a of the Small Business Act of 1958, SBA can make direct loans either by itself or in participation with banks; it can guarantee loans made by banks. The programs of the Small Business Administration encompass approximately 95 percent of all nonfarm industry. Such pervasive coverage of American business occurs because of the broad mandate contained in SBA legislation. Over 90 percent of the firms and industries facing the greatest abatement costs—foods, paper, chemicals, petroleum refineries, and primary metals—are classified as small businesses. The major benefit to hardship firms would be guaranteed access to loans for purchasing pollution abatement equipment and facilities. Payment over a ten-to-fifteen-year period would greatly reduce the cash flow burden that pollution abatement expenditures can cause.

The Economic Development Administration can offer financial and technical assistance to any plant or firm regardless of size if pollution abatement action should "tend to limit modernization, expansion or solvency of the facility." Usually such a plant must be in a county which is designated as a "depressed area." Nearly one-third of the land area is currently designated as depressed. EDA can also serve small areas. An area as small as a set of census tracts in New York City was designated as depressed because of the curtailment of work at the Brooklyn Naval Shipyard. In all areas, including those outside depressed areas, EDA can pay the entire cost of technical studies for the purpose of identifying least-costly methods of abating pollution for plants in towns or sections of cities threatened by reduced economic activity.

Another alternative is assistance offered to industry based solely on the burden to each plant or firm unrelated to the ability of the firm to handle the burden. The determination of relative burden could be based upon pollution abatement expenditures as a percentage of the value added for each plant. Once eligibility was determined, all assistance could be offered heavy burden cases.

There are, however, a number of administrative problems with this type of assistance which should be recognized. Assistance will require some measurement of hardship and it is not clear over what period of time this hardship should be measured. Assistance for a relatively short period is a desirable guidepost. Over the long run, the marketplace should determine success or failure for each plant and firm.

A further difficulty is whether assistance should be used to build a new plant. Inasmuch as entrepreneurs now generally know the ground rules for pollution abatement, it is felt that new plants should be excluded from receiving assistance.

Multi-plant firms present another problem. If plant "A" of a multi-plant firm is shut down for pollution reasons and relocated, would this plant be eligible for pollution assistance? Also, if a plant is shut down in a multi-plant firm, is this of the same severity as a shutdown of a single-plant firm? The answer should depend in part on whether the multi-plant firm is located in a one-plant town. Therefore, proper criteria and administrative discretion would have to built into such a policy alternative.

Finally, in some cases, the determination of the least-cost method of pollution abatement could involve the interference with the management prerogatives of the firm. For example, it might be possible to reduce the pollution from a plant by slightly altering the firm's product or its rate of output. Pollution control in a sulphuric acid plant is enhanced if the rate of production is slowed. A coffee roasting plant which changes its coffee blending techniques might have significantly fewer pollution problems.

Yet another alternative would be to offer grants or other forms of assistance on the basis of reduction in measured, damaging waste loads. Such a subsidy could be based on the marginal effort to abate and thus would be highly efficient and facilitate enforcement. This approach has the advantage of acting as a carrot.

Unfortunately, performance measures have not been perfected and therefore grants based on performance must wait for the future. But with the current effort to improve pollution measuring devices, a performance program may be feasible within the relatively near future.

From the economist's point of view, the control of air and water pollution could be facilitated if a price were charged for fouling the environment. The advantage of the price solution is that individuals and society explicitly value the resources that are devoted to pollution abatement. This valuation of the costs and benefits of abatement should lead to a socially optimal solution provided the income distribution which gives rise to the range of relative prices is considered desirable.

The implementation of such a plan requires the evaluation of the damage done by the emission of an incremental quality of pollution at a given time and place. Subsequent to this evaluation, an emission charge is assessed to the responsible parties based on the amount of damage. Presumably, those with the capability to reduce emissions at a cost which is less than the pollution charge will do so, and the proper amount of abatement will be obtained by means that are least costly. If the charge is too low, it will not constitute adequate inducement to reduce the wastes disposed and, if the price is too high, it will induce more control than is necessary and will be uneconomic in its effect. Experience through the use of such fees will help reduce this uncertainty. Experimentation could be fruitfully pursued in a few river basins now.

There is considerable experience with user charges[6] for industrial waste treatment service in collective public facilities. It has been successful in providing revenues to communities for replacement facilities, in encouraging sound industrial waste treatment practices, and in providing a businesslike way of managing a vital community service. Some pollution control experts see the establishment of regional waste treatment facilities for the acceptance of all wastes on a user charge basis as the appropriate solution to the water pollution control problem. The regional facility would be operated in accord with the hydrologic situation and environmental standards. Waste treatment facilities in the case of air pollution control on a collective basis are less applicable. However, the principle of regional management is equally attractive.

The only experience in America in this area has been the use of user charges by municipalities and other organizations handling wastes. Effluent or emission charges have yet to be tried extensively, although numerous task forces and studies have specifically recommended their experimental use. So far, there is no experience with charges for air pollution control, although the advantage of using them is likely to be significant.

---

[6] The term effluent or emission charge is used to refer to the price charged for direct disposal to the environment. In contrast, the term user charge refers to the price charged for waste treatment service provided in a treatment facility. The level of the effluent charge for direct disposal to the environment may alternatively be based on the cost of reducing or treating the particular wastes in a treatment facility. The treatment facility would be designed and operated to modify the wastes sufficiently to meet the environmental standards.

It is apparent that many difficulties are involved in setting and administering effluent charges, especially in the determination of the right price, and the surveillance and monitoring of performance.

In the air pollution situation, there is yet no opportunity to use the cost of treating emissions as a measure of the proper emission charge. Certainly it is wise to state that effluent and emission fees should be tried in demonstration projects and experimental programs during 1970. Current legislative authority would permit such projects or programs.

Summary

In summation of this discussion, it should be emphasized that tax and expenditure assistance are already being provided. Additional tax assistance would be ineffective and costly due to its multiple drawbacks. Moreover, it is not an incentive. There are already existing programs which can more effectively alleviate hardship if it occurs. Finally, there is evidence that the demand for abatement is far greater than its costs; it now remains to be supplied in an economical manner.

C

Revenue Sharing

Except for the recent surge in federal outlays in connection with the Vietnam conflict, state and local government expenditures have been growing much faster than federal expenditures. States and their localities, on their own, are now spending at the rate of over $100 billion annually. This amounts to almost $500 per capita in 1970 compared with less than $100 per capita in 1946. In 1946, federal tax receipts amounted to 21 cents per dollar of personal income, while state and local tax receipts were just over 6 cents per dollar of personal income. In 1970, federal tax receipts had not substantially changed as a proportion of personal income but state and local tax receipts had risen to 12 cents per dollar of personal income. Yet, an increasing demand for services continues to add significantly to the burden of state and local governments. Thus, state and local governments need additional revenues to finance the public services for which they assume responsibility.

The proposal to authorize the federal government to share its revenues with state and local governments is regarded by the Nixon Administration as an essential part of the President's domestic program. The two readings reflect the arguments for and against revenue sharing. The first reading, "The Need for Revenue Sharing," by Murray L. Weidenbaum, Assistant Secretary to the Treasury for Economic Policy, presents the arguments for revenue sharing. The second article, "Comments on Revenue Sharing," by Congressman Wilbur D. Mills, Chairman of the House Ways and Means Committee, presents the arguments against revenue sharing.

The Need for Revenue Sharing*

We all like to talk about the need to strengthen our Federal form of government, about moving government from Washington closer to the people. Most of the time, let us face it, that is just talk. However, we in the Nixon Administration are really trying to decentralize government and to take specific action to strengthen state and local government so that they can meet the fiscal crisis which is now facing so many communities and taxpayers.

The idea that is at the heart of this effort is the program of sharing a portion of Federal revenues with state and local governments, to, in effect, truly Federalize the income taxes collected by the Department of the Treasury. The mechanism that we have selected is financial because we believe that sharing responsibilities and work more effectively within the public sector requires a sharing of the fiscal resources necessary for the task—a sharing of public revenues.

Before getting into the details, one fundamental point needs to be made. We are not recommending just another program of sending Federal dollars around the country; there certainly is no shortage of ways of doing that already.

We are proposing a shift of decision-making power to state and local governments. Revenue sharing is unlike any existing grant-in-aid program. Under revenue sharing, the money that state and local governments obtain from the U. S. Treasury becomes their money. The Federal Government does not tell them how to use the money. For example, revenue-sharing money can go into a county's general fund, and it is up to the county council to decide how to spend it.

The following is an outline of the revenue-sharing proposal. First, the annual size of the fund will be fixed by law at 1.3 percent of the Federal personal tax base. States and localities will be able to count on it in their long-term planning. The annual amount will increase steadily as the economy and the tax base grows.

Second, the distribution among states will be made according to each state's share of the national population, with a simple adjustment for relative revenue effort.

Third, the distribution within each state to the cities and counties will be established by formula clearly spelled out in the Federal

---

*Murray L. Weidenbaum, unpublished paper furnished by Murray L. Weidenbaum, Assistant Secretary of the Treasury for Economic Policy, December 1970, pp. 1–9.

statute. The key point is that each city and county will be able to get its share as a matter of right and will not have to negotiate with the Federal or state government. There will also be a local option in our plan, whereby the local governments and the state legislature in a given state can get together and set up an alternate plan for the intrastate distribution of the money.

Fourth, the allocation of the money to specific programs will be made by the state or local government receiving the money. There will be no plans to submit for Federal review and no matching requirements.

Several key questions on how revenue sharing will work come up time and again. Here are some responses to the more serious points that have been raised.

Will all the money go to the state governments exclusively? The answer is no. Each city, county and town will get a portion of the revenue-sharing fund automatically. A guarantee has been developed which both protects the local governments and maintains the Federal form of government. This is different from most earlier revenue-sharing plans.

It is true that initially the U.S. Treasury will make payments to the states but each state, in order to qualify for the Federal money, will have to pass on to each city and county a predetermined share— the share spelled out in the Federal law (unless the "local option" is exercised by the state and its localities). This provision is called the mandatory pass-through. It was developed in joint consultations with the National League of Cities, the U. S. Conference of Mayors, the National Governors Conference, the National Association of Counties, and other key organizations.

Will the proposal provide enough money for the large urban areas? The amounts will be quite generous, particularly in view of the national budgetary situation.

Our approach is to distribute revenue-sharing funds within a state to each city and county in proportion to general revenue collections. So-called "tax havens" with low tax collections and a narrow range of functions will receive very small shares. In contrast, cities with heavy program responsibilities and, hence, large tax revenues will get bigger amounts, even if their populations are the same.

In practice, nearly every large city will receive not just absolutely more money but also more per capita than its smaller neighbors. However, the large central cities will get more revenue-sharing money not just because they are bigger, but because they bear a larger fiscal burden.

Why bother to make the expensive "round trip" of tax dollars to

Washington—why not leave the money in those states and localities where it originates? Actually, the Department of the Treasury has lower tax collection costs than any state or local government agency. Since revenue sharing will not require any new Federal agency or bureau (all that is required is a simple check-writing procedure) the round trip will be quite economical.

Do we really have any excess Federal revenue to share—won't revenue sharing increase the budget deficit? This question apparently results from some confusion over the purpose and operation of a revenue-sharing program. Revenue sharing is an expenditure for a basic national purpose—strengthening our Federal system of government. We would not be sending back to the states "excess" revenues left over from Federal program requirements, but rather rearranging existing Federal program priorities.

Revenue sharing will not raise the existing Federal tax burden. The alternative to revenue sharing is not a smaller Federal deficit. The alternative is a higher level of Federal spending in some other— and, in our view, lower priority—program areas.

In modern Federal budget-making, the levels of expenditures and revenues are determined as a part of the Nation's overall economic policy. In general, Federal expenditures are set at a level which makes a strong but noninflationary contribution to economic growth (noninflationary because keeping expenditures within the revenues that the economy generates at full employment—as we are trying to do avoids creating inflationary pressures).

Hence, funding a revenue-sharing program in the context of the present-day budget means that we are selecting this program, rather than some other, for a major share of the automatic annual growth in Federal revenues. We believe that this is a wise choice of priorities.

Are state and local governments competent to use revenue-sharing money effectively? This question presents a real challenge. We believe that strengthening our Federal form of government by helping state and local governments is an objective worthy of an investment of several billion dollars a year.

Frankly, no one can guarantee that all of the money will be used wisely. Of course, neither are we certain that all direct Federal spending or indeed that all private spending is sensible. To be sure there is nothing inherent in the revenue-sharing concept which would encourage wasteful spending. Public responsibility must be tied direct to the individuals in charge of conducting government programs, regardless of the source of financing.

The revenue-sharing plan does provide that each state and local government receiving revenue-sharing funds will assure proper accounting for the payments received and will provide regular reports to the Secretary of the Treasury on the disbursement of the funds. There is no intention of "second guessing" a state or local jurisdiction's determination to spend the money on education or health or safety, etc. We do want to be able to assure the President and the Congress that the money was spent for a lawful governmental purpose. The ultimate success of revenue sharing, therefore, will depend on the ability of states and localities to make the most efficient and judicious use of these funds.

The Nixon Administration maintains a large measure of confidence in the ability and willingness of local government to respond positively to those particularly local problems which require public solutions. A major purpose of revenue sharing is to enhance the financial ability of the levels of government closer to the people to respond effectively to the urgent problems that face us today. All governments are beset with problems, and the potential for effective management of social and public systems is high at the local level.

Does revenue sharing separate the responsibility for raising taxes from the act of spending tax revenues? While this may appear to have a logical ring to it, I believe that it is misleading. It ignores two important facts. At the national level, we have the precedent that the Federal Government already "shares" $30 billion annually, in the form of categorical grants, with state and local governments. At the state level, there is the precedent that every state shares revenue with its local governments, many in a completely unrestricted manner.

The real question is the control over the funds. It seems quite clear to me that there will continue to be some separation of the taxing power and the spending power—via rising amounts of Federal aid to the states, counties and cities. What revenue sharing does represent is an opportunity for state and local governments to have discretion over the allocation of a modest portion of these funds. In any event, the very real and present fiscal crisis facing so many states, cities, and counties makes updating political theory a very real political necessity and reality.

We believe that revenue sharing will help meet the current fiscal crises facing so many states and localities. Revenue sharing will also help to reduce the upward pressures on property taxes. Revenue sharing will, in addition, have a desirable employment impact—by providing the critical margin of additional funds, it will enable states and localities to hire and keep on the public payrolls more policemen, firemen, school teachers, and other key public employees.

In essence, revenue sharing represents a cogent response to today's problems—and a response which provides a durable, long-term solution to the challenge of providing essential public services without adding to the already heavy burden on the taxpayer.

Comments on Revenue Sharing*

The President announced in his State of the Union message that one of his six goals is the adoption of a revenue sharing program. Although I do not have the details of the program, I understand that it is a $16 billion program, of which $5 billion represents the general revenue sharing program along the lines previously presented, where funds are distributed to the States on a no-strings-attached basis. The remaining $11 billion may be referred to as revenue sharing, but in reality it is a series of block grants for 6 areas: law enforcement, elementary and secondary education, rural development, urban development, manpower training, and transportation. Of this $11 billion, $10 billion would be a reallocation of amounts provided under present law for specific programs in the 6 areas I have referred to, and $1 billion represents new money. This means, if I understand it correctly, that the same $10 billion will be available for the 6 areas as provided under prior law, but presumably with fewer Federal restrictions. The new money in this area is the $1 billion additional.

In very general terms, therefore, I think the program should be viewed as $6 billion of additional money, of which $5 billion is shared under a revenue sharing formula and $1 billion is added to the block grants. In the case of $10 billion of existing programs, apparently some restrictions are removed and the funds may be distributed somewhat differently than under prior law. We do not know how these funds are to be distributed. The major change, of course, is the $5 billion of revenue sharing and it is this to which I am directing my remarks at this time. Any meaningful discussions of the changes in the $11 billion of block grants must await further information.

Even before the President's statement relative to his goal for revenue sharing, it was difficult to pick up a paper without finding an article by someone as to why we must have revenue sharing. Al-

*Wilbur D. Mills, unpublished paper furnished by Congressman Wilbur D. Mills, January 26, 1971, pp. 1–10.

though I have said relatively little on the subject, what I have said—and some of the things I haven't said—have been aired widely. I thought it might be useful if I were to comment on the topic generally, recognizing however, that with a topic having so many facets, my comments at this time will necessarily be fragmentary.

Let me start by saying that I fully recognize that a significant number of urban areas are faced with very serious fiscal problems. Perhaps this is also true of some States as well, although there is some uncertainty on this.

I think it is clear that government taken as a whole—at all levels—must find answers to these serious fiscal situations. I recognize also that the Federal Government through the proliferation of grant-in-aids programs—without considering the fiscal impact of these programs on State and local revenues—has contributed to the problem. I think it is clear, however, that the root causes of the problem go much deeper than this. It is not the purpose of my comments today to dwell upon this aspect of the problem, but I think it is clear that increasing urbanism, and the complexities which it has brought to our society, is the chief culprit in this regard. I suspect, however, that the disorder of State and local financing is not far behind.

We see so many articles written on the need for revenue sharing that we are likely to lose our perspective with respect to the problem. The Federal Government has not been unaware of the fiscal problems of State and local governments in recent years despite what many of the articles we see in the press these days suggest. The Federal budget for the fiscal year 1971 shows that in 1959, Federal aid to State and local governments amounted to $6.7 billion. The 1971 estimate shows this growing to something like $27 1/2 billion. This represents a growth from 7 percent to nearly 14 percent of total Federal outlays. If outlays for defense, space, and international programs are set aside, this is a growth from 16 percent to 23 percent of total Federal domestic outlays—a not inconsequential proportion of Federal domestic spending. Federal aid also is significant even relative to the growth which has occurred in State and local revenues. In 1959, Federal aid to State and local governments was equal to 13 1/2 percent of their total revenue. By 1970 it is estimated that it grew to slightly over 18 percent of their current revenues.

It seems to me that we are faced with a concerted campaign to force the Federal Government willy-nilly into a revenue sharing program. It seems to me that the more rational way of acting when we are faced with a problem is first to analyze it carefully, then to outline possible alternative solutions, next to evaluate the strengths and weaknesses of the different possible answers to the problem, and finally to make a choice based upon as careful a weighing of these considerations as possible.

While we have heard a great deal about the need of the States and localities for revenue sharing, we have heard very little about why revenue sharing is the best answer to the problem. I thought it might be interesting for us today to explore as best we can the reasons why many view revenue sharing as the desired solution.

Certainly one of the effects of revenue sharing is a redistribution of income among the States. I say this because every dollar of revenue shared most obviously has to come from *some* source, and all of these sources originate in the 50 States. Of course, these sources are not the governments of the States or localities, but rather the people of the States or localities. I recognize that to the officials involved, this may be an important distinction. But the people of the various States may have a different point of view. I think it is time we explore these redistributional effects to see whether or not they correspond appropriately with the objectives of revenue sharing.

There are, of course, uncertainties in any analysis of this type. Some, for example, believe that the revenue share will displace Federal expenditures which might otherwise be made but even if this were true, it would be difficult to know what kinds of expenditures they will displace. While I wish that if we had revenue sharing, it would displace other expenditures, I cannot in reality believe that this will be the case. I suspect that if we are to have revenue sharing, it is more likely to take the form of additional spending. This might initially represent increased borrowing but in the long run the debt can only be paid for by additional taxes—probably either income taxes or some form of sales tax, such as the value added tax that we have been hearing so much about recently.

I thought it might be interesting if we were to explore, under these different assumptions, which States would receive more under revenue sharing than they would pay and which would receive less. Unfortunately, our statistical material on this subject is rudimentary. Because of this, I have asked the staffs to do what they can, and to work with other government agencies, in trying to improve this material. I think improvements can be made in the data but even with these improvements, we still will not have the exact information we need. This is true because if expenditures are to be displaced, we cannot tell now which expenditures these will be. They represent future decisions of budget officials, the agencies, and the Congress. If, as I think is more likely, revenue sharing is paid for by increased taxes, here too there are future decisions to be made. The decisions still remaining for the future include the questions as to whether there will be increases in income taxes—and what will be the distribution among the various income classes of these increases—or whether there will be some form of sales tax—which again can vary widely as to distributional impact according to the nature of future decisions.

Despite what I have said as to the uncertainties as to the distribution of the burden of revenue sharing, I believe some exploration of this today—as incomplete as our data may be—is useful. Because without some analysis in this direction, we will be making changes in our fiscal and economic structures without any realization of their impact.

Let us assume first that other government expenditures are cut back (or not made) in order to provide the funds for revenue sharing. Since we cannot tell exactly which expenditures will be reduced (or not made), let us assume for purposes of illustration that all expenditures are cut back proportionately. If this is true and we were to enact the revenue sharing formula proposed last year by the Administration, we would find the people of some States losing substantially and those of other States gaining substantially. The Legislative Reference Service of the Library of Congress for the period 1965 to 1967 attempted to trace Federal expenditures to the point at which they were made. This study is currently being updated but the figures now available probably do not depart too much from what the new distribution will show. Based upon these expenditures figures and the Administration revenue sharing formula for the States presented last year, we find that some States would lose under revenue sharing very substantially. If these data are correct, the 15 big losers would be:

> Alaska, District of Columbia, Connecticut, Virginia, Hawaii, Maryland, Rhode Island, Missouri, Kansas, Texas, California, Montana, Georgia, North Dakota, and South Carolina.

The 15 States which would gain the most under this type of a redistribution and under the assumption of an expenditure cutback are:

> Wisconsin, Michigan, Oregon, New York, Minnesota, Idaho, Mississippi, Indiana, West Virginia, Louisiana, Iowa, Nevada, Arkansas, Vermont, and Pennsylvania.

Under these assumptions, States like Alaska could lose twice as much from revenue sharing as they would gain. States like Wisconsin might gain under revenue sharing close to half as much more than they would lose.

States with large defense or civilian installations under this type of redistribution of expenditure programs would tend to lose and those where such installations are small, would tend to gain. In any event, it is not clear that such a redistribution of revenues would serve any real purpose in meeting the problems of today. Despite the presence of New York and Pennsylvania among the States which would benefit, most of those in this group are the less urbanized States.

Another alternative, still assuming that revenue sharing displaces expenditures, is that categorical aid programs will be reduced by the amount of the revenue sharing. We have already seen that $10 billion of the proposed block grants are a replacement of categorical aid programs, but we cannot tell whether there are, or will be, further reductions in categorical aid to offset the proposed revenue sharing. If this occurs, of course, the State and local governments in the aggregate will be no better off that they were before, although obviously some would benefit and others would be hurt. Let me give you the lineup of the 15 States that would be hurt the most if revenue sharing displaces categorical aid:

> Alaska, District of Columbia, West Virginia, Vermont, Montana, Oklahoma, New Mexico, Kentucky, Wyoming, Arkansas, Mississippi, Alabama, Rhode Island, South Dakota, Utah.

The 15 States which would be helped the most if we substituted revenue sharing for categorical aid programs would be:

> Wisconsin, Florida, Indiana, Michigan, Iowa, Maryland, Delaware, Nebraska, New Jersey, Oregon, Minnesota, Kansas, Washington, Virginia, North Dakota.

This is indeed a curious lineup. There is no rational justification for such a division of the States among gainers and losers. Indeed, among the States that would benefit the most are those with relatively less serious welfare problems and relatively high per capita incomes; while among the States that would be losers are those with very serious welfare problems and with relatively low per capita incomes. It is difficult to say what purpose is served if we bring about this kind of a redistribution of income.

Let me turn now to what I believe would be the most likely result if we were to have revenue sharing; namely, that it would require additional taxes at the Federal level. Distributions based on income and sales are still being prepared but I have at hand distributions of the existing Federal tax burdens as prepared by the Legislative Reference Service for the period 1965 to 1967 and by Tax Foundation for the fiscal year 1970. While these distributions differ in detail, interestingly enough they show a high degree of correlation as to the States which would be helped and the States which would be hurt if revenue sharing along the lines the Administration proposed last year is paid for out of additional taxes distributed in the same manner as the present tax burden. The tabulation based upon Legislative Reference Service data shows that the States which would be hurt the most are:

> Delaware, Connecticut, Illinois, District of Columbia, New Jersey, Ohio, Pennsylvania, Missouri, New Hampshire, Massachusetts, Rhode Island, New York, Maryland, Indiana, Michigan.

It shows those which would be helped the most to be:

> Mississippi, North Dakota, New Mexico, Louisiana, South Dakota, Alabama, Arkansas, Idaho, Arizona, South Carolina, Wyoming, Hawaii, Kentucky, Utah, Alaska.

This is quite an interesting lineup of States. It suggests that the distributional effects of revenue sharing would hurt most the urban States where we hear the most about the need for revenue sharing. You will recall that in my list of those which would be injured the most were Illinois, Ohio, Pennsylvania and New York, while the States which would benefit the most are those with less density of population. It seems to me that this actually is the reverse of facing up to the urban problem that we have been hearing about.

These data, preliminary though they are, have raised a great many questions in my mind, and I hope yours, as to whether the distributional effects of revenue sharing really meet the problems with which we are faced today.

Let me turn now to a second advantage claimed for revenue sharing. In various ways, it is suggested that the Federal tax system is a more efficient tax structure than the States and often it is claimed that it is better because it is based to a larger extent upon the income tax—which is a better measure of ability to pay that the sales and property taxes on which the States and localities depend to an important extent. It is also pointed out that the income tax grows more than the property and sales taxes as the economy grows.

To the extent that the superiority of the Federal system is based on the fact that it depends on the income tax rather than property and sales taxes, it seems to me that the States too are free to impose greater tax burdens by using the income tax if they consider this desirable. Most States have recognized this and I think you will find that much of the growth in State revenues in recent years is attributable to income tax increases. All but 14 States, in fact, now have an individual income tax and in a significant number of cases where the State does not have an income tax, many of its localities do.

I recognize that the income tax in the hands of a larger government, such as the Federal Government, may be a more efficient revenue device than in the hands of smaller governmental units. There are what the economicsts call economies of scale, that is, savings in collection devices which can be made more readily by the larger governmental units.

In this connection, the Federal Government has taken a number of steps in recent years which make it possible for the States to share in some of the economies of scale on the part of the Federal Government. I think this is a factor in an increasing number of States making their income tax base the same, or nearly the same, as the Federal base, and in some cases in actually making their tax a percentage of the Federal tax. The degree of cooperation of the Internal Revenue Service in helping the States find those cases where the proper amount of taxes is not being paid is already a major collection device used by State and local governments. I am sure improvements can be made in this area.

It is also possible to explore the possibility of collecting the State tax at the same time, and in the same mailing, as the Federal tax. In such a case, the State taxes collected by the Federal Government would be turned back to the State governments, but the State governments would maintain their full right to impose their own tax rates. Whether this is a good idea or something the States would want, I am not certain. But it is certainly one possibility we could explore if the States believe this would improve the efficiency of the State tax systems.

Another reason sometimes given for levying and collecting taxes by the Federal Government for the States and local governments to spend is the competitive problem among States in imposing high tax rates. It is sometimes suggested that States are inhibited in imposing higher income taxes by the fact that if the rates become too high, wealthy persons will move to other States where the rates are lower.

I think the importance of this point can be overemphasized. States which maintain low tax burdens in some respects may be attractive to wealthy taxpayers but they also tend to provide lower levels of services and this can detract from them particularly from the standpoint of employers who are also concerned with the welfare of their employees.

In addition, it is possible to deal with this problem to the extent it is a serious problem by providing credits of various types against

Federal taxes for the imposition of State or local taxes. While I am inclined to think that devices of this type present difficulties, certainly if this competitive problem is a serious factor, credits are an alternative we can consider.

I believe, however, that there is an answer to this problem of interstate competition. When people talk about the Federal government having preempted the income tax by getting there first and imposing the higher rates of tax, I find that I agree with the statement made by Governor Nelson Rockefeller of New York on Federal-State-Local Fiscal Relationships before the Tax Institute of America in 1967. At that time he said, "As far as the State saying that the Federal government has preempted the best tax fields, in my opinion this is a complete misrepresentation of the facts. When we raised our income tax to its present rates, which are almost as high as any State in the country—and a progressive tax at that—a taxpayer could deduct the money he paid under the State income tax from his Federal income tax. Thus, the Federal government hasn't entirely preempted the income tax field, because we can still obtain some of our State revenue by cutting into the Federal receipts. This works, though, only when a legislator and a governor take the necessary action."

This highlights an advantage of the States in imposing an income tax which the Federal government does not have; namely, the fact that State and local income taxes are deductible in computing the Federal tax. The reverse, of course, is not true—Federal taxes are generally not deductible in computing State or local taxes. The effect of this is that when a State increases its income tax part of the revenue raised by the State government in reality is not paid by the taxpayer since he is making smaller tax payments to the Federal government. This is an important and often overlooked advantage to the States in the field of income taxes. It seems to me that it may well outweigh the competitive factor referred to previously.

The third factor accounting for the popularity of revenue sharing by State and local officials is that it is so much easier not to have to face up to the responsibility of raising taxes to cover increases in expenditure programs. We who have the responsibility of raising taxes at the Federal level recognize the difficulty of raising taxes and often wish, as the Congress increases expenditure programs at the Federal level, it were possible to avoid making commensurate increases in taxes. As a result, I can understand why it is not pleasant for State and local government officials to take the responsibility for covering their expenditure increases with higher taxes.

It is, undoubtedly, feelings of this type which caused the Advisory Commission on Intergovernmental Relations in a recent publication, after referring to advantages of the Federal tax system, to go on and say that these "enable the Congress to raise far more revenue at far less political risk than can all of the State and local officials combined," or again, in another part of the same publication, when expressing opposition to a Federal tax cut which would leave additional funds available for State and local tax increases, making the following statement:

> "Such a policy would place governors and mayors in the untenable political position of wresting from the citizenry the tax reduction granted by the Federal authorities. National policymakers would reap all the political credit for granting tax reduction while State and local policymakers would be denounced for short circuiting this beneficent Federal policy."

Still elsewhere in the same document, references are made to taxpayer resistance as tax rates are pushed higher. We, at the Federal level, also recognize this resistence to higher tax rates and we see no reason why this type of restraint should not be shared with State and local governments.

What worries me most about not imposing taxes at the same level of government responsible for the expenditures is that this means there is no balancing of priorities between taxing and spending. In saying this, I do not mean that expenditures should not increase, but rather that if they are to increase, there should be an evaluation of these expenditure programs, not only one with another, but also with the effect of tax reductions or, if not tax reductions, at least with the prospect of foregoing tax increases.

I should say I am not merely worried about the 5 billion or so dollars which the Administration currently would schedule for revenue sharing; rather, my concern is that once this road is begun, where does it end? Obviously, from the standpoint of State and local governments, nothing could be nicer than having no-strings-attached-funds for which they bear no responsibility for raising. As a result, once the 5 billion or so dollars is obtained in this manner, what could be more natural than at some future time to demand in the strongest terms possible, further increases in funds available.

In my view, we already have too little restraint on spending programs at the present time. If the revenue sharing machine is to be cranked up, I fear we will lose much of what restraint we now have. I am not at all sure that this was not really the intent of some of the originators of the idea of revenue sharing. For example, let me quote from a recent article by Mr. Joseph Pechman who is often referred to as one of the authors of this proposal:

> "In present circumstances, Federal fiscal assistance should flow directly into State and local government treasuries to avoid use of the Federal funds for tax reduction."

In pointing out what I believe are the three principal reasons why revenue sharing is advocated, I have also expressed my view as to one of the major problems in going the revenue sharing route—namely, that to do so means there is no examination of the priorities in spending increases versus tax increases. But there is another major flaw in revenue sharing that needs to be brought out in the open and discussed freely.

If the purpose of revenue sharing is to meet the needs of our economy today, then revenue sharing is a poor and wasteful means of attaining these ends. Why do I say that it is wasteful? Because under any of the formulas that have been developed so far, substantial funds are given to States and localities where there is little or no need, as well as to those where there is need.

Let us examine the formula the Administration proposes for allocating funds from the Federal government to the 50 States. I understand at the State level the formula proposed this year is the same as that proposed previously. The formula, first of all, is on a per capita basis multiplied by a fraction in which the numerator is the revenue raised by the State and local governments and the denominator is the personal income level of the State and local governments. In many respects this is not too bad a formula in that the income level reflects the relative ability of the States to raise revenue, while the revenue which they already raised is a way of expressing their effort to raise the needed funds. However, the only attempt to measure need in such a formula is the reference to population; yet we all know that the number of people in a given area is a poor measure of need since this varies widely on a per capita basis. As a result, the revenue sharing formula advocated by the Administration is wasteful in that it shares revenue with States with little relative need, as well as with those where there is a substantial need.

The formula, which I understand is being proposed for the distribution of the funds among the localities of the various States, has still more problems in it. This formula would divide the money going to the localities on the basis of the proportion of the local revenue raised by each locality. This formula contains serious defects. If the revenues are divided on the basis of the revenues raised locally, this means that those localities which are the wealthiest and best able to raise revenue will receive the largest shares of the Federal revenue.

Essentially the same problem exists with respect to the formula used in determining how the funds are to be divided between the States and localities.

On the other hand, if the sharing were to be based on the relative expenditures of each locality—another formula which I understand has been considered—the formula then would become a positive inducement for a spending spree. It would give the most funds to the localities which spend the most, regardless of their need. Either of these formulas—that based on revenues and proposed by the Administration, or that based on expenditures—or a combination of them, ignore need and the relative ability of the communities to raise revenue. Instead, they tend to help the richer communities or those which are the freest spenders.

In making these comments about the formulas the Administration proposes for use in revenue sharing, I do not mean to be critical. I recognize the limitations within which they must work. Statistical data frequently are not available to develop the types of standards which they might like to have for distributing the revenues. Even more important, the tax systems and conditions are so diverse from State to State and from locality to locality within each State, plus the problem of dealing with overlapping local government jurisdictions, that I believe there is considerable question as to whether it is possible to come up with *any* distribution formula which will be fair and yet distribute the funds according to need and relative effort of the various tax jurisdictions throughout the country. In a much more limited area, looking only to distributions for education, this seems to be borne out by the comments of two research specialists of the Federal Reserve Bank of Boston, Mr. Steven J. Weiss and Mr. Robert W. Eisenmenger, who said the following:

> "We found, however, that there simply is no way to measure the tax base and tax effort of each and every school district. The differing tax structures within each State and the varying distributions of functional and financial responsibilities of States, counties, townships, and special districts make it impossible to evaluate—across State boundaries—the relative needs of individual districts.

Think how much more difficult the problem is when we try and take into account the differing needs in the whole spectrum of State and local expenditure programs!

Of course, these difficulties in State and local financing can be dealt with by means other than revenue sharing. It seems to me that when we have a proposal which is obviously defective, at the very least we should not rush into it without examining the alternatives.

Revenue sharing basically is the distribution of Federal revenues to States and localities under distribution formulas but on a no-strings-attached basis as far as use of the funds is concerned. Block grants, which the Administration has also espoused, differ from revenue sharing in this respect in the sense that the broad general purpose for which the funds are to be spent is specified by the Federal government. Block grants share most of the same problems as revenue sharing, although, in this case, there is at least some indication that the funds will be spent for purposes where there are recognized needs. It seems to me that if more funds are to be needed by States and localities, these are not the only ways of accomplishing these results.

Others have suggested that we should make an effort to aid the States and localities in improving their own tax systems. As I indicated earlier, this can be done by permitting the States and localities, if they use the Federal tax base, also to make use of the Federal tax collection system. Under this arrangement, the States will still be responsible for imposing the taxes and setting their own rate structure. The increased efficiency in collecting State taxes, which this might bring about, should free-up substantial additional revenue for State and local governments.

Others have suggested that credits should be allowed for State income taxes which are imposed. This is proposed as a way of removing the competitive problem, which some believe States are faced with when they increase their income taxes. I have doubts as to the desirability of trying to direct the States and localities in developing their tax structure, but at least this alternative should also be explored.

Another, and perhaps a more fruitful method of dealing with the program, is to review the categorical aid programs, which we have at the present time, with the intent of both simplifying them and making them available on a broader basis. This would make it unnecessary for the States and localities to go into programs which they believe are undesirable merely to obtain the Federal funds, since the same Federal funds might also be available for other programs which they believe their State and localities need.

In this same area, it is also possible to aid the States and local governments fiscally by changing the grant-in-aid formulas so that a larger portion of the total is borne by the Federal government. This, in effect, is what we have been doing in our consideration of the welfare programs through provision for the Family Assistance Plan. I believe this alone should do much to take the fiscal pressures off the States and localities.

Actually, if we were to reconsider the grant-in-aid programs in the areas of education, welfare, hospitals and health, we would be dealing with the areas which account for nearly 60 percent of the State and local government expenditures. Certainly changing the formulas so that the Federal share is increased somewhat in the case of programs of this type would do as much, if not more, than developing a new Federal revenue sharing program to be superimposed on top of the existing grant-in-aid programs.

Finally, to put this problem in perspective, I would like to stress that there are few things that could help the States and localities as much as a responsible fiscal policy which would help contain inflation and provide for a stable price level. We are told that one of the problems of State and local financing is that each time the price level goes up, the financial costs of State and local governments are increased more than their tax receipts. The moral of this, I think, is quite clear. Federal expenditures must be kept at reasonable levels and proposals for additional spending including revenue sharing should be scrutinized carefully in light of their possible inflationary impact.

Let me close by again stressing that bad as the fiscal problems of the State and local governments are, it is not clear that they are any worse than the fiscal problems faced by the Federal government. In a recent article, the economists, Mr. Richard A. Musgrave and Mr. Mitchell Polinsky, estimate that by 1975 State and local expenditures will be $191 billion after allowing for the increased workload due to rising population and for quality improvement at past rates. In this article, revenue in 1975, including Federal aid, expanding at normal rates is estimated at $174 billion, leaving a deficit of $17 billion. The authors go on to say that of this, $11 billion will be covered by normal borrowing, leaving a gap of $6 billion. They point out that this could be met by a 5-percent increase in tax rates at the State-local level; an increase which they suggest seems well within the reach of State-local governments given their past record of rate increases.

On the other hand, we are currently faced with very substantial deficits at the Federal level of possibly as much as $15 billion, which are likely to continue at least until we approach full employment levels. It seems to me that this at least should flash a caution light for us to go slow with these proposals for giving away Federal revenues.

D

Health Care: A National Problem

Perhaps the most important issue of the 1970's is the provision of adequate health protection for all Americans. The cost of health care is a national problem. In 1960, $25.9 billion was spent by all Americans on health care; by 1970 the amount increased to $67.2 billion or almost seven percent of the gross national product. Moreover, it is estimated that by 1980 the cost of medical care will amount to $172.5 billion. The problem involved is that few Americans can afford the cost of any type of an extended illness. Even though most Americans have some type of health insurance coverage, the protection typically is inadequate, except with respect to rather basic types of illnesses. Usually some type of protection is missing. Many insurance policies provide no coverage for diagnostic procedures; few provide payments for out-of-hospital prescription drugs. Because health insurance has become a major factor in wage negotiations, many policies are tied to employment by a specific company. When unemployment occurs, the policies are canceled.

There is general agreement that a federal role is necessary to provide all Americans with more adequate health protection. However, there is disagreement over the financial approach. The approach which is favored by the Nixon Administration is to provide more comprehensive coverage through existing private insurance companies, with the federal government financing the cost of insurance for low income families. An alternate approach, which has been developed by Senator Kennedy, would create a national health insurance system, financed by taxes on employers and employees. Additional costs would be financed out of general federal revenues. The features of the Nixon and Kennedy health insurance measures are the subject matter of this section.

The reading, "Health Care Resources," by Rita Ricardo Campbell, discusses some of the basic characteristics of the health industry. The second and third readings present the alternative health care measures of President Nixon and Senator Kennedy. The important thing to note is the difference in approaches.

Health Industry Resources*

Gradually over the last two decades, government decisions have become increasingly more important in the U.S. health industry. More recently, Medicare and Medicaid, both enacted in 1965, have increased the effective demand for health services above the increase which would have occurred without these programs.

Between 1965 and 1967, government payments jumped from 21 percent of total personal health care expenditures to 33 percent, and by 1968, to 35 percent. Establishment of heart, stroke and cancer clinics and new programs for comprehensive health planning and services, including the regional programs, are drawing into government service large numbers of clinical physicians. Moreover, increasing government expenditures on medical research, now 90 percent government-supported as against 80 percent in 1960, are attracting younger doctors who might have otherwise become general practitioners. From 1963 to 1967, the number of physicians in teaching, administration and research (both government and private) increased by 5,000, the number of physicians in federal service by nearly 6,000.[1] Although the number of physicians in private clinical practice increased by nearly 10,000 over this period, the potential increase was considerably greater. At the same time, private demand for medical care, already increasing due to rising incomes, a better educated public and advances in medical science, has been bolstered by the new government subsidies provided under Medicare and Medicaid. It is no wonder, therefore, that prices have been rising.

*Rita Ricardo Campbell, from *Economics of Health & Public Policy* (Washington: American Enterprise Institute, 1971), pp. 9-26.
[1] U.S. Public Health Service, *Health Resources Statistics* (Washington: U.S. Government Printing Office, 1968), p. 124; hereinafter referred to as *Health Resources Statistics*.

Expansion in Health Care Resources

The suppliers' response to this growing demand has been significant, despite the popular belief to the contrary. In 1967, there were 3.4 million workers in the health field as against 2.8 million in 1965, the year Medicare and Medicaid were passed. Moreover, for several years there has been a continuous increase in allied health manpower —for example, in x-ray technicians, physical therapists, nurses (registered and practical), and nursing aides—which reflects the changing structure of the labor supply in the health service area. In 1950, there were only 30,800 radiologic technicians but by 1960, there were over 60,000; and, in 1967, between 75,000 and 100,000.[2] In 1950, there were 249 registered nurses per 100,000 population; in 1960, 282; and in 1968, 331.[3] Physical therapists increased from 4,600 in 1950 to over 13,000 in 1967.[4]

Are There Enough Doctors?

Even the much touted projections of a large shortage of physicians in the U.S. by 1970 are now being questioned. For example, the Bane Committee's 1959 projection[5] of the number of physicians that would be practicing in 1965 turned out to be 30,000 physicians short. A recent careful analysis reports:

> This came about because more graduates were produced than had been anticipated, fewer physicians retired, and the inflow of foreign physicians into the U.S. continued to increase . . . the adjusted projections of changes in requirements and supplies proved to be almost 20 percent too low over a period of only six years.[6]

Evidence indicates that physician productivity has also increased. Details about how the unanticipated supply of physicians came about are lacking. Nevertheless, it is evident that supply does respond to demand in the more or less classic sense, in both the health industry generally and in medical care services specifically, despite monopolistic factors such as licensure laws and professional, trade-union-like associations that operate on the supply side. This is not to

---

[2] *Health Resources Statistics, op cit.*, p. 171.
[3] *Ibid.*, p. 138.
[4] *Ibid.*, p. 159.
[5] See the report of the Surgeon General's Consultant Group on Medical Education (Frank Bane, chairman), "Physicians for a Growing America." (Washington: U.S. Government Printing Office, 1959).
[6] W. Lee Hansen, "An Appraisal of Physician Manpower Projections," *Inquiry*, March 1970, p. 110.

say that the supply adjustment would not have been greater and faster without these monopolistic factors, but only to point out that the law of demand and supply does work to a very considerable extent in the health services market.

A few years ago economists, physicians, and government policy decision-makers all agreed that there was a general shortage of physicians and other health workers in the United States. Today at least one economist, Professor Eli Ginzberg of Columbia University, denies that the shortage exists. Several others make the somewhat sophisticated point that there will always be a shortage but primarily only in a statistical sense, that is, in the sense that physicians can and do create the demand for their services—mainly by telling their patients if and how often to return for further treatment and by controlling the decision as to whether procedures are performed by the physician or by paramedical workers.

With the paucity of statistical data available, the determination of whether, or to what degree, there is an overall shortage of physicians, in contrast to specific shortages in certain areas and of certain kinds of physicians, is a matter of judgment and not of mathematical exactitude. The author believes that some overall "shortage" exists— at least in the sense that, at current medical care prices (admittedly largely paid by third parties), individuals' demands for medical care are not being met without "queuing." In many communities, doctors are busy and the would-be patient is waiting for an operation or for an appointment with his physician. However, statistical proof of the extent of this situation is difficult to find. One service that the federal government could provide would be to construct a statistical index based on various measures of "waiting" (bed vacancies, et cetera). Such an index would take much of the guess work out of determining whether there is or is not an overall shortage of physicians, or other health manpower resources, in the United States today.

Whatever the overall picture may be, a shortage of general practitioners is developing in the United States. This has been recognized by the American Medical Association—which has established a new specialty, the family physician—and by the U.S. Congress—which passed a bill in 1970 authorizing federal funds to help hospitals and medical schools provide professional and technical training in the field of family medicine.[7] In 1940, 24 percent of M.D.'s in private practice were specialists; in 1965, 64 percent; in 1967, 67 percent.

[7] Contained in S. 3418 passed by the Senate on September 14, 1970 and in a related version passed by the House December 1st, and vetoed by the President on December 26th.

The decline of the general practitioner relative to the specialist is evident in many other countries of the world and may be an inexorable trend that has only been hastened by government research grant policies in the U.S. In any event, the relative decline in the numbers of general practitioners is developing pressure to train "physician assistants," to increase the use of multiphasic screening units run by technicians, and to develop other new means for directing would-be patients to their most suitable sources of medical care.

Increased specialization may mean better scientific medicine, but often at the expense of greater fragmentation of care and thus, potentially, confusion on the part of the patient. Increased specialization also may mean greater costs, although for a better product or service. Recent increases in costs have not been offset, as in the 1940s, by the introduction of antibiotics and shorter hospital stays. The substitution of more costly, higher quality and more specialized medical care for lower priced, less specialized care may be socially desirable. However, the part this plays in increasing costs should be recognized, its effect on other variables should be analyzed, and the question of consumer preferences should be considered. As to the latter, there is some evidence that consumers do not prefer costly, specialized medical care in all circumstances. Where no life-saving emergency is involved, some consumers may prefer lower cost, impersonal and generally more Spartan medical care to high cost, personal and luxury care. The third party payment umbrella, as is shown in the next chapter, makes this choice non-meaningful. In the extreme circumstance of impending death from irreversible causes, a patient may prefer to choose whether or not to accept the advanced modern medical techniques that will prolong life but at a high cost in both physical suffering and dollars.

Economic or effective demand for physicians' services is demand backed by intention to pay for the services, not demand created by "need" with no requirement for payment. To help evaluate when, if ever, the federal government should underwrite demand by *all* individuals for health care, statistically accurate measurements of shortages of key health manpower are needed. Price increases in a situation where bills are largely met by third party payments and where maldistributions of supply are extreme, as indicated by current shortages in rural and inner-city core areas, are not sufficient evidence of *general* shortages. In Soviet Russia, where the government supplies virtually 100 percent of medical care services and where health manpower to some degree is assigned to particular locations, urban-rural maldistribution still exists. And this is the case despite a tremendous increase in the total number of physicians (from 140 per 100,000 population in 1950 to 205 per 100,000 in 1963) and despite comparatively high usage of medical assistants and midwives. There is no reason to believe that maldistribution of supply would be corrected in the United States by merely greatly increasing the total supply.

Greatly increasing the supply of physicians will emphasize another problem. One economist has stated: "Given the alternatives of high average earnings for a taut supply of physicians and a loose supply, lower fees and over-doctoring, I opt unequivocally for the first."[8] Although the author does not agree with this judgment, there is considerable truth in the presentation of the choices as stated. A greater misallocation of resources or "over-doctoring," could occur in "loose supply" conditions because of consumer ignorance. But, since the role of price in the allocation of medical resources has been largely abnegated by the third party umbrella, considerable "over-doctoring" can be and already is taking place with a short supply and high fees. Peer review by committees of physicians appointed by local medical societies is one way to approach this problem. However, effective review is difficult to achieve even in formal organizations, such as hospitals and large group practices, and may be impossible to achieve among physicians practicing alone. Since the economic and professional success of physicians often depends on referrals from other physicians, it is naive to believe that colleagues will be as critical of each other's performance as they perhaps ought to be. Here, as in many areas of health services, better education of the consumer is badly needed.

Are There Enough Hospital Beds?

There are two major types of hospitals, the long-term hospitals, which are primarily psychiatric hospitals, and the short-term or general hospitals. The latter comprise over 80 percent of all hospitals but provide only about 40 percent of all beds. The nonfederal, short-term or community hospital is the one most commonly thought of as "the hospital." They are the major providers of acute diagnostic and therapeutic services and have a rapid turnover of patients. About 90 percent of their revenues come from third party payers.

Hospitals may be classified by ownership into three types—government-owned, voluntary nonprofit, and profit-making or proprietary. Of the 7,144 hospitals in 1969, only 10 percent were profit-making, and these had less than 3 percent of total hospital beds. Growth of profit-making hospitals is discouraged by the laws of some

---

[8] Eli Ginzberg and Miriam Ostow, *Men, Money and Medicine* (New York: Columbia University Press, 1969), p. 110.

states. Voluntary nonprofit hospitals represented 48 percent of the total and had about a third of total beds. Thus government hospitals constitute almost one-half of all hospitals and contain well over one-half of all beds. Federal and state government hospitals are usually long-term hospitals with emphasis on psychiatric care. County and city government hospitals are usually short-term, general community hospitals.

In the period from 1960 to 1969 the total number of hospitals has increased slightly from 6,876 to 7,144, or by 4 percent, but the number of beds has dropped by one-half of one percent. In the same period the number of general hospitals has increased by 8 percent and their number of beds by 29 percent. Long-term hospitals, on the other hand, have been declining in number of beds because the short-term general hospitals are now giving care to many patients who would have formerly been in long-term mental and TB institutions. In addition, nursing homes have increased their role in the care of aged long-term patients not needing the facilities of an acute general hospital. Most long-term hospitals are government-owned.

Although there are still bed shortages in inner-city core areas, the overall suppliers' response to recent increases in demand for hospital beds appears, on the surface, to have been adequate. This may be largely due to the influence of the federal Hill-Burton Act of 1946 which gives direct grants to construct and equip public and nonprofit voluntary hospitals. Under this act, construction in rural areas has been favored. Its 1970 extension provides, in addition to new construction money, $235 million for modernization of nonprofit hospitals and nursing homes over a three-year period.

It is of interest that many economists believe that hospital beds provide an exception to the usual rules of supply and demand in that whenever a community obtains an increase in hospital beds, the demand for the beds also increases so that an equilibrium is never reached. There are direct and indirect pressures on hospital boards of trustees, physicians and staffs to fill all or nearly all hospital beds in order to justify tax rates or bond issues for recent and anticipated hospital additions. The philosophy that appropriations from tax monies or bond flotations are difficult to obtain if last year's appropriation is not fully spent applies here. The high rate of utilization of beds in veterans' hospitals may be partly a reflection of this factor.

Incentives to use in-hospital rather than out-hospital facilities are always present. For the physician, it is far more convenient to care for patients if they are under one roof than if they are scattered in several facilities or homes. For the patient, it may be necessary to hire household help or home nursing care if he is an outpatient rather than an inpatient. Moreover, additional incentives for using in-hospital rather than outpatient facilities exist whenever insurance third party payments cover only in-hospital care. Outpatient care is covered, however, by major medical expense insurance contracts, which now insure 60 percent of all those with health insurance,[9] or about a third of the population. Moreover, "about 80 percent of persons insured for regular medical expenses [some 60 percent of the population has regular medical expense coverage] under the basic group policies have coverage for out-of-hospital diagnostic, X-ray and laboratory expenses."[10] Thus roughly 60 percent of the population has some form of coverage for "out-of-hospital" expenses.

Some increase in a hospital's bed occupancy rate (ratio of patient census to beds) is expected whenever the percentage of aged persons in that hospital's bed population increases. The occupancy rate in nonfederal, short-term general hospitals was 76.3 percent in 1964, dropped slightly to 76.0 percent in 1965 and thereafter rose steadily to reach 78.8 percent in 1969.[11] The percent of hospital beds occupied by the aged has been increasing since the beginning of Medicare. Aged persons take longer to recover from illness than younger persons and are much more likely to require a second admission if prematurely discharged. Physicians try to avoid this eventuality by keeping them in the hospital longer.

A recent study, based on data as of 1963, compared hospital utilization in Sweden—where, except for special accommodations, there are no direct costs for hospital care to the patient—with utilization in the U.S. The study found that although admission rates were about the same in the two countries, the mean number of hospital days per person once admitted was 24.3 per year in Sweden compared to only 14.5 in the U.S. The fact that Sweden has six short-term hospital beds per 1,000 population as compared to the U.S.'s 3.7 per 1,000 is believed to be partly responsible for this difference in utilization.[12] An economist and observer of the British health scene, where again length of hospital stay is greater than in the U.S., concludes: "The evidence presented . . . shows that supplying enough beds to 'satisfy demand' is likely to be an impossible task."[13]

[9] J. F. Follmann, Jr., "Health Insurance Plan Design Trends—Coverage and Benefits," *Pension and Welfare News*, February 1969.

[10] *Ibid.*

[11] *Hospitals*, August 1, 1970, Part 2 (Guide Issue), p. 473.

[12] R. Anderson, B. Smedby, O. Anderson, *Medical Care Use in Sweden and the U.S.—A Comparative Analysis of Systems and Behavior* (Chicago: University of Chicago Press, 1970), p. 21; all data as of 1963.

[13] Martin Feldstein, *Economic Analysis for Health Service Efficiency* (Amsterdam, Holland: North Holland Publicity Co., 1967), p. 200.

There has been a marked suppliers' response, notably by private industry, to the fact that Medicare and Medicaid pay for patient care in extended care facilities or convalescent centers. Such facilities differ from nursing homes in that they primarily care for patients recovering from surgery or serious illness while nursing homes primarily care for long-term cases, often involving those not expected to recover.

In July 1967, there were 740 extended care facilities in full compliance with Medicare standards, and 3,210 in "substantial compliance." By July 1969, the respective figures were 1,374 and 3,402 for a total increase of 826 (21 percent) in two years.[14] Extended care facilities offer a specialized and needed service at much lower prices than the hospitals, with their expensive equipment and higher staff-patient ratios, can afford. Thus they are replacing hospitals for patients recovering from surgery and serious illness. Using mass purchasing and standardized management techniques, large motel chains have entered this field. These chains include Sheraton Corporation of America, Medi-Centers of America, Inc. (an offshoot of Holiday Inns), Safecare-Careage, American Institutional Developers, and others—not to mention Four Seasons Nursing Corporation, which failed in the early summer of 1970. Profit-making extended care facilities are now an accepted part of the U.S. system of medical care.

Nursing home facilities have also been increasing. In the 12 months to January 1, 1969, the number of beds in licensed nursing homes increased 12 percent. However, there are still shortages, especially of acceptable quality, low-cost nursing homes. The major problem is that "acceptable quality" is very difficult to provide at low cost, and the financial resources of the patient, or his family, are often insufficient to meet the bills. Demand will continue to increase rapidly as medical science prolongs life resulting in greater need for nursing care in the later years of life than formerly. Financing of long-term medical care needs analysis. In fiscal 1969, of the $2.4 billion spent for nursing home care, $1.8 billion was paid out of government monies.

Organization of Delivery

One of the major criticisms of the way medical care is delivered in the U.S. is that it is a "nonsystem." If we believe that a "system"

---

[14] U.S. Senate, Committee on Finance, "Medicare and Medicaid—Problems, Issues, Alternatives," Staff Report, February 9, 1970, p. 95; hereinafter cited as Senate Staff Report.

requires centralized organization or control, then medical care is indeed a "nonsystem." However, there are also systems, such as the capitalist system, where the organization or direction of the whole is provided through a decentralized mechanism. Medical care delivery more nearly fits this definition.

The capitalist or market *system* posits a market place where goods and services are bought at mutually agreed upon prices, and where the "hidden hand"—the desire of each individual to improve his position via higher profits and lower buying costs—automatically operates to produce optimum resource allocation. The virtue of the "hidden hand" of the market system is that each individual makes his buy or sell decisions based on the type of product or service he demands (or supplies) and the price he is willing to pay (or ask). Demand and supply are balanced by the price and profit mechanism and no interference from government or other outside authority is needed.

The markets of the medical care industry meet this model only to a degree. Suppliers *have* increased in number in response to higher prices and greater profits, although perhaps not as freely as they would have if no restrictions—for example, licensure and accreditation—had existed. Moreover, buyers and suppliers of medical care *do* interact to negotiate prices, but not so much as in some other markets, for several reasons: One reason is the individual buyer's incentive to negotiate has been weakened by the continuing growth of third party payments for the services. However, recently, these third parties—government and insurance companies—have become more active in price negotiation. In addition, the buyer's ignorance of what the product is worth may be greater in the medical services market than in other markets. Finally, the many nonprofit hospitals are only partially within the market system.

Thus, the capitalist market system, which operates largely by competition, does not work perfectly in the medical care industry. There are two general approaches for solutions: one, to make the decentralized system we have work better by improving competition and resource allocation within the industry, or two, to impose a central control or authority.[15]

A brief description of the present organization of delivery of care in the U.S. follows. Demand for medical care is channeled through a physician. The physician may be in solo practice, group practice or

[15] Such a central authority or control would probably need to be governmental, since autonomous and effective cooperation by the suppliers of medical care is unlikely and, in any case, would probably be in violation of antitrust laws.

connected to a hospital's emergency room or outpatient department or a clinic's outpatient department. His compensation may take the form of a fee for each particular service rendered, an annual prepaid per capita fee, a salary, or, very rarely except for obstetricians, payment "by the case." A would-be patient cannot obtain *initial* medical care from a nurse or other medical technician except in the uncommon instance of the very new and scarce "physician assistants." After the patient has seen a physician, subsequent care can be given by a nurse and/or medical technician under the M.D.'s direct supervision.

The structure of health manpower contains a large gap in terms of training, income and duties between the physician and the registered nurse. Attempts to fill this gap are being made. One promising new approach, pioneered by Duke University, involves college training programs (normally two years or less) leading towards a "physician's assistant" degree. Although the annual training costs of physician assistants and medical students are about the same, the former can be trained faster and therefore more cheaply.

Very few physician's assistants are now working, but over one hundred training programs have developed in the past few years, primarily for ex-army medical corpsmen and registered nurses, and additional colleges are planning to enter the field. Among the programs are "Medex" at the Washington School of Medicine at Seattle, a Child Health Associate Program at the University of Colorado, and a Surgical Associates Program at Yale University. Stanford University has both a program for medical corpsmen and nurses and a longer program for "high school graduates or . . . [persons] with some additional training or college," who meet certain other requirements and who "demonstrate a real motivation to be directly involved in the delivery of health care."[16]

Before physician's assistants and other new types of health workers can be utilized to their full potential, problems of legal status and malpractice insurance will have to be worked out in many states. Both the American Hospital Association and the Health Manpower Council of the American Medical Association have called for a nationwide moratorium on licensure of additional health occupations by the states until a solution is reached that will not impede the anticipated growth of new health workers.

Advances in medical technology and the breaking up of complicated tasks into smaller, more specialized and more quickly learned functions have created a large number of new health occupations.

[16] Stanford University Medical Center, News Bureau Release, October 19, 1970.

This is also tending to close gaps in the vertical manpower structure of the health industry.

There are approximately 300,000 physicians in the United States, representing only a tenth of the 3 million or so total workers in the health field. Some of the 3 million—notably about 2,000 social scientists (i.e., anthropologists, medical sociologists and health economists)—have little to do with the primary delivery of health care. Others, for example 1.75 million nurses of varying levels of training, are directly involved in day-to-day delivery of care.[17]

Group Practice

Group practice is generally defined as a formal organization employing three or more full-time physicians and assorted nurses, laboratory technicians, et cetera. In 1965, only 11 percent of all physicians giving patient care were in group practice, 90 percent of them on a full-time basis.[18] Of these groups, 34 percent were multi-specialty, 50 percent single specialty and 15 percent general practice. The multi-specialty groups employed 60 percent of all M.D.'s in group practice.[19]

Groups may also be classified by the manner in which they are formally organized. In 1965, 78 percent were partnerships, 8 percent corporations, 11 percent "associations, foundations, or other" and 3 percent "single owner groups in which the owner employs the other physicians in the group."[20] Eighty-three percent of groups pay physicians on the basis of share of net income. In most multi-specialty groups, income is derived not only from payment of physicians' fees for services rendered (or alternately a prepaid monthly fee per person), but also from charges for x-rays, laboratory tests, physical therapy procedures, and other items which the group, rather than an independent laboratory, may sell. An individual physician's share of net income may be determined by various formulae depending on the group's organization.

What are the economies of scale derived from group practice? Savings in overhead costs of office space, expensive equipment, clerical and paramedical staff services and in purchasing are present in different degrees in all groups. Large groups, and especially the very large groups with several clinic buildings, may benefit from central purchasing, computerized billing and record keeping, and a specialized central management staff. Furthermore, the chances of expen-

[17]*Health Resources Statistics, op. cit.*, p 8.
[18]American Medical Association, *Survey of Medical Groups in the U.S.*, 1969, p. 6; hereinafter referred to as AMA *Survey of Medical Groups.*
[19]*Ibid.*, p. 5.
[20]*Ibid.*, p. 10.

sive equipment and specialized personnel being idle are less in large groups. For groups growing in size, however, there are discontinuities in adjustments, such as crowded schedules for physicians and waiting by patients until an additional physician is hired. Once hired, the additional physician may, for a period, have idle time. Similar discontinuities occur in the case of specialized expensive machinery.

To the author's knowledge no study has been made of what is the optimum size, in the economist's sense of lowest average cost per unit of output, of a multispecialty group in an urban area of given population range. Groups with lower average unit costs may tolerate longer periods of tight scheduling than some less "efficient" groups. One by-product of tight scheduling resulting in lower costs may be a structuring of patient demand. Thus the patient who feels that he needs immediate attention may not wait for an appointment but seek care outside of the group, even though his medical expenses for care provided within the group are prepaid and expenses for those provided outside of the group come out of his own pocket.

In 1958, prepaid subscriber families in the Kaiser-Permanente Program, probably the best known of the prepaid per capita groups, obtained about 16 percent of their care outside of the Kaiser plan. This included 12.4 percent of total short-term hospital care and 27 percent of physician visits (the latter including industrial and school physicians).[21] A 1968 study of prepaid groups including HIP-Montefiore, Kaiser-Permanente and the Labor Health Institute (LHI) states "that outside physicians are used for 37 percent of surgical operations in HIP, 14 percent of all paid physicians' services and 33 percent of home calls in Kaiser-Permanente, and 23 percent of physicians' and dentists' services in LHI."[22]

This rather high outside utilization may primarily reflect structuring of demand (consciously or unconsciously) by the prepaid group, resulting in lower average costs per patient to the prepaid plan. A survey of why persons in the Labor Health Institute Plan used outside care found that 57 percent liked "own doctor" or dentists, had "started with him, or disliked LHI doctor or dentist" (13 percent); 20 percent found it inconvenient because of "distance, time, waiting," 9 percent said it was an "emergency"; the remainder, 15 percent, cited various other reasons.[23]

[21] U.S. report of the National Advisory Commission on Health Manpower, Volume II, November 1967, p. 210, footnote 4; hereinafter referred to as *Report of the Health Manpower Commission.*

[22] Health Insurance Association of America, "Insurance Companies and the Prepaid Group Practice of Medicine," *Medical Economics Bulletin*, No. 3, 1968, p. 7.

[23] *Ibid.*, p. 8.

To spread the overhead cost of expensive x-ray equipment and laboratories, group ownership is not necessary, although it is a logical consequence of growth in the size of physician groups. Such equipment can be and is owned by other than physicians in centrally located medical buildings in many U.S. cities. It may be more convenient for the patient if these ancillary services are available in the building where his physician is. But, even for this, group organization is not necessary. Medical buildings may rent space to solo practitioners and to independent laboratories in one and the same building. Studies comparing fees charged by physician-group laboratories and by independent laboratories should be made.

One study of solo and group practices noted the importance to a group of fees for other than physicians' services. The author stated:

> ... gross revenues derived specifically from the sale of laboratory and x-ray services amounted to less than 5 percent of total internist billings in the solo practices; in the largest multi-specialty groups revenues from laboratory and x-ray services approached 40 percent of the total billings of the internists. As size increased, even within single-specialty internist group practices, there was a distinct and steady increase in the proportion of laboratory and x-ray billings to total billings—again attributable to the ability of the larger practices to diversify and profit from their offerings of services. Thus it is obvious that the measures of billings by physicians in dollars should not be used to prove that the greater earnings of large-scale practices are a result of greater efficiency. Rather, the higher earnings appear to reflect the fact that different services are being sold in the various forms of practice. These additional services contribute to the gross revenue of the practice, but they do not meet our technical concept of greater production of services rendered by the physician.[24]
> ... it is to be expected that the presence of these ancillary facilities within a group practice—coupled with their use positively affecting the physician's income—may, at the margin, result in higher usage than where these incentives do not exist.[25]

The groups referred to above were "fee-for-service" groups in the San Francisco Bay area. The study concludes that:

> ... the average fees charged for outpatient visits in our study showed ... [that] fees per visit and average fees per hour of work were generally higher in the large multi-specialty group practices than in the smaller-scale practices. Physicians thus imply that their time is more valuable in group practice.[26]

[24] Richard M. Bailey, "A Comparison of Internists in Solo and Fee-for-Service Group Practice in the San Francisco Bay Area," *Bulletin* (New York Academy of Medicine, November 1968), p. 1299.

[25] *Ibid.*, p. 1301.

[26] *Ibid.*, p. 1300.

This study is quoted at some length because studies of physician incomes and patient charges in group practices are rare and because it raises the question of the degree to which the cost advantages of group practice, if any, are passed on to the consumer.

It is possible, of course, that large, multi-specialty groups attract as patients a higher than average number of both healthy individuals who want a *"complete* physical" and ill individuals whose illness is difficult to diagnose. In both instances, more tests are likely to be prescribed than would be the case if an average population were being served.

The recent development of automated multiphasic testing centers whose facilities are open to all physicians in a community means that the productivity gains of modern medicine and of greater use of allied health workers are no longer necessarily limited to group prac-tice. One such center is maintained by The George Washington University. It is open to referrals from any physician and to any individual without referral who specifies a physician to whom the test results are to be sent. In this center, most diagnostic measure-ments—from ocular tension and vital capacity to even height and weight—are made electronically and the data are fed into an on-line computer. "Medical hostesses" with no prior health training shoot x-rays, draw blood, and take Pap smears, "tasks that in many other centers must be performed by technicians, registered nurses or doctors."[27]

It is possible that solo practitioners making use of competitive laboratories that provide x-rays and clinical tests and the newer auto-mated multi-test centers can provide care just as efficiently or more efficiently than group physicians having their own facilities of this type. A group may have greater unused capacity of its specialized equipment and personnel than a laboratory which services a larger number of physicians.

It is often claimed that group practice yields greater productivity per man-hour of physician labor because greater use of paramedical personnel is made to perform tasks otherwise performed by physi-cians. Data are not available to prove this and, although it seems logical, the one study quoted above maintains that there is "no dis-cernible pattern of differences" in the use of paramedical personnel between solo and group practitioners.[28] Another study of medical care delivery indicates that determined efforts to use physician assis-

[27]James Reynolds, "Catching On: Complete Physicals Without M.D.'s," *Medical Economics,* December 21, 1970, p. 81.
[28]Richard M. Bailey, *op cit.,* p. 1297.

tants and other paramedical employees, especially in pediatrics, have resulted in some increased productivity by the physician.[29]

To what degree group organization is necessary to increase physician productivity and what size group can best utilize paramedical personnel for this purpose are questions that also need study. Such studies would face a major obstacle at the outset. The term physician productivity is usually, and probably has to be, loosely defined to mean the number of patients a physician sees per hour. Although different weights may be used for different types of visits (history, diagnostic, follow-up, et cetera) there still is an uncontrollable factor that probably cannot be quantified, and that is quality. Paradoxically, low quality care may result in a high number of patient visits per hour and vice versa. Thus high quality care would be associated with fewer visits per hour and lower physician productivity.

Prepaid, Per Capita, Group Practice

In discussing group practice, it is important to distinguish between groups which are paid fees-for-service and those which are paid wholly or in part on a prepaid, per capita basis. The large Kaiser-Permanente Foundation, Inc. provides a good example of the prepaid approach. Its medical care programs establish by contract with a group of physicians a fixed amount of income per member served.

> Any excess of costs over the budgeted amount directly reduces the income of the individual physicians in the Medical Group. Conversely, any savings below the budgeted amount add to physicians' income. . . . In the California regions, the negotiated contract also contains a feature, termed a 'contingency contractual payment,' or CCP, that provides the Medical Groups with incentives to avoid lowering their costs by transferring expenses to Kaiser Hospitals . . .[30]

Wherever prepayment plans are tied to group practice, similar financial incentives may exist for physicians if their salaries, or prorated shares, are in some way a ratio of the net from the plan. The Kaiser system may be an excellent management technique to keep costs down, but dependency by the patient for quality care relies here more heavily on the professional idealism and altruism of the physicians involved than under some other systems of payment. This is not to say that the actual quality of care is lower under such arrangements, but only that "other things being equal"—and here

---

[29] A. Yankauer, J. P. Connelly and J. J. Feldman, "Task Performance and Task Delegation in Pediatric Office Practice," *American Journal of Public Health* (July 1969), pp. 1109, 1111.

[30] *Report of the Health Manpower Commission, op. cit.*, p. 219.

this phrase refers specifically to the training and ability of the physicians giving care—the opportunity is created for reaction to develop in this direction.

The primary claim made for the Kaiser-Permanente prepaid plan is a considerably lower utilization rate of hospital days by its members than by the general population: 612 hospital days per 1,000 against 891. The data are from a 1965 study comparing Kaiser patients and the general California population, corrected for age but not for socioeconomic status. It shows a much lower hospital admission rate by Kaiser patients than for the state as a whole and a slightly longer length of stay for Kaiser patients once hospitalized.[31] The inference is that Kaiser has been more successful than other medical practices in limiting hospitalization to medically justified cases.

The validity of this inference needs to be explored. A recent study points out that the utilization rate of hospital days by Blue Cross members in all Pacific states was 683 per 1,000 in 1967 and 686 in 1968.[32] These non-age adjusted data are much closer to the Kaiser figures than to those cited above for California's population as a whole. Whether the Kaiser patient's lower utilization of hospital days can be attributed solely to the Kaiser plan or to a combination of factors, including the socioeconomic class of users of both the Kaiser and Blue Cross plans, is an interesting question.

Current discussion in academic and government circles tends to assume that physicians in prepaid group practice will always respond to long run, not short run, monetary incentives. Thus, it is further assumed that they will always emphasize preventive care, early diagnosis, annual physical examinations, et cetera; and it is held that, in the long run, total per patient costs will be lower and quality of care higher under prepaid group than under other forms of practice that have no financial incentive to keep *long run*, per capita costs low. In any given prepaid group practice, it may be that at all times the combined effect of anticipated long run monetary gain and altruistic desire to give the highest quality care outweigh any effect on choice of treatment by an anticipated *short run* net gain to the group Yet, the structure of the group is such that the possibility exists for suppliers with high valuations of present versus future income to

---

[31] *Ibid.*, pp. 209, 210. No correction for use of hospital outside of Kaiser Plans, "Averaging the figures for non-Kaiser hospital care and physician visits . . . gives the result that these families ['a small sample . . . in 1958' (p. 209)] obtained about 16 percent of their care outside of the Kaiser Plan," p. 210, footnote 4.

[32] Margith Pachl, "Use of Hospitals by Blue Cross Members in 1968," *Blue Cross Reports*, Res. Ser. No. 3, December 1969, p. 8.

select, consciously or unconsciously, courses of action which net more in the short run than in the long. In periods when labor costs (for nurses, laboratory technicians, et cetera) are rising rapidly and the government is bringing pressure to hold prices of medical care stable, the temptation to restrain short run costs by cutting quality would seem to increase.

Any underwriting by government of prepaid per capita group practice should be accompanied by measures that protect the quality of care given to the consumer. If the government grants low-interest loans to prepaid groups and/or guarantees annual per capita fees for those defined as poor, additional suppliers will be attracted into prepaid group practice. Such suppliers may not be so altruistic as the original pioneers who had an interest in proving the superiority of this organizational form. Moreover, in the stress of competition, the well-established, older groups may succumb to the attractions of short run gains.

Patients' complaints against prepaid group practice are often the same as those raised against any form of group practice and sometimes the same as those against any form of medical care, including solo practice. The more common complaints are fragmentation of medical care, impersonality and, more rarely, lack of privacy At a 1967 National Conference on Group Practice sponsored by the U.S. Public Health Service, the surgeon general of the United States stated that prepaid group practice plans

> reached a plateau some years ago and are having trouble in leaving it. The number of people covered by prepaid group practice plans increased from 3.3 million in 1955 to 4.2 million in 1965—surely not a precipitous rise in a decade marked by social change. I understand that more recent figures indicate only three new prepaid group plans established in 1966.[33]

Coverage of group practice prepayment plans was about 3.5 million people in 1961, 4 million in 1967,[34] and in the neighborhood of 5 million in early 1970.[35] Currently, according to President Nixon's 1971 health message to Congress, the enrollment in Health Mainte-

[33] U.S. Public Health Service, "Promoting the Group Practice of Medicine," Report of the National Conference on Group Practice, 1967. Statement of William H. Stewart, p. 9.

[34] Louis S. Reed and Willine Carr, "Private Health Insurance in the United States, 1967." *Social Security Bulletin* (Washington: U.S. Government Printing Office, February 1969), p. 14.

[35] "Report of the Task Force on Medicaid and Related Programs," U.S. Department of Health, Education, and Welfare (Washington: U.S. Government Printing Office, June 29, 1970), p. 32; hereinafter referred to as *Medicaid Task Force Report.*

nance Organizations (HMO's) is about 7 million.[36] Because the health message defines HMO's as a single organization, providing a comprehensive range of medical services "for a fixed contract fee which is paid in advance by all subscribers," it is unclear whether or not the 7 million includes some people served by the neighborhood clinics or the community health comprehensive centers originally funded by the Office of Economic Opportunity and subsequently transferred to Department of Health, Education, and Welfare. Recently, in addition, under the "Partnership for Health Program" (PL 89–749) prepaid groups organized by private institutions, such as the Harvard Community Health Plan, Inc., have received federal grant monies.[37]

In general, prepaid group practice has been growing more slowly than all group practice. (Perhaps the full effects of recent federal encouragement to the former have not yet occurred.) Why has this been so? Among the usual explanations given are legal restrictions in some state laws, shortages of good administrators, and problems of communication within the group and between group and patient. However, these are not sufficient. An additional explanation lies in the economics of group practice in an inflationary period. In such a period when costs are rising, a prepaid group has the disadvantage of a fixed monthly income, whereas a fee-for-service group has a steadily increasing income resulting from an increasing number of services sold in response to rising demand and at higher prices. Thus, one would expect prepaid groups to increase during deflation and fee-for-service groups to increase during inflation. In recent years, inflation has created a more favorable climate for fee-for-service groups than per capita groups.

Two other arguments should also be considered: (1) healthy individuals are reluctant to commit sizeable monthly amounts for medical care in advance, and (2) prepaid group practice may interfere, in some fashion or other, with the establishment of a satisfactory patient-physician relationship. Data relating to the first are difficult to find. To the extent that individual commercial insurance contracts suffer from adverse selection, this argument is substantiated. However, many healthy individuals do, in fact, prepay for health in the form of sizeable health insurance premiums. Prepaid groups generally provide more comprehensive care than health insurance contracts,

[36] President's Message to the Congress on Health and Hospitalization, February 18, 1971.
[37] U.S., Public Health Service, *Public Health Reports*, Volume 85, No. 1 (Washington: U.S. Government Printing Office, January 1970), p. 87.

and therefore their fees are probably higher on average than health insurance premiums.

It is often simpler for an employer to pay health insurance premiums for his employees than to pay per capita fees to one or more group practices. If he pays to only one group, he limits the choice of his employees. Moreover, in many areas there is only one group practice or sometimes none, and not all employers are willing to take the time—nor is it really their function—to promote prepaid group practice so that a choice will exist. Generally, therefore, employers prefer to pay health insurance premiums and leave the choice of medical care supplier to their employees.

To what degree healthy individuals are willing to prepay monthly sums as high as $50 under the newer, open-to-all-community-residents group plans[38] is not yet really known. Community-based plans are relatively new and few in number.

Analysis of the second argument, the possibility of poorer patient-physician relationships, depends upon recognition that this complaint appears to be more prevalent for prepaid groups than for group practice in general. It may be that with a prepayment system—as is also true in varying degrees with other forms of prepayment, such as private insurance and some government third party payments—the physician is not necessarily 100 percent the patient's agent. At the extreme of interference with the relationship would be a government medical care plan which requires physician certification of disability for absence from work and/or collection of cash sickness benefit. Under such a plan, the government may exert pressure on the physician to limit certification and thus save government monies. Here the physician is partly an agent of the government, and it is not difficult to conceive of circumstances within this framework where the confidentiality of the physician-patient relationship would be impaired. This situation does not exist in the U.S., except possibly under the workmen's compensation plans and some state temporary disability insurance plans. But it is not an inaccurate description of medicine as it is practiced in Soviet Russia.[39]

If the third party is a private insurer or an employer paying premiums to a prepaid group, the physician can also become—but to a lesser degree—the partial agent of the insurer or employer. Recent statements of insurers—commercial, Blue Shield and Blue Cross—

---

[38] The monthly premium for a family of four under Harvard Medical School's Community Plan is $50; Johns Hopkins Medical School Plan's premium is $43.50 a month per family regardless of number of children.

[39] See Mark Field, *Soviet Socialized Medicine* [New York: The Macmillan Company (Free Press), 1967].

indicate that in striving for lower hospital utilization via such devices as utilization review and emphasis on *oupatient* diagnostic tests, they may be placing pressures on the physician to be less than 100 percent the patient's agent. Moreover, in prepaid groups, a physician may be influenced by anticipated short run gain or loss to the group, since the level of the group's income may be affected by his decisions.

A recent review of the literature on prepaid group practice summarizes the problem of future growth of prepaid group practice as follows:

> Although prepaid group practice has appealed to enough people to ensure a slow but steady growth, its acceptability to broad segments of potential recipients and providers of care remains in considerable doubt. Attachments to the traditional, and more familiar, forms of medical care run deep. But they can be strained or ruptured. There is much to suggest that prepaid group practice becomes acceptable to consumers to the extent that they become alienated from traditional practice. But the future growth of group practice need not depend merely on dissatisfaction with what now exists. There is evidence that consumers are able to judge rival plans on the grounds of their relative merits and to select what best meets their own needs as they see them. Insufficient information, rather than rejection, may be the major obstacle.[40]

Assessment of Group Practice

A patient in a prepaid or fee-for-service group may complain in broad terms that medical care is "fragmented" and that he does not have a "personal physician." Fragmentation is largely the result of technological change and specialization and so, to some extent, is impersonality and lack of privacy. But impersonality is more apparent to the patient when he goes to a group clinic than when he sees his physician or consulting specialist in a solo office situation. As the practice of medicine becomes more scientific and less personal,[41] groups may gain favor because then the consumer's choice would become more of an economic choice based solely on price—with or without the refinement of a budgeted price as offered by prepaid per capita group.

Any form of group practice, whether prepaid or not, may dilute

[40] Avedis Donabedian, "An Evaluation of Prepaid Group Practice," *Inquiry*, Volume VI, No. 3, September 3, 1969, p. 25.

[41] At least one physician dissents: "I see no reason for scientific equipment to interfere with the personal relationship with the patient." Letter to the author from Dr. F. A. Barrett, Cheyenne, Wyoming, December 4, 1970. The author believes that the great increase in number of tests and medical procedures performed by other than physicians generally impersonalize the physician-patient relationship.

the patient's privacy, because it provides a common meeting place where physicians can informally discuss their patients. On the other hand, this factor along with the ready availability of specialists may be to the patient's benefit because it produces higher quality care. Turnover rates of subscribers in different prepaid groups would be useful data for judging the degree of consumer satisfaction.

Group practice may be more efficient than solo practice. To what degree any efficiency gains are reflected in higher income to the group's physicians or higher quality or lower prices to the patient, or some combination of these, is unknown. Income data show "that physicians in partnerships earn more than solo practitioners."[42] Among those reporting a net profit in 1966, "the average was $25,500 for sole proprietors and $32,700 per partner for partnerships ($34,500, if special payments to partners are included)."[43] If the data for solo practitioners are corrected for the effect of part-time practice by eliminating income figures for those earning less than $10,000 in 1966, "the average net income from self-employment practice of the well-established solo practitioners, giving full time to private practice, was in the neighborhood of $33,000."[44] This amount is slightly below the net income, $34,477,[45] of *all* members of partnerships reporting a net profit. Some of these, of course, are also not full-time practitioners and receive a pro-rata share, depending on their hours of work, of the group's income. One explanation of this may be that the "better" physician practices with a group and not alone. This seems unlikely and, at any rate, would be impossible to prove either way. Data also indicate that physicians in groups work fewer hours than full-time solo practitioners, and take more vacations and more time off to attend educational meetings. More adequate analysis of physicians' incomes would be possible if Bureau of Labor Statistics' data on physician fees were broken down into fees charged by solo practitioners and by groups.[46] There is little evidence that any cost savings resulting from group tech-

[42] Louis Reed, "Studies of the Incomes of Physicians and Dentists," U.S. Department of Health, Education, and Welfare (Washington: U.S. Government Printing Office, December 1968), p. 33.

[43] *Ibid.*, p. 59.

[44] *Ibid.*, p. 21. Part-time practice includes "moonlighting" by some interns, residents and salaried physicians.

[45] *Ibid.*, p. 10, text and footnote 5; $32,701 plus $1,776 ("guaranteed payments made to a partner for services or the use of capital where such payments were determined without regard to income of the partnership") equals $34,477.

[46] For type of data referred to, see U.S. Social Security Administration *Research and Statistics Note*, "Magnitude and Frequency of Physicians' Fee Increases for Selected Procedures, December 1965–December 1969," Note No. 11, July 16, 1970.

niques are necessarily passed on to consumers in the form of lower prices.

HEW's income data for group practice plans show a net income to total income ratio in 1969 of 6.7 percent for "private medical clinics," 3.0 percent for "employer-employee union" plans, and zero (representing break-even) for "community" plans.[47]

Observations indicate that successful group plans in urban areas reinvest savings in plant and equipment and that they grow in size. Not only does a large established group have advantages in borrowing money but it may also have surplus funds. Analytical studies of what happens to surplus income, if any, are needed. The Kaiser Foundation's 1969 report on its medical care program states that "commercial lenders have advanced us approximately $75 million during the past decade as the basis for more than $200 million worth of needed construction."[48] Further, the 1969 financial report of the Kaiser Foundation Health Plan shows about $5 million deducted from working capital for "additions to land, buildings, and equipment"[49] and similarly, the Kaiser Foundation hospitals' net income statement for 1969 shows $31 million for "addition to land, buildings, and equipment."[50] In other words, large, prepaid group practice can apparently be financially successful.

It is recognized today that the individual's state of health or illness is a continuum, ranging from optimum adaptation to environment and no disease to maladaptation with various levels of disease. This concept puts stress on prevention and early detection of disease—as well as on the care of symptoms and, if possible, rehabilitation. However, today with physician shortages in many areas and with the mobility of urban populations, there is little opportunity for the traditional physician-patient relationship to develop. Also, the physician is unlikely to know his patient outside of his office practice, unlike the situation among middle-income groups 50 years ago. A solo practitioner does not usually have enough contact with a given patient over a period of years to provide as a matter of course "a continuum of care" whether by himself or by referrals to other health workers.

Today's socioeconomic climate is favorable to the development of team practice involving the use of many types of health practi-

[47] U.S. Department of Health, Education, and Welfare, *Research and Statistics Note No. 27* (Washington: U.S. Government Printing Office, December 24, 1970), Table 3.

[48] *Kaiser Foundation Medical Care Program 1969*, The Foundation, California, p. 2.

[49] *Ibid.*, p. 25.

[50] *Ibid.*, p. 28.

tioners in addition to the physician and the nurse. But team medical care does not necessarily require the group approach. Solo practitioners can and do refer their patients to specialists, therapists, laboratory technicians and others. However, in general they do not make as great a use of the wide variety of allied health workers that are available as do physicians in groups or clinics. Moreover, coordination of all the different levels and types of health practitioners needed for an individual's care may be a more costly process for the solo practitioner than for the group. Cost comparisons of this nature would be complex and are not available.

National Health Insurance Partnership Act of 1971*

By Mr. Bennett (for himself, Mr. Jordan of Idaho, Mr. Hruska, Mr. Hansen, Mr. Fannin, Mr. Griffin, and Mr. Scott):

S. 1623. A bill to amend the Social Security Act to require employers to make an approved basic health care plan available to their employees, to provide a family health insurance plan for low-income families not covered by an employer's basic health care plan, to facilitate provision of health services to beneficiaries of the family health insurance plan by health maintenance organizations, by prohibiting State law interference with such organizations providing such services, and for other purposes. Referred to the Committee on Finance.

National Health Insurance Partnership Act of 1971

Mr. Bennett, Mr. President, on behalf of the administration, I introduce the National Insurance Health Partnership Act of 1971, a legislative proposal designed to fulfill the President's desire to build a national health strategy and to enable the Government, the American people, business and labor, the insurance industry, and the health profession to work together in a national partnership to assure that all Americans who are unable to protect themselves against the cost of medical care are able to do so.

Joining me today in introducing this proposal are the Senator

*President Richard M. Nixon, "National Health Insurance Partnership Act of 1971," *Congressional Record*, April 22, 1971.

from Idaho (Mr. Jordan); the Senator from Nebraska (Mr. Hruska); the Senator from Wyoming (Mr. Hansen); the Senator from Arizona (Mr. Fannin); the Senator from Michigan (Mr. Griffin); and the Senator from Pennsylvania (Mr. Scott).

Few people today in the United States would disagree that we face a major health care crisis in our country. What there is little agreement on so far, however, is what should be done about it. On the one hand, we hear that our people have a right to health care but that the evidence is overwhelming that we are confronted with a crisis in the availability and the delivery of essential health services, that the cost of health care simply overwhelms the vast majority of our people, and that if we are to avoid the collapse of our health care system we must take drastic action, and we must take it soon.

On the other hand, Mr. President, we hear that while health care is a right, there is much that is right today with American medicine. We have developed startling new medical techniques, discovered powerful new drugs, and designed and constructed a dazzling array of medical facilities—to the betterment of us all. Clearly, the American health care system has reached new heights. Health care expenditures have been expanding at a rapid rate, our resources have been growing spectacularly, and there has been a marked rise in health insurance coverage for all members of our population.

Efforts of the Public Sector

I maintain, Mr. President, that these two views are not incompatible. There is a massive crisis facing America's medical system, and that crisis is deepening. But behind all of the rhetoric is the fact that much good has been accomplished in health care by both the public and private sectors. For example, in the last decade, our spending on health care has risen from $26 billion a year to $70 billion. In 1960, we devoted 5.3 percent of our gross national product on health; today, we are spending almost 7 percent of our gross national product on health care. This growing expenditure in health care costs has been led by the Federal Government. Ten years ago, Federal health expenditures were $3.5 billion, or 13 percent of the total; this year, the Federal Government will spend $21 billion—or about 30 percent of the Nation's health care spending. I hardly need to point out that the medicare programs alone has eased the financial burden of health care for millions of older people and their families, so that today it is the Nation's largest health insurance program.

Efforts of the Private Sector

The private sector has not lagged behind. In the last 20 years, the private insurance industry has made coverage more readily available so that the segment of our population owning health insurance has grown from 50 percent to 87 percent and the portion of medical bills paid for by insurance has gone from 35 percent to 60 percent. In 1950, about one-half of employed workers were covered for hospitalization; today, some 80 percent are so covered. In 1950 also, only a third of all employees were covered for surgical benefits—over 70 percent are today; 16.4 percent were covered for regular medical benefits—over 60 percent are today; and none had major medical expense insurance, while almost one-third have this type of protection today.

Problems in our Health Care System

Despite the impressive growth of both the public and private sectors, there are serious problems in our Nation's health care system that merit immediate attention and action by the Congress.

In his Health Message to the Congress last month, the President suggested that four of these problems, which this legislation is designed to solve, exist in our present system of providing health insurance protection:

First, many private health insurance policies today cover hospital and surgical costs and leave critical outpatient services uncovered. Although some 80 percent of our people have some hospitalization insurance, only about half are covered for outpatient and laboratory services and less than half are insured for treatment in the physician's office or the home. Because money is available for hospital care people will demand such care rather than less costly noninstitutional care. The result is unnecessary and expensive overutilization of acute health care facilities. The average hospital stay today is a full day longer than it was 8 years ago. Studies show that over one-fourth of the hospital beds in some areas are occupied by patients who do not really need them and could have received equivalent or better care outside the hospital.

A second problem is the failure of most private health insurance policies to protect beneficiaries against the costs of major illnesses and accidents—what is generally referred to as catastrophic costs. Only 40 percent of our people have catastrophic cost insurance of any sort and most of that insurance has upper limits of $10,000 or

$15,000. This means that insurance often runs out while expenses are still mounting. For many American families, a serious illness is often so expensive that it may take years for them to recover financially from the high cost of the medical care required.

A third problem with much of our private health insurance at the present time is that it cannot be applied to membership in a prepaid organization, or as referred to in this legislation, a health maintenance organization—and thus effectively precludes such membership. No employee will pay to join such a plan, no matter how attractive it might seem to him, when deductions from his paycheck—along with contributions from his employer—are being used to purchase another health insurance policy.

The fourth gap we must correct in present private health insurance coverage is its failure to help the poor gain effective access to our medical system. Just one index of this failure is the fact that 50 percent of poor children are not even immunized against common childhood diseases. The disability rate for families below the poverty line is at least 50 percent higher than for families with incomes above $10,000. Those who need care most often get care least. A vicious cycle is thus reinforced—poverty breeds illness and illness breeds greater poverty. This situation will be corrected only when the poor have sufficient purchasing power to enter the medical marketplace on equal terms with those who are more affluent.

The legislation which I introduce today is designed to fill these gaps and correct these inadequacies by building on our present insurance system which has been developing impressively over the past decade or two. At the conclusion of my remarks, I shall include a section-by-section analysis of the bill so that my colleagues may have the opportunity to examine the details of this bill. At this time, however, I would simply like to call attention to the major provisions of the bill.

National Health Insurance Standards

First. A National Health Insurance Standards Act would be established as a new title under the Social Security Act, which would require employers to provide basic health insurance coverage for their employees—except religious, Federal, State, and local employees, and persons eligible for medicare—who have been employed for 25 hours a week in 10 out of 13 weeks, or 350 hours in 13 weeks. Precedents for this proposal are laws which assure workers a minimum wage, provide them with disability and retirement benefits, and set occupational health and safety standards. This legislation goes one step further and guarantees that all workers will receive adequate health insurance protection.

The minimum health insurance program required under this act would pay for hospital services, physicians' services—both in the hospital and outside of it—full maternity care, well-baby care—including immunization—laboratory services, and certain other medical expenses, such as the cost of children's annual eye examinations. To protect against catastrophic costs, benefits would include not less than $50,000 in coverage for each family member during the life of the policy contract. The minimum package would include certain deductible and coinsurance features. As an alternative to paying separate fees for separate services, workers could use this program to purchase membership in a health maintenance organization.

The Federal Government would pay nothing for this program: the costs would be shared by employers and employees, much as they are today under most collective bargaining agreements. A ceiling on how much employees could be asked to contribute would be set at 35 percent during the first 2 1/2 years of operation and 25 percent thereafter. To give each employer time to plan for this additional cost of doing business, this program would not go into effect until July 1, 1973.

I understand that a bill will be introduced in the House next week which will contain a different formula for dividing this insurance cost but to me this is not crucial because the committees could normally be expected to consider and perhaps adopt changes anyway.

As the number of individuals enrolled in the private insurance plans rises, the costs per insured person can be expected to fall. The fact that employees and unions will have an even higher stake in the system will add addition pressures to keep quality up and costs down. And since the range within which benefits can vary will be somewhat narrower than it has been, competition between insurance companies will be more likely to focus on the overall price at which the contract is offered. This means that insurance companies will themselves have a greater motivation to keep medical costs from soaring.

There are several other requirements for the employer plan that I believe bear mentioning. Hospitals providing services for which reimbursement may be made under the plan must have a utilization review plan in effect; reimbursement for services are subject to the reasonable cost and reasonable charge limits imposed under medicare; appropriate arrangements must be made by the private insurance organization underwriting the plan to avoid duplicate coverage;

the employer may continue coverage at the same rate of employer participation in the premium for up to 90 days after termination of employment if he has had coverage for 13 weeks or more; and quality control standards would be applied by professional standards review organizations in accordance with regulations promulgated by the Secretary of Health, Education, and Welfare.

Family Health Insurance Plan

Second. This legislation would also establish a new Family Health Insurance plan to meet the special needs of poor families who would not be covered by the proposed National Insurance Standards Act or by the medicare program—those that are headed by younger unemployed, intermittently employed, or self-employed persons. A poor family would be defined as one whose annual income is less than $5,000 for a family of four—with comparable amounts for families of other sizes—and whose family resources do not exceed $1,500. Excluded from this amount are family dwellings and certain other things such as land that is necessary for a family's maintenance.

What the new Family Health Insurance plan would do is eliminate that part of medicaid which covers most welfare families, and in its place substitute a health insurance scheme fully financed and supported by the Federal Government. Few would agree that with respect to poor families, the medicaid program has not accomplished its goals. Because it is not a truly national program, its benefits vary widely from States to State. Sixteen States now get 80 percent of all medicaid money and two States—California and New York—get 30 percent of Federal funds though they have only 20 percent of the poverty population. Two States have no medicaid program at all.

In addition, medicaid suffers from other defects that now plague our failing welfare system. It largely excludes the working poor—which means that all benefits can suddenly be cutoff when family income rises ever so slightly—from just under the eligibility barrier to just over it. Coverage is now provided when husbands desert their families, but is often eliminated when they come back home and work. The program thus provides an incentive for poor families to stay on the welfare rolls.

Some of these problems would be corrected by the proposal to require employers to offer adequate insurance coverage to their employees. No longer, for example, would a working man receive poorer insurance coverage than a welfare client—a condition which exists today in many States. But we also need an additional program for much of the welfare population—a Family Health Insurance plan.

Eligibility with respect to the income levels under the plan would be determined prospectively for 6-month periods and would generally be based on income for the preceding period, unless the Secretary finds that circumstances have changed. Redeterminations could be made during the 6-month period if there have been changes affecting eligibility. Termination of eligibility would be effective at the end of the 6-month period in which the finding of ineligibility is made, unless the individual is not eligible for coverage under the National Health Insurance Standards Act or medicare, in which case termination would not be effective for an additional three months.

Under the family health insurance plan, benefits in a calendar year for each family member would include: 30 days of inpatient hospital care—or equivalent days of extended-care services or home health services—emergency services, physicians' visits, additional physicians' visits for well-child care—including immunizations—laboratory services in connection with physicians' services, maternity care, and family planning services.

Various medicare provisions would be applicable, such as the provisions on reasonable cost, reasonable charges, and utilization review, and the same exclusions as are in medicare would also apply except that physical checkups would not be excluded. Cost quality controls would generally be provided by professional standards review organizations.

For the poorest of eligible families, this program would make no charges and would pay for basic medical costs. As family income increased beyond a certain level—$3,000 in the case of a 4-person family—the family itself would begin to assume a greater share of the costs—through a graduated scale of premium charges, deductibles, and coinsurance payments. This provision would encourage cost consciousness on the part of program recipients as income rises. But unlike medicaid—with its abrupt cutoff of benefits when family income reaches a certain point—this program would provide an incentive for families to improve their economic position.

The family health insurance plan would go into effect on July 1, 1973. In its first full year of operation, it would cost approximately $1.2 billion in additional Federal funds—assuming that all eligible families participate. Since States would no longer bear any share of this cost, they would be relieved of a considerable burden. In order to encourage States to use part of these savings to supplement Federal benefits, the Federal Government would agree to bear the costs of administering a consolidated Federal-State benefit package. The Federal Government would also contract with local committees to review local practices and to insure that adequate care is being provided in exchange for Federal payments. Private insurers, unions, and employees would be invited to use these same committees to review the utilization of their benefits if they wished to do so.

To review, then, this is how these two new plans would work to complement existing programs and thereby help to bring into being a comprehensive approach to providing adequate health insurance protection for almost all Americans: The Family Health Insurance plan would meet the needs of most welfare families—though medicaid would continue for the aged poor, the blind, and the disabled. The National Health Insurance Standards Act would help the working population. Members of the Armed Forces and civilian Federal employees would continue to have their own insurance programs, and our older citizens would continue to have medicare. The program would also require the establishment in each State of special insurance pools which would offer insurance at reasonable group rates to people who did not qualify for other programs—the self-employed, for example, and poor-risk individuals who often cannot get insurance.

Limitations on the Medicaid Program

I mentioned previously that under this legislation medicaid would continue for the aged, blind, and disabled. These are people who are either receiving cash assistance under a State plan, or whose incomes and resources are so low as to meet the requirements of the plan. Since the Family Health Insurance plan would meet the health cost needs of most families with dependent children, this category of recipients for medical assistance would no longer be included in medicaid. The bill does require, however, that State plans continue to include children receiving foster care. State medicaid plans may optionally include the aged, blind, and disabled who are medically indigent whether or not they meet the income and resources tests of the State plan.

Inapplicability of State Laws

I also previously mentioned that a major problem with much of our private health insurance is its failure to encourage people to enroll in prepaid groups or organizations—health maintenance organizations. This legislation would take a large step forward to solving this problem. Under the proposed National Health Insurance Standards Act, the minimum insurance plan provided by an employer would have to offer the employee the option of joining a health maintenance organization. Under the proposed family health insurance plan, the Secretary could contract with health maintenance organizations to provide services to families covered under the plan.

To insure that the Federal Government reaps the advantages of health maintenance organizations—chiefly that they increase the value of the services a consumer receives for each health dollar because of a strong financial incentive to provide better preventive care and to operate more efficiently—this legislation also preempts certain State laws in favor of the contracts entered into by the Federal Government with HMO's to provide services to family health insurance plan beneficiaries. Archaic laws prohibiting or limiting the group practice of medicine exist in 22 States, and laws in most States prevent doctors, from delegating certain responsibilities—like giving injections—to their assistants.

There is one other feature of this bill about which I am most enthusiastic and strongly urge my colleagues to keep clearly in mind—and that is the provision for the participation of professional standards review organizations. As you may recall, I sponsored the inclusion of the PSRO provision in the ill-fated social security bill of last year out of a firm conviction that major new steps were required if we were ever to stem the tide of rising costs and utilization.

We are all aware of the failure of the existing methods of attempting to control the rising costs of health care—in large part, this failure is a consequence of our failure to encourage and stimulate more active participation by physicians in the review and evaluation of the utilization of services and facilities.

My PSRO proposal was designed to do just that—not only encourage, but make it possible for physicians to play a major role in determining whether our health system is being effectively and appropriately used. I am gratified by the administration's endorsement of the PSRO concept by its incorporation by reference in this bill.

The formal language and PSRO amendment apply to all programs, medicare, medicaid, and this act will be introduced and discussed fully later in the session.

Section 102 of the Bill. Technical amendment.

Section 103 of the Bill. Specifies an effective date of July 1, 1973.

Section 104 of the Bill. Transitional provision.

Provides that the 25 percent limitation on contributions to premiums established in section 603 shall apply only to the period beginning January 1, 1976. For the period July 1, 1973, through December 31, 1975, the limitation shall be 35 percent.

Title II of the Bill—Family Health Insurance Plan

Section 201 of the Bill. Adds to the new title VI of the Social Security Act a new part—part B—entitled "Family Health Insurance Plan."

Part B—Family Health Insurance Plan

Section 620. Short Title. Part B may be cited as the "Family Health Insurance Act."

Section 621. Purpose. The purpose of the new part is to assist low-income families with children to obtain adequate insurance coverage to meet their health needs, in a manner which will encourage the efficient and economical use of resources for health care, through the establishment of the family health insurance plan.

Section 622. Eligibility. Each family as defined in section 625, which includes one or more members who are not entitled to Medicare hospital insurance or to health insurance under the National Health Insurance Standards Act (Part A of title VI) is entitled to health insurance benefits under this new part B, provided that the total annual family income does not exceed $1500. Income limits range from $2500 for one-member families to $7000 for families of seven or more members. The limit for a family of four is $5000.

Family health insurance coverage is required with respect to any family member who receives cash benefits under the Family Assistance Plan or under a State program supplemental to the Family Assistance Plan.

Eligibility and premium amounts will be determined within 30 days following the family's initial filing for family health insurance coverage and every six months thereafter. The Secretary will estimate the family's income for the forthcoming six-month period, basing his estimate, ordinarily, of the family's income for a preceding period. Redeterminations of eligibility and premium amounts will be made whenever the Secretary has reason to believe they are needed.

To the extent that he finds them relevant, the Secretary, in making determinations of eligibility and premium amounts, may adopt determinations of family income made under the Family Assistance Plan or under a State program supplementing the Family Assistance Plan.

The Secretary may by regulations determine when income received, or expenses incurred, in one period shall be considered as income received or expenses incurred in another period or periods.

Each family member whose coverage is terminated will be so advised by the Secretary and the termination will take effect with the close of the six-month period in which notice is given. Where the terminated beneficiary is not entitled to Medicare's hospital insurance and is not a member of a family covered by The National Health Insurance Standards Act, the termination will take effect with the last day of the quarter following the six-month period in which the coverage determination is made.

Provision is made for setting special income limits for purposes of eligibility on a family's gross income from a trade or business (including farming).

Section 623. Meaning of Income. Both earned and unearned income are counted. Specific definitions are provided. Family assistance benefits and State supplementary payments are counted, but food stamps (and other than in-kind benefits based on need) are not counted, nor are amounts received for care of foster children.

The amount of income attributed to each member of an eligible family will be determined by dividing the family's total income by the total number of family members eligible for coverage under this part and assigning an equal share to each member.

For purposes of determining premiums, deductibles and coinsurance amounts, families are classified by number of eligible members and their total income in accordance with a table included in the bill.

Section 624. Resources. In determining "resources," the Secretary will exclude the family home, household goods, personal effects, and property so essential to family self support as to warrant its exclusion. Regulations will specify the effect that disposition of a family's property will have on eligibility.

Section 625. Definition of a Family and Child. The terms "family" and "child" are defined. A parent (or spouse of such parent) who is absent because of employment or search for employment will be counted as part of the family. A "child" must be under age 18 or, if between 19 and 22, must be attending a college, university, or other school in preparation for employment.

In determining eligibility and premium amounts, income of any person that is not available to the family will not be counted (except for the income of a parent or spouse of a parent). Where the person is a child, he will be included in determining the family's eligibility but not in determining its premium amount.

Section 626. Benefits. In each calendar year, each covered member of a family is eligible for coverage of 30 days in inpatient hospital care (or equivalent days of extended care or home health services), physicians' services during these 30 days (or the equivalent number while receiving extended care or home health services), emergency services, outpatient physicians' services on 8 occasions, and other services. Also provided are well-child care, with the number of occasions of such care being limited by the child's age; one routine eye examination for a child under 12 years of age; and maternity care and family planning services and related drugs and devices. Psychiatric care, prosthetic devices and drugs to outpatients (other than those related to maternity care or family planning services), are excluded.

Deductibles and coinsurance vary in accordance with the income class of eligible families. (The classes range from 1 to 5, with 5 being the highest eligible income class.) A deductible of one day of charges for room and board in a hospital is provided for families in income classes 2, 3, or 4, and 2 days for families in income class 5. The deductible for services other than well-baby care, maternity care, and family planning services is $50 per family for those in income classes 3 and 4, and $100 in class 5. Coinsurance is at the rate of 10 percent for income class 4 and 25 percent for income class 5. There is no coinsurance for families in income classes 1, 2, or 3.

Hospitals providing services must have a utilization review plan; reimbursement for services is subject to reasonable cost and reasonable charge limits under title XVIII (Medicare); appropriate arrangements must be made by the carrier to avoid duplicate coverage; Professional Standards Review Organization provisions of title XI (which would be added by H.R. 1) as they apply to payments under titles XVIII and XIX would apply to the extent determined by the Secretary; the same exclusions that apply under title XVIII would apply, except that physical checkups are covered; and State agencies, intermediaries, carriers, and other private agencies or organizations, will be utilized by the Secretary to the extent he finds appropriate in carrying out the program.

Section 627. Premiums. Premiums are based on the family's income class, taking into account the family's size. (A family in income class 1 pays no premium.) Premiums are to be paid as prescribed in regulations. They may be deducted from payments due any member of the covered family under any title of the Social Security Act. The Secretary may request that premiums be deducted from State benefits supplementing Federal Family Assistance benefits. Family members who are dissatisfied with any determination made under the program have opportunity for hearing and review.

Section 628. Payments to Health Maintenance Organizations. Provision is made for families to choose to receive covered services through a health maintenance organization. The HMO option is like that proposed for Medicare under H.R. 1.

Section 629. Consolidated Federal-State Health Benefits. States may enter into agreements with the Secretary under which the State would provide benefits supplemental to benefits under this new part, with the State paying the administrative costs.

Section 630. Definitions. The terms "inpatient hospital services," "physicians' services," "medical and other services," "extended care services," "home health services," "provider of services," and "carrier" have the same meaning as when used under title XVIII. The term "pediatric nurse associate" is defined.

Section 202 of the bill. Sets July 1, 1973, as the effective date of the program.

Title III of the Bill—Restriction of Medical Assistance Programs to Aged, Blind, Disabled and Children in Foster Care

Title XIX of the Social Security Act is amended to provide that the only mandatory coverage groups under State Medicaid plans will be the aged, blind, and disabled within the meaning of title XVI who are either receiving cash assistance under the State title XVI plan, or whose income and resources meet the requirements of such plan—and also children receiving foster care under a State plan approved under part A of title IV. State Medicaid plans may optionally include the aged, blind, and disabled who are medically indigent (whether or not they meet the income and resources tests of the title XVI plan) and also medically indigent children who are under 21 years and are ineligible for coverage under part A or part B of title VI.

Title IV of the Bill—Inapplicability of State Law to Health Maintenance Organizations

Health maintenance organizations providing services pursuant to agreement with the Secretary under title VI of the Social Security Act (National Health Insurance Standards Act and Family Health

Insurance Act) would be exempted from State laws or regulations inconsistent with the agreement or with the Secretary's regulations.

Physicians affiliated with such health maintenance organizations may delegate any of their functions to employees, either of the physicians or of the organization, subject to the Secretary's limitations and requirements, notwithstanding any State laws or regulations; no State law or regulation may prevent, interfere with, or penalize any such physician, employee, or organization for so doing.

Health Security for America *

Mr. Kennedy. Mr. President, on behalf of Senator Cooper, Senator Saxbe, and myself, together with Senators Bayh, Case, Cranston, Gravel, Harris, Hart, Hughes, Humphrey, Inouye, Javits, Magnuson, McGee, McGovern, Metcalf, Mondale, Moss, Muskie, Pastore, Pell, Randolph, Stevenson, and Tunney, I introduce for appropriate reference S. 3, The Health Security Act of 1971.

The bill is a legislative proposal to establish a Health Security program for all Americans. Through the mechanism of comprehensive national health insurance, it will bring health security to our people and end our current health crisis by improving each of the three basic aspects of our health care system—the organization, delivery, and financing of personal health services. We commend this legislation to our colleagues in the Senate for their favorable consideration and early action.

I believe that in America today, health care is a right for all, not just a privilege for the few. The basic goal of the Health Security program is to make that right a continuing reality, not just the empty promise it is today. Just as the Social Security program of the decade of the 1930's brought hope and new faith to a nation mired in the social crisis of the great depression, so I believe the Health Security program in the decade of the 1970's can guarantee high quality health care to our people and lead us out of the current crisis of confidence in our health system.

We know from recent experience that changes in the organization and delivery of health care in the United States will come only by an

*Senator Edward M. Kennedy, Speech in the Senate on "S.3—Introduction of a Bill to Create a National System of Health Insurance," *Congressional Record*, January 25, 1971.

excruciating national effort. Throughout our society today, there is perhaps no institution more resistant to change than the organized medical profession. Indeed, because the crisis is so serious in the organization and delivery of health care, there are many who argue that we must make improvements in the organization and delivery system first, before we can safely embark on changing the financing system through national health insurance.

I believe the opposite is true. We must use the financing mechanism to create strong new incentives for the reorganization and delivery of health care. Thomas Paine declared at the founding of our American Republic, echoing the words of the ancient Greeks, "Give us a lever and we shall move the world." I say, give us the lever of national health insurance, and together we shall move the medical world and achieve the reforms that are so desperately needed.

The fact that the time has come for national health insurance makes it all the more urgent to pour new resources into remaking our present system. The existing organization and delivery of health care are so obviously inadequate to meet our current health crisis that only the catalyst of national health insurance will be able to produce the sort of basic changes that are needed if we are to escape the twin evils of a national health disaster or the total federalization of health care in the 1970's.

The use of the phrase "national health disaster" is not too strong. That the danger is great and imminent is a point on which both President Nixon and I agree. In July of 1969, President Nixon told a news conference that the Nation faced a massive crisis in health care, and that unless action was taken both administratively and legislatively to meet the crisis within the next 2 or 3 years, we would have a breakdown of our medical care system.

Our view of the problem is the same, but—on the basis of the information available about the administration's health program—we differ profoundly on the solution to be proposed. The central issue is how we can begin to move the health care system from where we are today to where we want to be tomorrow and in the years ahead. Neither the Health Security program nor the administration's program seeks revolutionary change in health care. The change that comes must be evolutionary change, but it must also be change that is capable of reaching the goals we share.

In essence, our difference is over the question whether the existing health care system needs a major overhaul or simply a minor tuneup. The question is whether a coordinated and comprehensive new approach is needed, or simply the sort of patchwork approach we have been using for too long. To be sure, we do need health insurance for the poor, catastrophic illness insurance for middle America, more assistance for medical schools, a moonshot against cancer and a manhattan project against sickle-cell anemia, incentives for health maintenance, and all the other items likely to be unveiled in the administration's arsenal. But we cannot afford to take these steps alone. Such divided and categorical approaches have been tried under Government or private sponsorship in the past, and they have met with uniform frustration and defeat.

We propose that the Nation cannot afford to repeat the mistakes of the past. We must begin now to develop a more coherent health care system which provides for the efficient use of existing health services and resources, which encourages better services and resources for the future, and which offers a comprehensive, balanced and proportioned approach to the health care system as a whole. This is the goal of the Health Security program.

The experience of medicare and medicaid has demonstrated that money alone and health insurance alone are no longer adequate to deal with the health needs of the Nation. So long as the resources are insufficient and the organizational arrangements are inadequate, money alone will only make the problem worse. National health insurance is necessary, but it must now and for the years ahead be part of a broader program of Health Security.

To those who say that the Health Security program will not work unless we first have an enormous increase in health manpower, health facilities and our ability to deliver health care, I reply that until we being moving toward such a Health Security program, neither Congress nor the medical profession will ever take the basic steps that are essential to improve the system. Without something like the Health Security program to galvanize us into action, I fear that we will simply continue to patch the present system beyond any reasonable hope of survival.

If we are to reach our goal of bringing adequate health care to all our citizens, we must have full and generous cooperation between Congress, the administration, and all the health professions. I believe that we shall have this cooperation. We know the dedication of the health professions, the heroic efforts of hospitals and other institutions, the conscientious efforts of Federal, State, and local government agencies and their health personnel. We know their strong desire to end the limitations under which they struggle today to meet the growing national need for better health care. We share a common goal, and I am confident that we shall prevail.

It is highly appropriate that we in the Senate launch this new debate over health care on this, our first day of legislative business in the 92d Congress. At last, the debate over health care has shifted from the halls of the universities to the hearing rooms of Congress. The anguished pleas of millions of our people are being heard.

In the weeks and months to come, a great national debate will take place. As the new chairman of the Senate Health Subcommittee, I intend to take this issue to the people in all parts of the country, and to make every effort to insure that the promise of good health care becomes a reality for every citizen.

Although the debate will be nationwide, the primary focus will be on Congress and the response we make to the challenge that so clearly exists. More and more, in recent years, Congress has shown itself capable of meeting great challenges with great responses, and I am confident that the 92d Congress will do no less. Indeed, there could be no finer tribute to the 92d Congress than to be recorded as the Congress that at last ended the crisis of health care in America and brought health security to all our people.

The Current Crisis

If one thing is clear in the United States of 1971, it is that health care is the fastest-growing failing business in the Nation—a $70 billion industry that fails to meet the urgent needs of our people. Today, more than ever before, we are spending more on health care and enjoying it less.

In spite our vaunted research and technology, unequalled by any other nation in the history of the world, America is an also-ran in the delivery of health care to our people.

Almost every family knows the cruel burden of worry, frustration, and disappointment that mark our search for better health care. The average American lives in dread of illness and disability. He lives with the uncertainty of not knowing whether to seek medical care, or when to seek it, or where to find it, or how to pay for it.

For millions of our citizens, health care of any sort is simply not available at any price. For millions more, the quality of care available is so poor that it may be fairly said that the citizen will be worse off because of his contact with the system.

There is not a person in the Nation who has not felt the heavy burden of the soaring cost of medical care. There is not a family in the Nation that does not live in fear of sickness and ill health, and the very real prospect of financial ruin and worse because of accident or serious illness.

Our current health crisis cuts across all political, social, economic and geographic lines. It affects rich and poor, black and white, old and young, urban and rural alike. Of all the pressing domestic problems we face, none is more pervasive or more difficult to resolve than the deterioration of our once proud system of health care. Never have so many different elements in our population been so united in their demand for action.

Comparisons With Other Nations

We know very well the dismal health record of the United States compared to the other major industrial nations of the world. Our rates of sickness and mortality lag far behind the potential of modern health care in America, or the reality of such care in many foreign nations. Year after year, the statistics tell us how little progress we have been making in health care in recent decades compared to other nations. Our record is getting no better. Unless we stop the slide, the crisis will get worse, and the result will be disaster.

The comparisons are shocking:

In infant mortality, among the major industrial nations of the world, the United States today trails behind 12 other countries, including all the Scandinavian nations, most of the British Commonwealth, Japan, and East Germany. Half of these nations were behind us in the early 1950's.

We trail six other nations in the percentage of mothers who die in childbirth. In the early 1950's, we had the lowest rate of any industrial nation.

Tragically, the infant mortality rate for nonwhites in the United States is nearly twice the rate for whites. And nearly five times as many nonwhite mothers die in childbirth as whites—shameful evidence of the ineffective prenatal and postnatal care our minority groups receive.

The story told by other health indicators is equally dismal. The United States trails 17 other nations in life expectancy for males, 10 other nations in life expectancy for females, and 15 other nations in the death rate for middle-aged males.

The Role of Private Health Insurance

The comparison with other nations, reveals one other very important point. The United States today is the only major industrial Nation in the world without a system of national health insurance or a national health service. Instead, we have placed our prime reliance on private enterprise and private health insurance to meet the need.

I believe that the private health insurance industry has failed us. It fails to control costs. It fails to control quality. It provides partial benefits, not comprehensive benefits; acute care, not preventive care. It ignores the poor and the medically indigent.

Despite the fact that private health insurance is a giant $12 billion industry, despite more than three decades of enormous growth, despite massive sales of health insurance by thousands of private companies competing with each other for the health dollar of millions of citizens, health insurance benefits today pay only one-third of the total cost of private health care, leaving two-thirds to be paid out of pocket by the patient at the time of illness or as a debt thereafter, at the very time when he can least afford it.

Nearly all private health insurance is partial and limited. For most citizens, their health insurance coverage is more loophole than protection. In 1968, of the 180 million Americans under 65:

Twenty percent, or 36 million, had no hospital insurance;

Twenty-two percent, or 39 million, had no surgical insurance;

Thirty-four percent, or 61 million, had no in-patient medical insurance;

Fifty percent, or 89 million, had no out-patient X-ray and laboratory insurance;

Fifty-seven percent, or 102 million, had no insurance for doctors' office visits or home visits;

Sixty-one percent, or 108 million, had no insurance for prescription drugs;

Ninety-seven percent, or 173 million, had no dental insurance.

As a result, it is fair to say that private health insurance today is a major part of our current crisis in health care. Commercial carriers syphon off the young and healthy, leaving the old and ill to Blue Cross, vulnerable to escalating rates they cannot possibly afford.

Too often, private carriers pay only the cost of hospital care. They force doctors and patients alike to resort to wasteful and inefficient use of hospital facilities, thereby giving further impetus to the already soaring cost of hospital care and unnecessary strains on health manpower.

Valuable hospital beds are used for routine tests and examinations which, under any rational health care system, would be conducted on an out-patient basis.

Unnecessary hospitalization and unnecessarily extended hospital care are encouraged for patients for whom any rational system would provide treatment in other, less elaborate facilities.

Unnecessary surgery is encouraged. We know that far more surgery takes place in the United States than in other nations with far better health records. We know that under the Federal Employees Health Benefits program, more than twice as much surgery takes place on Federal employees enrolled in the indemnity reimbursement plan as on those enrolled in prepaid group practice plans in the Federal program. The figures are especially striking for female surgery and for surgical procedures like appendectomy and tonsillectomy.

This, then, is where we stand today. Private health insurance has done no more than this to provide health security for American families.

The Source of Our Health Crisis

Our system of health care is in crisis today largely because our knowledge of health care has evolved at a much greater rate than our ability to deliver health care. We are the richest Nation in the world in Nobel Prizes for medicine, yet we are among the poorest nations of the world in our ability to translate the triumphs of medical research into the reality of better health care. Our success in the laboratory is hollow indeed, in light of the cruel truth that good health care is simply not available to millions of our people.

In large part, our health care system has been buried under our magnificent advances of medical research. We have allowed ourselves to become so preoccupied with developing techniques to treat disease that we have ignored the delivery of health care. To be sure, the delivery system has evolved, but it has evolved more by neglect than design, to the point where it can no longer be called a system in a meaningful sense. We have severe shortages of family doctors and dentists, and a surfeit of surgeons. Rural practitioners retire, and hundreds of counties and thousands of small communities in America find themselves without access to a physician. Patients everywhere face a bewildering array of health personnel who know more and more about one disease or organ, but less and less about the whole patient.

It is important to understand how our present health crisis came about. At the turn of the present century, medical care in the United States began to take firm root in the emerging modern science. Soon after 1910, medical education itself became a university undertaking with a solid foundation in science.

The explosion of scientific knowledge made vast new resources available to medicine. The science and art of medical care developed at an unprecedented rate. As a result, specialization in medicine became necessary, and a number of specialties began to develop in medical schools and in the practice of medicine. The family physician began to disappear, replaced by an increasing variety of specialists, according to ages of life, categories of disease, organs of the body, and medical techniques.

Medical care became increasingly fractionated. No adequate resources were developed to take the place of the disappearing family physician, to provide primary medical care, or to coordinate services of the emerging specialties. The quality and effectiveness of medical care became increasingly uneven.

The specialization of physicians was accompanied by an increasing variety and number of allied practitioners. And, inevitably, along with the increasing complexity in the function of physicians, a similar complexity developed in the services provided by hospitals—the essential workshops of most of the new specialists.

As a consequence of these developments, the cost of medical care began to rise, progressively pricing more and more medical care beyond the reach of more and more people.

At the same time, the system of medical practice in the Nation—which had developed over the centuries when medical care was simple and uncomplicated—became increasingly rigid and unchanging, and began to impede the availability of medical care for more and more people. It began to interfere with the development of the personnel, facilities, and organizations needed to make medical care actually available to the people.

In turn, the stagnation of the health care system had two further unfortunate developments—an increasing unavailability of medical care despite increasing public expectation and demand for better medical care; and steeply increasing costs. The system resisted the development of needed resources for the delivery of medical care, and it resisted organizational improvements to moderate the steep rise in costs.

These developments and progressions were not peculiar to the United States. They were also taking place in all developed countries of the world. As one nation after another faced the problem, it acted to deal with the situation. Some countries developed national health insurance programs. Others developed national health services. They met their problems as best they could, according to their own needs and resources.

The United States alone stood apart from these worldwide developments. We preserved our faith in the private sector. Although government did become involved in the effort to upgrade health care, the effort was always limited, categorical, and inadequate. We chose to leave basic planning and development of health care to professional leadership and to the play of the marketplace.

The crisis today reflects the fact that professional leadership alone was not capable of meeting the national needs, and that the demands and needs of medical care do not lend themselves to satisfaction solely through the forces and the dynamics of the marketplace.

The Development of the Health Security Program

Recently, an important new chapter began in the long history of American health needs and social policy. Walter Reuther, the late president of the United Auto Workers, was among the first to see that financing programs like medicare and medicaid or extensions of private health insurance could not resolve the crisis of disorganization and the spiraling cost of health care. Walter Reuther understood that the Nation needed to take a bold step forward. In November 1968, he announced the formation of the Committee of One Hundred for National Health Insurance. As he said, in establishing the mandate of the committee:

> I do not propose that we borrow a national health insurance system from any other nation. No nation has a system that will meet the peculiar needs of America. I am confident that we have in America the ingenuity and the social inventiveness needed to create a system of national health insurance that will be uniquely American—one that will harmonize and make compatible the best features of the present system, with maximum freedom of choice, within the economic framework and social structure of a national health insurance system.

Joining Walter Reuther on that committee were Dr. Michael E. deBakey, president of Baylor College of Medicine; Mrs. Mary Lasker, president of the Albert and Mary Lasker Foundation; Mr. Whitney M. Young, Jr., executive director of the National Urban League; and other outstanding citizens from the fields of medicine, public health, industry, agriculture, labor, education, the social services, youth, civil rights, religious organizations, and consumer groups. I have had the honor of serving on that committee, along with my Senate colleagues, John Sherman Cooper and William Saxbe, and my former colleague, Ralph Yarborough.

In its efforts over the past 2 years, the committee has worked to develop a sound program for improving the organization, financing and delivery of health services to the American people. The committee's deliberations were based upon the premise that progress toward a more rational health system should be orderly and evolutionary. The members of the committee felt that a better system of health care for America should rest upon the positive motivations and interests of both consumers and providers of health services. They believed that no system could succeed if it were imposed by fiat through rigid legislation and administrative regulations.

Throughout its deliberations, the committee has been guided by the work of its distinguished technical subcommittee, chaired by Dr. I. S. Falk, professor emeritus of public health of Yale University and the most eminent authority in the field of health economics in the Nation. The committee consulted extensively with representatives of professional associations, consumer organizations, labor unions, business groups, and many other interested organizations. The Health Security program is the result of these efforts, and it gives careful consideration to the recommendations of all of these groups.

Last August, Senators Cooper, Saxbe, Yarborough, and I, together with 11 other Senators, introduced the original version of the Health Security program as S. 4297 in the 91st Congress. In September, the Senate Committee on Labor and Public Welfare held 2 days of hearings on the legislation, the first hearings to be held in Congress on comprehensive national health insurance since the critical problems of health care in America first became paramount 20 years ago. With the exception of the administration, testimony from a broad spectrum of witnesses was immensely favorable to the bill, and generated increased momentum for introduction of the bill in the 92d Congress.

At the time the bill was originally introduced last year, Congresswoman Martha Griffiths of Michigan had already introduced legislation in the House of Representatives to create a national health insurance program similar in overall concept to the Health Security program, and her bill had received the strong endorsement of the AFL-CIO, under the leadership of President George Meany.

Before the 91st Congress adjourned last year, we had decided to pool our efforts and introduce a common bill in the 92d Congress. Hundreds of detailed differences between the two previous bills have been resolved, and the debate over the preparation of the new bill has led to the stronger Health Security program we introduce today.

As these and other developments make clear, we are now seeing the uniting of major American institutions to support the goal of Health Security. It is an issue destined to grow and remain before the American public until the goal of adequate health care for all is finally achieved.

Major Provisions of the Health Security Program

The Health Security program is intended to be comprehensive and extensive. At the conclusion of my remarks in the Congressional Record, I will include a section-by-section analysis of the bill and the text of the bill itself, so that the details of its provisions may be widely available to all. At this time, however, 1 would like to call attention to its main provisions:

Basic Principle

Basic Principle

The basic principle of the Health Security program is twofold: to establish a system of comprehensive national health insurance for the United States, capable of bringing the same high quality health care to every resident; and, to use the program to bring about major improvements in the ogranization and delivery of health care in the Nation.

The Health Security program does not envisage a national health service, in which Government owns the facilities, employs the personnel, and manages all the finances of the health care system. On the contrary, the program proposes a working partnership between the public and private sectors. There will be Government financing and administrative management, accompanied by private provision of personal health services through private practitioners, institutions, and other providers of health care.

Persons Eligible for Benefits

Every individual residing in the United States will be eligible to receive benefits. There will be no requirement of past individual contributions, as in Social Security, or a means test, as in Medicaid.

Starting Date for Benefits

July 1, 1973. The 2-year tooling-up period prior to that date will be used to prepare the health care system for the program.

Covered Benefits

With certain modest limitations, the program will provide comprehensive health benefits for every eligible person. The benefits available under the program will cover the entire range of personal health care services, including the prevention and early detection of disease, the care and treatment of illness, and medical rehabilitation. There are no cutoff dates, no coinsurance, no deductibles, and no waiting periods.

For example, the program provides full coverage for physician's services, inpatient and outpatient hospital services, and home health services. It also provides full coverage for other professional and supporting services, such as optometry services, podiatry services, devices, and appliances, and certain other services under specified conditions.

The four limitations in the otherwise unlimited scope of benefits are dictated by inadequacies in existing health resources or in management potentials. They deal with nursing home care, psychiatric care, dental care, and prescription drugs, as follows:

Skilled nursing home care is limited to 120 days per benefit period. The period may be extended, however, if the nursing home is owned or managed by a hospital, and payment for care is made through the hospital's budget.

Psychiatric hospitalization is limited to 45 consecutive days of active treatment during a benefit period, and psychiatric consultations are limited to 20 visits during a benefit period. These limits do not apply, however, when benefits are provided through comprehensive health care organizations or comprehensive mental health care organizations.

Dental care is restricted to children through age 15 at the outset, with the covered age group increasing annually until persons through age 25 are covered. Persons eligible for coverage through age 25 will remain eligible for coverage throughout their lives.

Prescribed drugs are limited to those provided through hospital in-patient or out-patient departments, or through organized patient care programs. For other patients, coverage extends only to drugs required for the treatment of chronic or long-term illness.

Inevitably, simply stating these four limitations gives them a prominence they do not deserve. In all other respects, covered health services will be available without limit, in accordance with medical need.

Administration

The administration of the Health Security program will be carried out by a five-member full-time Health Security Board, appointed by the President with the advice and consent of the Senate. Members of the Board will serve 5-year terms, and will be under the authority of the Secretary of Health, Education, and Welfare.

A statutory National Advisory Council will assist the Board in the development of general policy, the formulation of regulations, and the allocation of funds. Members of the Council will include representatives of both providers and consumers of health care.

Field administration of the program will be carried out through the 10 existing HEW regions, as well as through the approximately 100 health subareas that now exist as natural medical marketplaces in the Nation. Advisory councils on matters of administration will be established at each of these levels. However, the Board will guide the overall performance of the program. It will coordinate its functions with State and regional planning agencies, and it will account for its activities to Congress.

Financing the Program

The program will be financed through a Health Security Trust Fund, similar to the Social Security Trust Fund. Income to the Fund will derive from four sources:

Fifty percent from general Federal tax revenues;

Thirty-six percent from a tax of 3.5 percent on employers' payrolls;

Twelve percent from a tax of 1 percent on employees' wages and unearned income up to $15,000 a year;

Two percent from a tax of 2.5 percent on self-employment income up to $15,000 a year.

Employers may pay all or part of their employees' health security taxes, in accord with arrangements established under collective-bargaining agreements.

Payment Mechanism

The essence of the payment mechanism and the central cost control feature of the program is that the health care system as a whole will be anchored to a budget established in advance. A given amount of money will be made available for the program each year, based on the available estimates of the needs to be met and the services to be provided, with due regard for the resources of the system. As in every area of our economic life, the health care system will be obliged to live within its budget. In this way we can end the unacceptable escalation of costs within our present system. In this way we can end the long financial binge in which health care has had a signed blank check on the whole economy of the Nation.

Each year, the Health Security Board will make an advance estimate of the total amount needed for expenditure from the Trust

Fund to pay for health care services in the program. The Board will allocate funds to the several regions, and these allocations will be subdivided among categories of services in the health subareas. Advance estimates, constituting the program budgets, will be subject to adjustments in accordance with guidelines in the act. The allocations to regions and to subareas will be guided initially by the available data on current levels of expenditure. Thereafter, they will be guided by the program's own experience in making expenditures and in assessing the need for equitable health care throughout the Nation.

Compensation of Doctors, Hospitals, and Other Providers

Providers of health services will be compensated directly by the Health Security program. Individuals will not be charged for covered services.

Hospitals and other institutional providers will be paid on the basis of approved prospective budgets. Independent practitioners, including physicians, dentists, podiatrists, and optometrists, may be paid by various methods which they may elect: by fee-for-service, by capitation payments, or in some cases by retainers, stipends, or a combination of such methods. Comprehensive health service organizations may be paid by capitation, or by a combination of capitation and methods applicable to payments to hospitals and other institutional providers. Other independent providers, such as pathology laboratories, radiology services, pharmacies, and providers of appliances, will be paid by methods adapted to their special characteristics.

Foundations, sponsored by medical or dental societies, or other specified nonprofit organizations, are specifically recognized as a class of providers with which the Board may contract for services. Foundations would be required to have an enrolled population and to permit participation by all qualified physicians in the area. Foundations would be reimbursed by the same formula used for prepaid group practice plans.

In addition, drug addiction and alcoholic treatment centers are specifically included as eligible providers of services under the program.

Resources Development Fund

An essential feature of the program is the Resources Development Fund, which will come into operation 2 years before benefits begin. In the first year of this "tooling up" period, $200 million will be appropriated for the fund; in the second year, $400 million will be made available. Once the program benefits begin, up to 5 percent of the Trust Fund—about $2 billion a year—will be set aside for resources development. These funds will be used to support innovative health programs, particularly in areas like manpower education, training, group practice development, and other means to improve the delivery of health care. The principal attribute of the Fund is that it can be used to channel far more money into areas like education and training than is possible under the existing system of congressional authorization and appropriation for ongoing programs.

Quality Control

The Health Security program includes various provisions designed to safeguard the quality of health care. The program will establish national standards more exacting than medicare for participating individual and institutional providers. Independent practitioners will be eligible to participate if they meet licensure and continuing education requirements. Specialty services will be covered if, upon referral, they are performed by qualified persons. Hospitals and other institutions will be eligible for participation if they meet national standards, and if they establish utilization review and affiliation arrangements.

In addition, the Health Security Board is authorized to require prior consultation with an appropriately qualified specialist before the performance of designated nonemergency surgery, in order to allow administrative monitoring of surgical procedures that are frequently abused.

Incentives

Financial, professional and other incentives are built into the program to move the health care delivery system toward organized arrangements for patient care, and to encourage preventive care and the early diagnosis of disease.

In the area of health manpower, the program will supplement existing Federal programs. It will provide incentives for comprehensive group practice organizations, encourage the efficient use of personnel in short supply, and stimulate the progressive broadening of health services. It will provide funds for education and training programs, especially for members of minority groups and those disadvantaged by poverty. Finally, it will provide special support for the location of increased health personnel in urban and rural poverty areas.

Relation to Existing Programs

Various Federal health programs will be superseded, in whole or in part, by the Health Security program. Since persons of age 65 or over will be covered by the program, medicare under the social security system will be terminated. Federal aid to the States for medicaid and other Federal programs will also be terminated, except to the extent that benefits under such programs are broader than under the Health Security program. However, the bill does not affect the current provisions for personal health services under the Veterans Administration, temporary disability, or workmen's compensation programs.

Cost of the Program and Federal Revenue Sharing

On the basis of data available for the fiscal year 1970, a total of $41 billion was expended for health care benefits that would have been covered by the Health Security program had the program been in effect for that year. In other words, if the Health Security program had been in effect in 1970, the cost of the program would have been $41 billion.

The $41 billion figure represents approximately 70 percent of the total actual expenditures for personal health care in the United States for that year. These expenditures consist of $30 billion in private health insurance payments and private out-of-pocket payments, $8 billion in payments by the Federal Government, and $3 billion in payments by State and local governments.

The cost of the health security program has been the source of enormous confusion and misunderstanding since the original version of the Health Security Act was introduced last year in the 91st Congress. The crucial point is that in no sense does the hypothetical $41 billion price tag for the Health Security program in 1970 represent new money. Rather, this is what Americans are already paying for personal health care under the existing system.

Thus, the Health Security program is not a new layer of Federal expenditures on top of existing public and private spending for health care. Instead, the Health Security program simply redistributes the health expenditures that are already being made. Although, of course, *Federal* expenditures in 1970 would have risen from $8 billion under the existing system to $41 billion if the Health Security program had been in effect, individuals and organizations throughout the Nation would have been relieved of $30 billion of *private* health insurance expenses and out-of-pocket payments for health care, and State and local governments would have been relieved of $3 billion, representing costs incurred largely in medicaid and other public assistance programs, and in city and county medical programs.

In a very real sense, therefore, the Health Security program is a direct form of Federal revenue sharing. It offers $3 billion in substantial and immediate Federal financial relief to State and local governments, thereby freeing scarce State and local funds for other urgently needed purposes.

Over the long run, by revitalizing the existing health care system and ending the excessive inflation in the cost of health care, the Health Security program will be far less expensive than the amount we will spend if we simply allow the present system to continue.

Even at the beginning, moreover, the Health Security program will provide more and better services without increasing the cost, since the initial savings achieved by the program will be sufficient to offset the cost of the increased services. In other words, from the day the Health Security program begins, we will guarantee our citizens better value for their health dollar and achieve a substantial moderation of the current exorbitant inflation in health costs. Even in the first year of the Health Security program, the comprehensive health services provided will be available for the same cost we would have paid for the partial and inefficient services of the existing system.

In 1970, for example, spending for health exceeded $70 billion. For the first time in our history, expenditures for health rose above 7 percent of our gross national product. If we continue to do nothing, the annual cost will exceed $100 billion in only 3 years.

Conclusion

In sum, the Health Security Act we submit to the Senate and to the people of the United States differs from all previous proposals for health care or national health insurance. It is not just another financing mechanism. It is not just another design for pouring more purchasing power into our already overstrained and overburdened nonsystem for the delivery of health care. It is not just another proposal to generate more professional personnel or more hospitals and clinics, without the means to guarantee their effective use.

Ours is a proposal to give us a national system of health security. Under this program, the funds we make available will finance and budget the essential costs of good health care for generations ahead. At the same time, these funds will be building new capacity to bring adequate, efficient and reliable health care to all families and individuals in the Nation.

I invite all Members of the Senate to study this proposed legislation and to join with us in seeking early enactment of the Health Security program.

Mr. President, in order that the details of this legislation may be widely available to all, I ask unanimous consent that the bill may be printed at this point in the Record, together with a section-by-section analysis of the bill.

Index